Crossing over the Line

CROSSING

THE

The Chicago
Series in
Sexuality,
History, and
Society
Edited by John C. Fout

OVER
LINE

Legislating
Morality
and the
Mann Act

DAVID J. LANGUM

THE UNIVERSITY OF CHICAGO PRESS • *Chicago and London*

The University of Chicago Press, Chicago 60637
The University of Chicago Press, Ltd., London
© 1994 by David J. Langum
All rights reserved. Published 1994
Paperback edition 2006
Printed in the United States of America

15 14 13 12 11 10 09 08 07 06   2 3 4 5

ISBN: 0-226-46880-1 (cloth)
ISBN-13: 978-0-226-46870-9 (paper)
ISBN-10: 0-226-46870-4 (paper)

Library of Congress Cataloging-in-Publication Data
Langum, David J., 1940–
    Crossing over the line: Legislating morality and the Mann Act /
David J. Langum.
    p.   cm.—(The Chicago series in sexuality, history, and
society)
    Includes bibliographical references and index.
    1. Prostitution—United States—History.   2. Sex customs—
United States—History.   I. Title.   II. Series.
KF9449.L36   1994
306.74′2′0973—dc20   94-13292
                                                                CIP

⊗The paper used in this publication meets the minimum re-
quirements of the American National Standard for Information
Sciences—Permanence of Paper for Printed Library Materials,
ANSI Z39.48-1992.

FOR THE VICTIMS OF THE DEPARTMENT OF JUSTICE

Contents

Illustrations

Acknowledgments

My first thanks are to my school, Cumberland School of Law of Samford University. I have many thanks to give to individuals here. Dean Parham H. Williams, Jr., has consistently nurtured and supported scholarship in many direct and indirect ways. Edward L. Craig, Jr., of our library, successfully found many hundreds of items through interlibrary loan, many very obscure. An entire squad of research assistants helped me, including, at various times, Leigh Mattox Dulaney, Mary Warner Godofsky, Mark Hull, N. DeWayne Pope, Earl J. Reuther, D. Wayne Rogers, Jr., and Joan Bledsoe Sheffield. I thank them all. Messrs. Pope and Reuther, at the very end and beginning of the project, respectively, were particularly helpful. My colleague and fellow historian, William G. Ross, carefully read every chapter and offered excellent advice and insights. He has been a model of collegiality, and I am greatly indebted to him. Patsy L. Campbell and Faye P. Lovelady also assisted on various matters.

The federal government and its agencies have been generally helpful. The FBI supplied one major document that I requested, but it also promised, over eighteen months before press deadlines, many more that were never delivered. On the other hand, the National Archives was consistently helpful. I want to thank specifically James Gregory Bradsher, Washington National Records Center; Mary Ann Hawkins, National Archives—Southeast Region; and James K. Owens and Stanley P. Tozeski, National Archives—New England Region. Personal friends, Laura Redoutey and Ann Schumacher, read much of the manuscript and made extensive comments. Good editors always see things an author cannot. My editors at the University of Chicago Press, John Tryneski and Kathryn Kraynik, have helped me make this a better book than it would have been otherwise.

Some of the research was undertaken, and some of the manuscript written, while I was in New York as a Golieb Fellow at the New York University School of Law. Even more was written here in Birmingham in the main reading room of the Linn-Henley Research Library. It is a beautiful place and an ideal location to transcend the temptations which otherwise encompass me to waste time.

By the nature of the crime, women were as much involved in Mann Act violations as were men. Any historical appraisal of the Mann Act and its place in American society depends very much, therefore, on the historian's own view of women's strengths and weaknesses, and particularly their sexual autonomy. The subjective sense of things hopefully can be set over in a corner and objective evidence brought to center stage. However, historians are never completely free of the pervasive and sometimes subtle, even unconscious, influences of their own times and personal pasts. Therefore, I want to briefly acknowledge and thank those women whose personal relationships have been the most dominant in forming my own impressions of womanhood in these regards: Bernadette, Carole, Dee Ann, Grace, JoAnne, and Lucie. I particularly want to thank Grace for having put up with me while I wrote this book.

David J. Langum
Birmingham, Alabama

How Times Have Changed

It is hard to believe how things once were.

On November 14, 1934, Maurice Shannon left his home in Erie, Pennsylvania. Shannon may not have had much money, but he did own a Graham Paige sedan. He hoped it would take him and his girlfriend, Eleanor Becker, to a better life in the South. They both could be certain the South would warm them during that bleak November in the middle of the Great Depression.

The couple headed for Mobile, Alabama. Money was hard to come by then. Without doubt they had to stop several times along the way and seek work to pay for the gas to continue their trip. Maurice and Eleanor had to camp outdoors at night en route to their promised land. They were lovers and would not think it strange that they camped together as man and wife, although they knew they were not, at least not yet.

Finally, against many odds, the Graham Paige Sedan brought them to Mobile. The couple spent the week of Christmas camped outside of the city, huddling together in the rain, and dreaming of the unfolding of their new beginnings. Then on December 27, 1934, their luck changed. They were treated to a Christmas present of Southern hospitality.

On December 27, 1934, a deputy sheriff of Mobile County arrested Maurice and Eleanor and turned them over to a Special Agent of the United States Department of Justice, who charged them with three felonies. It seemed, according to the local federal authorities, that the two lovers had engaged in a criminal conspiracy. By traveling as a couple from Pennsylvania to Alabama, they had conspired together to transport the woman with the intention that she "would engage in the practice of submitting her body to carnal illicit sexual intercourse with the said defendant, Maurice Lorenzo Shannon."

There was no money for bail, and the couple had to remain in jail until the Grand Jury could be summoned to hear the details of their heinous crime. That took over a month, since the honest Christian burghers of the town were enjoying the felicities of the season. On January 30, 1935, they were formally charged with their terrible offense, in the quaint language quoted above.

There was still no money, after a month in jail, for lawyers or a trial. Neither Eleanor nor Maurice could afford that much justice. So on the day following the indictment, they did the only thing practical for them. They pled guilty and relied on the mercy of a federal judge. But the Christmas bells had ceased their chimes, and that unmerry official handed Maurice six months in the New Orleans federal jail and gave his lover, Eleanor, six months of probation. Perhaps the judge even thought that this was merciful, that six months of the life of a poor man would not count for much. They would both be branded as felons, many jobs would be closed to them, and they would be unable to vote.[1]

But this is not a story about the South.

In late January 1942, Marco Reginelli, a 45-year-old bachelor, took a trip from his residence in Camden, New Jersey, to Miami. The trip was fine but he missed his lady friend, Louise. In fact he showered her with endearing telegrams and telephone calls. Since he had written that he wished she were there, she suggested she might join him in Florida. At first, Marco seemed to frown on the idea, but soon agreed.

Louise took a cab from Camden to Philadelphia. She picked up a ticket Marco had reserved for her and flew to Miami. Marco met her at the airport and they drove off together to his hotel in Miami Beach. Louise enjoyed a ten-day vacation in Miami, and at night, quite naturally, she occupied the same bed as Marco and from time to time they had sexual relations.

But a stern federal prosecutor found them out. The U.S. Attorney of Trenton accused Marco Reginelli of aiding and assisting the transportation of Louise, his willing, adult girlfriend, with the purpose to entice her "to engage in an immoral practice, to wit, the practice of illicit sexual intercourse with him." The sex was not the crime so much as the transportation, and the prosecutor was able to file the charges in New Jersey, not Miami.

Unlike Maurice Shannon, Marco Reginelli had the means to buy plenty of justice. With a small battery of lawyers, Reginelli went through trial to a jury verdict. Guilty! Six months and $1,500. Reginelli had the resources to afford an appeal. Affirmed! He sought review in the United States Supreme Court. Refused! He sought rehearing of this refusal. Denied! Although this was a stable relationship, and would last for at least fifteen more years, involved an adult woman, willing and single, the Miami sojourn cost Reginelli dearly. The ten-day vacation, and resulting felony conviction, was the basis upon which Reginelli, born in Italy, was denied naturalization. He narrowly escaped being deported.[2]

What is going on here? Why these ridiculous prosecutions for harmless activities?

They are prosecutions for violations of the White Slave Traffic Act, more commonly known as the Mann Act. Many Americans have some vague recollection of a federal law that makes it illegal to transport women across state lines for "immoral purposes." Some believe it applies only to prostitutes; others, only to underage girls; still others, only to coerced, forced transportation. They are wrong.

The Mann Act has been used to punish far broader sexual activities of an interstate character. Men have been imprisoned where the prohibited "immoral purpose" involved purely consensual relationships, noncommercial in nature, between unmarried consenting adults. The federal government has jailed men where the "immoral purpose," although sexual, did not include intercourse. Mann Act defendants have transported women to work as B-girls, as erotic dancers, and as models for nonpornographic nude photographs.

The statute, dating from 1910, has now been significantly amended. However, Congress has never had the courage to repeal an absurd law, that has been used, and still could be used, to interfere with inoffensive private activities or to persecute selected individuals that particular U.S. Attorneys just happen not to like.

The Mann Act was born of strange parents. Hysteria was the mother and an international treaty obligation was the father. The United States had committed itself in 1908 to an international agreement for the repression of trade in white women, and in part the White Slave Traffic Act was adopted to honor the national commitments undertaken through that treaty. Additionally, during the years from 1907 to 1914 a genuine hysteria seized the United States, a phenomenon more carefully explored in Chapter 2.

It was widely thought and feared that large-scale rings of "white slavers" were preying upon young women in the nation's cities. These gangs, so it was thought, were coercing women into prostitution through threats, intimidation, and force. Thereafter, these women were kept in brothels under conditions of near slavery. This fear had a special poignancy for middle-class Progressives. There was a sharp tension between the prevailing image of women as precious, domesticated, virtuous beings and the historically unprecedented fact of middle-class women moving into the crowded urban areas and living alone, without the male protection of a father, brother, or husband. The virtuous daughters of the middle class might be the victims of evil white slavers.

In enacting the Mann Act, Congress aimed at a very specific problem. Unfortunately, it used general language. The wording of the Act by its terms applied to the movement of prostitutes who were plying their trade voluntarily. Furthermore, the statute used words that could be read as including even totally noncommercial, boyfriend-girlfriend travel, if done for a purpose the federal judiciary might deem immoral. That was the path that was eventually chosen by the Supreme Court in its famous *Caminetti* decision in 1917.

Furthermore, the violation was complete upon the woman's crossing of the state line if the man at that time merely *intended* that the purpose of her travel be for any "immoral purpose." Because of this construction of the law almost every adult American male, especially those reaching maturity prior to 1986, has violated the Mann Act at least once in his life. Any man who has ever driven his girlfriend from New York to New Jersey, with the hope of sexual activities that evening, or has urged his girlfriend to come from Boston to Chicago to visit him, with the same hope, has committed a federal felony. It did not matter whether the wish was father to the deed. Sex need not occur for the felony to be complete. What was required was the crossing of the state line, transportation or enticement by the male, and the illegal intention in the man's mind at the time of the transportation. Today these sorts of noncommercial peccadillos are ignored. In the 1920s such moral transgressions earned men several months in jail, and if the woman were married or young children were abandoned, several years.

The Mann Act has many interesting ties to broader themes in American culture. The enactment related to several strains of Progressive thought in relation to sexuality, and its early enforcement was a significant factor in the growth of the Federal Bureau of Investigation. Over the years the Mann Act furnished material for many expressions of American culture, through movies, novels, and jokes. Its entire history is interesting, but no part is more fascinating than that of the 1960s and 1970s, when the courts, faced with decades of rigid judicial precedent and a Congress too cowardly to repeal or amend the Act, were forced to reconcile the archaic statute with the social fact of the Sexual Revolution. Certainly one significant aspect of this study is that the history of the Mann Act is itself fascinating and has never before been studied in detail.

However, in addition to its own inherent interest, the story of the Mann Act illustrates important aspects of the American impulse toward reform, especially the American proclivity to use coercive legislation to accomplish it. For more than two centuries, the United States has had reform movements and social uplift organizations. But in the first half of the nineteenth century these were most frequently aimed at conditions external to individual human beings; the abolition of slavery and the improved treatment of the poor, prisoners, sailors, and the insane are examples.

The nature of reform changed somewhat during the later nineteenth century. The primary focus changed from outer-directed to inner-directed. There were still many reforms urged against external conditions, such as trust busting, or economic schemes such as Henry George's single tax. But to a considerable extent the reformers of the late nineteenth century wanted to make individual human beings better. The Temperance Movement may have had its origins in a reaction to the New Immigration's rejection of the Protestant norm of temperance.[3] But a major focus of its concern was on the individual drunkard and the effect of insobriety on the family. In a like manner, the Purity Movement originally focused on the sexual purity of the individual, to be achieved through moral uplift, exhortation, more open discussion of sexuality, and other means explored more thoroughly in the following chapter. These reform movements were concerned with sobriety and morality of humans as individuals; they were not focused on evil institutions or legal conditions. Although another major reform movement of the late nineteenth century, suffrage for women, most certainly was aimed at eliminating a legally disabling condition, arguments were frequently advanced that the women's vote would be a tool for legislation leading to the control of liquor, the raising of the age of consent, and so forth. The case for women to vote was often made on the basis of what it would do to aid other reform movements that were focused on individual human conduct.

This new spirit of reform, prevalent in the late nineteenth century, took a sharp turn when it encountered the "can-do" mentality of the Progressive years, roughly between 1890 and 1925. The Progressives were preoccupied with making order out of the chaotic conditions that arose from rapid urbanization, unrestrained industrialization, and an explosion of population, largely from immigration.[4] They tended to place great reliance on professional expertise and did not flinch from social engineering that would impose solutions for social ills upon the populace, willy-nilly, whether desired or not.

The combination of reform interested in specific human conduct together with the social engineering of the Progressives led to a uniquely American spirit for the dealing with social concerns. Throughout history there have been reformers who have concerned themselves with the social conditions, for example, of alcoholism and prostitution. They have been ameliorators, attempting to control and reduce drunkenness and debauchery. No one had ever thought they could be eliminated altogether.

But the Progressives regarded drugs, vice, and insobriety, not as simply social conditions, but as social *problems* that could be *solved*. This was an aspect of the profound pre-war faith in social progress, the Progressive reflection of "the Victorian faith in the individual and confidence in the inevitability of human progress."[5] By the proper use of social engineering, often employing the coercion of the federal government, individual human behavior could be controlled and changed through legislation. Men could be forced to be good and social evils conquered forever. No one articulated this new spirit better than the Chicago Vice Commission, which in 1911 adopted as its fundamental recommendation: "Constant and Persistent Repression of Prostitution the Immediate Method: Absolute Annihilation the Ultimate Ideal."[6] This spirit of suppression leading to absolute annihilation of human behaviors resulted in three major coercive enactments engineered by the Progressives: the Mann Act (1910); the Harrison Narcotic Drug Act (1914), the opening shot of the so-called War on Drugs; and the Prohibition Amendment (1919).

The history of the Mann Act illustrates the problems associated with this sort of coercive legislation. One problem is philosophical, yet fundamental to the nature of the liberal state. The classical liberal state is dedicated to the flowering of her individual citizens. This sort of liberalism, which is the sort that Thomas Jefferson honored, in effect creates a presumption against governmental activity. If the purpose of government is to secure the individual citizen's right to life, liberty, and the pursuit of happiness, to paraphrase the Declaration of Independence, then the legitimate use of governmental coercion is where one individual's actions interferes with another individual's own life, liberty, and pursuit of happiness. Government coercion, the essence of criminal legislation, which is designed simply to make citizens "good" and not to stop actions causing specific harm to others, does not meet this test. Reasonable minds and different times might differ about the meaning of "harm" as concerns sexuality. People often engage in conduct that in a psychological sense hurts others, especially spouses and parents. Yet surely government cannot become so intimately involved with our lives in a free society so as to attempt to extirpate actions that merely dismay family and friends.

However, in the 1910s and 1920s a great many Americans probably saw real harm to the women themselves who engaged in sex outside of marriage. Today, most people would see no harm to either a man or woman consenting to an interstate journey to facilitate sexual activity involving only the pair, notwithstanding that it may dismay third parties. Others might see the risk of possible spread of venereal disease or unwanted pregnancies, with accompanying strains on the public purse, as actual social harms. Yet these potential harms are only the result of a lack of precautions, not sexual activity itself. In any event, the rhetoric behind the enforcement of moral norms has seldom been this narrowly tailored and almost always condemns conduct for its own sake.

Furthermore, the invocation of governmental coercion to blunt a basic human desire for sex, simply to prevent certain noninevitable results, evokes an Orwellian vision of Big Brother and his "Anti-Sex League." The prohibition goes too far. It cannot be said with honesty that noncommercial and consensual violations of the Mann Act ever were prosecuted primarily with a view of addressing the threat of unwanted pregnancies or venereal disease. At least in the years between 1913 and 1928, it was repressive American puritanism, largely religiously inspired, opposed broadly to sexuality outside of marriage, that was at work. It was a demand that people be good.

Moreover, morals legislation for the purpose of coercing "goodness" is specifically contrary to the spirit in which the *federal* government was

formed. The national government was designed to be a limited government of only specifically delegated powers. The federal Bill of Rights
once proclaimed with meaning that, "The powers not delegated to the
United States by the Constitution . . . are reserved to the States respectively, or to the people."

Other problems associated with coercive legislation such as the
Mann Act are quite practical. The Progressive hopes for elimination of
humanity's ills were "dashed by the First World War and the stubborn-
ness of the human character."[7] But the failure of such laws was predicted in advance. Walter Lippmann pointed out in *A Preface to Politics*
(1913), that repressive legislation was "the method of the taboo, as naive
as barbarism, as ancient as human failure." It never works. He wrote:

> What reformers have to learn is that men don't gamble just for the
> sake of violating the law. They do so because something within them
> is satisfied by betting or drinking. To erect a ban doesn't stop the
> want. . . . The taboo—the merely negative law—is the emptiest of all
> the impositions from on top. . . . the impulses, cravings and wants of
> men must be employed. You can employ them well or ill, but you
> must employ them. A group of reformers lounging at a club cannot,
> dare not, decide to close up another man's club because it is called a
> saloon. Unless the reformer can invent something which substitutes
> attractive virtues for attractive vices, he will fail.[8]

The inevitability of failure of repressive legislation thwarting the
human desire for sexuality and stimulants is far from the only problem,
however. Coercive legislation, requiring men and women to be good by
denying the employment of their impulses, is like a dam hastily thrown
across a stream. It may block the water for a time from entering the area
immediately underneath the obstruction, but eventually the water will
flow around the dam, creating new and different waterways. In other
words, there are collateral consequences that result from repressive
morals legislation, and these new channels of water, the collateral consequences, are often far worse than the alleged evils that the coercive
legislation was designed to suppress. Again Walter Lippmann:

> It is impossible to abolish either with a law or an axe the desires of
> men. It is dangerous, explosively dangerous, to thwart them for any
> length of time. The Puritans tried to choke the craving for pleasure
> in early New England. They had no theaters, no dances, no festivals.
> They burned witches instead.[9]

All of these great coercive experiments of the Progressives led to terrible results. National Prohibition led to the rise of gangsters and profound disrespect for law. The so-called War on Drugs has led to a vast increase in urban crime and a deplorable disregard for the Fourth Amendment and its guarantees against unreasonable searches and seizures. An important aspect of this book will be to demonstrate that the Mann Act as a coercive device to require "correct" moral conduct likewise failed. But perhaps the most important lesson is in the collateral consequences generated by the attempt of the federal government to use its powers for this purpose.

One byproduct of the Mann Act was the growth of an entire industry of blackmailing. It was built upon violations of the statute by men with women who were members of blackmailing organizations. This was an evil that was predicted at the time of enactment, and an entire chapter is devoted to its exploration.

Another consequence was the power given federal prosecutors to prosecute selectively and their abuse of that power. United States Attorneys ignored some moral transgressors and vigorously persecuted others. Like the later tax laws, the Mann Act was used to target specific defendants, such as gangsters and con men. But with far more menace to a liberal state, in which government ought to be neutral with respect to its citizenry, federal prosecutors also used the Mann Act as a club against blacks who dated white women and defendants who espoused unpopular political beliefs.

Under the most extended libertarian argument imaginable, men who would drug and kidnap women, force them to prostitute themselves, and hold them as prisoners are clearly legitimate and most appropriate targets of government power. They should be stopped and vigorously punished precisely because they are interfering, most seriously, with their victims' liberty. Had the Mann Act stopped with actual "white-slavers," were there any, few would criticize. But it did not stop there, and, instead of fostering, it interfered with liberty. The Act covered consensual transportation of willing prostitutes and then it was judicially extended to noncommercial, boyfriend-girlfriend travel. The case could be made that government ought not interfere with consensual prostitution, that whatever a woman willingly wants to do with her body is her own business. It is not necessary to go that far for the purpose of this study. However, it seems clear enough that interstate travel for the purpose of the mutual enjoyment of sexuality by a man and a woman, as lovers and friends, is activity that imposes no tangible harm on anyone. Its suppression is at odds with the American system of limited government and ought to be abhorred by all who respect liberty. Therefore, one of the most significant collateral consequences of the Mann Act was the denial of this liberty interest that is implicit in the foundation of our nation.

One of the ironies of the Mann Act's evolution is that women, as the protected class of the statute, in fact became its chief victims. The Act originally reflected the mentality of male legislators, who assumed that men generally were the villains and women the passive victims. Indeed, it was enacted at the height of concern that women were being drugged and carried off to be unwilling prostitutes. But even when the Act was perverted into a proscription against boyfriend-girlfriend travel, there was an implicit assumption of feminine weakness. As one federal judge wrote, "Congress passed the Mann Act to protect 'weak women from bad men.'"[10] As the century progressed, the notion of feminine weakness became increasingly attenuated, and, indeed, never existed to the extent believed by male legislators and judges. The number of Mann Act cases involving actual coercion was extremely small.

Women could be and were prosecuted for transporting other women, for example, madams who took prostitutes across a state line. But in noncommercial cases women were in a strange twilight in which they were both victims and villains. They were victims in that they were regarded as "weak." Yet between 1915 and 1932, dates associated with particular court cases, women were prosecuted along with their boyfriends for conspiracy to arrange their own transportation by agreeing to go along on the trip. The males were prosecuted for a direct violation of the Mann Act for transporting their "weak" girlfriends, the victims. Then, at the same time, the women were prosecuted for conspiring with their boyfriends in that same transportation.

However, authorities most frequently used the threat of conviction for criminal conspiracy only as a lever, designed to induce women to confess to details of the trip that could in turn be employed to turn up hard evidence, such as hotel registration ledgers, to convict their male companions. The women involved in these interstate affairs of the heart often were released on probation or with very modest sentences. But there were also some substantial prison sentences handed to women for crossing a state line with a boyfriend.

The most substantial harm to women was more subtle. The statute distinctly inhibited women from taking trips with their male friends. It not only deprived women of opportunities for vacations and travel but effectively prevented women from using the vehicle of interstate travel as a method of expressing their own sexuality. Women were deprived of a fundamental human activity which caused no harm to anybody. They were also subjected to a double standard, since males could travel in interstate commerce to meet women, but no couple without fear of prosecution could allow the woman to similarly travel to meet the male. As a group, American women were far more victimized by the Mann Act than by so-called white slavery.

Blackmail, selective prosecution by prosecutors, and significant deprivation of freedom in consensual sexuality are three significant harms that resulted from the coercive aspects of the Mann Act. There are two others of a more general nature that follow from almost any repressive statute.

The Mann Act is a classic example of repression imposed through a tyranny of the majority against a dissident minority, the greatest failing of a democratic state. After the statute was passed, there were occasional "scares" that the statute might be amended to exclude noncommercial travel. When that happened, letter-writing campaigns ensued, and individual citizens and church groups flooded Congress and the Department of Justice with letters, petitions, and resolutions. They all urged that Congress not "weaken" the Act by excluding consensual sexual activities from its scope. These church groups and individuals exulted in the imposition of their own standards of morality upon others who did not believe as they did. It is easy to scoff at the simple-minded morality expressed in some of these communications. Yet they probably did represent the majority of American thought. Especially in the early days of its enforcement, there were thousands of letters sent to individual United States Attorneys and the Department of Justice that accused various persons of immoral conduct and requested prosecution. The case can be made that the public actually pushed the government to go farther in its interpretation and enforcement of the statute than government itself originally wanted to go. The Mann Act is a classic example of both the tyranny of the majority and also the federal judiciary's failure to protect those who dissented and acted differently.

The history of the Mann Act also demonstrates a second danger of repressive legislation. It is far easier for Congress to pass such a statute than later to repeal or significantly amend it. This statute was passed in response to a popular outcry over an alleged problem of kidnapped women and coerced prostitution. But after it was enacted, the law acquired a large constituency in the form of church groups, purity organizations, and moralists who favored its purposes and who applauded the imposition of federal coercion to advance their visions of "proper" conduct. This constituency did not waiver and even was encouraged by the subsequent interpretation of the Act to include sexual activities between consenting adults. The fervor of these supporters prevented amendment and repeal until the 1970s and 1980s and even then probably accounted for the rather disguised and disingenuous techniques adopted by Congress to change the law.

Thus, there is much to be gained from a study of the Mann Act. This book attempts to describe not only the narrative history of its enforcement, but also to delineate these collateral consequences. A few words describing the organization of the book will aid the reader: Chapter 2, which follows this introduction, describes sexuality in America, between 1870 and 1910, and the immediate background for the enactment of the White Slave Traffic Act. It outlines the Purity Movement of the years from 1870 to 1890 and the several strains of Progressive thought in relation to sexuality: anxiety over young women in urban areas without the protection of fathers or brothers as symbolic of the degeneration of society generally, nativist concerns over shifting patterns of immigration and its effect on prostitution, and the concern over the relation of low wages and prostitution. The Red Light Abatement and Vice Commission movements are briefly sketched, as well as the specific white slavery hysteria and congressional response that led to the passage of the Mann Act.

Chapter 3 examines the early enforcement of the White Slave Traffic Act, between 1910 and 1917. It describes how the (Federal) Bureau of Investigation used the Act to begin its rapid expansion as the national police. It is in this period that public opinion played its greatest role in pushing the federal government into a more expansive interpretation of the statute than the Department of Justice originally wanted to take.

Chapter 4 takes up blackmail and extortion specifically, the extent of its existence, and the efforts of the FBI and other agencies to combat the use of the Act for these other illegal activities. It also describes some of the more famous celebrities, including Frank Lloyd Wright, threatened with Mann Act prosecution by estranged wives and blackmailers. The pivotal case of *Caminetti v. United States,* wherein the United

States Supreme Court definitively extended the Mann Act to purely noncommercial consensual activities, is the focus of Chapter 5. It describes the affair itself, the political scandal set in motion by charges the Wilson administration delayed the prosecution because of political favoritism, the trial, and closes with an extensive analysis of both the majority and dissent in the Supreme Court.

Chapter 6 follows with a consideration of what influences led the Court to follow the path it took. It describes the very different understanding, both popular and legal, of the word "prostitution," as it was used then, compared with now. This suggests that the conduct of the two women in the Caminetti case, from a contemporary viewpoint, either was prostitution or something so close to it that the statute did cover that conduct.

The period immediately following *Caminetti*, namely, from 1917 through 1928, became virtually a morals crusade. Federal officials claimed that noncommercial prosecutions were limited to abusive situations. Chapter 7 appraises this claim. It draws on prosecutorial records obtained from the National Archives, FBI reports, and trial records, in order to gain an understanding of the average case, not just the spectacular cases that found their way to appellate courts.

After 1928, noncommercial prosecutions became much more selective as juries became increasingly unwilling to convict ordinary interstate fornicators and adulterers. Chapter 8 describes a shift in focus whereby the federal government used noncommercial violations, not abusive in nature, to target specific individuals and types of individuals, much as the tax laws were used to imprison Al Capone. The better known of these targeted defendants include Machine Gun Jack McGurn, the Capone hitman; Charlie Chaplin, prosecuted because he was a radical; and Jack Johnson the boxer and Chuck Berry the singer, blacks who dared to have sexual relationships with white women.

Chapter 9 examines a renewed judicial skepticism about the value of noncommercial purpose prosecutions and the beginnings of effective national control over local federal indictments. It also describes a high public awareness of the Mann Act, vividly demonstrated by a spate of incidents where a car would pull up to a state line, women would get out and themselves walk over the line to re-enter the car on the other side. Time and again courts were asked whether this conduct would be enough for the women's male companions to evade the Mann Act.

Chapter 10 discusses how the federal courts dealt with noncommercial cases in the 1960s and 1970s, faced with the social fact of a sexual revolution, hard precedent that placed boyfriend-girlfriend travel within the proscriptions of the Mann Act, and also with a Congress unwilling or politically unable to amend the statute. Some courageous District Judges simply defied precedent and refused to enforce the Act in noncommercial cases. Others redefined the meaning of "immoral purpose" to exclude activities, such as strip shows and nude photography, that in the 1930s and 1940s had been included.

Chapter 11 examines the growth of male prostitution and juvenile prostitution and pornography in the 1970s and 1980s. These developments finally enabled Congress to amend the Mann Act, first by making it applicable to the transportation of males as well as females, and second, by redefining the focus of the statute itself. In 1986, Congress significantly changed the illegal purpose of the interstate transportation and essentially removed the necessity for federal judges to define "immoral purpose." The chapter concludes the study by arguing that the collateral consequences set in motion by the Mann Act far outweighed any benefits. In particular, the noncommercial prosecutions facilitated blackmail, permitted a tyranny of majoritarian views, deprived Americans of freedom of interstate movement in consensual sexual relationships, and allowed individual prosecutors to crush individuals selected for persecution for reasons having nothing to do with the Mann Act.

The court cases that interpret the dry language of a statute give it life. This is certainly true of the Mann Act. Particularly interesting are the consensual noncommercial prosecutions, and throughout we will focus somewhat more on these than on the prostitution transportation cases. But before looking at the development of the Mann Act enforcement and interpretation, we should go further backward in time and discuss the growing concern over sexuality in America, during the years from 1870 to 1910, and then, the immediate events leading to the passage of the White Slave Traffic Act.

Prostitutes, Progressives, and Moral Panic, 1907–1914

During the years from 1910 to 1914, America worried about prostitution with an intensity never before or after equaled.[1] During those years, the "social evil," as it was often called, became the focus of at least six feature motion pictures, about the same number of plays and novels, and at least twelve "white slavery narratives," a special genre hovering uncomfortably between fact and fiction. Over thirty-five local, state, and national commissions probed the causes, practice, and possible eradication of prostitution.

A glance at the *Readers' Guide to Periodical Literature* tells the story. In the twenty years between 1890 and 1909, thirty-six entries appear under the heading "prostitution." Forty-one entries appear in the ten years, between 1915 and 1924. But for the mere five years between 1910 and 1914, "prostitution" carries no less than 156 separate entries.[2] In the Victorian age anything sexual was a matter of hushed, guarded reticence. But by 1914, a contemporary recorded that prostitution had become "a subject for polite conversation at the dinner table."[3]

Of course, this did not happen in isolation. Several historians have convincingly argued that this intense interest in prostitution was a product of three different developments that were causing angst in Progressive America. Prostitution became a symbol of decline and a manifestation of weighty concerns and social dislocations. Prostitution gave meaning to deeper problems of immigration, urbanization, and above all, the dramatic changes in the status and roles of women that threatened traditional forms of sexual control and traditional ideas of civilized morality.[4]

In 1900, the population of the United States was 76 million. Between that year and 1914, 13 million immigrants would reach American shores. Unlike the earlier immigration from Scandinavia, Britain, Germany, and Ireland, this newer wave of migration, the so-called New Immigration, between 1880 and 1917, came primarily from southern and eastern Europe. It was heavy with "unassimilable" Roman Catholics and Jews from Italy, Poland, and Russia. Middle-class America deplored their open acceptance of liquor. It fretted the country was losing her ethnic identity and becoming mongrelized. Middle-class America also feared the new immigrants' sexuality.[5] One middle-class observer in 1908 feared the "accumulation of undesirables in our land" and noted:

> We no longer draw from Northern Europe. . . . [Today] this enormous influx hales from Russia, Austria, Hungary, Italy, and the southern countries about the eastern end of the Mediterranean,—men of alien races, mixed in blood and of many tongues and often the last resultants of effete and decaying civilizations. . . . We no longer receive accessions from the best peoples beyond our borders but from the mediocre and the worst.[6]

America was rapidly becoming urban in the opening decades of the twentieth century. In 1920, for the first time, more Americans lived in cities than in the country. Urbanization went far to disintegrate the traditional patriarchal family by luring young people to the cities. In particular, the typewriter, new department stores, and offices created employment opportunities for young, single women. The social worker Jane Addams and many other middle-class observers saw possibilities of great evil in the city:

> The social relationships in a modern city are so hastily made and often so superficial, that the old human restraints of public opinion, long sustained in smaller communities, have also broken down. Thousands of young men and women in every great city have received none of the lessons in self-control . . . These young people are perhaps further from all community restraint and genuine social control than the youth of the community have ever been in the long history of civilization. Certainly only the modern city has offered at one and the same time every possible stimulation for the lower nature and every opportunity for secret vice.[7]

With the increased opportunities for a measure of economic independence and their movement into the cities, women experienced a considerable freedom. Correspondingly, the first two decades of the twentieth century saw an alarming liberalization in sexual habits and attitudes, at least among young people of the working class.[8] A widespread belief held that women had a unique claim to "the charm and beauty of life" and held a "purity of thought and heart."[9] Overt sexuality of young women in the cities, however, challenged this conventional view of women as asexual, passive, and primarily interested in the ideals of domesticity: the management of home, care of husband, and rearing of children. Some men doubtless feared a loss of sexual control over women by their increasing freedom—and even worse, enjoyment—of sexual autonomy.[10]

Many sexual tensions centered on the temptations women faced in the city.[11] It was true, as Jane Addams lamented, that "never before in civilization have such numbers of young girls been suddenly released from the protection of the home and permitted to walk unattended upon city streets and to work under alien roofs."[12] In the same years that women moved to the cities, the older system of courtship where a man called at the woman's parlor, was being supplanted by the dating system, under which the couple would go out to a show, a dinner, a park, or a dance. Actually the dating system was originated by the urban lower classes, which did not have access to parlors in crowded tenements. The shift from parlor courtship to dating, where men paid for the costs of activities, brought about an inequality in the relationship. Men controlled the "date" and expected some sort of sexual return, ranging from a simple good night kiss to actual intercourse.[13] There was a sense of implicit obligation, and we shall see that this "treating system," as it was called in the Progressive era, sometimes led to arrangements that were regarded as close to prostitution.

The "problem" of prostitution became a flash point for all three of these social tensions, immigration, urbanization, and the sexuality of women. Prostitution was directly related to the New Immigration, even apart from the hysteria of white slavery. The *New York Times* editorialized that by 1905 "scores of thousands of women had been imported into this country for immoral purposes."[14] In 1913 a New York probation officer wrote that "the great majority of them [prostitutes] are of foreign birth or extraction."[15] A vice investigator in 1913 concluded that a majority of the brothel owners in New York City were "foreigners by birth. Some of them have been seducers of defenseless women all their lives."[16] The pimps were foreigners too, but it was not clear of what nationality. The United States Senate's Immigration [Dillingham] Commission in 1909 thought that there were two important organizations of pimps, "one French, the other Jewish," whereas in the same year the muckraker George Kibbe Turner believed that the typical New York City procurer "in the past was almost always Jewish; now the young Italians have taken up the business in great numbers."[17]

All of the ethnic groups took umbrage at their linkage with prostitution. But none protested as vehemently as the New York Jews.[18] However, Jews were conspicuously involved in prostitution, certainly in image, and uncomfortably enough in reality. The Jewish response was the most pronounced of all the ethnic groups. There was a concerted effort by Jewish organizations to fight prostitution generally and especially Jews involved with prostitution.[19] In 1909 the Council of Jewish Women of New York adopted a plan to obtain the names of every Jewish girl entering the United States, to find suitable lodging and employment, and to follow through with visits.[20] At the same time the Jewish Uplift Society of New York City was formed with the purpose to "rescue fallen women and to protect innocent women . . . particularly those of the Jewish faith, . . . and to suppress disorderly houses."[21]

Although the initial Jewish response was denial, once the widely publicized disclosures of Jewish participation in prostitution, fanned by nativism and prejudice, reached the point of palpable reality, the Jewish community acted swiftly. Following the early efforts in 1909, B'nai B'rith in 1912 decided to create special watchers at railway stations and ports, paralleling the Travelers' Aid efforts, and to create information bureaus to inform young girls about prostitution and procurers. This effort would be concentrated in Central Europe and the United States.[22] Finally, between 1912 and 1917, the Kehillah, a formal Jewish community organization, maintained a Bureau of Social Morals, really a sort of secret service that fought vice in the Jewish quarters of New York.[23]

It was not enough of an evil that the prostitutes, pimps, and owners of brothels were foreigners. It was thought they were introducing special forms of perversions and depravity, which generated the slang "French" for oral sex and "Greek" for anal sex, and that these practices would corrupt the youth of America. Again from the Senate Immigration Commission's official report:

In many instances the professionals who come have been practically driven from their lives of shame in Europe on account of their loathsome diseases; the conditions of vice obtaining there have even lowered the standard of degradation of prostitution formerly customary here. . . . The vilest practices are brought here from continental Europe, and beyond doubt there has come from imported women and their men the most bestial refinements of depravity. The inclination of the continental races to look with toleration upon these evils is spreading in this country an influence perhaps even more far-reaching in its degradation than the physical effects which inevitably follow it.[24]

Some observers related prostitution not only to immigrants but also to city conditions, "a result of unfortunate social and economic conditions . . . particularly in the congested sections of our large cities—and also by reason of the great influx of foreigners who usually have but little capital and no business or profession."[25] Social purity journals, such as *The Light,* regularly ran articles with titles such as "What Are the Dangers of City Life for a Country Girl?" (1909), "Commercialized Vice and the Farm. Are Our Farm Girls in Imminent Danger From This Foe" (1914), and "The Assault of Society Upon the Country Boy" (1911).[26]

Women's entry into prostitution, especially of innocent American farm girls, seemed to be caused by the city itself. Addams was disturbed by "the dangers implicit in city conditions" and wrote:

the increasing nervous energy to which industrial processes daily accommodate themselves, and the speeding up constantly required of the operators, may at any moment so register their results upon the nervous system of a factory girl as to overcome her powers of resistance. Many a working girl at the end of a day is so hysterical and overwrought that her mental balance is plainly disturbed.[27]

It was hard for a girl thrilled by the "city excitements and eager to share them, to keep to the gray and monotonous path of regular work. Almost every such girl of the hundreds who have come to grief, 'begins' by accepting invitations to dinners and places of amusement. She is always impressed with the ease for concealment which the city affords."[28] Of course, many young women saw the autonomy of city life as an opportunity for pleasure and excitement. Working girls flocked to the dance halls and other places of amusement, often as a means of finding male companionship, and the open sexuality of their behavior, the new and untraditional dance forms, the drinking, and the hugging and kissing in public, shocked middle-class Americans.[29]

Middle-class America was certain this sexual independence would lead to ruin and ultimate prostitution. "The danger begins the moment a girl leaves the protection of Home and Mother," wrote Florence Mabel Dedrick in 1909; another reformer, Charles Bryon Chrysler, echoed her: "Independence has been the cause of the ruin of many girls."[30] Although greatly overblown, there was some truth to this. There was a class of young women in the cities who regularly traded sex, not for money, but for excitement, a good time, or, very often, shoes, clothing, or other presents. The women who traded within this furthest extension of the "treating system" were called "charity girls," because they did not demand money for sexual favors, but gave them for free, or at least not a definite monetary consideration. Naturally, the various vice investigations paid close attention to these women, thoroughly disapproved of their conduct, and, as we shall see in chapter 6, the Progressive period drew no sharp distinction between this conduct and prostitution for money.[31]

Of course, most urban young women were simply enjoying themselves, were in no sense recognizable to the modern mind "ruined," and were not swept up into prostitution. Nevertheless, some did engage in a clandestine prostitution, taking advantage of city concealment, keeping their day jobs, and practicing prostitution on an occasional basis as a sideline.[32] Naturally, these women would be more likely than most to slip into full-time, professional prostitution.

At times, the effort to link immigration, the cities, and changing sexual mores bordered on an attack on modernity itself. It is hard to read the comments of B. S. Steadwell, president of the World's Purity Federation, in an article entitled "Some of the Causes of Present-Day Immorality," as other than a diatribe of pure disgust at the modern world:

> The advent of electricity brought us the telephone which is a necessity to any modern house of shame whether located in the city or in the country, and connects every home with these dens of infamy . . . it made possible the degrading picture show, and inventions which have been used largely to promote and cultivate immorality. During the past fifty years girls and women have taken their places beside boys and men in schools, colleges, stores, offices, factories and shops, and have in constantly increasing numbers entered commercial life.

This close association has brought opportunities for sexual gratification of which full advantage has been taken. The automobile . . . has made possible the "joyride," and has built up the palatial "roadhouse" or country brothel. Luxurious transportation facilities have also ushered in immoral practices never before known.[33]

This concern over prostitution evoked two responses. One response was characteristic of the Progressives' regulatory and perfectionist thought, founded on firm moral convictions. This channel of thought wanted to do no less than rigorously repress prostitution and ultimately stamp it out entirely.[34] A second response, entirely different in tone, was the white slavery hysteria, during the approximate years of 1907 to 1914.

In the closing decades of the nineteenth century and the first decade of the twentieth, every American city of significant size supported a segregated district wherein prostitution was practiced openly. Prostitution in this form was not legal as such, but it was tolerated so long as it was kept within the boundaries of the district and did not impose too greatly on middle-class sensibilities. The districts had colorful names. San Francisco had her "Barbary Coast"; Chicago her "Levee"; New York her "Tenderloin"; and New Orleans her "Storyville." But lesser towns had districts too. In Washington, D.C., the place to go was the "Division"; in Salt Lake City, the "Stockade"; and in Fort Worth, "Hell's Half Acre."

Nineteenth-century middle-class Americans supported segregated districts while themselves becoming increasingly moralistic, perhaps to meliorate fears of rape and seduction of their own women and to protect their own respectability.[35] However, in 1870 an event occurred which would set in motion a mass movement to change this cozy arrangement and which also nicely illustrates Joseph R. Gusfield's thesis of law as a symbolic statement of preferred norms.[36] In that year St. Louis took the step of legalizing prostitution by ordinance, regulating what had previously been de facto arrangements, licensing brothels, and requiring periodic medical inspections.[37]

Sparked by a spontaneous women's reaction to the assault upon their normative values represented by legalized prostitution, a mass middle-class movement began to attack vice. This Purity Movement had many different facets.[38] It lobbied to raise the age of consent, which in some American states was still as low as ten; it attacked the theory that men had a physical necessity to engage in sexual intercourse, a common

nineteenth-century justification for prostitution; it urged more open-
ness in the discussion of prostitution and sexuality generally, decrying
the Victorian reticence that had precluded open consideration of sexual
topics. The Purity Movement also made a feeble effort to "rescue"
prostitutes, but its methods here were largely those of moralistic regen-
eration and exhortation.

Above all the Purity Movement contested the double standard,
whereby men were allowed their "wild oats" but women were disgraced
and ruined by a premarital affair. One of the ironies of history is that
this assault on the double standard, launched in the closing decades of
the nineteenth century, has so completely succeeded in the closing
decades of the twentieth, but not in the way the purity crusaders could
possibly have imagined. Instead of men's moral conduct rising to the
"purity" of women's, as the reformers wished, in our age women have
taken on the freedom formerly reserved exclusively for men.

The early period of the Purity Crusade had an evangelistic flavor. It
attracted many old-time abolitionists, and William Lloyd Garrison
himself wrote in 1875 that the new crusade had "the old ring of uncom-
promising warfare against sin."[39] Gradually, the movement expanded
to include broader issues of concern to women and spawned such other
groups as the Women's Christian Temperance Union and the Young
Women's Christian Association. In the Progressive period, the Purity
Movement was taken over by male leaders. Typical of the period's faith
in experts, self-styled purity experts began forming purity organizations with pretentious names such as American Purity Alliance,
National Vigilance Committee, and American Vigilance Association.
The revamped movement also attracted such leading educators as
David Starr Jordan of Stanford and Charles W. Eliot of Harvard. These
organizations were unstable and constantly merged and regrouped, but
in their time were responsible for an entire genre of purity publications,
including such journals as *Vigilance* and *The Light.*

One of the goals of the original women's movement was to convert
the medical profession away from a belief in the regulation of prostitution to the Purity Movement's view that prostitution ought to be suppressed and the segregated districts broken up. In this it also enjoyed
complete success, but not on the moralistic grounds originally
advanced. By the turn of the century, doctors had discovered the medical basis of venereal disease. Syphilis and gonorrhea could no longer be
considered signs of moral condemnation when the diseases could so

easily be passed to demonstratively innocent wives and children. Doctors began to form social hygiene groups.[40] Dr. Prince A. Morrow, one of the leaders of this social hygiene movement, published his influential *Social Diseases and Marriage* in 1904 and the following year founded the American Society of Sanitary and Moral Prophylaxis.

As was true with the purity groups, there was at first a plethora of social hygiene organizations, eighteen by 1912.[41] Eventually in 1914, the leading purity group, the American Vigilance Association, merged with the leading social hygiene group to become the American Social Hygiene Association. The co-option of the women's Purity Movement, first by men, and later by doctors, was complete.

The social hygiene movement was committed to repression of prostitution, as opposed to regulation. It also supported a single standard of morality, which was assumed would be that of women.[42] The middle class was still trying to extend its values to the lower class but, in conformance with the Progressive style, the tone had changed from moralistic fervor to coldly scientific reasoning.[43]

An international equivalent of the American Purity movement ran along somewhat parallel lines. Josephine Butler, William Alexander Coote, and William T. Stead waged a crusade in England against an alleged international traffic in women among brothels throughout the world. Stead caused considerable stir with an 1885 article in the *Pall Mall Gazette* alleging a trade in very young girls. The reformers also charged that women were being transported against their will and held in bondage.

This agitation resulted in an international conference and the 1902 proposal of an international arrangement for the suppression of the traffic of young girls and women. A formal international treaty was promulgated in 1904. This treaty was aimed at international recruitment or transportation of young girls, or unconsenting adult women, for the purposes of prostitution, and required surveillance of ports of entry, exchange of information, and criminal sanctions. The United States prohibited the importation of women for the purposes of prostitution as early as 1875. In March 1905 the United States Senate consented to the international treaty and on June 15, 1908, President Roosevelt proclaimed the American adherence to its terms.[44] This treaty obligation would become the basis of Section 6 of the Mann Act.

One of the specifically legal efforts undertaken to suppress vice, and an effort supported by the purity and social hygiene groups, was the

Red Light Abatement Movement. This was designed to make it far easier for courts to enjoin the operation of brothels and summarily close
them down. At Common Law brothels were regarded as a public nuisance. One of the peculiarities of the Common Law was (and is) that a
public nuisance, one affecting a substantial amount of the public, cannot
be abated, that is legally enjoined or halted, by an individual citizen
complainant unless he can show that the nuisance damages him far
more and in some special way than the average citizen. A private citizen
can suppress only a *private* nuisance, a neighbor's activities peculiar in
their effect to the complainant's property. The local prosecutor, acting
on behalf of the entire community, is the person authorized to seek a
court order suppressing a *public* nuisance.

The problem was that there were constant allegations that the segregated prostitution districts operated in connivance "with whatever
political organization is in power."[45] The police and municipal authorities were thought to be "either implicated or else helpless."[46] The
reformers saw this legal rule as a great impediment to efforts to close
the districts, since local prosecutors, as representatives of the municipal
authorities, would not file actions to suppress the brothels.

The novelty of the red light abatement laws was that they permitted
a private citizen to file a private action to suppress and enjoin a brothel,
even though it was really a public nuisance. An individual purity leader,
or a local crank: either could file such a lawsuit. The movement started
in Maine in 1891. By 1915, seventeen states and the District of Columbia had such a statute, and by 1917 the reform extended to thirty
states.[47]

Another typically Progressive response to prostitution was to
appoint a local commission to study the problem. New York's Committee of Fifteen showed the way when it issued its study in 1902.[48] The
Chicago Vice Commission issued its well-regarded *The Social Evil in
Chicago* in 1911. New York appointed a special grand jury to investigate
after George Kibbe Turner published a muckraking article, "The
Daughters of the Poor," on the eve of the 1909 elections and charged
the complicity of Tammany Hall in local prostitution.[49] Tammany
called it a "grossly exaggerated partisan campaign story" and her may-
oral candidate called Kibbe a "political and racial bigot . . . [with] the
traits of ignorance, superficiality, recklessness, and irresistible propen-
sity to falsify."[50] The New York City court appointed John D. Rockefeller, Jr., to head a special grand jury to learn whether there was an

organized business of prostitution in New York and whether city officials were in complicity with it.[51] After his grand jury duty was finished, Rockefeller organized the influential Bureau of Social Hygiene and hired George J. Kneeland to prepare his *Commercialized Prostitution in New York City* (1913).

After this beginning in Chicago and New York, other American cities began to discover they had vice problems and appointed vice commissions to investigate and report. These commissions hired professional vice investigators such as George J. Kneeland and Abraham Flexner to come to their communities and study local conditions. It became the thing to do, and eventually, over thirty-two municipalities and states would issue vice reports, including such unlikely nests of vice as Lancaster, Pennsylvania (1913), Bay City, Michigan (1914), and Lexington, Kentucky (1915).[52]

The vice commissions all recommended the suppression of the segregated districts.[53] Since almost all of the districts existed only by tolerance and lacked any legally protected status, these recommendations and the force of public opinion formed by the purity and social hygiene movements ended the system of tolerated prostitution districts. Mayors and city councils simply ordered their police to enforce existing laws. Most of the vice commission reports also criticized the relationship between dance halls and saloons and between saloons and brothels, urged their municipalities to provide more parks and other recreational facilities for youth, and discredited the theory of male sexual necessity. Most also found that the low wages of working women bore a causal relationship to urban prostitution.[54]

There was considerable controversy, between 1909 and 1914, over the entire question of the relationship of low wages to prostitution. Doubtless, low wages led many women to rely extensively on the "treating system," but did it actually induce them to become professional prostitutes? Many pointed out that urban girls were paid a wage of $6 per week, while studies indicated they needed a minimum of $8 per week in order to live independently. Others replied that most working girls either lived at home or in the company of other women. Both the purity press and mainline publications were filled with articles bearing such titles as "Wages and Sin" and "Are Low Wages Responsible for Women's Immorality?"[55] The issue became further politicized by the resulting drive for a minimum wage for women.[56]

There were many who clung to the older view that it was only defect of character that caused a woman to become a prostitute. A priest in 1913 thought that women did so mostly "because they have indulged their curiosity, vanity, gluttony, idleness, love of pleasure, disobedience, sensuality, from childhood, and have never attempted any self-restraint."[57] A night court judge in New York laced his easy answers with Social Darwinism: "The greater proportion of prostitutes are in the business because they want to be, generally because by that life they can get money more easily than by hard work. . . . it is all part of the great question of efficiency. The woman who cannot secure a living wage is generally the inefficient woman, the inefficient woman is the woman who is not up to par mentally."[58]

Beyond these extreme views, however, more sensitive observers were unsure of a direct relationship between low wages and prostitution. A female investigator for the federal government, Mary Conyngton, wrote in a 1910 report that "not one [social] worker assigned poverty or low wages as a direct and immediate cause of immorality. It was agreed that indirectly their influence is great . . . the need of money is far more potent in keeping women in the life [i.e., prostitution] than in causing their first wrong step."[59] Jane Addams saw a causal "connection between low wages and despair, between over-fatigue and the demand for reckless pleasure," that was more nuanced than a reductionist equation of poverty and prostitution. "In addition to the monotony of work and the long hours, the small wages these girls receive have no relation to the standard of living which they are endeavoring to maintain. Discouraged and over-fatigued, they are often brought into sharp juxtaposition with the women who are obtaining much larger returns from their illicit trade." The prostitute herself always assigns poverty, "even when the immediate causes have been her love of pleasure, her desire for finery, or the influence of evil companions."[60]

This discussion of poverty and prostitution, the recommendations of the various vice commissions, the purity, social hygiene, and red light abatement movements are like calm ponds of rationality viewed alongside the stormy seas of the white slavery hysteria. We must review it in detail, since the white slavery hysteria was the immediate cause of the Mann Act. The term "white slave" had an earlier history and had been used to refer to prostitutes at least as early as 1857,[61] even on occasion to Mormon plural wives.[62] But this is quite different from its meaning, first in Chicago in 1907 and 1908, and then in the rest of the nation. Throughout the hysteria, the term "white slaves" was a constant reminder to middle-class America both of the alleged coercion involved, but also that it was not the lowly Negro that was being enslaved, but women of their own kind.

It was appropriate that the white slave hysteria began in Chicago as the city was teeming with reform currents involving such disparate elements as social justice, municipal reform, and evangelical Christianity.[63] It began with an article published in *McClure's Magazine* by the muckraker George Kibbe Turner in 1907. In it he charged that a "loosely organized association . . . largely composed of Russian Jews" was furnishing most of the women for the Chicago brothels, with the connivance of city officials.[64] Then Clifford G. Roe, a crusading Chicago prosecutor, apparently recovered a note thrown from a brothel in which a young prostitute claimed she was held as a "white slave." Roe began a sensational series of prosecutions, charging that brothels were holding young girls in actual confinement. Soon there were allegations of sales and auctions of women held as slaves. On October 17, 1909, the *Chicago Tribune* published a vivid cartoon depicting a young seminaked girl, sobbing into a handkerchief with shame, while buyers bid for her at auction as a new acquisition for their brothels. The accompanying article quoted Roe's triumphant acclamation:

> Chicago at last has waked up to a realization of the fact that actual slavery that deals in human flesh and blood as a marketable commodity exists in terrible magnitude in the city today. It is slavery, real slavery, that we are fighting. . . . The white slave of Chicago is a slave as much as the negro [sic] was before the civil war [sic] . . . as much as any people are slaves who are owned, flesh and bone, body and soul, by another person, and who can be sold at any time and place and for any price at that person's will. That is what slavery is, and that is the condition of hundreds, yes of thousands of girls in Chicago at present.[65]

Panic quickly spread to the rest of the nation. Soon a substantial segment of the population believed that young girls in America's cities were being lured to brothels by false pretenses, or pricked by poisoned darts or hypodermic needles and then dragged off to dens of iniquity. They were held there as slaves, bought and sold as chattels. Worst yet, playing on the political Progressive's fear of large enterprise, the whole thing was thought controlled by an far-flung, evil syndicate running this evil as a business.[66] As of 1910, as the federal officer in charge of suppressing vice put it:

It might almost be said that unless a girl was actually confined in a room and guarded—owing to the clever devices of these white slave traffickers—there was no girl, regardless of her station in life, who was altogether safe. . . . There was need that every person be on his guard, because no one could tell when his daughter or his wife or his mother would be selected as a victim.[67]

The writers on the topic were extreme in their assertions. "Today no one questions the fact that girls are bought and sold in America even as cattle and sheep and hogs are bought and sold" (1914). "There . . . now are, organized societies for the express purpose of debauching little girls . . . organized agencies to drag them down; slaves sold or pushed into the vicious life, and held there by iron bands" (1913). "Intoxication and drugging are often used as a means to reduce the victims to a state of helplessness, and sheer physical violence is a common thing. . . . Once a white slave is sold and landed in a house or dive she becomes a prisoner" (1910).[68] Nor were these sentiments issued by irresponsible persons. J. W. Jenks, a professor at Cornell and a member of the Federal Immigration Commission, stated that "girls . . . are secured through promises of employment, or at times through outright capture. Then they are held in a condition of practical slavery."[69] The superintendent of the Illinois Training School for Girls warned in 1910 that "some 65,000 daughters of American homes and 15,000 alien girls are the prey each year of procurers in this traffic. . . . They are hunted, trapped in a thousand ways . . . sold—sold for less than hogs!—and held in white slavery worse than death."[70]

Mainstream journals took up the cry. *The Outlook* wrote that "to deny that the traffic in enslaved girls exists is to presume on the ignorance of the public" (1909), and "we know without further investigation that girls are systematically both enticed and forced into prostitution" (1913).[71] Even the *New York Times* at first believed in white slavery. In a December 9, 1909, editorial, "There Is a White Slave Traffic," it wrote that the "belief that the white slave trade is a great as well as a monstrous evil . . . has the support of all the commissions and individuals who have given the matter examination at once honest and careful."[72] Nor was the hysteria regional. The *San Francisco Examiner* demonstrated its feeling of certainty with the arresting column headline "Slavers Kidnap 60,000 Women Each Year" on March 16, 1913.[73]

The hysterical pronouncements were often linked to the concerns we have noted as to immigration, urbanization, and sexual indepen-

"MY GOD! IF ONLY I COULD GET OUT OF HERE"
The midnight shriek of a young girl in the vice district of a large city, heard by two worthy men, started a crusade which resulted in closing up the dens of shame in that city. (See page 450.)

1. From Ernest A. Bell, ed., *Fighting the Traffic in Young Girls, or War on the White Slave Trade* (n.p. 1910).

dence of women. While the immigrant pimps and brothel owners were damned in print, there was considerable sympathy for the young Jewish and Italian girls forced to prostitute themselves by brutal masters. Such a girl was, in the language of the Immigration Commission, "ignorant of the language of the country, knows nothing beyond a few blocks of the city where she lives, has usually no money, and no knowledge of the rescue homes and institutions which might help her."[74] The muckrakers devised more lurid images of "little Italian peasant girls, taken from various dens, where they lay, shivering and afraid, under the lighted candles and crucifixes in their bedrooms."[75]

One would think that sexually experienced women might be more resistent to the wiles of the white slavers, but not according to Stanley W. Finch, in 1912 the Special Commissioner for the Suppression of White Slavery, a division of the (Federal) Bureau of Investigation. "No man's daughter, sister, or wife—if she be young and attractive—is safe from the artifices and devices of these traffickers," he said in a speech before a conference of the World's Purity Association. However, the white slavers were especially "quick to perceive and to single out girls, who . . . are inclined to be somewhat careless, and those who, through lack of, or distaste for, parental restraint, undertake to select their own companions, amusements, and occupations,"[76] in a word, young women who were independent.

Above all, it was the wicked city that was behind the evil. Edwin W. Sims, United States Attorney in Chicago and a personal friend of Representative James R. Mann, fanned the flames higher, both by a series of federal white slavery trials directed at foreigners and also by his public pronouncements:

> I can say, in all sincerity, that if I lived in the country and had a young daughter I would go any length of hardship and privation myself rather than allow her to go into the city to work or to study. . . . The best and the surest way for parents of girls in the country to protect them from the clutches of the "white slaver" is to keep them in the country. . . .
>
> One thing should be made very clear to the girl who comes up to the city, and that is that the ordinary ice cream parlor is very likely to be a spider's web for her entanglement. This is perhaps especially true of those ice cream saloons and fruit stores kept by foreigners.[77]

In the years of the hysteria the newspapers were filled with stories reporting the "sales" of women, often stating the prices. To the extent there was any truth to these accounts, the "sales" were probably agents' fees for locating a willing prostitute to move to another brothel. One spectacular trial illustrates the process of the hysteria. On April 30,

THE FIRST STEP

Ice cream parlors of the city and fruit stores combined, largely run by foreigners, are the places where scores of girls have taken their first step downward. Does her mother know the character of the place and the man she is with? (See page 71.)

2. From Ernest A. Bell, ed., *Fighting the Traffic in Young Girls, or War on the White Slave Trade* (n.p. 1910).

1910, the *New York Times* carried as its major headline on the first page "White Slave Traffic Shown to Be Real." The story noted that District Attorney Whitman had "unmistakable evidence" that two female investigators had "bought" two girls. According to the District Attorney the girls "gave their ages as 17 and 18, but even [the defendant] says they are younger. It is understood that they are only 16. And these are white girls. . . . [one was] a girl, so little and so childish that she wept when they took her from one house to another because she had had to leave her Teddy bear behind. . . . The other . . . freed from a house where she had been kept ever since last September, brought nothing with her except a tattered doll, which she still cherished."[78] The next day the District Attorney claimed that the arrest of these "sellers" had netted "the leaders in the traffic for this city."[79]

On May 2, in an editorial, "Facts That Cannot Be Denied," the *Times* said that the case provided an answer to those who denied the existence of the trade. "There were slaves for sale," it declared.[80] The matter was quickly brought to trial amid considerable publicity. It developed that the female investigators had approached the defendants, a brothel owner and a madam, and asked if they knew of any prostitutes who would like to work in Seattle. The two defendants looked around and referred them to the women described by the prosecutor as the little girls. For this service, the two defendants were paid a fee of $120, in effect a finder's fee. To facilitate the transaction the police agents had spent over $3,000 to entertain the various madams, pimps, and prostitutes involved.[81]

Both of the "girls" who had been sold testified for the prosecution. One was twenty-five years old, had been married, and was a professional prostitute. The other testified that she was twenty-three and was a prostitute. The *Times* article noted that she "looked the part" and that throughout her testimony she swung a "patent-leather toe in the neighborhood of the stenographer's left ear." She said that she had been approached by their "buyers" and asked if the two of them would like to work in Seattle. The two prostitutes talked it over and agreed. The police investigators, the "buyers," then asked if the women needed money; they said yes and spent it on clothes for the trip.[82]

The two defendants were convicted. They had violated a statute that prohibited "receiving money for and on account of procuring and placing women in the custody of another person for immoral purposes." But this was hardly a "sale" in the usual sense of the term. The *Times* was greatly disappointed. It was "not a victory of which anybody connected with the prosecution can or should be very proud, and there was not in it anything obviously relevant to the traffic in 'white slaves.'"[83] A letter to the editor asked, "Are they the only kind of white slaves we have? Is not the whole thing buncombe—the most despicable kind of buncombe?" Another letter writer had a telling insight into the crusader and reformer mentality. He charged that the whole drama was "designed to reflect an effulgence of great purpose upon the authors thereof."[84]

This trial of Belle Moore, one of the two defendants, was a defining moment for the *Times*. It no longer supported the crusade against white slavery. By July 1914 it declared that "sensational magazine articles had created a belief in the existence of a great interstate 'white slave' trust. No such trust exists, nor is there any organized white slave industry anywhere."[85] By 1916 it referred to the "myth of an international and interstate 'syndicate' trafficking in women" as merely "a figment of imaginative fly-gobblers."[86]

An entire literary genre developed around white slavery. Novels, such as Thomas Nelson Page's *John Marvel, Assistant* (1909) and Estelle Baker's *The Rose Door* (1913), depicted young women's seduction or abduction and descent into prostitution. The best known was Reginald W. Kauffman's *The House of Bondage* (1910), which went through eleven printings in less than nine months.[87] Dramas followed, including two controversial plays, *The Lure* and *The Flight,* which opened on Broadway amid threats of censorship in 1913.[88] In addition to their "immorality," some social workers criticized the lurid nature of the white slave novels and plays as contributing to the "state of hysteria."[89]

The white slavery hysteria inspired a new form of literary creation, books filled with lurid case studies and grossly distorted real events combined with chapters contributed by public officials and social workers. These white slavery narratives have been placed in the American tradition of captivity narratives.[90] Some examples are Ernest A. Bell, ed., *War on the White Slave Trade* (1909), Clifford G. Roe, *The Great War on White Slavery; or, Fighting for the Protection of Our Girls* (1911), and Jean Turner Zimmermann, *America's Black Traffic in White Girls* (1912). There were dozens of these books, and all enjoyed large printings. There was even a statuette, created by Abastenia St. Leger Eberle, of an unclothed, cowering girl in the process of sale by an evil white slaver. The May 3, 1913, cover of *The Survey* featured a photograph of the statuette and touched off a letter-writing campaign that extended for weeks.

The white slavery movies caused the biggest sensation. They displayed innocent women from the country lured to vice and immigrant girls fresh off the boat drugged and dragged off unconscious, then confined in a brothel and held against their will. "The Fatal Hour" (1908), involving Chinese white slave traffic, was probably the first.[91] The best was Universal Picture's "Traffic in Souls" (1913), which sold thirty thousand tickets in its first week and at one time played simultaneously to twenty theaters in the New York City metropolitan area.[92] This was quickly followed by "The Inside of the White Slave Traffic" (1913), more documentary than melodrama. It had a huge initial popularity but was suppressed. A film version of the "House of Bondage" (1914) followed, as did films with titles such as "The Little Girl Next Door" (1916) and "Is Any Girl Safe?" (1916).[93] These white slavery films, while popular, were quite controversial.[94]

It was a strange sort of moral panic. First, people had different definitions of what "white slavery" meant. Second, there were many contemporaries who did not believe in it at all. For that matter, modern historians are in disagreement as to whether there was any considerable amount of coerced prostitution. Third, the official commissions appointed to investigate often issued self-contradictory reports.

The term "white slavery" varied in meaning from coerced, imprisoned women to a psychological bondage to purely voluntary prostitution.[95] Some writers and vice commissions clearly distinguished a free-will prostitute from a white slave.[96] Others thought that prostitution and white slavery were the same thing, and the white slaver was simply a male who procured or exploited women, regardless of their consent.[97]

Many contemporary observers rejected the whole notion out of hand.[98] Frank Moss, an assistant district attorney in New York, felt that prostitution was almost entirely voluntary.[99] Brand Whitlock, a former mayor of Toledo, thought the hysteria was "one of those strange moral movements which now and then seize upon the public mind" and slyly suggested that the reformers had an economic motive to stir things up so that they could raise funds to carry on their "work."[100] He saw the vice commission reports and the white slavery narratives as a "sort of pornography to satisfy the American sense of news . . . rendered aseptic by efforts of officials, heated to a due degree of moral indignation, to bring the concupiscent to justice." He ridiculed the stories of the "shanghaied innocent . . . trapped in precisely the same way by the minions of a huge system, organized like any modern combination . . . [with] its own attorneys, agents, kidnappers, crimpers, seducers, panderers and procuresses all over the land."[101]

Even the social workers disagreed. Addams thought that there were "young girls who, in evil houses, are literally beaten and starved by the dissolute men whom they support" and that "a number of women have entered [prostitution] against their own volition."[102] But John Sumner of the New York Society for the Suppression of Vice thought that "comparatively speaking there is only a small amount of compulsion."[103] And A. W. Elliott, president of the Southern Rescue Mission, wrote that "there never was a joke of more huge proportions perpetrated upon the American public than this white slave joke. There is scarcely a simmering of truth in the various stories of so-called white slavery. . . . I surely do not believe that there are a dozen girls in America to-day that are in houses of ill fame that could not walk out if they wanted to." He also suggested the stories of reformers were told to raise funds.[104]

Subsequent historians have disagreed about white slavery. Many students of the period have attributed the entire hysteria to a moral panic.[105] Others have accepted that a considerable number of women were coerced prostitutes,[106] while still another estimates that the extent of unwilling prostitutes was only about ten percent.[107] The *New York Times* carried about a dozen accounts alleging abduction, deception, or coercion for prostitution during the period from 1910 to 1914. In some, the context clearly suggests an attempt by the woman to absolve herself of guilt in the eyes of husband or parents, but some of them may have been true. In a study published in 1933, Walter C. Reckless examined the court files of the white slave prosecutions in Chicago for the years 1910 to 1913. He found no evidence of organized gangs and little evidence that there were any attempts purposely to trap girls. He did find that some cases, less than five percent, involved holding women as prostitutes against their will.[108] This seems an appropriate conclusion generally and as close to the truth as we can come. There was indeed *some* coerced prostitution at the time of the white slave hysteria, but very little. Nor was there any syndicate or organization.

The American public's collective mind was not soothed by the internal inconsistency of several of the vice commission reports. The three most significant commissions were the Senate [Dillingham] Immigration Commission, which reported in 1909; the Rockefeller Grand Jury, appointed in response to Turner's sensational article, and which reported in 1910; and the Chicago Vice Commission, whose findings were published in 1911. The Dillingham report had the most serious inconsistencies.

On the question of the voluntariness of the immigrant women's prostitution, the report stated on the one hand: "The majority of women and girls who are induced to enter this country for immoral purposes have already entered the life at home and come to this country as they would go elsewhere, influenced primarily by business considerations. They believe they can make higher profits here. . . . To guard against the sensational beliefs that are becoming prevalent, it is best to repeat that the agents of this commission have not learned that all or even the majority of the alien women and girls practicing prostitution in the United States . . . were forced or deceived into the life."[109]

On the other hand, the commission also reported that prostitutes "are beaten and threatened, sometimes with murder, if they attempt to escape. . . . alien women and girls in considerable numbers have been so deceived or taken advantage of by procurers that they have found themselves in conditions which practically forced them into practicing prostitution. . . . If she tries to leave her man, she is threatened with arrest. . . . she may be beaten; in some cases when she has betrayed her betrayer she has been murdered."[110]

The commission was also inconsistent on the question of whether the white slavers were organized. "There has been much talk in the newspapers," the report stated, "of a great monopolistic corporation whose business it is to import and exploit these unfortunate women, trafficking in them from country to country. The commission has been unable to learn of any such corporation and does not believe in its existence." However, on the other hand, "doubtless the importers and pimps have a wide acquaintance among themselves, and doubtless in many instances they have rather close business relations with one another . . . there are two organizations of importance, one French, the other Jewish. . . . They [the importers] have also various resorts where they meet and receive their mail, transact business with one another, and visit. Perhaps the best-known organization of this kind throughout the country was one legally incorporated in New York in 1904 under the name of the New York Independent Benevolent Association."[111]

The Rockefeller Grand Jury and the Chicago Vice Commission also seemed to speak with two minds on the question of whether the vice trade was systematic and organized. The Rockefeller Grand Jury reported in 1910:

> We have found no evidence of the existence in the county of New York of any organization or organizations, incorporated or otherwise, engaged as such in the traffic in women for immoral purposes, nor have we found evidence of an organized traffic in women for immoral

purposes. It appears on the other hand . . . that a traffic in the bodies of women does exist, and is carried on by individuals acting for their own individual benefit, and that these persons are known to each other, and are more or less informally associated. We have also found that associations and clubs, composed mainly or wholly of those profiting from vice, have existed, and that one such association still exists. These associations and clubs are analogous to commercial bodies in other fields, which, while not directly engaged in commerce, are composed of individuals all of whom as individuals are so engaged.[112]

While a trade association may not be a corporation or even a syndicate, it still came uncomfortably close to the trust-like organization the public imagination had in mind. The Chicago Vice Commission reached essentially the same ambiguous conclusions about conditions there. "It has been demonstrated that men and women engaged in the 'white slave traffic' are not organized. Their operations, however, are so similar and they use the same methods to such an extent that it is safe to infer that they are in some way working together."[113]

But the reformers did not reflect the ambiguities of the official reports. They saw events in a black and white mode. Allegations that the white slavery talk was hysteria were simply dismissed. William Burgess wrote in *Vigilance* that "it was to be expected that just as soon as a real awakening began on this most serious of all social problems, somebody would see in it an 'epidemic of frenzy.'"[114] The head of the (Federal) Bureau of Investigation snapped that "some hysteria always accompanies important changes and important steps forward in the life of a nation," but did suggest it be replaced by "sincere, earnest and unrelenting efforts . . . until the White Slave Traffic is indeed annihilated."[115]

The irresponsibility of statements by certain public officials is hard to believe. Worst still, these public officials fanned public apprehension by playing on alleged official information available to them in their governmental status. In a 1912 speech, Stanley W. Finch, Special Commissioner for the Suppression of White Slavery, told his audience that "it is a fact that there are now scattered throughout practically every section of the United States a vast number of men and women whose sole occupation consists in enticing, tricking, or coercing young women and girls into immoral lives. . . . Moreover, their methods have been so far developed and perfected that they seem to be able to ensnare almost any woman or girl whom they select for the purpose. This is indeed an extraordinary statement, and one almost passing belief, but that it is absolutely true no one can honestly doubt who reviews any considerable portion of the mass of evidence which is already in the possession of the Attorney General's Bureau of Investigation."[116]

The most irresponsible statements of all were those made by Edwin W. Sims, the United States Attorney in Chicago. They were the most sweeping and also played on information available to him in his official capacity. They were the most important because they were picked up and repeated in numerous other formats, newspaper and magazine articles, sermons, and purity publications. Compared with the ambiguities of the vice commission reports, the clarity of this federal prosecutor was irresistible to many. "The legal evidence thus far collected," he wrote in 1909:

> establishes with complete moral certainty these awful facts: That the white slave traffic is a system operated by a syndicate which has its ramifications from the Atlantic seaboard to the Pacific ocean, with "clearing houses" or "distributing centers" in nearly all of the larger cities; that in this ghastly traffic the buying price of a young girl is from $15 up and that the selling price is from $200 to $600 . . . that this syndicate . . . is a definite organization sending its hunters regularly to scour France, Germany, Hungary, Italy and Canada for victims; that the man at the head of this unthinkable enterprise it [sic] known among his hunters as "The Big Chief."[117]

The ravings of Sims and men like him drowned out weaker voices urging calm. The white slavery hysteria led to demands for government to "do" something, and by 1910 it was already the federal government that was thought most appropriate. Then too, the beliefs of the hysteria itself lent an appropriateness to action on the federal level. If white slaves were being sold and then shipped from coast to coast, it was more than a state problem. Federal power was needed to prevent even the initial procurement of the white slaves. The House report to the Mann bill claimed that as "the traffic involves mainly the transportation of women and girls from the country districts to the centers of population and their importation from foreign nations the evil is one which cannot be met comprehensively and effectively otherwise than by the enactment of federal laws."[118] In fact, the Senate's Immigration Commission had already recommended the criminalization, surprisingly on a gender neutral basis, of "the transportation of persons from any State, Territory, or District to another for the purposes of prostitution."[119]

The crusading United States Attorney in Chicago, Edwin W. Sims,

3. Edwin W. Sims, United States Attorney, Chicago, and probable draftsman of the White Slave Traffic Act. From Ernest A. Bell, ed., *Fighting the Traffic in Young Girls, or War on the White Slave Trade* (n.p. 1910).

consulted with his friend, James R. Mann, the Congressman from Chicago. Mann acknowledged to Congress that Sims first brought his attention to the possibility of federal action against white slavery.[120] While the Act was pending, Sims wrote that he took the matter up with Mann because of Mann's position as Chairman of the House Committee on Interstate and Foreign Commerce.[121] Several years later Mann again acknowledged Sims's role in bringing the matter to his notice, but contended that when he had asked Sims to draft appropriate legislation, the draft Sims prepared dealt only with immigration. Mann claimed for himself the idea of using the interstate commerce clause as the basis of federal jurisdiction. Although Sims later prepared a draft based on interstate transportation, Mann said he rewrote it and that he introduced his own final version which ultimately became the White Slave Traffic Act, or Mann Act.[122]

Sims never directly claimed the authorship of the Act. However, it is more likely than not that he drafted the bill. Another of the Chicago crusaders, Ernest A. Bell, contemporaneously wrote that Sims drafted the bill.[123] When Representative Mann and President Taft consulted together about the proposed legislation just before it was introduced, Sims's role was important enough that he came to Washington to participate in the conference. At the conclusion of the conference, on November 24, 1909, Mann issued a statement praising Sims's work in Chicago and stated that most of the American girls who became white slaves "are enticed away from their homes in the country to large cities."[124] His concern was both a justification for federal action and a description of the national angst.

Sims's involvement in the national legislation is also seen in the legislative committee reports. Mann both sponsored the bill and also guided it through the committee he chaired, the important Interstate and Foreign Commerce Committee. The committee's report cribbed several paragraphs, without attribution, of material Sims had previously published.[125] The Senate report is a virtual copy of the House report.[126]

Mann introduced his bill on December 6, 1909, and it was referred to his own Committee on Interstate and Foreign Commerce.[127] Within a few days, in his annual message to Congress, President Taft gave his opinion that it would be constitutional for federal law to prohibit the transportation of persons across state lines for the purpose of prostitution.[128] Several different purity organizations and publications urged their members and readers to write their congressmen to urge the passage of Mann's bill and later congratulated themselves on their good work.[129] As it made its way through Congress, Mann's bill competed with other proposed legislative cures to the white slavery problem,[130] but none had the broad scope of Mann's bill. The House Committee on Interstate and Foreign Commerce reported it out on December 21, 1909. The bill was based on the interstate commerce clause of the Con-

4. Congressman James R. Mann, sponsor of the White Slave Traffic Act.
Courtesy of the Library of Congress.

stitution and also on the 1904 international treaty for the suppression of
the white slave traffic. The committee report clearly shows the legislative intent behind the enactment, a clear history that was later ignored
by the United States Supreme Court when it extended the statute to
noncommercial interstate transportation.

The legislation is needed to put a stop to a villainous interstate and international traffic in women and girls. The legislation is not needed or intended as an aid to the States in the exercise of their police powers in the suppression or regulation of immorality in general. It does not attempt to regulate the practice of voluntary prostitution, but aims solely to prevent panderers and procurers from compelling thousands of women and girls against their will and desire to enter and continue in a life of prostitution.[131]

That seems clear enough as to what Congress was attempting; but the report goes on to describe what white slavery meant and thereby underlines that the congressional intention was to attack coerced prostitution.

There are few who really understand the true significance of the term "white-slave trade." . . . the inmates of many houses of ill fame are made up largely of women and girls whose original entry into a life of immorality was brought about by men who are in the business of procuring women for that purpose—men whose sole means of livelihood is the money received from the sale and exploitation of women who, by means of force and restraint, compel their victims to practice prostitution. . . . these women are practically slaves in the true sense of the word [and] many of them are kept in houses of ill fame against their will [and] force, if necessary, is used to deprive them of their liberty.

The characteristic which distinguishes "the white-slave trade" from immorality in general is that the women who are the victims of the traffic are unwillingly forced to practice prostitution. The term "white slave" includes only those women and girls who are literally slaves—those women who are owned and held as property and chattels—whose lives are lives of involuntary servitude.[132]

Again and again, in unmistakable terms, Mann's report underlined the statute's narrow purpose. "In order to insure her continuance in the degraded life, to which she has unwillingly been forced to submit, the procurer has resort to physical violence and the maintenance of a system of surveillance which makes her, to all intents and purposes, a prisoner."[133] The committee flatly stated that "it is the purpose of the proposed laws . . . to protect women and girls against *this criminal traffic*"[134] (emphasis added). Even for this narrow purpose there was opposition. A minority report by Representative William Richardson of Alabama, and concurred in by two other members of the committee, opposed the bill on the grounds of states' rights.

The real correct analysis of this bill is, that it proposes to turn over to the jurisdiction of Congress, under the pretense and guise of regulating commerce among the States, the authority to exercise police power that is inherent to, and remains with, the States. It is an attempt to exercise police authority by the General Government over those things subject only to the police authority of the States.[135]

The bill sailed through Congress with only token, verbal amendments. There was no debate in Congress on what the expression "any other immoral purpose" really meant. The only reference to that phrase in the legislative history is the committee report reference to the Supreme Court's interpretation, for purposes of an amendment to the immigration act, that "immoral purpose" included the importation of a woman to be a personal, private mistress.[136] No one in Congress suggested that there might be a truly radical interpretation of the meaning of "other immoral purpose" or the vastly increased police powers that would land in the federal government's lap if it were so interpreted. And there was no need to raise this issue. As Representative Andrew J. Peters of Massachusetts pointed out, "the considerations which prompt the support of this bill are so widespread and its objects are so well understood and meet with such universal approval."[137] That universal understanding, of course, was the smashing of white slavery. No one gave a thought to boyfriend-girlfriend travel.

The little opposition that was raised centered on the interstate commerce clause, federal powers, and states' rights. Richardson said that he knew "that a man puts himself in a position . . . to be criticised by standing up here on the floor of this House and undertaking to resist a bill of this kind. I am aware of that." Another southern representative said that he wished "to make only a few remarks—not, however, in defense of prostitution of women. We are all opposed to that."[138]

Mann spoke on behalf of his bill along the lines of his report, quoted above. He warmed to the subject sufficiently to make the incredibly ludicrous remark that "the white-slave traffic, while not so extensive, is much more horrible than any black-slave traffic ever was in the history of the world." Representative Coy of Indiana joined in this comparison, calling the newly discovered white slavery "a thousand times worse and more degrading in its consequences and effects upon humanity than any species of human slavery that ever existed in this country." The remarks of other members demonstrate that they understood the purpose of the statute to be exactly the same. Representative Edward W.

Saunders of Virginia referred to "conditions of restraint, and compulsion, which have been aptly, and universally styled, 'white slavery,'" and warned that "an organized society exists both in this country, and abroad, formed for no other purpose than to exploit innocent girls for immoral purposes. This syndicate has headquarters and distributing centers in New York, Chicago, San Francisco, Denver, and many other American cities."[139]

Representative Thetus W. Sims of Tennessee agreed that there was a "regular system, a chain of criminal traffickers" and that whenever he thought "of a beautiful girl taken from one State to another . . . and drugged, debauched, and ruined . . . [sold] to any brute who will pay the price, I cannot bring myself to vote against this bill."[140] Nor could Representative Gordon J. Russell of Texas who saw in favor of the bill "every pure woman in the land . . . every priest and minister of the Living God . . . [and] men who reverence womanhood and who set a priceless value upon female purity. Upon the other side you would find all the whoremongers and the pimps and the procurers and the keepers of bawdy houses. Upon that other side you would find all those who hate God and scoff at innocence and laugh at female virtue."[141]

It was a foregone conclusion that the bill would pass handily. It did and was signed into law by President Taft on June 25, 1910.[142] "It owed its passage," a wiser *New York Times* editorialized six years later, "to a misapprehension or misrepresentation of its real language and inevitable result, and to a sort of moral panic in Congress, the reflection of the spasms of amateur sociologists and mythmakers of the magazines."[143]

It will be helpful to describe the actual language of the Mann Act as it was enacted in 1910. The original provisions, reproduced in the appendix, were not amended, except for simplification and modernizing of language, until the 1970s. However, the Act as passed in 1910 was a classic example of redundant legalese. It contained eight sections.

Section 1 made a commonsense definition of "interstate commerce," and Section 7 extended the term "territory" to include unorganized American possessions and defined "person." Section 5 permitted prosecution in any judicial district from, through, or into which the woman was transported in violation of the Act. This section was of some practical consequence. It permitted prosecutors to select that state, and even portion of a state, in which the moral climate was such as to most likely assure conviction. Section 8 gave the short title of the statute, declaring that the statute "shall be known and referred to as the 'White-slave traffic Act.'"

Of the four sections defining criminal activity and ordaining punishment, sections 2, 3, 4, and 6, Section 6 was longest and least important. This section was specifically responsive to the nation's international treaty obligation to suppress international traffic in women. It designated the Commissioner General of Immigration as the American official responsible for obtaining information concerning the international movement of women for prostitution or debauchery and required him to maintain certain records. It required the filing of a statement by every person who maintained or harbored any alien woman for the purpose of "prostitution, or for any other immoral purpose" within three years after the woman had entered the United States. The statement to be filed required such information as the name and age of the woman, the facts concerning her nationality and entry into the country, and the place at which she was kept.

The Act provided that a person filing such a statement could not be prosecuted under any *federal* law concerning its disclosures. The statute does not mention it, but the federal authorities could hand the information obtained through the statements to *state* prosecutors for the filing of pandering and prostitution charges or the closing of the brothel disclosed. On the other hand, a failure to file the statement was declared a misdemeanor, not a felony, with punishment not to exceed a $2,000 fine, two years imprisonment, or both. Although Section 6 was an integral part of the Mann Act, it was less vigorously enforced and had far less impact on most Americans than the better-known sections concerning interstate travel.

Section 2 penalized "any person" who transports, or aids or assists in the transportation, of a "woman or girl" for a prohibited purpose or intent, in interstate or foreign commerce, or "in" any territory or the District of Columbia. Therefore, while a female had to be transported, the transporter-defendant could be male or female. The federal government has general police jurisdiction over its territories and Washington, D.C. Transportation *within* those territories violated the Act. In cases not involving a federal territory, the Mann Act was clearly based on the constitutional powers conferred by the interstate commerce clause, and a state line had to be crossed.

Interstate transportation of women could hardly be absolutely prohibited. To violate the law the travel had to be for the prohibited purposes of "prostitution or debauchery, or for any other immoral purpose." Alternatively, the transportation or assistance in transportation was criminalized if accomplished with the defendant's "intent and purpose to induce, entice, or compel such woman or girl to become a prostitute or to give herself up to debauchery, or to engage in any other immoral practice."

This alternative penalization, of purpose or intent, meant that the Act was violated even though the immoral purpose was not accomplished. If the defendant held the wrong mental state as the woman crossed the state line and intended that she be prostituted, debauched, or engage in any other immoral sexual activity, then he was guilty of the Mann Act. It would not matter that the intended seduction or other sexual activity never occurred. The violation of this Section 2 was declared a felony and punishable by a fine not exceeding $5,000, five years imprisonment, or both.

Section 3 was an entirely different crime. A defendant could violate 2 without 3, vice versa, or violate both. Section 3 prohibited any person from persuading or forcing, or assisting in persuading or forcing, a woman to travel in interstate or foreign commerce, or within any federal territory, for the same prohibited purposes or intent. The section specified that the woman's consent did not matter. So much for white slavery as slavery. It is puzzling in light of the strong statement of legislative purpose to combat coerced prostitution, "true" white slavery. It may be that the purpose of consent not being a defense, as well as the inclusion of "other immoral purpose," was simply to prevent subterfuge and evasion. Section 3 also required that, as a result of the persuasion, the woman or girl "be carried or transported as a passenger upon the line or route of any common carrier." Violation of this section was a felony and punishment was the same as Section 2, with imprisonment not to exceed five years, a fine not to exceed $5,000, or both.

The requirement of a common carrier in Section 3, the persuasion and enticement section, and its absence in Section 2, the transportation section, led to an interesting and apparently unintended consequence. Trains, planes, and buses are common carriers, but a private automobile is not. If a man himself drove his girlfriend by car to an adjacent state with a prohibited purpose, he would be guilty of Section 2. If he called his girlfriend on the telephone and persuaded her to drive over from an adjacent state to visit him, he might be free on a technicality. If he paid for the gas he would be guilty under the aid or assist provision of Section 2, where no common carrier was required. However, if the girl-friend paid for her own gas and drove over in her own car, he did not violate the Mann Act. He did not transport or assist the transportation. His persuasion may have resulted in an interstate travel but not "upon the line or route of any common carrier," required under Section 3. These distinctions led to some anomalous cases.

Section 4 was patterned after Section 3. It penalized any person who persuaded or coerced a female "under the age of eighteen years" to engage in interstate travel for the same prohibited purposes. It did not penalize the person who merely assisted in these activities, as did Section 3, but did require that the transportation be by common carrier. Like Sections 2 and 3, but unlike Section 6, it was a felony violation with doubled punishment, presumably because of the youth of the so-called victim. Punishment could not exceed ten years imprisonment, $10,000, or both.

The Progressives had a deep concern with prostitution, although this masked even deeper anxieties about immigration, urbanization, and changing sexual mores. One response to prostitution was characteristic of the Progressive period—a reliance on experts, commissions, and changes in law. The other response was the hysteria represented by white slavery. The hysterical response led to the enactment of the Mann Act. Now we shall see the first fruits of this child of panic, its early enforcement.

Early Enforcement, 1910–1916

The stereotypically swarthy white slavers proved to be in as short a supply as their stereotypically coerced virginal victims. It was appropriate that the nation's first arrest for violation of the Mann Act took place at the Union Station in Chicago, July 8, 1910. But it was both ironic and telling that the first culprit taken prisoner under the White Slave Traffic Act was a woman, a madam escorting five apparently perfectly willing prostitutes from Chicago to her brothel in Houghton, Michigan.[1] The transportation of adult, willing prostitutes would always constitute the great bulk of Mann Act prosecutions.

By early fall, the Department of Justice and the Commissioner-General of Immigration concluded an arrangement whereby Justice would enforce the transportation sections of the Act and Immigration would be primarily responsible for enforcement of the sixth section, which dealt with the filing of statements concerning alien prostitutes. The Department of Justice sent copies of the Act itself and the nature of the jurisdictional agreement to all United States Attorneys on October 31, 1910. In the circular, Attorney General George Wickersham wrote that it was his desire that "special attention be given to the enforcement of this act" and directed consideration to the section dealing with under-aged girls. There was no mention of the scope of the statute, the meaning of "debauchery," or whether it covered noncommercial immorality of an interstate nature.[2]

Since the Department of Justice was to handle the major burden of enforcement, that in turn meant that its police division, the Bureau of

Investigation, would be responsible for such investigation and apprehension as was not entirely local. Prior to 1908 the various federal agencies had a makeshift system of borrowing detectives from other agencies or hiring private detectives whenever an investigation was needed. Particularly popular was the borrowing of Secret Service agents. In May 1908 Congress forbade the Department of Justice and other executive departments from using Secret Service agents, probably because the members were piqued by their recent investigations of various members' alleged land frauds. This development had a potentially crippling effect on executive agencies, and President Theodore Roosevelt directed Attorney General Bonaparte to create an investigative bureau within the Department of Justice. Bonaparte did so by order of July 26, 1908. The following year the Taft administration gave the subagency the name of Bureau of Investigation, ultimately to be renamed the now familiar Federal Bureau of Investigation.[3]

When the subagency was created in 1908, it had only a director and twenty-three agents, and because there was substantial fear of a national police force it was given only a limited jurisdiction.[4] Its investigations were confined to antitrust and postal act violations and an assortment of miscellaneous crimes. It really did not have much work to do.[5] By 1910, under the directorship of Stanley W. Finch, the Bureau had grown to thirty-five investigators, but it still lacked any significant field offices and operated almost entirely out of Washington.[6] This changed with the acquisition of Mann Act jurisdiction.

The Mann Act resulted in the Bureau's first major field office, in Baltimore, and a dramatic increase in manpower. Later jurisdictional grants, such as the prohibition laws and espionage, would ultimately prove more important, but the Mann Act provided the real takeoff for the FBI. One historian of the FBI wrote that "the enforcement of the Mann Act began the transformation of the Justice Department's police bureau from a modest agency concerned with odds and ends of Federal law enforcement to a nationally recognized institution, with agents in every State and every large city."[7] Most students of the FBI have agreed.[8] As of April 1912 the white slave investigations overshadowed the entire balance of the Bureau's work.[9]

In addition to the help of the Bureau of Investigation, the Attorney General hired an individual named Henry J. Dannenbaum of Houston to be his special assistant to assist in the prosecutions of violations of the White Slave Traffic Act. Dannenbaum is somewhat of a shadowy figure. He was hired on April 1, 1911, and paid an extraordinarily large salary for the time, $500 per month.[10] He set up a sort of headquarters in New York. Occasionally he made some specific suggestions to Wickersham or to Finch, and on a few occasions he appeared in court in regard to prosecutions. He departed, apparently amicably and with the department's satisfaction with the value of his services, by the end of the summer of 1911. His chief value, as Wickersham put it later, was "in securing the co-operation of various non-government organizations and in bringing about, in various quarters, a realization of the importance of this class of prosecutions."[11]

Dannenbaum had some sort of public relations role, and it may well have had to do primarily with the railroads, which in 1911 were still the most important means of interstate travel. In May 1911 Dannenbaum advised Finch that several railroads had issued circulars to their ticket agents about the White Slave Traffic Act, including specifically the L&N, Illinois Central (see figure 5), and the Southern. Other railways, including the Union Pacific and Southern Pacific, invited suggestions as to how they could assist the federal effort in suppressing white slave traffic.[12]

And, indeed, the railroads were co-operating. The circulars of Illinois Central and Chicago and Northwestern were typical. Illinois Central advised its ticket agents not to deliver prepaid tickets to women or girls "known to reside in the so-called segregated districts" nor to accept deposits from persons residing in such districts for prostitution for the delivery of tickets to women, regardless of address.[13] The traffic manager of the Chicago and Northwestern Railroad sternly warned their employees that "this company will not directly or indirectly solicit, aid, encourage or facilitate any known effort for the movement of so-called white slave traffic."[14] Still other lines, such as Southern Railway, took advantage of the pamphlets containing the White Slave Traffic Act printed by the Government Printing Office and mailed copies to passenger representatives.[15]

The early investigative activity came at a price, and appropriations proved difficult to obtain from a tight Congress, still suspicious of the Bureau of Investigation. For the two fiscal years, 1911–12 and 1912–13, Congress appropriated only a general sum to the Department of Justice under a rubric entitled Detection and Prosecution of Crime. The estimates of the funds actually spent on enforcement of the White Slave Traffic Act seem inconsistent, but they suggest approximately $75,000

Illinois Central Railroad Company
Indianapolis Southern Railroad Company
The Yazoo & Mississippi Valley Railroad Company

Passenger Department
(File No. 70-481)

CHICAGO, ILL., September 15, 1910

To Ticket Agents:
To Passenger Department Representatives:

Below please find copy of Sections 1 and 2 of

"An Act to further regulate Interstate and Foreign Commerce by prohibiting the transportation therein for immoral purposes of women and girls, and for other purposes."

This Act became effective June 25, 1910

White Slave Traffic Act

"*Be it enacted by the Senate and House of Representatives of the United States of America in Congress assembled*, That the term 'Interstate Commerce,' as used in this Act, shall include transportation from any State or Territory or the District of Columbia to any other State or Territory or the District of Columbia, and the term ' Foreign Commerce,' as used in this Act, shall include transportation from any State or Territory or the District of Columbia to any foreign country and from any foreign country to any State or Territory or the District of Columbia.

Sec. 2. That any person who shall knowingly transport or cause to be transported, or aid or assist in obtaining transportation for, or in transporting, in interstate or foreign commerce, or in any Territory or in the District of Columbia, any woman or girl for the purpose of prostitution or debauchery, or for any other immoral purpose, or with the intent and purpose to induce, entice, or compel such woman or girl to become a prostitute or to give herself up to debauchery, or to engage in any other immoral practice; or who shall knowingly procure or obtain, or cause to be procured or obtained, or aid or assist in procuring or obtaining, any ticket or tickets, or any form of transportation or evidence of the right thereto, to be used by any woman or girl in interstate or foreign commerce, or in any Territory or the District of Columbia, in going to any place for the purpose of prostitution or debauchery, or for any other immoral purpose, or with the intent or purpose on the part of such person to induce, entice, or compel her to give herself up to the practice of prostitution, or to give herself up to debauchery, or any other immoral practice, whereby any such woman or girl shall be transported in interstate or foreign commerce, or in any Territory or the District of Columbia, *shall be deemed guilty of a felony, and upon conviction thereof shall be punished by a fine not exceeding five thousand dollars, or by imprisonment of not more than five years,* or by both such fine and imprisonment, in the discretion of the court."

Requests from persons depositing the value of tickets, or from other persons, to deliver tickets to conductors or to retain baggage checks as security for the delivery, at destination, of women or girls for whom transportation is prepaid, must be declined.

Effective at once, do not issue prepaid orders for tickets to be used by any woman or girl, in traveling from one place to another, for the purposes stated in the *White Slave Traffic Act*; agents will deny to such depositors, or others interested in the transportation of women or girls, for the purposes stated, any aid or assistance of any kind or character, through the reservation of space in Pullman cars, or otherwise; prepaid tickets must not be delivered to women or girls *known to reside in the so-called segregated districts in cities or who reside in localities, residences, or other buildings in cities, towns or villages, which are known to harbor women or girls of the character described, nor shall deposits for the delivery of tickets to women or girls* (regardless of their address) *be accepted from persons known to reside in so-called segregated districts, localities, residences or other buildings, which are known to harbor women or girls of the character described, and no aid or assistance of any kind or nature which would facilitate the transportation of such women or girls should be given.*

If prepaid order is received to furnish ticket or tickets to women or girls whom you think are to be transported for immoral purposes, do not deliver the ticket or tickets; and advise agent who placed order with you that same will not be delivered. In such cases, Agent accepting deposit will advise the depositor (without assigning any reason) that the company cannot make the delivery, and refund the deposit in accordance with Rule 123, Book of General Instructions, No. 4.

Acknowledge receipt.

A. H. Hanson
Passenger Traffic Manager.

J. G. Hatch
General Passenger Agent.

IC1 2632 10 (.900)

---

5. Circular, Illinois Central Railroad Company to Ticket Agents, regarding enforcement of White Slave Traffic Act. Attached to letter, Illinois Central Railroad Company to George W. Wickersham, Attorney General, May 27, 1911, Records of the Department of Justice, General Correspondence, Record Group 60, Class 31-0, Box 2620 National Archives, Washington National Records Center.

for 1911–12 and $150,000 for 1912–13.[16] Funds internally allotted to the Mann Act enforcement were sometimes crowded out, as in 1911, by more urgent needs of antitrust and neutrality law enforcement.[17] But then sometimes funds were "stolen" for the white slave work through money taken from the general fund.[18]

At times in the early years there was just no money, or almost none, available for the Mann Act work. In October 1911 the department ran out of appropriated money and it became necessary to curtail the white slave investigations until the following spring; in July 1912 Congress failed to pass a new budget and the continuing appropriations under the former year's formula forced a two-month suspension; and once again, in the spring of 1913 there was a slowdown in activity.[19]

Effective at the end of April 1912, Attorney General Wickersham created a new sub-subagency, the office of the Special Commissioner for the Suppression of the White Slave Traffic, a special division within the Bureau of Investigation. It is a sign of the importance of the white slave work that the director of the Bureau itself, Stanley W. Finch, resigned his directorship in order to become the Special Commissioner, reporting to the position that he had quit. Finch opened offices in Baltimore because there was no additional room in the Department of Justice, there was insufficient money to rent additional offices in Washington, and there was a congressional limitation on the employment of clerks in Washington offices that could be evaded outside the seat of government.[20]

Different explanations were given for creation of this new office of Special Commissioner for the Suppression of the White Slave Traffic. The Attorney General's version was that a "tremendous increase in violations" reported to the department had necessitated a special office to formulate a "comprehensive plan" to enforce the Mann Act.[21] Finch stated that from January 1912 he had been more and more absorbed in the white slave work, which had grown to the point that he was soon really working two jobs, up until midnight or one o'clock every night, and supervising two distinct sets of records and field officers. The white slave work was becoming a "much bigger and more difficult job than the entire balance of the work of the bureau" and the division was therefore a natural process.[22] The somewhat cynical chairman of the House committee considering the Sundry Civil Appropriations had a different interpretation. He charged that "this segregation of work [i.e., creation of Special Commissioner office] occurred after Congress declined to

6. Stanley W. Finch, Special Commissioner for the Suppression of the White Slave Traffic. Courtesy of the Library of Congress.

increase the salary of the chief of this bureau, and you [Finch] were then transferred out of that place and appointed to this other position at $6,000 a year." Finch quarreled with the interpretation, but admitted that two years earlier a request had been made to increase his salary to $4,000 per year, but Congress had limited it to $3,500, and that, indeed, he was being paid $6,000 per year as Special Commissioner.[23]

To avoid having funds requisitioned for other work, and to extend the system Finch had devised for local officers to register prostitutes, the Department of Justice requested a $200,000 appropriation specifically for the Special Commissioner for fiscal 1913–14. Even with the huge increase, it was explained, some funds in the remaining general account of $300,000 for Detection and Prosecution of Crime, the entire balance of the Bureau's budget, might be diverted toward Mann Act enforcement.[24]

The separate appropriation was denied by Congress.[25] However, although it was not coming smoothly, funding was increasing. In part, that was due to the pressures of constituent correspondence brought to bear on congressmen. At the end of 1911, the World's Purity Association offered to use its influence for greater appropriations to be devoted for ending the white slave traffic.[26] It made good on its promise and its journal, *The Light*, continuously urged members to write to their congressmen. It called upon "churches, reform societies, temperance and uplift associations, women's clubs, lodges, and all other organizations that stand for higher things" to pass resolutions demanding support "for Mr. Finch and his work" and forward such resolutions to their members in Congress.[27] By September 1912 it congratulated its readers that they had flooded Washington with petitions, telegrams, and letters from every state.[28]

Indeed, Washington was flooded. By spring of 1912, Representative Joseph R. Knowland of California, a man sympathetic to the purity movement, was receiving "a number of letters from California women" and groups urging him to use his influence to obtain additional appropriations for the white slave effort.[29] The California women's clubs were especially active, with their civics sections sending letters to every Congressman.[30] The Attorney General wrote that he daily received "letters from individuals and philanthropic organizations in various parts of the country urging this Department to increase its activities in the suppression of the white slave traffic, and expressing the view that additional funds should be secured for this purpose."[31]

In the summer of 1912, Special Commissioner Finch thanked the World's Purity Association for "the splendid support which we have received through you . . . in our efforts to secure funds for our work. . . . The many letters and petitions . . . have, undoubtedly, had a powerful influence in securing the increased appropriation. . . ."[32] That was far from the only group involved. Another large purity organization, the American Vigilance Association, declared in May 1912 that its policy would be "to encourage and maintain the Bureau's activity, to sustain the Bureau in its request for substantial appropriations for the enforcement of these laws and to make the results of the Bureau's work known to the public."[33] In addition to these two large organizations, there were hundreds of smaller purity associations, churches, and, of course, individuals, who sent letters to Congress.

One of the reasons offered to the public why the Attorney General had created the Special Commissioner for the Suppression of the White Slave Traffic was so that the commissioner might formulate a comprehensive plan to implement the Mann Act. There may well have been more to it, most strikingly the seventy-percent pay raise Finch received as special commissioner that had been denied him by Congress as mere director of the bureau itself. But regardless of this, Finch did in fact formulate a general plan. The plan was previewed by the Attorney General in his 1912 annual report, who said it "involves the selection of local white-slave officers, who render service for nominal compensation."[34] By the following year he boasted that a "corps" of local white-slave officers were "stationed at most of the principal cities of the country" and that this corps had already passed along "a large amount of useful information."[35] In reality, the plan was considerably more complicated and proceeded much more slowly.

The idea was to employ local, part-time officers, eventually in all cities with a population over five thousand in which there appeared to be any likelihood of violations of the White Slave Traffic Act. Private individuals having other regular employment were obtained; preference was given to men having a legal education, and local agents would not be hired in cities where there were regular agents of the Bureau.[36] Cities were selected by sending circular letters to postmasters, chiefs of police, and others, "inquiring as to whether or not there are any houses of prostitution in their towns."[37]

Most postmasters co-operated and passed on information that was of general knowledge locally. The only one to complain, apparently, was the postmaster in Detroit. But as a result of his complaint, Attorney General Wickersham halted the postmaster circulars in July 1912.[38] The next change of administration brought about a different spirit. Two years later, under Woodrow Wilson, the Postmaster General informed the Attorney General that his department and its postmasters desired to "cooperate so far as practicable"[39] with plans to obtain information about prostitutes.

When a new city was selected, a regular Bureau agent went there to find a competent attorney willing to act as a local white slave agent. The two then visited the local police chief and requested him to cooperate by assigning a police officer to assist them. According to Finch, almost all police chiefs cooperated. Next, the three-man teams went to all of the local brothels, many of which, in 1912, were still operating openly. The policeman instructed the madam that they had to cooperate with the federal agents or the local police would close them down. The federal agents would then post notices for the prostitutes to read, concerning the Mann Act, the Peonage Law, and other federal laws pertaining to obstruction of justice and kidnapping.[40]

Envelopes addressed to the local white slave agent would be left for the madam to report any information she heard regarding violations of the Mann Act. But the heart of the system was the census of prostitutes. Forms were filled out at the brothel by the regular Bureau agent with information on each prostitute, including names by which she had been known, age, identifying statistics, country where her parents were born, and detailed information on addresses and owners of all houses in which she had practiced prostitution. For each new prostitute who arrived at the brothel the madam was asked to fill out such a form and send it to the local white slave agent.[41]

The idea was that the local part-time agent would become familiar with the local prostitutes, and when a new face appeared he would recognize her and demand information on where she came from. In addition, the madams and prostitutes allegedly were jealous of each other and would report others' violations to the local agent. Local agents would also feed information to the local police on pandering or pimping charges and, in turn, obtain information from them on federal violations.[42] In these ways, the local white slave agents could obtain information on probable Mann Act violations, spot and return missing girls, and cooperate with local U.S. Attorneys in investigations and prosecutions.

The local part-time agents were paid a pittance, a fifty-cent fee for reporting the arrival of a prostitute from another state and a superficial investigation as to a Mann Act violation. If a fuller investigation were warranted, the pay was $2.50 per day, with a maximum of two days at any one time. Upon conviction of a white slaver, the local agent received a $10.00 reward, with a limitation of $50.00 per month. The average local white slave agent received $20.00 per month, approximately ten percent, as Finch pointed out, of the cost of a regular full-time Bureau agent.[43] Both Special Commissioner Finch and Bureau Chief Bielaski maintained that the great bulk of the local agents were attorneys who served not for the compensation but for the altruistic purposes of suppressing the white slave traffic and benefiting their communities.[44]

Finch extended his plan systematically, although always hampered by lack of funds. The first three cities to be covered by the census were Baltimore, Richmond, and Washington, and that was completed by the spring of 1912.[45] By September the system was established in Ohio, West Virginia, Maryland, the District of Columbia, Virginia, North and South Carolina, most of Tennessee, and a part of Kentucky.[46] Two hundred cities had local white slave officers by December, and in the following month, January 1913, local white slave officers were stationed in fourteen states in the east.[47] By February, Finch's plan was operating in eighteen eastern states east of the Mississippi, and he had just begun work in Missouri and Arkansas to the west.[48]

Before he began the local white slave agent system, in the spring of 1912, the Bureau of Investigation had employed forty full-time agents, in many different cities, working nearly exclusively on white slave traffic. Finch's plan reduced the need for so many full-time agents. In February 1913, the special commissioner's office employed ten full-time field agents, six extending the plan to other states, and four supervising a total of 220 local white slave officers. In his headquarters the special commissioner had an assistant, twelve clerks, and two messenger boys.[49] This, of course, was in addition to the regular Bureau agents, assigned full-time to the larger cities.

The fact that Finch's "system" was in operation in a particular state meant only that local white slave agents were stationed there; by no means does this imply that the complete census he hoped for had been accomplished. It also must be emphasized that there were many Mann Act prosecutions in states to which the local white slave officer system had not been extended. Local U.S. Attorneys could often depend on the cooperation of local police, church groups, purity groups, fathers, and husbands to report violations which they, the local federal prosecutors, could prosecute without the assistance of the Bureau of Investigation.

The efforts of these local groups were important in the early enforcement of the Act. In May 1911 the Cincinnati Vigilance Society claimed credit for nine Mann Act arrests.[50] Readers of the purity journals were regularly advised to report white slave violations to the special commissioner. And these efforts were taken seriously and were encouraged by the Department of Justice. In March 1911 the "Secret Law and Order League" of Ballston Spa, New York, claimed prostitutes were being brought in from Canada, held in clearing houses in Troy and Albany, and then shipped to Chicago and St. Louis. It was assured by the department that if the league obtained "positive evidence to support your belief" the department would assign an agent from the Bureau.[51] Similarly, in September 1912, the "State Law and Order Alliance" (New York) was told to "communicate the facts in any cases which may come to your attention directly to this Department either by telegram or letter as the necessities of the situation may require."[52]

As of January 1, 1914, the office of the Special Commissioner for the Suppression of the White Slave Traffic was abolished, the Baltimore offices closed, the clerks dismissed, and the white slave work became a part of the regular operations of the Bureau of Investigation. The Bureau continued under the leadership of A. Bruce Bielaski, who had taken the directorship when Finch became the special commissioner. The Attorney General explained the changes as an effort to assure that "all of the investigating work of the department might be under one head and possible friction and unnecessary expense avoided."[53] Finch himself departed. Probably he had become restive under the continual fight for funding and had left for a private philanthropic effort to "reclaim" former prostitutes, financed by John D. Rockefeller, Jr., and which had, as Finch put it, "no embarrassment for funds."[54]

Even without Finch personally, and without the office of the Special Commissioner, the local white slave officer system tottered on for a time, reaching a crest tide in 1916 when it covered thirty-seven states.[55] But it subsided, and during the reign of J. Edgar Hoover, Mann Act cases were investigated by full-time agents "in the usual course of business with all of the other crimes."[56] In part, the local white slave officer system was abandoned because of the growing professionalization of the Bureau itself. But also, in large part, the reorganization of the prostitution business was making the local agents unnecessary.

The special segregated districts for prostitution that existed in almost every American city at the turn of the century were closed on a city-by-city basis by local authorities, primarily during the years between 1912 and 1916. This occurred by virtue of the activities of the vice commission movement and the change in attitude of the medical profession and the public generally from one favoring a system of regulation of prostitution to one favoring its suppression. Neither the Mann Act nor the actions of the military during World War I were responsible for closing down the red-light districts. That this happened *before* the entrance of the United States into the War is clearly established by contemporary observers.[57] The military authorities in World War I merely pushed over the hard cases, such as New Orleans and her Storyville, that had refused to go along with the national trends. By January 1916, a leading vice investigator claimed that red-light districts had been "almost universally abolished in American municipalities. . . . on a recent trip through the country I was able to find but two cities where the existence of these districts was frankly conceded—New Orleans and San Francisco."[58]

No one pretended that prostitution was gone; it had just moved underground. As the Bureau of Social Hygiene of New York City put it: "Vice still exists; but its amount has been greatly reduced. . . . In 1912, prostitution was open, organized, aggressive, and prosperous; in 1916, it is furtive, disorganized, precarious, unsuccessful." Such few houses as existed, the Bureau said, were "hard to find, still harder to enter; they lead a brief, uncertain, day-to-day existence."[59] In January of the following year, 1917, an investigator claimed that "there is not in the entire city of New York a disorderly house of the old type in operation."[60]

Finch had always emphasized *houses* of prostitution, saying that "a house of prostitution is primarily the marketplace for the white slave."[61] His census was designed to develop a catalogue of "every house of ill-fame in the whole country, with the name and history of every owner and of every inmate."[62] With the submergence of prostitution into a clandestine twilight, the local officer's role, that of gathering information about obvious prostitutes in identified houses, became moot. The result was that, as a 1921 study of American prostitution put it, "the records kept by the so-called white slave officer in the various cities ceased to be of much use in securing adequate information."[63]

The results obtained from the early investigations and independent work of the United States Attorneys were generally regarded as gratifying. The Attorney General reported in mid-1913 that "very material progress has been made, particularly during the past year, in suppressing the most vicious features of the traffic," and then again in 1914, that "the continued vigorous enforcement of this act is beginning to make itself felt . . . the interstate traffic of women for immoral purposes is decreasing."[64] Likewise, Bureau chief A. Bruce Bielaski was optimistic, writing in 1915 that "the open and notorious interstate transportation of women for immoral purposes is no longer practiced."[65] Finch reported one collateral gain. The posting of the Peonage Law in the brothels subject to his system had altogether broken up the practice whereby women were held against their wills to pay for expensive gowns and money advanced by madams.[66]

Actually, in the early years there was some criticism by purity groups of a lack of enthusiasm in prosecutors and low sentences from judges.[67] Frederick H. Whitin, Secretary of the Committee of Fourteen, in New York City, was philosophical. What was needed, he wrote, was "education of the judges that they may be abreast of the moral sentiment of the day." The problem was that the federal judges were "men of the older generation [and] do not, therefore, look upon the commercializer of prostitution, if he is not a white slaver in the stricter meaning of that term, with the abhorrence which is growing so rapidly in the younger generation."[68] The Bureau chief, Bielaski, believed that in the early years federal judges looked with disfavor on the Mann Act, thinking that it brought before them "mere police cases" that lowered the dignity of the Federal Courts. But by 1915, he thought the attitudes of the Judges had changed "almost entirely."[69]

In reality, there was not much change in total sentences given over this period. If one takes the total number of convictions and divides that into total months of imprisonment and once again into total fines, the average prison term during the first three years, 1910 through mid-1913, is twenty months and the average fine $160. The averages for the longer period of 1910 through mid-1916 are nineteen months and a $112 fine.[70] This is hardly evidence of changed attitudes on the part of sentencing judges. For one year only, 1912, the Attorney General's *Annual Report* showed individual cases, from 1910 through mid-1912, and the disposition of each. What is most impressive about the sentences for convictions is their extreme variability. There are $50 fines, thirty days in jail, and five years in the penitentiary. The average in these early years of Mann Act enforcement means very little. The gross results in terms of convictions or other disposition for the country as a whole is shown in the following table:[71]

Fiscal year	Convictions	Acquittals	Dismissals
1911	76	14	10
1912	261	21	not available
1913	266	35	19
1914	357	53	46
1915	302	57	52
1916	334	45	54

Although the reports of the Attorneys General, Finch, and Bielaski were all upbeat and optimistic over progress being made in this early period between 1910 and 1916, still they sought various amendments and further legislation. In 1912 Finch called for new legislation criminalizing the use of interstate mail or telegraphs for the purposes of prostitution, pointing to the existence of large numbers of bogus job offers negotiated by the mails. He also urged legislation under the Thirteenth Amendment to make it a federal crime to hold any woman, regardless of interstate movement, for the purposes of prostitution or the payment of a debt. Finch also wanted to abolish spousal immunity in Mann Act prosecutions, devise easier methods to obtain search warrants, create a separate offense of an attempt to violate the Mann Act, and impose minimum sentences with no possibility of suspension.[72]

The purity journals editorialized in favor of these changes, and Finch's successor, A. Bruce Bielaski, called for the abolition of spousal immunity in order to make the wife a competent and compellable witness against her husband. The Attorney General also pushed for legislation clarifying witness immunities.[73] Bielaski went further and asked the government to negotiate new extradition treaties, pointing out that there was "no country in the world" from which the United States could extradite a fugitive for violation of the Mann Act.[74]

All of these projects for legislative revision came to naught. However, as we will see, the proposal for abolition of spousal immunity was accomplished, largely by judicial classification of the Act's violation as a crime against the person of the wife and therefore falling within a common law exception to spousal immunity.

In the early years of the Mann Act there were serious doubts as to its constitutionality. The United States Supreme Court had been striking down federal legislation as unconstitutional, notwithstanding the invocation of the congressional right to regulate commerce. There were three significant arguments against the Act's constitutionality. First was that the Constitution's interstate commerce clause was not broad enough to allow Congress to regulate the private purposes of individuals' travel. In other words, immoral purposes of travel had nothing to do with the safety or efficiency of the process of interstate commerce and therefore was not within the power to regulate. The second was that the law violated the privileges and immunities clause, in that evil persons, including prostitutes, had a fundamental right to travel in interstate commerce. The third was that the Mann Act invaded the police powers reserved to the states by the Tenth Amendment by regulating the private morals of the people.

From the earliest days the lower courts had upheld the constitutionality of the statute, the first challenge coming as early as November 1910.[75] Some lower courts upheld the statute extremely reluctantly, with one judge writing that the Mann Act attempted to exercise purely police powers "under the guise of regulating commerce."[76] It was a prescience of the technique utilized by the federal government for the remainder of the twentieth century to enhance its power.

The United States Supreme Court determined the issue in the case of *Hoke v. United States*,[77] decided along with three companion cases in 1913. *Hoke* involved fraudulent representations to young women and elements of actual coercion. The Court stated that the scope of the commerce clause was the heart of the case since if the Mann Act were "a valid exercise of that power, how it may affect persons or States is not material." The Court then reasoned that if Congress could deprive the facilities of interstate commerce to lotteries, obscenity, diseased cattle, and impure drugs, all cases recently decided, it could certainly withhold interstate movement from persons transporting or enticing women and girls for prostitution and debauchery.

The Court dismissed the fundamental right to travel contention as urging "a right exercised in morality to sustain a right to be exercised in immorality." Fundamental rights only exist for "beneficial exercise" and may not be used to "justify baneful exercise," all as defined by the federal government. As to the police powers of the states, the Court held that the federal government's interstate commerce power is "complete in itself, and . . . Congress . . . may adopt not only means necessary but convenient to its exercise, and the means may have the quality of police regulations."[78] The rhetoric virtually pitches the Tenth Amendment, with its guarantees to the states and people of all powers not granted to the federal government, into the ashcan of history.

Naturally, the vigilance press praised the decision. But, significantly, there was a favorable reaction among general publications[79] and among legal writers.[80] Contemporary observers recognized the case as a significant extension of the federal government's powers under the commerce clause. The *New York Tribune* called the case "one of the most significant interpretations of the Constitution as a grant of national power . . . which has been made for years"; the *Survey* noted that *Hoke* was "the most advanced step yet taken" in construing the federal power of interstate commerce; and the *Outlook* called the decision "one of the great monuments that mark the history of Constitutional interpretation."[81]

In actuality, the steady expansion of federal power by means of the interstate commerce clause was not to begin for a number of years. The Supreme Court still vacillated. As late as 1918, in *Hammer v. Dagenhart*,[82] the Court held that Congress exceeded its powers under the commerce clause by attempting to ban the interstate movement of goods manufactured by child labor. It reverted to earlier theories of the limited role of federal government, noted that there was nothing inherently wrong with the goods so manufactured, and viewed labor as a matter for state regulation. Of course, no one ever claimed either that prostitutes were plying their trade on interstate railroads or that minors were operating the trains themselves. The interstate aspect of the movement was clearly a pretext for federal regulation.

The Court's views as to appropriateness of the interstate commerce clause as a pretext for congressional regulation of the interstate movement of women and the inappropriateness of the interstate commerce clause to regulate child labor are, of course, inconsistent. In *Hoke*, the Court argued that "it must be kept in mind that we are one people,"[83] in order to justify federal regulation of sexuality and the interstate movement of women. In *Hammer*, the Court argued that "it must never be forgotten that the Nation is made up of States"[84] to strike down federal regulation of child labor. A double standard was being applied, the Court making it far easier for the federal government to regulate morality than to regulate business.

No one ever can know exactly why the Supreme Court decides cases the way it does. However, one can speculate that the reason why the Court permitted the federal regulation of women's movement was that the country was caught up in a moralist fervor over prostitution and white slavery. Very, very few Americans opposed the Mann Act or its early enforcement, and of those who did, virtually no one opposed the Act on the basis of the inappropriateness of sexual regulation. The only opposition was based on states' rights or fear of blackmail. On the other hand, there were still many, many arguments being made over the appropriateness of governmental regulation of business. It was still a lively political issue. The prevailing popular beliefs made it a much easier judgment call for the Court to expand federal power in the field of morals than in the field of business.

In the years following *Hoke,* the Supreme Court continued to define the meaning of the Mann Act. In 1916, the Court narrowed the meaning of the Mann Act's sixth section, that requiring the filing of statements concerning aliens practicing prostitution. It held that the filing of that statement with the Commissioner of Immigration could take place only in Washington, D.C., and that therefore the only appropriate district in which an indictment could be made for a failure to file would be in Washington, D.C.[85] This had a practical effect of limiting prosecutions under that section of the statute, since it would usually be local U.S. Attorneys, not those stationed in Washington, who would have the knowledge and will to prosecute brothel owners. Yet only prosecutors in far-off Washington, with much less enthusiasm, could bring actual indictments. Although there continued to be an occasional prosecution under the filing section of the Mann Act, it largely passed into obscurity, far outshadowed by the transportation sections.

In another important early case the Court read the statute expansively. In a 1914 case, *Wilson v. United States,*[86] the two defendants, husband and wife, owned a brothel in Chicago. They hired a man to bring two willing prostitutes, apparently adults, from Milwaukee to Chicago to work in their brothel. Once they arrived in Chicago, the defendants, for reasons that are not clear, refused to admit the women and would not allow them to work in their house. The husband and wife defended a Mann Act charge by asserting they had voluntarily abandoned their immoral intention before anything happened; the girls never prostituted themselves in the state of destination, at least insofar as the defendants had anything to do with it.

The Court held that this was not a defense. The offense was complete upon the interstate transportation of the woman with the illicit intent of the person transporting or directing the transport.[87] The federal courts have consistently interpreted the statute as criminalizing the actual transportation accompanied by bad intent of the transporter, regardless of what happened at the destination. A judge put it well in a 1939 case:

> [T]he offense is complete the moment the female has been transported across the state line with the immoral purpose or intent in the mind of the person responsible for her transportation. The immoral conduct and relations of the parties are, of course, in no sense, elements of the offense.[88]

This doctrine held tremendous implications once the Mann Act was extended to noncommercial, boyfriend-girlfriend travel, an extension that was definitively made through the *Caminetti* case in 1917. It meant that any man who has taken his girlfriend from New York City to New Jersey on a date, hoping for sexual romance that evening, has violated the Mann Act, regardless of the fact that the planned seduction never occurred. Likewise, the man who invites his girlfriend to fly by herself from Detroit to Birmingham for a visit, with the same hope, has committed a federal felony if he held that hope while she crossed the state line, notwithstanding that he is subsequently disappointed and no sexual conduct occurs. This Orwellian "badthought," plus transportation, defined the essence of the crime. This was true throughout the history of the Mann Act. As late as 1959 a federal judge wrote:

> Debauchery as used in the Mann Act is a broad term and includes all sexual immoralities, whether for hire or not for hire, or for cohabitation. . . . The crime is complete the moment the female has been transported across the state line with the intent to entice her into debauchery. Proof that he accomplished his illicit purpose is not necessary to conviction.[89]

But that was 1959, and in the early years it was murky whether noncommercial immoralities, boyfriend-girlfriend travel or the interstate tryst of adulterers, were within the statute. Not only was there confusion within the courts, but the position of the Department of Justice was far from clear.

At first, the Attorney General, George W. Wickersham, believed that the new statute ought not apply to noncommercial cases. In July 1911 he wrote to Dannenbaum that the Mann Act was directed against a "pernicious traffic in women" and was enacted as a result of an investigation that satisfied Congress that there was "a regular systematized course of business [where] young girls were lured or kidnapped . . . and transported like chattels from one State to another. . . ." It was only for the "purpose of reaching and breaking up this traffic [that] the language of the statute was necessarily comprehensive." Wickersham warned that the federal courts ought to interpret the law so as to avoid dealing "with that class of violations of the ordinary police regulations of the community which should be dealt with by the local tribunals."[90]

Wickersham made his position even clearer in correspondence the following year with the United States Attorney for Minnesota. An adult young woman, twenty-four years old, had traveled from Chicago to St. Paul in October 1910 at the solicitation and expense of a young man. The couple passed the time riding, eating, and drinking, and spent the night together. She spent three days with him in Minnesota and then returned to Chicago. She repeated the visit in June 1911, but apparently she did not obtain the results she wanted as in June of 1912 she applied for an arrest warrant, charging her lover with a violation of the Mann Act. The Minnesota United States Attorney wrote Wickersham that he did not believe that case was within "the spirit and intent of the Mann Act." But the woman had "enlisted certain club women . . . who are insisting on the arrest being made" and he asked for a departmental construction. Wickersham replied on July 23, 1912, that these facts did "not bring the matter within the true intent of the White Slave Traffic Act" and that no prosecution should be brought.[91]

Yet it was not clear that *all* noncommercial cases were outside the Act. The federal prosecutor from Arkansas wrote the department in December 1911. He had a case where two married men had passed themselves off as single and persuaded a seventeen-year-old girl to travel with them from Oklahoma to Arkansas. They claimed they had hired her to sell town lots, yet she had no training in sales and only a limited education. But the men were not white slavers and had no connection with the business of prostitution. Indeed, it was not clear that the men even had sex with the girl. Bielaski and Finch advised against the prosecution, arguing that there was no evidence that the men "intended to induce the girl to lead a life of prostitution." William R. Harr, Wickersham's Assistant Attorney General, a career official in Washington, wrote in his own hand over the letter: "I think this case should be prosecuted. The transportation was for an immoral purpose—need not necessarily be prostitution." The Arkansas prosecutor was directed to proceed with the prosecution.[92]

What emerged from the department was a grudging acknowledgment that the language of the Act went beyond its purpose. Harr wrote to another U.S. Attorney in February 1913 that "the Department has maintained that the White Slave Traffic Act does not apply to the ordinary case of illicit relations between a man and a woman, when interstate travel happens to be involved."[93] A fuller expression of his opinion came in an internal memorandum addressed to Wilson's Attorney General, James C. McReynolds, in August of that year. The timing is significant since the *Caminetti* case was breaking in California. This case involved a purely noncommercial relationship between consenting adults and was prosecuted amid allegations that the case had been delayed because of political favoritism, charges that will be considered fully in chapter 5. In this context Harr wrote:

> The doubt as to the meaning of the Act arises from the fact that it is not confined in terms to its declared object . . . however, it is apparent—especially when the history, the declared purpose, and the title of the Act are considered—that the language referred to ["other immoral purpose"] was not intended to cover the transportation of a woman or girl for the purpose simply of having immoral relations with her, but that it was intended to prevent . . . transportation for the purpose of having the woman or girl concerned take up or continue in an immoral life *as a vocation* [emphasis in original] . . . [Congress] evidently thought best to word it so as to reach every one who acts with any such nefarious purpose in view . . . nevertheless the Act, fairly construed, seems to require that the purpose of the offender in bringing about the transportation shall be to have the woman or girl concerned take up or continue in an immoral life as a business or vocation.[94]

In the same memo Harr acknowledged that in some situations where "exceptionally outrageous conduct concerning young girls of tender age was involved" prosecutions had been made in cases not involving prostitution. That would harmonize his view of the law with his earlier instruction to prosecute the two men who induced the seventeen-year-old girl to travel from Oklahoma to Arkansas, but that would seem to be the extent of the Department of Justice's thinking about noncommercial cases in the early years of the Mann Act. Even Stanley Finch while special commissioner thought that noncommercial traffic would be merely a "technical violation"[95] and that the federal government was "simply undertaking to prevent the interstate and international transportation of women for the purpose of prostitution,"[96] and that the "real purpose" of the Act "was to destroy the nefarious traffic which was known to be going on between the states . . . [of] women and girls . . . solely for the purpose of prostitution."[97]

Throughout the years from 1912 to 1916 the Department of Justice routinely responded to inquiries from U.S. Attorneys in the field as to noncommercial cases, urging that they should use their own discretion, consider the age and motives of the parties, and the circumstances of any aggravation. U.S. Attorneys also were routinely cautioned that the department had endeavored to confine noncommercial prosecutions to cases where there was more than the occasional immorality of mature persons that could more properly be dealt with in state courts.[98] Nevertheless, prosecutors were encouraged to proceed with noncommercial cases where "young girls have been enticed away from home."[99] At least on the aspirational level, as opposed to actual practice, it is true in the years between 1910 and 1916, as George W. Wickersham put it in his 1912 *Annual Report,* that "the department has been careful to refrain from instituting technical or trivial cases, or cases which more properly belong in the State courts, and has restricted itself to the class of cases at which the act was primarily directed."[100]

The reality was, however, that the Justice Department was being pressured to expand prosecutions to include noncommercial violations involving consenting adults. The pressure was coming from the public, zealous prosecutors, and the courts themselves. United States Attorneys received numerous complaints from women deserted by their husbands who left with other women for other states.[101] And some prosecutors were responding with considerable enthusiasm. One prosecutor in a purely noncommercial case argued to the jury that "the libertine is the most dangerous miscreant in the world. . . . Hell itself is moved and mocked by his excesses and his perversions." Sexual intercourse, unblessed by marriage, was "the demon that has dug more graves and sent more souls unshrived to judgment than all the pestilences that have wasted life since God sent the plagues to Egypt, and all the Wars since Joshua stood before the walls of Jerico."[102]

In the 1910s both courts and jurors responded well to such religious appeals. Federal judges began to go in different directions, some interpreting the Mann Act as including noncommercial "escapades," to use the contemporary term, and others not.[103] Some of these early noncommercial prosecutions involved girls under eighteen,[104] and others involved men enticing married women to leave town with them.[105] Still other successful prosecutions only technically involved prostitution, as where a man transported a prostitute across a state line for his own pleasure, as a customer and not as a pimp.[106] But the principle being established was broader than these situations themselves, and one appellate court had declared as early as 1913 that where a woman was persuaded to go from one state to another "for the purpose of engaging in illicit intercourse," those were "immoral acts analogous to prostitution, and come well within the letter of the statute."[107]

Nothing showed more clearly the drift of public opinion toward noncommercial prosecutions and also the religious sentiment behind that movement than the events of 1913. There was a national press release out of Washington, D.C., dated July 28, 1913, detailing "sensational disclosures" that the then Attorney General McReynolds had "issued instructions to district attorneys that no man is to be indicted and prosecuted . . . unless it is shown that he shared in the earnings of the woman."[108] Had this been true, it would have been a definitive interpretation that the Mann Act would not apply to noncommercial cases. Moreover, this alleged interpretation would be in the immediate wake of the political scandal that followed the Diggs and Caminetti arrests, taken up in detail in Chapter 5, involving two young men politically connected to the new Democratic administration and which involved a purely noncommercial incident.

It is true, as we have seen, that the department considered that the Mann Act did not properly apply to noncommercial cases, although technically it might. It had discouraged prosecution unless a minor female had been involved but had never issued blanket orders of any sort. But the political situation was so volatile that the next day the Democrats read into the *Congressional Record* a denial from the Attorney General that he had directed United States Attorneys "not to prosecute any white slave case where it was not charged that there had been traffic in women for gain."[109] For the next eight months church and purity groups denounced a directive that never had been made and in the process moved the federal government more and more toward a policy of vigorous prosecution of noncommercial violations.

The day following the publication of the "sensational disclosures," Mrs. Albert R. Hall, as president of the Minnesota Federation of Women's Clubs, wrote President Wilson expressing the "hope that the statement made is without foundation in fact" and that "myriads of lecherous men" should not escape punishment.[110] Most critiques of the nonexistent policy were filled with self-righteousness and implied threats of political retribution. The Chicago Church Federation Council, representing over six hundred churches, resolved in convention on September 29, 1913, to "call upon Christian churches and reform organizations and all men who desire the safety of our homes, and upon all good women and women's organizations, to support this law in its prohibition of debauchery, whether for gain or for personal indulgence, and we protest against any weakening of the Mann Act for the evil gratification of influential men." In transmitting the resolution to the Attorney General the executive secretary wrote that he hoped "the voice of United Protestantism will be heard in this matter."[111] The resolution was widely published in hundreds of journals, including the major purity publications.[112]

In October 1913, D. O. Hopkins, president of the Illinois Baptist State Convention, wrote to Woodrow Wilson, pointing out that his convention represented 153,000 Baptists from 1,225 churches in Illinois. The convention had resolved that "strong influences are now being brought to bear upon Congress to weaken this great law by amendment, and certain judges of our land have surprisingly declared that the law of the land does not concern itself with personal escapades. . . . We regard this great law as . . . increasingly needed in the work of protecting our youth and our homes against the social evil; and most respectfully demand that no amendment be made to this law that shall in any way curtail its scope or weaken its operation."[113]

The Presbyterians also weighed in. The moderator of the General Assembly of the Presbyterian Church of the U.S.A. wrote to President Wilson in April 1914 that "many of us are deeply concerned as to the continued efficiency and unchanged influence of the Mann Act and believe that any limitation of the law which discriminated between commercial prostitution or personal indulgence would be a grave weakening of its power and would have disastrous results. Surely the man who uses his wealth or influence to betray young womanhood is no less a menace to society than the man who directly commercializes the vice in the transportation of those already corrupt."[114]

Another preacher, also the superintendent of the International Reform Bureau, explained to the Attorney General in early 1914 that the Mann Act "distinctly prohibits" the movement of women by men "whether for their own carnal indulgence or to fill their pockets. Cases of greed and lust stand alike in the wording of the law. . . . It was on the strength of the petitions of purity experts that the large appropriation was secured for the enforcement of this law and some of us do not think that we are getting from it anything like the results that ought to be secured, in view of the wide prevalence of immorality."[115]

The rumors never ceased during 1913. At the close of the year there was yet another flurry, and Senator Wesley Jones of Washington introduced a resolution of disapproval of the alleged policy of nonprosecution of noncommercial cases. Almost immediately the Department of Justice was forced to issue another denial, stating explicitly that "no order to stop white slave prosecutions in cases not involving commercialism has been issued. . . . On the contrary the Department of Justice has adhered to the practice adopted immediately after the passage of the law and followed during the previous Administration."[116]

The political sentiment of America clearly favored prosecution of noncommercial libertines. The *Portland Telegram* mused about the possibility there might be an amendment or repeal of the Act in Congress. It acknowledged that the Mann Act "reaches farther and does more than originally intended," but applauded the result, since the broader spirit of the statute was aimed at the exploitation of women whether "from motives of passion or profit." The newspaper was curious to know "what sort of apology a Congressman would make to the American people, as he champions the repeal of this law. Would he say that the law was going too far in protecting the daughters of decent households from the evil machinations of the society young man about town; because heretofore society has tolerated this sort of thing as the sowing of wild oats. . . . We hardly think that in any community a Congressman could be elected on the promise to do his best for the repeal of the Mann Act." The Mann Act was so politically popular that shortly after its enactment a majority of states adopted "Little Mann Acts" prohibiting the transportation of women for prostitution into, within, or through their territories. However, only a minority of these states employed the phrase "any other immoral purpose" in these statutes.[117]

However, the issue was not entirely political; it was also legal. What would the United States Supreme Court say about the application of the Mann Act to noncommercial transgressions? Two of the three companion cases considered along with the *Hoke* case in 1912 had been commercial cases.[118] However, one of the four cases ruled upon by the Supreme Court in its initial round of cases had been noncommercial, at least in a sense, and many people saw it as the harbinger of an ultimate determination.

Athanasaw v. United States,[119] was the story of a naive young Southern girl lured to the big city. Almost literally, nothing happened to her, but the man who hired her to work in his chorus line and hustle drinks on the side was sentenced to prison for two and one-half years.[120] Agnes Couch, a girl of seventeen years, lived in Suwanee, Georgia. One day in September 1911 she saw an advertisement in Atlanta for a girl to dance in the chorus of the Imperial Musical Comedy Company at the Imperial Theatre, Tampa, Florida. She signed a contract in Atlanta, which included a provision that "All the ladies engaged in this Theatre are required to go in the boxes." The compensation was $20 per week for the first four weeks, and $15 per week for a second four weeks. In addition she was to receive "an amount of 20% allowed you on all drinks sold in the boxes."[121]

Couch traveled to Tampa from Atlanta by train, arriving at 6:30 in the morning. The owner of the theater, Louis Athanasaw, met her at the train, took her to her room, and she slept until 2:00 P.M. Then she went to the theater and rehearsed her singing for about one hour. That was followed by lunch at which "they were all smoking, cursing, and using such language I couldn't eat." Later that afternoon in her room, defendant Athanasaw came by to tell her "not to let any of the boys fool me, and not to be any of the boys' girl; to be his."

She testified that the middle-aged defendant "wanted me to be his girl; to talk to the boys and make a hit, and get all of the money I could out of them. . . . he told me he was coming in my room that night and sleep with me; and he kissed and caressed me."[122] Athanasaw denied making any such propositions, and the girl was impeached by the testimony of the United States Commissioner and a newspaper reporter that she had not mentioned any such activities or statements in the preliminary hearing, notwithstanding that she was asked broad questions about what had occurred at the Imperial Theatre.[123]

That evening at 9:00 P.M. she returned to the theater, entered one of the boxes, and was met by defendant's adult son and three other young men, who were "smoking, cursing, and drinking."[124] They encouraged her to drink beer and join their revelry, but one of the men after talking with Couch "thought she was a decent girl." He testified that "the boys were touching her and fooling with her. I thought she was decent because it took her so long to drink the beer. I took her out of the box and spoke to her. She said she wanted to get out." This man summoned a constable who "found the girl crying. She was in one of the Theater boxes. . . . she said she wanted to leave; that it was not the kind of place she thought she was coming to."[125] And she did leave; there was no rape, no seduction, no serious pressure.

The trial court gave the jury extremely broad instructions, rejecting defendants' contention that to justify conviction they must have had the deliberate intent for someone, one of them or somebody else, to seduce Couch. Instead, the judge instructed that all that was needed was an intent to put the young girl under conditions that would lead to her seduction by some unknown third person.

> Did they intend to induce or entice or influence her to give herself up to debauchery? It makes no difference whether the profits . . . came from the sale of liquor or other immoral purpose. The question here is of intent; what was the intent with which they brought her; that she should live an honest, moral and proper life? or that she came and they engaged and contracted with her for the purpose of her entering upon a condition which might be termed debauchery, or tends to or would necessarily and naturally lead her to a condition of debauchery just referred to? . . . There is no allegation that the defendants brought her here with the purpose or with the intent to debauch her; but to induce her or entice her, or influence her to enter upon a course of debauchery. . . . The term debauchery, as used in this statute, has an idea of sexual immorality; that is, it has the idea of a life which will lead eventually or tends to lead to sexual immorality . . . in this case as to whether or not the influences in which this girl was surrounded by the employment which they called her to, did not tend to induce her to give herself up to a condition of debauchery which eventually, necessarily and naturally would lead to a course of immorality sexually. . . . Was or was not it a condition that would necessarily and naturally lead to a life of debauchery of a carnal nature relating to sexual intercourse between man and woman?[126]

The United States Supreme Court unanimously held that "the instructions of the court were justified by the statute . . . [and] the plan and place justified the instructions. The plan might have succeeded if the coarse precipitancy of one of the defendants and the ribaldry of the habitues of the place had not shocked the modesty of the girl." It termed the defendants' theater "an efficient school of debauchery of the special immorality" toward which the Act was directed.[127] Conceivably this was an excessively wide holding. Temptations were thought to encompass all young women in the large metropolitan areas, and traditionalists were concerned that young men made propositions to women even in such neutral locations as the counters of department stores. Could it then be a violation of the Mann Act were a man to hire a woman to travel to New York for a bona fide job in a large department store, but in a location where male customers encountered her?

Some legal commentators were critical of *Athanasaw*. The *Virginia Law Register* wrote that "whatever may have been the intention of the law makers, it is certain that the courts have given this act a much wider meaning. . . . [We] ought to know what powers the United States government has arrogated to itself." Speaking of *Athanasaw*, it commented that "not only must [the male] refrain from debauching the girl himself, but he must not even *lead her into temptation*"[128] (emphasis in original). Other commentators were more temperate. One noted that *Athanasaw* seemed to be different from the other three first-round convictions affirmed by the Supreme Court since it involved "an apparently legitimate purpose—for the female's employment as a chorus girl." Nevertheless, "if this was but the ostensible purpose with the real intent to lead the female into a life of debauchery or prostitution, all of the cases would be upon the same footing."[129]

Whatever the true reasons for the *Athanasaw* decision, its broad holding was not followed. Its reasoning was rarely applied, and a general theory of "leading into temptation" for Mann Act violations never developed. Indeed, we shall see that the Supreme Court implicitly repudiated this theory in 1954. Probably the real basis of *Athanasaw* was the young age of the girl coupled with a conclusion that the women of the Imperial Theatre were expected to furnish sexual entertainment of some variety to the men in the boxes, as well as merely to sell drinks and perform on the stage. The Justice Department believed that to be true, as a report described the Imperial Theatre as "a drinking resort in which the girls were required to go out into the audience and endeavor to induce men to buy drinks and to entertain men in the rooms furnished by the manager."[130]

This expectation of sexual entertainment is supported both by the immediacy with which the men pawed Couch and a description of the boxes themselves. Agnes Couch described them as "looking over the stage; with a little opening looking onto the stage. There was a door in the back of it that could be closed and bolted. They were on the second floor. There were some chairs and a table in it." The constable testified that the upstairs boxes were "partitioned off, and have a window in each one of them . . . looking on the stage."[131] From their physical description it would not seem that watching the performance on the stage would be the primary purpose of the boxes.

What is absolutely clear is that *Athanasaw* did not stand for the proposition that interstate travel for noncommercial sexual purposes was within the statute. That came with the later *Caminetti* decision, and it is significant that Justice McKenna, who authored the unanimous decision in *Athanasaw*, dissented in *Caminetti*. So the confusion as to noncommercial travel continued. Yet noncommercial prosecutions were undertaken and convictions obtained. As of April 1914 the Department of Justice had a complete record for 530 convictions and had analyzed their classes. They broke down as follows:[132]

> Extreme white slave cases in which the woman had been the unwilling victim of either force or fraud at the hands of the defendant   75

> Cases in which she was at the time of the prosecution a more or less willing victim, but in which she had first been made a prostitute by the defendant   129

> Cases in which the woman had merely assented to her use by a pimp or madam, but in which she was already a prostitute before encountering the particular defendant   247

> Cases of simple fornication or adultery accompanied by the use of fraud or force by the defendant   28

> and the same sort of cases [simple fornication or adultery] without fraud or force   51

Thus as of April 1914, 71 percent of the White Slave Traffic Act convictions (second and third classes) involved the transportation of willing prostitutes, not the coerced victims of white slavers. "Fraud" is not defined in the report and might simply be successful persuasion by promise of marriage. In any event, noncommercial cases (fourth and fifth classes) amounted to 15 percent of total convictions, and cases involving no prostitution, no fraud, and no force (fifth class) constituted approximately 10 percent of total Mann Act convictions.

The trend continued. In 1915 the Attorney General reported that while the total number of Mann Act complaints continued to be large, "those involving commercialized vice are decreasing somewhat."[133]

The eagerness to punish those with different moral standards and convictions, seen in the religious fervor opposing the supposed 1913 policy on noncommercial enforcement, continued in America. But notwithstanding the convictions and the citizen pressures, the Supreme Court had not definitively spoken, and no one really knew whether mere immoral transgressions could be within the statute.

The *Atlanta Constitution* asked the question in 1913, "does a personal escapade that overlaps state lines render an individual liable? Or is the individual immune unless he or she imports or deports a girl for 'commercial' immoral purposes?" It answered that "no man knows, under existing conditions, just what is the proper interpretation of the law. Federal courts are in square contradiction." The newspaper opined that "upon an issue of this importance it is impossible that such a tangle should long continue." It believed that it was "only a question of a short time" before either Congress made the law more explicit or the Supreme Court settled the issue, so as "to eliminate the undesirable spectacle of tribunals of equal jurisdiction all over the country" reaching different conclusions.[134] However, the country would have to wait several more years, until the *Caminetti* appeal was heard in 1917, before receiving a definitive answer.

In the years from 1910 through 1913, the federal government appeared to be content with prosecuting pimps and such few genuine white slavers as it could find. Then came the wide publicity of the *Caminetti* arrest and trial in 1913 and the massive pressure campaign mounted in response to the supposition that the Department of Justice was about to limit Mann Act prosecutions to cases of commercial prostitution. This had the effect of pushing the government into a more extreme position than it originally wanted to take. Probably the government surrendered easily to these pressures for much the same reason as the Supreme Court went the way of increasing federal power in *Hoke* but the other direction in *Hammer*. There were lots of groups and individuals arguing that it should prosecute noncommercial cases, and few countervailing arguments and pressures that it should not.

Once the government reluctantly began to prosecute noncommercial cases, petty adulterers and ordinary lotharios became potential criminal defendants. In turn, that gave female "victims" an opportunity to extort their male "villains" by threatening exposure of a Mann Act violation. Through these developments, blackmail and extortion became a major collateral consequence of the Mann Act, a topic explored in the following chapter.

Blackmail and Extortion

From the beginning there were warnings that the Mann Act would lead to extortion by women who would lure men across a state line for the express purpose of blackmail. When Representative Adamson of Georgia opposed the Act as it was considered by Congress, he contended in debate before the House that "these provisions are liable to furnish boundless opportunity to hold up and blackmail."[1]

Apparently, the United States Attorney General agreed. On July 28, 1911, in the first of several Mann Act circulars addressed to the various United States Attorneys, Attorney General Wickersham charged local prosecutors to look to several factors in deciding whether to prosecute. Among those factors was "the motives of those urging prosecution," language that clearly contemplated extortion.[2]

Successful blackmail, by its nature, is a crime which never becomes public. It is therefore difficult to gauge its extent. But unsuccessful examples were quick to appear in the press. The *New York Times*, for example, in February 1914, reported the arrest on Mann Act charges of a wealthy California rancher, on the complaint of a young woman who alleged that he had taken her from New York to San Francisco for immoral purposes. The rancher reported that he had expected this trouble "for some time" and that it was "simply a case of blackmail." That sounds problematic, except that, before the arrest was made, he had complained to the San Francisco police that he was being black-mailed by the young woman. He further submitted, according to the newspaper account, documentary evidence to show that the woman was "a part of the Los Angeles underworld." Apparently, the woman's response was to leave town quickly.[3]

In the following year, 1915, there was a public account of a Providence, Rhode Island, man charged with violating the Mann Act by transporting his mistress from Los Angeles to Chicago. Simultaneously, the mistress was under indictment for having attempted to bribe federal officers into extorting her benefactor.[4] A legal journal argued in 1914 that the statute ought not to extend to noncommercial, private immoralities, a point not to be decided until 1917 with the Supreme Court's decision in *Caminetti*. It urged that the courts ought to consider "the opportunity for blackmail afforded by the statute, if it should be held to embrace the foibles of every couple who have dispensed with the marriage ceremony. A woman who can induce a man to go with her from Philadelphia to Atlantic City, or to leave New York on a Fall River boat, may hold over his head the threat of exposure and prosecution under the statute."[5]

The turmoil over blackmail was sufficient that in 1914 the *New York Times* headlined a critical editorial, "Uncle Sam, Blackmailer." The newspaper charged that the prosecution of cases of simple adultery with no commercial overtones had served as a "direct incitement to blackmail. Women have waited until the partners of their guilt carelessly crossed a State line, and have then confronted them with a demand for money, with the alternative of a prison term. . . . The law is in itself an absurdity. . . . It breaks up no 'white slave' traffic, but it does make the Federal Government the accomplice and instrument of blackmailers and facilitates their operations."[6]

Bearing in mind the recent hysteria over coerced prostitution of pure victims, criticism of the relation of blackmail to Mann Act prosecutions appeared in strange quarters. A. Bruce Bielaski, the director of the Bureau of Investigation, acknowledged in January 1915 that "many scheming women of the worst sort have levied blackmail by threatening to accuse men of violations of the White Slave Traffic Act."[7] At about the same time, Clifford G. Roe, a former state prosecutor and now leading purity official, wrote of a "growing tendency to blackmail by threatening prosecution under the Mann Act."[8] Bielaski later said that by January 1915 the blackmail problem had created a public sentiment hostile to the enforcement of the Act.[9]

The public outlook concerning blackmail implications of the Mann Act was improved during the spring of 1915 due to a decision handed down by the Supreme Court on February 1, 1915, in the case of *United States v. Holte.*[10] The indictment charged Chester Laudenschleger with transporting Clara Holte from Barrington, Illinois, to Milwaukee, Wisconsin, for immoral purposes. It recited the formula of "prostitution, debauchery, and other immoral practices," but apparently Clara Holte was married to someone else, no money was involved, and it was a case of simple adultery. In fact, Clara was forty-one years old and dominated young Chester, only twenty-one.[11]

The indictment contained one specific count alleging the immoral purpose as that of having "illicit sexual intercourse" between themselves, and another count alleged that the object of the conspiracy was that the couple might "more easily enter into, assume, and safely continue and maintain illicit sexual and libidinous relations."[12] In the majority opinion issued by the United States Supreme Court, Justice Holmes simply referred to the transportation as being "for the purpose of prostitution." The reader may well recall this case for Holmes's description of simple adultery as prostitution when considering, in chapter 6, the then contemporary confusion as to the meaning of the term prostitution.

The indictment also charged Clara Holte with conspiracy, insofar as she assisted Laudenschleger in her own transportation. The trial court threw out the indictment against the woman, saying that the woman "cannot be both slave and slaver."[13] The indictment for conspiracy truly was problematic.

A conspiracy is an illegal agreement to commit a criminal act. The law of conspiracy has developed the doctrine that if the criminal act necessarily requires two persons for its commission, then the mere cooperation of two persons to commit the act is not in itself a conspiracy. To illustrate, a duel requires two persons. A duel just cannot take place without the engagement of two persons. If two men agree to hold a duel, they may well violate a statute prohibiting dueling or, if they have not actually carried it out, they may be guilty of criminal attempt to commit a duel, but they have *not* conspired to violate the dueling law since the crime itself requires two persons. It would take the participation of three persons to make a conspiracy in this case. Another example of this concept would be criminal adultery. Consensual sexual relations between two persons married to others might well violate a criminal adultery statute, but it does not constitute a conspiracy to violate that law since it requires two persons for the crime's very commission.

No one doubted, in 1915, that a woman could violate the Mann Act by the transportation of *another* woman for immoral purposes, as with a madam taking one of her prostitutes across a state line. But by agreeing with a proposal for interstate transportation, could a woman conspire with a man for her *own* transportation? The Supreme Court in *Holte* said yes, in a decision written by Justice Holmes. The reasoning, a bit of sophistry, was that the crime itself could be committed if the woman were drugged or taken by force. Therefore, the woman's consent was an addition to the elements necessary for the complete commission of the crime and could constitute a conspiracy. The rhetoric was more important than the reasoning. Holmes wrote:

> Suppose, for instance, that a professional prostitute, as well able to look out for herself as was the man, should suggest and carry out a journey within the act of 1910 in the hope of blackmailing the man, and should buy the railroad tickets, or should pay the fare from Jersey City to New York, she would be within the letter of the act of 1910 and we see no reason why the act should not be held to apply. We see equally little reason for not treating the preliminary agreement as a conspiracy that the law can reach, if we abandon the illusion that the woman always is the victim.[14]

Of course, this is completely at odds with the original rhetoric that women were helpless victims of evil white slavers. The dissent of two justices followed the ideology of the original white slavery hysteria and wrote that the statute treats the woman who is transported only as a victim, "often a willing victim but nevertheless a victim." The woman, "whether coerced or induced, whether willingly or unwillingly transported" is regarded by the statute "as the victim of the trafficker and she cannot therefore be punished for being enslaved nor for consenting."[15] The dissent went on to analyze and criticize the purposes of the majority in terms that unmistakenly show the purpose of the majority was to combat blackmail:

> The fact that prostitutes and others have used this statute as a means by which to levy blackmail may furnish a reason why that should be made a Federal offence, so that she and they can be punished for blackmail or malicious prosecution. But those evils are not to be remedied by extending the law of conspiracy.[16]

The idea was that women would be discouraged from attempts to set men up for blackmail, through carrying out immoral interstate journeys, if they knew that they, too, could be charged with conspiracy by aiding or consenting to their own transportation. That might cut down on blackmail. It was understood, even before the appeal to the Supreme Court, that the clarification sought in the *Holte* prosecution was to combat blackmail.[17] But as the dissent pointed out, it would also make it more difficult to prosecute pimps or other white slavers, since the interpretation of the statute making the woman criminally liable for her own transportation would "tend to prevent her from coming forward with her evidence."[18]

In any event, the decision was immediately hailed. The *New York Times*, which had earlier denounced the government for being a blackmailer, now, on February 4, 1915, days after the *Holte* decision, bannered a new editorial, "A Blow to Blackmail":

> Again has the United States Supreme Court come to the rescue against the fanatical enforcement of a bungling law. This time it is the miscalled "white slave law," which as interpreted and enforced has been a law making the Government an accomplice in the business of the blackmailer. . . . The Mann law, through some oversight in wording, was immediately perverted into an instrument for blackmail. . . . What was a police court offense at most if committed at the end of a trolley ride became a Federal crime if committed at the end of a railroad journey. The blackmailers immediately saw their opportunity. All that was necessary was for the blackmailer to decoy her victim across a State line and then threaten him with the terrors of the law. . . . Her previous character, her consent, had nothing to do with the crime. The Supreme Court has now administered a check to this Government-aided blackmail business by a decision that the woman can be punished as well as the man. . . . This decision draws the teeth of the blackmailers, and this industry, which the Mann law has fostered and developed, will languish if the blackmailer finds Government aid withdrawn and a prison sentence awaiting her instead of a sympathetic hearing in the Grand Jury room.[19]

In the following year of 1916 an attorney in the District of Columbia reviewed the effect of the *Holte* decision. He agreed that in the first few years of the statute "blackmailing cases became so frequent as to require some special action" and saw that action in the prosecution of would-be blackmailing women for conspiracy where the woman had fully agreed to the transportation. He saw nothing but good as a result of the *Holte* case. "Since that recent holding of the Supreme Court the activity of the blackmailer has greatly diminished; indeed about ceased."[20] Bielaski was likewise optimistic during 1915, hailing the effects of *Holte* as having put an end to a "large measure" with the activities of female blackmailers because they realized that they could be prosecuted.[21]

But the hope of the *New York Times* and the observations of the Washington attorney were entirely too optimistic. Blackmail and extortion did not stop. With allowance for the difficulties of measuring a crime of secrecy, it seemed actually to increase. By 1916, the *New York Times* was back to editorializing against the Mann Act.

Even before this happened, however, another problem was felt. The *Holte* decision had caused a dislocation. As it was explained in a January 8, 1916, letter from T. W. Gregory, the Attorney General, to Senator Charles A. Culberson, Chairman of the Senate Committee on the Judiciary, the *Holte* case

> has had its deterrent effect on blackmailers, but it has also somewhat interfered with the effectiveness of prosecutions in commercial cases. It sometimes happens that women who are transported for the purpose of prostitution . . . go willingly and may, therefore, be prosecuted for conspiracy. In such cases the testimony of the woman transported is often desired by the government and, because she is liable to be prosecuted for conspiracy, she may decline to testify to such acts as would tend to incriminate her and the government has no method of compelling her to testify. Persons who have profited by the traffic in women . . . have frequently induced the principal witness to refuse to testify by holding over her the threat that she will also be prosecuted.[22]

Gregory went on to recommend that Congress amend the White Slave Traffic Act to provide that no person could refuse to testify, but that any person who does testify would be immune from prosecution as to those matters to which they testified.[23] In other words, the prostitute could be compelled to testify, but would gain immunity from a conspiracy prosecution directed at her. In his annual reports for both 1915 and 1916 the Attorney General publicly recommended amendment of the Mann Act to grant immunity to essential witnesses as a means to prevent them from refusing to testify. Bielaski repeated that recommendation before purity groups.[24]

Legislation to amend the Mann Act in this regard was introduced in January 1916 but was not enacted.[25] However, this negative effect of *Holte* did result in a Department of Justice policy, never fully honored and never articulated in a circular memo, that if a willing woman were transported for purposes of prostitution in a commercial case, ordinarily she should *not* be charged with conspiracy. In that way, she could be compelled to testify against the male.[26] This policy limited the conspiracy theory as brought against women to noncommercial cases.

In any event, the blackmail storm was about to break. On January 13, 1916, the press announced the arrest of one Don Collins, said by law enforcement officials to be the "head and shoulders of the worst gang of blackmailers in the country," specializing in victimizing men of wealth all over the country. Within days additional arrests were made. These six or seven men and women used fake warrants and phony badges to extort money:

> Their method was to shadow a man of wealth and observe closely his relations with any woman not his wife. If he took such a woman out of town, he would be followed by some member of the blackmailing gang to keep a careful record of the time and place of all meetings. Subsequently the prospective victim would be approached by a man who would show a Federal badge and represent himself as a United States Marshal, authorized to arrest the victim under the Mann White Slave act [*sic*] for taking a woman from one State to another.[27]

As an alternative to prosecution, "hush money" ranging from $500 to $20,000 was demanded. In this manner the gang collected over $200,000, an enormous sum for 1916. Should the process of letting "nature take its course" not be sufficient to generate a violation of the statute, the gang also "employed a number of attractive women to assist in creating evidence."[28]

Such press accounts became common in 1916. In April came news of the arrest of a New York gang of ten or twelve men. It operated a scheme that was more devious and one imagines much more likely to succeed. It marked as targets pairs of small-town businessmen, in New York on business, traveling together. Two girls, employed by the gang, would make the acquaintance of the men. After several nights on the town with the women, the men's trust would grow.

> The rest of the game, as it was told by one of the victims, is that about Friday, one of the girls, the companion of the man who has appeared to have the most money, suggests that he take her to Atlantic City for the week-end. He demurs on the ground that he may get in trouble. In an ingenuous manner the girl replies that she appreciates his reti-

cence, and suggests that she go all alone, providing only that he will give her the wherewithal. He does, and she departs.

"The next day," the victim's story continued, "the other girl called me on the telephone and told me that my 'friend' who had gone to Atlantic City wanted me there. She urged me to go and remarked that she was going herself to stay there over Sunday. Everything seemed all right and we two men went to Atlantic City Saturday afternoon.

"We returned Monday. Monday afternoon a man called on me, flashed a Federal officer's badge and informed me that he was a detective. He said he had been in Atlantic City on another case and had seen us there with our companions. He told me to be careful, because the girl I was with was a trouble-maker. He added, however, that he had no axe to grind and wished merely to warn me. He left his card with me and said that if she tried to make any trouble to call on him. He said he believed he could fix the thing up for $1,000. I thanked him and told him good-bye.

"The next day the girl called, and with her was a lawyer. They demanded $2,000 and put up a whole lot of arguments, but I ordered them out.

"On the following day the detective dropped in casually, and, in the course of conversation, asked me if I had heard any more from the girl trouble-maker. I told him I had and recited what had taken place. He said he believed he could hush the thing up for $500. 'If you believe can do it for $500 all-right,' I said. I gave him the money and that's all I heard from any of them."

The police related that they had heard nearly the identical story so many times they were certain it was a gang using a standard operation. The only thing that varied was the amount that had been extorted, which sometimes was as much as $1,700.[29]

Extortion also was used as pressure in business dealings. A person with whom one was negotiating a commercial transaction might use a threat of exposure to coerce concessions. That some businessmen, to their credit, absolutely refused to engage in this conduct helps to underscore the practice in other businessmen. A refusal is shown in the following snippet of conversation quoted in a letter dated May 19, 1916. At stake was an attempt to negotiate a settlement in a very complicated case involving coal land, tramway condemnation, and rights-of-way. The addressee is the General Counsel for the Denver and Rio Grande Railroad:

I arrived at Odgen shortly after noon, but did not get to see Mr. E. [LeRoy Eccles] until about 1:30 p.m. I went to his office in the Eccles Building at that time and had a conference which lasted about an hour and a half. . . . I thereupon remarked:

"I got some information some time ago that K. was making some effort to have C. indicted under the White Slave Act."

To this Mr. E. replied:

"Yes, I know all about it. Mr. K. followed the matter up and got all the details, even the name of the woman."

I said: "I understand that he came within an ace of getting C. indicted."

He replied:

"I was the one who pulled him off. I told him that if he pursued a course like this people would say that I was back of the whole thing because of our mutual relations, and that while I was perfectly willing to conduct a clean fight in the open, I absolutely refused to make any personal attack; so I told K. that he would have to drop this, as I would not stand sponsor for such a proceeding; and thereupon it was dropped."[30]

In the fall of 1916 readers of the press were treated to revelations about yet another gang, this one based in Chicago. This gang was larger, with estimates varying from twenty-five to sixty members, one-third of them women. It was national in scope and operated in New York City, Philadelphia, Atlantic City, and Chicago. And it was highly successful, with estimates of up to $1,000,000 in annual earnings. Week after week, additional arrests were made.

Lurid stories filled the newspapers with accounts of the gang's *modus operandi*. The primary scheme was for the female members to lure prominent and wealthy victims into interstate trips and assignations. Once engaged in a hotel room over the state line, confederates posing as federal officers and equipped with bogus badges and arrest warrants would break into the room. The female conspirator would become hysterical and plead that her parents, or husband, be spared the embarrassment of a Mann Act accusation. Thereupon, an alternative financial arrangement would be discussed.

This Chicago gang was somewhat more diversified than the others. Mothers were blackmailed for their sons' conduct, and some women were lured into compromising situations by male members of the group. This gang also netted larger fish than the others. Not only did they catch wealthy businessmen, but also a Pennsylvania Congressman and a judge. It is difficult to determine, in retrospect, whether all of these blackmailers were in fact members of a vast conspiratorial gang. To the Progressive mind they were, and the news accounts called them variously the "blackmail trust" and "the great Mann Act blackmailers' syndicate." Probably the numerous arrests in the fall of 1916 were of criminals of several different groups rather than one huge syndicate.

In any event, the blackmailers were treated leniently. The federal extortion statute called only for a two-year imprisonment and $2,000 fine as a maximum punishment. Although most of those arrested in the fall 1916 sweep might have been charged with the crime of impersonating a federal officer, in addition to extortion, the bulk of the defendants pled guilty to a single count of extortion, impersonation, or conspiracy and received a prison sentence of eighteen months.[31]

The federal authorities found it extremely difficult to gain the cooperation of male victims of extortion, even after a defendant's arrest. Generally wealthy businessmen, they feared either business repercussions from scandal or much more personal repercussions from their wives. Threats were dropped in the newspapers that the authorities might be forced to compel testimony. Eventually a brave soul would step forward with enough of an account to gain a plea of guilty as to some count of the indictment.

Actually, the federal authorities were generally quite solicitous of the victims' feelings. The prosecutors did not reveal the names of the persons extorted, although newspapers did when they obtained them. Even when threatening to force some victims to testify by subpoena, the authorities promised to first call "those who are unmarried or who are so situated that publicity will do them only temporary injury." Should their testimony prove sufficient, the names of the other men involved "will be kept secret."[32]

In another case, a wealthy Iowa merchant had been blackmailed for $10,000 with the Mann Act as a club. The man, a widower, appealed to the federal authorities to delay the arrest of the swindlers for about a month, until after the date of his daughter's wedding. In a virtual reprise of the father's plea in Verdi's opera *La Traviata*, the merchant claimed that "exposure now would wreck his daughter's happiness and might even cause the wedding plans to be canceled." The federal authorities accommodated the merchant.[33] The concern for the victims' feelings was a far cry from the current efforts of police officials, beginning in the 1970s, to lure men to attractive women dressed as prostitutes and then arrest them for the solicitation that would naturally result from those encounters.

As the Department of Justice prosecuted extortion arising from the use of the Mann Act as a club, it also reassessed its position on white slavery prosecutions themselves. On January 26, 1917, the department made its advice more explicit to local United States Attorneys that they use their discretion so as not to prosecute Mann Act violations where blackmail lurked in the background. The suggestion of the July 28, 1911, circular that local prosecutors consider "the motives of those urging prosecution" was strengthened, and U.S. Attorneys urged that "blackmail cases should, so far as possible, be avoided."[34] But the guidelines were not completely successful.

There was never any legislation amending the Mann Act to make blackmail more difficult. One of the reasons for the congressional inaction was the politician's cowardice in dealing with any controversial subject. But additionally, the American public truly thought with two minds on the issue of blackmail and the Mann Act.

The legal community expressed concern with the possibilities for blackmail in the Act. In a paper read to the Medico-Legal Society in January 1917, a New York attorney charged that "hundreds of men—captains of industry, bankers, and men of wealth and position—have been deliberately and easily blackmailed to a total of millions. The victim cannot squeal without making himself liable to prosecution." The lawyer doubted that there was a single member of Congress "who has the nerve to even introduce a bill to amend the law so as to limit its operation to cases of commercialized vice," but did suggest that the Act be amended to make the woman equally guilty with her male companion in cases where no commercialized vice was present, and further to make it a violation of the Act for a woman to entice a man from one state to another. However, the New York lawyer was not hopeful that there would be any amendment for "some years," and that, therefore, the "outlook for the professional blackmailers is roseate in the extreme." He offered the practical advice that if a man insisted on being a "devil," he ought to avoid interstate transportation by being "A Devil in His Own Home Town."[35]

Another legal commentator at about the same time was appalled by the "condition of affairs that has come into existence by virtue of the interpretations put upon the Mann Act. If we can credit the press and rumor, unscrupulous women are everywhere blackmailing men who unguardedly permit themselves so much as to be in their company; and there have been discovered conspiracies for carrying on this most lucrative crime in a wholesale manner." He thought that the existing state of affairs was "a most distressing one" that Congress should promptly relieve "by declaring that the act shall not be interpreted to apply to other than commercialized vice."[36]

Yet many more narrowly minded and singularly focused Americans did not agree. The members of the Illinois Vigilance Association, an organization of ministers and social workers founded to promote "personal morality and the suppression of vice both clandestine and commercialized" did not. The Illinois Vigilance Association and the Church Federation of Chicago took the same firm position against "polite corruptors" who ruined women without monetary motives but solely for their own "dishonorable indulgence" as they did against the "money-making exploiters," who presumably ruined women for less personal motivations. In a resolution passed at a joint meeting of March 29, 1915, the stalwart members of the two organizations observed that "men of blameless conduct have not been complaining that they have been blackmailed under the Mann Act." They urged the federal government to "punish impartially" both the commercial and noncommercial "corruptors of the innocent and the weak."[37]

If the Illinois Vigilance Association had no difficulty in analyzing the blackmail "problem," neither did the *New York Times*. As we have seen, this newspaper condemned the Act in 1914 for making the federal government "the accomplice and instrument of blackmailers." Then it praised the *Holte* decision as holding out hope for containment of extortionists. As soon as it was clear that prosecuting women for conspiracy to violate the statute was an insufficient deterrent to blackmail, the *Times* returned to its original position. As the evidence of blackmail gangs and arrests for extortion mounted in 1916, the *Times* thundered away at the Mann Act.

On January 14, 1916, it editorialized under the headline, "Government Aid to Blackmailers," that "a gang of professional criminals have been making use of the misnamed Mann White Slave law to blackmail rich men systematically. . . . the Mann law is chiefly a bid for blackmail and serves no other purpose worth mentioning."[38] On September 20, 1916, the *Times* suggested that the Act "ought to have been called the Encouragement of Blackmail act." It charged that while "the 'syndicate' of white slavers is a figment of imaginative fly-gobblers, the 'syndicate' of blackmailers is a reality. . . . The Mann law should be wiped off the statute books at the next session."[39] Four days later the editor acknowledged that, notwithstanding the absence of wholesale traffic in coerced women, the Mann Act may have prevented prostitutes from moving volitionally from one city to another. But the voluntary movement of prostitutes was a "trivial evil" compared with the "fostering of the crime of blackmail on a great scale with the aid of the National Government."[40]

The *Washington Post* was more moderate in its views. It noted following the January 1917 decision in *Caminetti* that the Supreme Court had "virtually conceded" that the law was used for blackmail and urged Congress to amend the statute promptly. People "need no legal training to tell them that a law that offers opportunity for blackmailers of both sexes is a bad law unless its form is altered."[41]

But if the Illinois Vigilance Association, the Church Federation Council of Chicago, and the *New York Times* are representative of American institutions that had firm views on the subject of blackmail and the Mann Act, many other Americans and American institutions were of two minds. Among those organizations that were ambivalent were the Department of Justice and the Supreme Court itself.

Following the *Caminetti* case and its definitive inclusion of noncommercial cases within the Mann Act, one anonymous official of the Department of Justice was quoted as saying that "under the construction of the law . . . the Mann act is a menace rather than a help to the public. It will serve no purpose other than that of the blackmailers, and under it, unless it is amended, I expect to see the already big army of blackmailers largely increase."[42] Yet letters from individual United States Attorneys to the department sometimes sounded a different note.

The U.S. Attorney in Milwaukee wrote the chief of the Bureau of Investigation in November 1914 that he had "never had a case involving blackmail presented to this office. I should, of course, not wittingly allow the law [Mann Act] to be used for that purpose, but it is true that in a proper case showing a violation, the motive prompting the complaining witness to make the complaint, would be immaterial."[43]

On January 31, 1917, the U.S. Attorney for the Southern District of Iowa wrote even more bluntly to the department:

> I have had no trouble, whatever, with the question of blackmail and
> believe that phase of it is very largely over-estimated and exaggerated

by those who are opposed to this law. I firmly believe there is no better statute on the books looking toward the suppression of sexual vice
than this one and I have no patience, whatever, with those who are
continually in the public press displaying great anxiety for the wel-
fare of some timid subject of blackmail.[44]

The judiciary was always alert to the connection of blackmail to the
Mann Act, especially when applied to noncommercial settings. As early
as 1914 a federal appellate court had noted that "the act, when applied
to merely unlawful sexual intercourse, has been used as an instrument
for blackmail or other oppressions." However, the judges still felt
bound to follow the plain meaning of the statute and held noncommercial immorality within the law.[45]

The ambivalence over blackmail was felt also by the justices on the
Supreme Court. The minority in *Caminetti*, arguing against the extension of the Act to noncommercial immorality, boyfriend-girlfriend
travel, charged that "blackmailers of both sexes have arisen, using the
terrors of the construction now sanctioned by this court as a help—
indeed, the means—for their brigandage. The result is grave and
should give us pause."[46] The majority opinion, while admitting indirectly that blackmail might be a consequence, deflected the problem to
Congress:

> The fact, if it be so, that the act as it is written opens the door to
> blackmailing operations upon a large scale, is no reason why the
> courts should refuse to enforce it according to its terms. . . . Such
> considerations are more appropriately addressed to the legislative
> branch of the government, which alone had [*sic*] authority to enact
> and may if it sees fit amend the law.[47]

Because of the sharply divergent views of many Americans, and the
differing strands of thought even within specific organizations, it was
unlikely that Congress would act. And, indeed, Congress did not
address the problem of blackmail and the Mann Act, not in 1916–17 or
ever to this day. And there is an abundance of evidence that blackmail
and extortion continued on in the 1920s, 1930s, and 1940s.

Some of the evidence for this later blackmail is merely circumstantial, consisting of books, articles, and other expressions of opinion that
it was happening. For example, a highly critical review of the Mann Act
that appeared in the *American Mercury* in 1936 charged that the statute
gave some women "a legal vehicle for coercion and blackmail."[48] A July

1933 law journal commented that, because of inclusion of noncommercial sex within the Mann Act, "if we can credit the press and rumors, unscrupulous women are everywhere blackmailing men who unguardedly permit themselves so much as to be in their company."[49] *Designs in Scarlet,* a book written in 1939 by a man with close ties to J. Edgar Hoover, the director of the Federal Bureau of Investigation, contains a vivid description of blackmail perpetrated by a female hitchhiker. It stated that there was "a small army of female blackmailers who today work the highways in the hope of finding a sucker who will be fool enough to spend a night with them—across a state line."[50]

Anecdotal evidence in the 1940s suggested that blackmail continued as a problem associated with the Mann Act. A 1944 book mentioned a Hollywood talent scout who "had once had a minor threaten him with charges based on the Mann Act."[51] Another writer asserted in 1946 that the interstate highways "have become avenues of potential blackmail, slander and libel."[52] *Time* magazine asserted in April 1944 that "the Act is a wide open invitation to blackmail and feminine revenge."[53] Even courts referred to blackmailing. One court in 1944 stated that it did not by a new interpretation wish to "open wider than it is the door to blackmailing."[54] A justice of the Supreme Court in 1945 mentioned the "evils of blackmail and persecution" caused by the Mann Act.[55]

Aside from these speculations, there is tangible evidence of extortion in actual prosecutions for Mann Act violations. In some of these situations the local United States Attorney requested authority from the Department of Justice to dismiss the pending prosecution. For example, in February 1928, the U.S. Attorney for the Western District of Michigan wrote the Attorney General that "there has come to my attention that the victim and her mother have attempted to extort money from subject [defendant]" and requested authority to dismiss the case. In April 1930 the United States Attorney for Topeka, Kansas, wrote that "immediately after the indictment word was received that this appeared to be a blackmail case on the part of the relatives of the victim. . . . In view of the above fact this office believes that the prosecution should be dismissed. . . ."[56]

But other prosecutors apparently took the attitude we have seen was held by the United States Attorney in Milwaukee that "in a proper case showing a violation, the motive prompting the complaining witness to make the complaint, would be immaterial." In the following three noncommercial cases, as examples, the prosecutors were aware before trial that the women or their families had attempted to extort money from the defendants. In *Carey v. United States* (1920), the prosecutor knew, as stated by the appellate court, that there was:

> a letter to accused from the attorney for the girl in a civil suit by her against accused, arising out of this seduction, and a conversation between accused and the attorney. The vital portion of this evidence was that, unless accused paid $500 in the civil suit, he would have "a white slave prosecution brought against him."[57]

In a 1924 case, the complaining witness "wrote the defendant's father a letter offering to go away and 'get Sam [the defendant] out of trouble' if the father would pay the money required by some unnamed boy, who would marry her on that condition."[58] The ultimate in evidence of blackmailing was an actual written receipt given to a defendant by the blackmailers, of which the prosecutor was aware in a 1933 trial for a noncommercial violation. A receipt signed by the so-called victim's aunt stated:

> I, the undersigned, herewith acknowledge receipt of the sum of Seventeen Hundred ($1700.00) Dollars from W. W. Yoder. The payment of said money to me by the said W. W. Yoder is for the purpose of preventing me, my sister, Mrs. Long, and my niece, Samuel Lee Young from prosecuting Roy Yoder for white slave traffic in which my niece Miss Young and Roy Yoder, went to Kansas and other states for immoral purposes. I agree with Mr. Yoder that we will not prosecute Roy Yoder for said offense and the payment of said money settles the entire transaction. Witness my hand this 8th day of October, 1931.[59]

In these three examples, the noncommercial violations were prosecuted notwithstanding clear evidence of blackmail and notwithstanding the Justice Department's guidelines urging the nonprosecution of cases involving blackmail. Blackmail usually is a silent crime and leaves no trace. These examples are merely evidence that blackmail continued throughout the period.

There was a particularized form of extortion practiced in the 1920s and 1930s whereby wives extorted additional money in divorce settlements by threats to have their husbands prosecuted for violations of the Mann Act involving other women. In 1928, one California wife threatened her husband with Mann Act prosecution, as a result of which he entered into a property settlement agreement. Nine years later he successfully sued his former wife to set aside the property agreement because of the fear in his mind caused by her extortion.[60]

In a 1939 Florida case the husband sought to set aside a property settlement for extortion. He charged that his wife had conspired with another woman who was to entice him into a trip to Atlantic City. He was successfully enticed, but once the philandering husband was ensconced with the temptress in their Atlantic City hotel room they were raided by hotel detectives. The wife thereupon threatened her husband with prosecution under the Mann Act if he did not sign a property settlement to her liking.[61]

Probably the best-known effort by a wife to extort a favorable divorce settlement from her husband was the 1926 arrest of the architect Frank Lloyd Wright for violation of the Mann Act, arranged in part by his estranged wife, Miriam. Wright's matrimonial and monetary difficulties in the period from 1924 to 1929 engendered numerous civil and criminal lawsuits. The full and complex story has been told elsewhere.[62] What follows is only a brief summary necessary to put the Mann Act charges in perspective.

Wright and his wife, Miriam Noel, separated in spring 1924, she moving out of his famous home, Taliesin, near Spring Green, Wisconsin. That fall, the fifty-seven-year-old Wright met Olgivanna Milanoff, a beautiful twenty-six-year-old woman from a prominent Montenegrin family. She was married, separated from her husband with their seven-year-old daughter in her custody.

Wright was captivated and pursued the young woman. In February 1925 Olgivanna moved into Taliesin and obtained a divorce from her husband a few months later. She bore Frank Lloyd Wright a daughter, Iovanna, by the end of the year. In the fall of 1925 Wright's wife, Miriam, filed for divorce.

Wright's legal entanglements accelerated during the following year. In June, Miriam unsuccessfully attempted to force her way into the Taliesin estate. That sent Olgivanna into hiding. In August, Miriam filed an alienation of affections suit against Olgivanna, after having previously complained to the Bureau of Immigration about Olgivanna's immigration status. Three significant events occurred in September. First, The Bank of Wisconsin foreclosed on Taliesin, generating a flock of subsidiary lawsuits. Second, Olgivanna's ex-husband brought a habeas corpus action to obtain custody of their daughter, Svetlana, and obtained warrants for Olgivanna's and Frank's arrest for violation of the Mann Act. Soon the former husband's attorney and Miriam's lawyer were actively cooperating in their pursuit of the couple. Third, Frank Lloyd Wright joined Olgivanna in hiding.

Their hiding place was a cottage on Lake Minnetonka, just west of Minneapolis. They were discovered there and arrested on October 20, 1926. They were charged with a state crime of adultery and also the federal Mann Act. After two nights in the Hennepin County Jail the adultery charges were dropped and, as to the Mann Act, they were released on $12,500 bail. The poet Carl Sandburg and several other prominent midwestern intellectuals petitioned the federal authorities to drop the white slavery prosecution. In March of 1927 the indictment was dismissed, although the difficulties in the divorce and litigation with Miriam would continue for two more years.[63]

Wright gave a moving description of their arrest in his autobiography:

> We had just dined. The baby put to bed. Svetlana asleep in her bed out on the porch. . . . Fire burned in the grate, all warm and cozy. . . . About half-past-nine came a rude knock on the door of the living room toward the street. I went to the door and opened it. A dozen or more rough-looking characters—lead by Miriam Noel's lawyer—now mutual with Svetlana's father—accompanied by members of the press, several of whom I had seen somewhere before. They shouldered their way into the room and surrounded us.
>
> "You are all under arrest," said the heavy-handed one, the bigger sheriff.

He sardonically portrayed the circuslike atmosphere created by the morals police and malicious press, at the time of his arrest and at the county jail:

> Cameras had already been set up around the house to illustrate the story as we came out the door. . . . I went out in the face of puffing flashlights, got into his car and was driven down to the sheriff at the county jail in Minneapolis. His name was Brown. Brown was a man of some parts in the Hennepin County community. A sheriff, but serving as a patriot without pay to clean up the Baptist belt and make it moral or something. . . . [At the sheriff's office] the crowd was busy now doing their daily stuff. In the next room they were word-painting the noble "volunteer" sheriff as a hero. This was his reward for

playing up to their game. Coming to me now was the sovereign insult
a free country has to offer one of her own sons.

Wright gave a detailed and understandably bitter account of his jail
experiences, the petty inflexibility of the law and its enforcers, and the
sensational press that pandered to the fantasies of the "hoi-polloi, rag-
tag and bobtail." Once the state charges were dropped, the federal
Mann Act had to be faced:

> We were to be held there in jail pending appearance before an arm-
> chair Federal, famous in the Northern Baptist Belt for "moral" ten-
> dencies. . . . We now went before this august limb of the Federal law
> on the charge of having violated that malign instrument of revenge
> diverted from its original purpose to serve just such purposes as this:
> the Mann Act. Mr. Mann and his wife used to sit across the aisle
> from me at my uncle's church: All Souls. His law was dead letter so
> far as public sentiment went. But for ulterior purposes a law just the
> same.[64]

There is one aspect of Miriam's chasing of her husband and her
Mann Act charges that is quite ironic. Many years earlier, in 1915, a dismissed housekeeper made accusations to the Department of Justice that
Wright was violating the Mann Act by taking his girlfriend back and
forth between Chicago and Spring Green, Wisconsin. Wright's then
girlfriend was the same woman, Miriam Noel, later his wife, who thereafter accused Wright of violating the Act with Olgivanna Milanoff. No
formal charges were brought as a result of the 1915 accusation, but
Wright took them seriously enough to hire Clarence Darrow to argue
his case before the federal prosecutors.[65]

Blackmail and extortion as by-products of noncommercial prosecutions under the Mann Act never disappeared. Federal efforts to prosecute blackmailers ultimately failed, as seen by the persistence of the
problem. It was precisely the attempt to control private morals by the
clumsy tools of felony prosecutions that facilitated this perverse use of
the Mann Act.

As we will see, beginning approximately in 1928 there was a curtail-
ment of prosecution for noncommercial offenses. With the close of the
federal morals crusade, blackmail and extortion waned. While noncommercial prosecutions were still possible after 1928, they were less likely.

With the decreasing probability of arrest for noncommercial violation, the blackmailers simply had less leverage to press against their victims and consequently less success in their efforts to extort.

It is by now apparent that *Caminetti* was a watershed case. We should step back briefly to look at how the case developed, and then move forward to its appellate status before the United States Supreme Court in 1917.

The Case of *Caminetti v. United States*

The reach of the Mann Act was undetermined until the Caminetti case was decided in January 1917. Specifically, it was unknown whether the statute prohibited the use of interstate commerce in matters of private immorality unconnected to purse or pocketbook. Did it apply to a man's transportation of a woman across a state line, or urging her to cross herself, when the immoral purpose was an adulterous tryst or a weekend seduction? It short, did the Mann Act apply to affairs of the heart?

As we have seen, some of the federal judicial circuits had applied the statute to noncommercial sexual irregularities, but some judges resisted and had dismissed indictments on that ground. As we have also seen, Attorney General Wickersham, in 1911, rendered a legal opinion that two weekends of wining, dining, and sex between a consenting couple did not constitute a violation of the Act, even though the man had paid for his companion's interstate transportation.

The Supreme Court had not yet resolved the question. True, the *Athanasaw* case had not involved prostitution. Agnes Couch had been hired for the chorus line and to hustle drinks as a B-girl. Still, the context of the operation of the Imperial Theatre was such that one might surmise that sexual activities would likely result. In any event, the context was clearly commercial. It was not an affair of the heart.

Doubts as to the scope of the Act were resolved in *Caminetti v. United States,* which held that the Mann Act did indeed apply to fully consensual, noncommercial, sexual encounters in which a male transported or encouraged the transportation of a woman in interstate commerce. *Caminetti* was decided along with two companion cases.[1] One involved Maury I. Diggs, who was tried separately from F. Drew Caminetti but was very much involved with the affair for which they were convicted. The other companion case concerned an unrelated defendant, L. T. Hays, and involved the interstate transportation of an admitted prostitute by Hays, not as a pimp but for his own private use.

The *Caminetti* case was decided by the Supreme Court on January 15, 1917. It had a history, going back to 1912, that may be conveniently divided into three earlier phases: first, the love affair itself; second, the political turmoil that enveloped the early prosecution of the case; and third, the trial and intermediate appeal to the circuit court, prior to its final resolution in the United States Supreme Court.

In the spring of 1913 Drew Caminetti was about twenty-seven years old and resided in Sacramento, California, with his wife and two children, one a baby. He was a buddy of Maury Diggs, twenty-six, also married and living in Sacramento with his wife and young daughter. Caminetti was a clerk in the State Board of Control and had an office in the state capitol. Diggs was an architect with offices in the Diepenbrock Building who worked for the state and also had a private practice.[2]

Both men were from prominent, wealthy families. Caminetti's father was a former Democratic state senator, recently appointed as Commissioner of Immigration by the incoming Wilson administration. Diggs was the nephew of another Democratic state senator and his father was a contractor in Berkeley.

A saloon keeper named Monte Austin introduced Maury Diggs to Marsha Warrington on the street one day in September 1912. Marsha was twenty, a stenographer, and lived with her father and stepmother. She had a close friend, Lola Norris, nineteen, who lived with her parents and worked in the State Library. These women, both unmarried, came from very respectable families, and some of the subsequent newspaper accounts characterized them as society girls.

Within a month the four of them began keeping company together, Diggs and Warrington as one couple and Caminetti and Norris as the other. The women knew that their companions were married, although they later claimed that both Diggs and Caminetti had represented their marital situations as unhappy. The young women introduced the men to their parents under fictitious names because they realized that their parents would forbid them to date married men had the parents realized their true identities.

Diggs had an automobile and the foursome traveled about the countryside, having picnics and visiting roadhouses. Diggs and Warrington entered into a sexual relationship by November 1912. The foursome held a party in Diggs's flat in December 1912 during a time when his wife was away. According to Diggs, he slept with Marsha in the marital bed on that occasion, an assertion she denied. She did acknowledge repeated visits to Diggs's offices, often with Caminetti and Norris, where they carried on activities the *New York Times* subsequently characterized as "champagne orgies." Marsha testified that she was pregnant by Diggs by February 1913.

The sexual aspect of the Caminetti and Norris affair was slower to blossom. In February 1913 the two couples took a trip to San Francisco and San Jose, with the girls giving their parents misinformation as to their destination. They stayed at hotels where the two couples each occupied separate rooms and registered as man and wife. Lola Norris, however, claimed an understanding that the girls were to occupy one room and the men the other. When Marsha and Maury disappeared into one of the two connecting rooms and locked themselves in, Lola beat on the door, only to eventually give up and sleep in a chair all night. Lola later testified that Drew Caminetti had not seduced her until their trip to Reno.

Because of their social prominence and also because they were indiscreet, it was not very long before the story of the affair began to circulate. The week preceding their March 10 departure for Reno was one of intense pressure upon all participants, although for different reasons.

Toward the end of February Marsha told the others of an article that had been planned for publication in the *Sacramento Bee*, the local newspaper, exposing their affair. It was squelched, she said, by a friend of hers. At the same time, her uncle was investigating matters and had called upon the saloon keeper Monte Austin. According to Caminetti, Marsha's uncle questioned Monte closely and threatened that Marsha's father would kill any married man who dated his daughter. On March 1, Maury Diggs's father arrived in town. He wandered around town looking for his son with a policeman in tow, anxious to arrest some culprits.

The senior Diggs called Caminetti and threatened his job with the state, asserting "I came up here from Berkeley to get him, and I am going to get you too." Diggs's uncle said that his brother was "around town acting like a wild man, that he had policemen with him, that he had telephoned all around the country, to all the surrounding towns . . .

and notified the police in those towns [to arrest his son, Maury, Caminetti, and the two women]."

This is not as implausible as it might seem today. In this time period parents wishing to stop their children's conduct often requested an arrest of the delinquent child. The senior Diggs clearly wanted the affair stopped and undoubtedly thought that any prosecution initiated on the basis of a state adultery statute or local ordinance could be dropped quietly later.

Maury was holed up at the Columbia Hotel, hoping to escape his father. He ducked out at times to hold furtive conversations with Marsha in the park. On a few occasions Caminetti and the two girls slipped in to visit him in his room. One day Diggs stopped at O'Brien's saloon, a watering spot he and Caminetti had frequented in quieter times. O'Brien told him his father was a "terror," that he was running around like a "maniac," with policemen. O'Brien said that the father had pounded on the bar and said that there were a "bunch of people" in Sacramento who were ruining his son and he was going to "put a stop to it and have everyone arrested."

On another occasion in that exciting week Diggs took his car out and went riding with Marsha Warrington. He was on the road leading toward Stockton when he spotted another automobile behind him. It was his father chasing him with an officer of the Juvenile Court. Diggs sped up to "fifty miles an hour for some minutes" and thus eluded them.

Meanwhile Drew Caminetti had been hearing about things from his wife. The two paramours were still technically minors, at twenty and nineteen, and Mrs. Caminetti threatened to haul them before the Juvenile Court. She told her husband that she and Mrs. Diggs had had several discussions about the matter and were going to bring some lawsuits if things did not stop immediately. She was particularly incensed that the girls were boasting of their affairs and claiming that they did not care if the men were married. "They should worry," the wife quoted the girls as saying.

Caminetti heard from Mrs. Diggs as well, probably because her own husband, Maury, was hidden out in the hotel but his partner could be reached. Mrs. Diggs called Caminetti at O'Brien's place and told him that he, Caminetti, had been "a snake to me" for a long time, but that now she was going to show him "what a real serpent is." She told him she knew all about their affairs and was going to tell the girls' parents and "you know what will happen to you." Caminetti persuaded her to hold off until he talked with her in person at her house.

He arrived for their 7:30 meeting in great fear, even hiding behind the door until he was certain Mrs. Diggs was not carrying a gun. She told Caminetti that she had suffered a great deal, as his own wife had also. She said she had not had any sleep that week, she was half crazy, and she intended "to make me and these two girls suffer everything that she had suffered." Meanwhile, Diggs's uncle told Diggs that his father had left town. Diggs left the hotel, and uncle and delinquent nephew arrived at the Diggs' residence, passing Caminetti at the house as he left.

During that hectic week and the few days following, there were many discussions between the four participants in the affairs about what to do about their fix. The sequence is hard to follow from the trial testimony, but it is clear that, at this point, the stories between the men and the women diverge. The women claimed that Diggs, principally, threatened them that a scandal was about to break in the papers from a story planted by his wife. Diggs also said that Mrs. Diggs would have them arrested and punished under the juvenile law, and they would be subjected to the "third degree," according to the women's recollections. The solution to their problem was to leave town with the two of them, Maury and Drew. The girls claimed that both Diggs and Caminetti professed their love and promised to get divorces and then marry them.

Lola Norris did testify at trial that "Mr. Caminetti did not, in any of those conversations, propose to me that I should go from Sacramento to Reno for the purpose of having sexual relations with him. . . . The subject of sexual intercourse or the subject of being a mistress was never discussed in any of those conversations. Never by anybody." Doubtless, it was implicit.

Caminetti's testimony was that on the day before their departure Diggs had told the foursome that his father was coming up soon to have Caminetti and the two girls arrested. Caminetti decided to flee the approaching storm, and the women refused to stay behind to face the consequences by themselves. Caminetti testified at trial that he had expressly told the girls that he did not want them "to leave with the idea" that they were going to have "any great or glorious or glittering future," apparently negating the idea of divorce and remarriage.

Diggs told the group that he preferred to leave town by himself. He testified that he had said that he had "too much to lose, and had a good home, and a good wife, and too nice a child." And at another point he said, "I've got lots before me in this town and I want this to blow over." But Warrington insisted she go too, and, according to Diggs, had asserted, "Well, old boy, believe me, you're not going away and leave me here. . . . I am going too." She then enlisted Lola Norris.

Diggs did acknowledge that Marsha asked him what the authorities might do to Lola and her, and admitted he told her that "owing to the fact that she was not 21 . . . I believed she [his wife] could institute proceedings against her [Marsha] through the Juvenile Court if she [wife] wanted to. I also told her that if she had any money my wife could sue her for alienation of her husband's affections." According to the men, the subject of possible legal actions against the two girls was discussed but not in the context of a threat they made. The girls insisted they were pressured; the men claimed they left town merely to avoid arrest and scandal.

A sort of comic farce followed the decision to leave town. There was loose discussion of where to go. They agreed to meet at a restaurant near the station. Caminetti arrived late and was drunk. He had forgotten his money and had to return for it. They missed one train. After they had reassembled and were finally ready, the next train out of Sacramento was headed eastward toward Reno. Had it been southward for Los Angeles, and that destination was discussed at one point, they would not have violated the Mann Act. In the early morning hours of March 10, 1913, the two women, Diggs, and Caminetti slipped out of Sacramento on a Southern Pacific train, the China Mail, and headed up the Sierra Nevada mountains, crossing over that fatal state line fourteen miles before the Reno depot.

The foursome took a drawing room and Lola and Drew settled into the upper berth while Marsha and Maury took the lower berth. The train pulled into Reno mid-morning on Monday, March 10. After eating breakfast at a cafe, the men left the women at the Riverside Hotel and rented a cottage. They told the real estate firm that they were cattle buyers and would be in Nevada for several months. Apparently the bungalow would not be ready until the following day, and for the Monday evening the two couples rented a suite of rooms at the Riverside Hotel. Diggs registered himself and Marsha as C. E. Enright and wife and Caminetti registered as F. F. Ross and wife. The next day they ordered provisions and moved into the cottage at 235 Cheney Street, Maury and Marsha occupying the front bedroom with Drew and Lola in the back bedroom.

Their departure had become notorious in Sacramento. By Tuesday, lurid articles appeared in the local newspapers about their flight and, by Wednesday, authorities charged them with child abandonment, contributing to the dependency of minors, and other California statutes. On the morning of March 14, that Friday, the Reno Chief of Police arrested the foursome. Sacramento authorities arrived and escorted them under arrest by train to California. The officers took them first to Truckee, just over the California line, for questioning. They then proceeded to Auburn, where they detrained for transportation by car the short distance into Sacramento. The police hoped this maneuver would avoid anticipated crowds at the Sacramento station, but word had leaked out and they were confronted with a crowd in Auburn, anxious to look at the culprits. Within three days, John L. McNab, the United States District Attorney for Northern California, announced that he would prosecute Caminetti and Diggs under the White Slave Traffic Act and the state actions were suspended.

The subsequent prosecution resulted in a sharp, if short-lived, scandal. Well before trial, and far from California, the *Caminetti* case appeared on the front pages of the *New York Times* every day for six days beginning June 22, 1913, and on four of those days it was on the front page.[3] The improprieties in the prosecution of the case reached high into the Wilson administration, involving two cabinet officers, and were resolved only by the personal intervention of President Wilson.

In due course after their arrests, Caminetti and Diggs were held to answer by the federal commissioner, admitted to bail, and then formally indicted. McNab, the United States District Attorney, was a holdover Republican, still serving in the new Democratic administration. In early May, as a routine matter, McNab advised the Democratic Attorney General, James C. McReynolds, concerning the status of the case. On May 16, 1913, McReynolds asked McNab for a full report, which was sent to McReynolds on May 21 and which reached him on May 27. In that report McNab warned the Attorney General that it was "being openly charged that political influence would stop the cases and that the prosecution would be 'fixed'" and demanded instructions to proceed.

On May 21, C. K. McClatchy, editor of the *Sacramento Bee*, wired the federal government that there was in California "strong intimation from certain leading Democrats" that a "systematic effort is being made with the authorities at Washington to have the white slave cases" against Diggs and Caminetti dropped and postponed for the "weakening of the prosecution." McClatchy charged that this would be an "infamous outrage" that would demonstrate that "there is one law for wretches without friends and a totally different law for wretches with a political pull." In California, it was asserted that the two young defendants were boasting that their political influence would be used to halt the prosecutor.

Before he took office, Anthony Caminetti, Wilson's newly appointed Commissioner of Immigration and the father of the defendant Drew Caminetti, had advised his superior, the Secretary of Labor, that it would be necessary for him to take a leave of absence in order to be present at the trial of his son. As the late June trial date approached, the elder Caminetti twice contacted McNab with a request, or demand as characterized by McNab, that the trial be postponed. McNab twice refused, advising the elder Caminetti on May 27 that his "well-known political prominence has already brought forth suggestions that the case has been continued for political reasons."

On May 27, the date McReynolds received McNab's full report on the case, McReynolds wired his instructions to go forward with the prosecution. On May 28, McNab wrote the Attorney General warning of political pressures that would be brought in Washington to defer or dismiss the cases. On June 3, McNab wrote McReynolds again, advised him of the repeated attempts by the elder Caminetti to obtain a postponement, and cautioned McReynolds that the "Government's case will be impaired by a long delay."

In mid-June, Commissioner of Immigration Caminetti reminded W. B. Wilson, the Secretary of Labor and his superior, of his earlier request for a leave of absence so he could attend the trial of his son. The Secretary informed Caminetti that a leave of absence was impossible due to the formative stage of the department, the press of business, and the desirability of Caminetti being fully familiar with the immigration operations so that he could inspect their stations when he traveled to the West Coast. Wilson asked Caminetti whether it might be possible for Caminetti to obtain a postponement. Perhaps somewhat disingenuously Caminetti replied that he did not know whether a postponement could be obtained. Then the Secretary of Labor offered to talk with the Attorney General McReynolds.

On June 18, Secretary of Labor Wilson telephoned McReynolds, laid out the circumstances, and asked for a postponement. McReynolds would later report to the president that postponements are not unusual, that it did not occur to him that anyone would malign his motives, but that he had not stopped to go through the files and refresh his recollection of the specifics of the case before he wired McNab, also on June 18. In his telegram he recited that the "Secretary of Labor advises it is a matter of public importance that Commissioner of Immigration Caminetti remain at his post here. [that is, Washington] . . . In view of all the facts, you are instructed to postpone the trial of these cases until the Autumn."

Subsequent scholarship has indicated that, while McReynolds may have lacked good, practical political judgment, he did not act from improper motives. The postponement was not a product of any conspiracy to obstruct justice.[4] Yet this was not clear at the time, and the motives could certainly be questioned by a partisan political opponent.

McNab wired his resignation to President Wilson. He recited his earlier warnings of influence, called the Caminetti-Diggs affair a "hideous crime," warned that there had been attempts to corrupt government witnesses, and that friends of the defendants were publicly boasting that wealth and influence would stay the prosecution's hand. He concluded that "in bitter humiliation of spirit, I am compelled to acknowledge . . . that the Department of Justice is yielding to influence which will cripple and destroy the usefulness of this office. I cannot consent to occupy this position as a mere automaton and have the guilt or innocence of rich and powerful defendants . . . determined in Washington on representations on behalf of the defendants. . . . Neither my sense of honor nor public duty can permit me thus to destroy the prestige of this office." In his parallel message to McReynolds, McNab wired that "corruption and subornation of perjury will weaken and destroy the cases long before Autumn is here."

McNab turned over copies of his telegrams to the press on June 21, and they appeared on the front page of the *New York Times* the following day. The press caught up with McReynolds near Baltimore on June 21, a Saturday, at a wedding he was attending. His initial reaction was less than brilliant. The Attorney General stated that "a Republican District Attorney has resigned, and I am shedding no tears." The next few days would force him to reconsider his statements.

The next day, Sunday, he did a bit better, suggesting that he did not think the cases would suffer by postponement. Administration officials gave out the line that McNab was attempting to make political capital as he was said to be a candidate for the Republican gubernatorial nomination.

By Monday, June 23, the Republican press across the country took up McNab's cause, charging wicked corruption and political influence. On that day, three resolutions were introduced in Congress demanding an investigation and requiring the administration to turn over all documents to House committees. The demands included an unrelated case, that of the Western Fuel Company, about which McNab had also charged influence, but over which the excitement chilled quickly. It lacked the juicy prurience of white slavery allegations.

Representative Julius Kahn, of San Francisco, and Representative James R. Mann himself were the leaders of the House attack. Mann challenged President Wilson to "appoint a new Commissioner General of Immigration on the ground that the present Commissioner has used his political and official influence to prevent his son from being brought to a speedy trial under the Mann act for one of the most horrible of all offenses." Even the San Francisco federal grand jury got into the act, indicating that it was going to take up McNab's charges, although its ultimately adverse report was rejected by the federal judiciary.[5]

Meanwhile, the Wilson administration was becoming weary under the charges. On Tuesday, June 24, the *New York Times* reported that "high officials of the Administration are evidently much concerned over the McNab affair." President Wilson called for a report from McReynolds and brought the matter to his cabinet's attention the following day for what was reported to be a "long discussion." McReynolds recited the facts as he understood them, including a written report from Secretary of Labor Wilson. McReynolds charged that McNab should have sent another dispatch to alert him again to the peculiar facts of the case before publishing his telegrams. Had he, McReynolds, realized the construction put upon his act he would have been "scrupulously careful to avoid it. . . . I do not even hope to escape mistakes, but I am profoundly conscious that my actions are free from unworthy motives."

Wilson accepted McNab's resignation with regret that he had "acted so hastily, and under so complete a misapprehension of the actual circumstances." The president wrote McReynolds expressing satisfaction that the Attorney General had acted previously with sound and impartial judgment but that now the cases had to be pressed with the "utmost diligence and energy." He agreed with McReynolds's suggestion that a special prosecutor be appointed, "the ablest we can obtain," and thanked his Attorney General for his anticipated "personal attention to the immediate and diligent prosecution."

The Republicans tried to keep the scandal alive. Clayton Herrington, in charge of the [federal] Bureau of Investigation in San Francisco and the agent who had prepared the Diggs-Caminetti cases, appealed for the removal of McReynolds. He was promptly suspended and then fired.[6] McNab decried the lack of candor in McReynolds's report of the earlier warnings he had been given. They had been alluded to by McReynolds, but not nearly as clearly as McNab detailed them to the press on June 26.

Congressman Mann charged that the president and Attorney General had acted like "frightened rabbits," maligned the elder Caminetti's lack of dedication to office that he would want a leave of absence, and suggested the "manly course" for Wilson would have been to refuse the resignation and ask McNab to try the cases.[7] On July 3, the House Judiciary Committee issued a report disclosing a portion of the correspondence relating to the postponement,[8] but no full investigation was ever held. There were snipes at the first special prosecutor appointed, since allegedly he had been a friend of the senior Caminetti, and he was forced to withdraw.[9]

Representatives Kahn and Mann still pursued their cause. When the Democratic leadership would not allow Kahn to deliver a peppery speech he had prepared, Mann conducted a successful filibuster. Ultimately, after two weeks of parliamentary maneuvering, at the end of July 1913, the Republicans obtained five hours in which to debate the postponement of the cases.[10] Although there had been considerable debate in Congress,[11] the scandal sputtered to a halt.

The two men were tried separately, both in San Francisco and both before the same federal judge, William C. Van Fleet. Diggs went first and his trial began on August 5, 1913.[12] Almost immediately Judge Van Fleet ruled that the character of the women would not be admitted, but he did allow evidence of Marsha Warrington's sexual activities with Diggs on an enticement count. On August 13 the Judge startled the jurors by questioning them as to whether any of them had spoken with anyone connected with Diggs or Caminetti. No one responded, and he admonished them again not to converse with the defendant or his counsel. The following day he explained that he had not meant to imply that there was any well-founded suspicion, but a member of his staff had

7. Maury I. Diggs (left) and F. Drew Caminetti during trial, from the *San Francisco Examiner,* August 9, 1913, p. 2.

suggested that someone who looked like a member of the jury "had been seen talking with some one connected with the defence of this case."

Diggs was accompanied at the trial by his wife, mother and father, and three aunts. Caminetti also attended Diggs's trial, accompanied by Mrs. Caminetti. On August 15, 1913, a squad of newspaper photogra-

8. Marsha Warrington (left) and Lola Norris, from the *San Francisco Examiner*, August 12, 1913, p. 3.

phers confronted Diggs and his family as they left the Federal Building through a side entrance. The women tried to run, but the photographers kept up with them, snapping pictures on the run. Somebody snatched at a camera, a free-for-all ensued, and Diggs was arrested for assault.

Nellie Barton, a government witness and friend of Lola and Marsha, testified that Diggs and his attorney had attempted to use her to convey messages to the two girls to influence their testimony. Both of the "victims" testified for the government that they were pressured by threat of exposure and Juvenile Court prosecution and attracted by protestations of love into taking the interstate journey. Both wives testified to the nervousness and worry that characterized their husbands in the week before their departure, aiding the defense contention that the journey was simply a flight in panic and lacking immoral purpose.

There was considerable public interest in the trial. A circus atmosphere prevailed and pushy photographers and large crowds attempted to pack into the courtroom. Lola and Marsha were a big draw, but newspapers also reported that "handsomely gowned women stood two hours without luncheon in the corridors of the Federal Building" to have an opportunity to hear Diggs. Reports of the trial were banned in Boston, a sure sign of public interest. Word reached the mayor of this cradle of puritan America that a moving picture of the trial was being prepared, and he issued orders to the licensing clerk that "under no circumstances" would he permit its showing in Boston.

In closing arguments the federal prosecutor alluded to the sensationalism and popularity of the proceedings. "The eyes of not only the people of the state of California are upon you, gentlemen of the jury," he told them, "but the people of all these United States; 60,000,000 or 90,000,000 people are awaiting your verdict . . . an acquittal in this case would be a miscarriage of justice."

The judge gave a broad interpretation to the statute, setting the stage for the later appeal to the Supreme Court. He charged that neither previous chastity nor prior intercourse with the defendants mattered. Furthermore, "even if you find that the defendant and his companion Caminetti were actuated in their departure or flight from Sacramento by a fear of exposure or arrest, but that nevertheless in taking these two girls with them, there existed the intention to subject them to the immoral purpose charged, the defendant is guilty." The judge practically directed the verdict, and the jury convicted Diggs of four counts, but acquitted him of the inducing and enticing count.

Caminetti's trial began on August 27, 1913.[13] To a large extent it was a repeat of the Diggs case. Diggs and both the wives attended the Caminetti trial. The senior Caminetti was not present. Lola Norris admitted that in her initial statements to the authorities she had lied about a platonic relationship with Caminetti and that she had done that "to save the man she loved and whom she then trusted." The jury also heard a reading from a statement in which Caminetti admitted to a court reporter shortly after his arrest that he had promised to marry Norris. According to press accounts, Mrs. Caminetti made "a willing and even eager witness for her husband," testifying to her own threats to take Norris to Juvenile Court and her husband's nervousness and sleeplessness just prior to his departure for Reno.

Caminetti's jury acquitted him of any responsibility for Marsha Warrington's transportation and, more significantly, acquitted him of the charges that he had induced or enticed Lola into the interstate journey. It found him guilty only of actually transporting her for immoral purposes.

Maury Diggs was on trial once more in September, charged along with one of his attorneys, Charles B. Harris, with subornation of perjury, by attempting to cause Nellie Barton to intercede with Marsha Warrington to color her testimony favorably to the defense. They denied the charges, and evidently this third jury thought there had been enough federal persecution for it acquitted them after an hour and a half of deliberation.[14]

Judge Van Fleet sentenced the two men on September 17, 1913, giving Diggs a prison term of two years and a fine of $2,000, the equivalent of almost $30,000 in 1994 dollars. Caminetti drew eighteen months and a fine of $1,500. Although the judge insisted that the language of the Act covered noncommercial cases, he agreed with defense counsel that the offense as committed by the defendants was not as grave as those committed for monetary gain. Further, he acknowledged that "the act originally did not contemplate cases of this character."

The judge clearly revealed his own rigid mind-set through his observations in sentencing that it was "the laxity of social conditions and the lack of parental control [that] made it possible. All through this case there is evidence that drink had its paralyzing influence upon the morals and the minds of these men and the young girls with whom they went on that trip to Reno. The terrible, debasing influence of the saloon and the roadhouse is too disgustingly apparent, and I make the observation here that society must pay the price for permitting the existence of these highly objectionable places."[15]

The defendants were free on bond pending appeal. The chief point of the appeal was that the statute ought not be interpreted to apply to noncommercial immorality.[16] The panel of the Circuit Court of

Appeals that heard the appeal split two to one to affirm the conviction in a decision rendered in March 1915. Curiously, neither the majority nor the dissent focused on the issue of whether noncommercial vice was within the Act. They brushed that aside in favor of extended analysis of less important issues in the case involving the scope of cross-examination of the accused and the testimony of an accomplice.[17]

Diggs and Caminetti next asked the United States Supreme Court to review their convictions. Joseph Weldon Bailey, a Texan lawyer and graduate of Cumberland School of Law, represented both Caminetti and Diggs in the Supreme Court. A prominent congressional Democrat, Bailey served in the House of Representatives for ten years and was elected twice to the Senate. He retired from public life in 1912 to resume his law practice.[18]

On June 14, 1915, the Supreme Court denied their petition for a writ of certiorari to review the case, but a week later changed its mind.[19] The petition for rehearing emphasized the confusion surrounding the question of whether noncommercial immoralities were within the Act. The petition argued that "it is held by some district courts of the United States that the law applies to cases involving acts of mere immorality, while in other district courts of the United States it is held that the law applies only to cases in which there is an element of commerce or coercion."[20]

Bailey's major contention was that the Mann Act did not apply to affairs involving mere immorality lacking elements of commerce or coercion, mere "escapades," to use the terminology of the times.[21] The defendants emphasized that "Congress intended to legislate only against commercialized vice, and no conduct, however immoral, which is free from coercion and commercialism, is within the statute. . . . To hold that the act includes mere escapades transforms into a felony what all of the States have regarded as a misdemeanor for many years, and renders men infamous for conduct which, at its worst, might be no more than a transgression of the moral law."[22] He brought the opinion of Attorney General Wickersham to the justices' attention.

Bailey also pointed out the strong legislative history and that Congressman Mann's report to the House from the Committee on Interstate and Foreign Commerce, recommending the statute, had noted that "the characteristic which distinguishes 'the white-slave trade' from immorality in general is that the women who are the victims of the traffic are unwillingly forced to practice prostitution. The term 'white slave' includes only those women and girls who are literally slaves."[23] The statute itself declared that it should be known as the White Slave Traffic Act. The briefs argued that this congressional declaration of purpose for the legislation and its definition of "white slave" should be read into the Act's interpretation to exclude consensual immorality.

However, the majority of the Court held otherwise and branded the weekend seducers and adulterers who traveled in interstate commerce as felons, regardless of the lack of coercion or compensation. The majority was comprised of Justices Day, Holmes, Van Devanter, Pitney, and Brandeis. Justices McKenna, Clarke, and Chief Justice White dissented. McReynolds, recently appointed to the Court, did not participate, obviously disqualified because of his prior association with the case as the Attorney General about whose head the earlier political storm had broken. Day wrote the majority opinion and McKenna served as spokesman for the dissenters.

Day, writing for the majority, did not duck, as had the Circuit Court, the primary contention that, as he put it, "the conduct for which the several petitioners were indicted and convicted, however reprehensible in morals, is not within the purview of the statute when properly construed in the light of its history and the purposes intended to be accomplished by its enactment." He conceded that "in none of the cases was it charged or proved that the transportation was for gain or for the purpose of furnishing women for prostitution for hire."[24] Justice Day and the majority nevertheless relied on two separate grounds of reasoning to support their decision affirming the convictions.

First, Day relied on the plain meaning rule of statutory interpretation, as he said, "that the meaning of a statute must, in the first instance, be sought in the language in which the act is framed, and if that is plain, [and the law is otherwise constitutional] the sole function of the courts is to enforce it according to its terms." In other words, the Court could feel free to simply ignore what Congress said about the purpose of a law if the language were clear.

Day then went on to say that there was no ambiguity in this statute and that the conduct charged seemed to be within the plain meaning of "any other immoral purpose." He reasoned that the transportation "would be more culpable in morals and attributed to baser motives if accompanied with the expectation of pecuniary gain," as, for instance, the transportation of a prostitute by her pimp. Yet that would not prevent noncommercial immorality, "the lesser offense against morals of furnishing transportation in order that a woman may be debauched, or become a mistress or a concubine from being the execution of purposes within the meaning of this law. To say the contrary would shock the common understanding of what constitutes an immoral purpose when those terms are applied, as here, to sexual relations."[25]

Nor would the majority consider the title of the act, "White-Slave Traffic Act." It merely reflected that one of the purposes of the statute was to stop the white slave conditions that had existed in 1910. But to Justice Day that was not the end of the inquiry, since "the name given to an act by way of designation or description, or the report which accompanies it, cannot change the plain import of its words. If the words are plain, they give meaning to the act, and it is neither the duty nor the privilege of the courts to enter speculative fields in search of a different meaning."[26]

Thus, no matter how clear Congress was in its intent, it counted for nothing if the Court later determined that the language of the statute was plain enough for it to interpret without any help from the body that enacted it. Today this complete avoidance of any consideration of congressional intent seems arrogant. But it was not so then.

The basic problem exists today as well as in 1910. Congress passes a statute. The language is general in scope, but there is very clear evidence of what Congress meant and it is much narrower than the generality of the language. Or it can be the converse. Congress passes a law, using reasonably clear language that is not broad enough to cover what the legislature made clear it wanted to accomplish. And there are gradations of ambiguity of intentions and language employed running the range between these poles. The courts, by necessity, are often called upon to interpret just what a law means. Does it cover a particular factual situation?

In the late nineteenth and early twentieth centuries the "plain meaning rule" was a common method of statutory interpretation among generally conservative judges who used this method of interpretation to reduce the scope of a statute. The canon of this construction was that courts should not look beyond the exact language of a law unless the literal language was itself confusing. Otherwise, they were to act as though they were men from Mars, descended upon our planet in total ignorance of social, economic, or political context. They were to ignore the legislature and focus with tunnel vision upon the text of the statute. The language itself would be the final meaning of what the legislature intended. Usually this led to a "cleaving to the letter rather than the spirit of such laws."[27]

Conservative judges often employed this rule to cut away the clearly intended scope of laws enacted by more liberal state legislatures and Congress. There is considerable irony in the invocation of the plain meaning rule in *Caminetti,* since the effect was to expand the scope of the statute beyond that probably intended by the legislature. Increasingly throughout the later twentieth century, the American legal system has come to be dominated by statutes, and the judiciary's former reliance on the plain meaning rule has been replaced increasingly by use of legislative history and other sources extrinsic to the words of a statute to interpret its meaning.[28]

Writing for the dissent, Justice McKenna attacked Day's use of the plain meaning rule on the ground that "immoral" is not a plain, clear word. Rather it "is a very comprehensive word. It means a dereliction of morals. In such sense it covers every form of vice, every form of conduct that is contrary to good order. It will hardly be contended that in this sweeping sense it is used in the statute. But if not used in such sense, to what is it limited and by what limited? . . . By its context, necessarily, and the purpose of the statute." He then turned to the title and legislative history, the congressional debates and reports, and concluded that there was no uncertainty as to what conduct "white-slave traffic" had reference. "It is commercialized vice, immoralities having a mercenary purpose."[29]

McKenna chided his colleagues by referring to several earlier cases in which the Court had disregarded the literal words of a statute in order to effectuate the intent of the congressional framers. McKenna acknowledged that the clear language of a statute generally foreclosed dispute as to its meaning. But he claimed that to occasionally overlook the literal language of a law, to employ a rule of liberal construction, in order to effectuate its spirit or purpose is "the dictate of common sense. Language, even when most masterfully used, may miss sufficiency and give room for dispute. . . . [liberal construction] rescues from crudities, excesses and deficiencies, making legislation adequate to its special purpose. . . . Nor is this judicial legislation. It is seeking and enforcing the true sense of a law notwithstanding its imperfection or generality of expression."[30]

Turning to the specifics of the Mann Act, McKenna declared that the Supreme Court "should not shut its eyes to the facts of the world and assume not to know . . . that there is a difference between the occasional immoralities of men and women and that systematized and mercenary immorality epitomized in the statute's graphic phrase 'White-slave traffic.' And it was such immorality that was in the legislative mind and not the other."[31]

Day, writing for the majority, had another argument, a second arrow in his quiver; he argued from precedent. The immigration acts of 1875 and 1903 had forbidden the importation of women for the purpose of prostitution. By amendment of February 20, 1907,[32] Congress inserted the phrase "or for any other immoral purpose" (precisely the same clause subsequently used in the Mann Act) after the word "prostitution," thus extending the prohibition to the importation of women "for the purpose of prostitution, or for any other immoral purpose."

After that new amendment was passed a man named John Bitty was indicted for importing Violet Sterling from England for "an immoral purpose," that is, "that she should live with him as his concubine." The criminal prosecution had came to the Supreme Court in 1908.[33] There is nothing in the record to indicate whether Bitty was paying compensation to Violet for her services, but at a minimum he was supporting her as she was to live with him.

In *Bitty* the Supreme Court had reasoned that the phrase "or for any other immoral purpose" must mean something other than prostitution, or Congress would not have added it. The defendant relied on a rule of legal construction called *ejusdem generis*. This rule operates to determine whether some particular thing or activity is within a legal rule when the rule describes a series of purposes, things, or objects, starting with specifics and ending with generalities. Suppose, for a humorous example, a statute were written to regulate "rockets, airplanes, and other dangerous things." The rule would require that the general phrase, "other dangerous things," be directly related to the specific things mentioned before it. Thus, interpreting this ludicrous statute, a handgun, notwithstanding it is a very dangerous thing, would *not* be included within its scope, while a glider might very well. The gun would not be regulated because it has no real relationship to the rocket or airplane. It does not fly. The glider, if regarded as a "dangerous thing," would be included because it has the same fundamental aspect of moving through the air that the specifics mentioned, rockets and airplanes, also share.

In 1908 the defendant Bitty had argued that *ejusdem generis* required that the law prohibiting the importation of women for "prostitution, or for any other immoral purpose," could only be interpreted very strictly. Only if a woman were imported as a procuress, madam, or other agent directly related to prostitution would her importation be illegal. The Supreme Court rejected that argument in reasoning that Day found later to be significant for *Caminetti*.

In *Bitty* the Supreme Court acknowledged the *ejusdem generis* rule but found it did not help the defendant since "the immoral purpose charged in the indictment [namely, to live with him as his concubine] is of the same general class or kind as the one that controls in the importation of an alien woman for the purpose strictly of prostitution. The prostitute may, in the popular sense, be more degraded in character than the concubine, but the latter nonetheless must be held to lead an immoral life, if any regard whatever be had to the views that are almost universally held in this country as to the relations which may rightfully, from the standpoint of morality, exist between man and woman in the matter of sexual intercourse." Therefore, it held that "Congress intended by the words 'or for any other immoral purpose,' to include the case of anyone who imported . . . an alien woman that she might live with him as his concubine."[34]

Day made use of this earlier case in his second ground for holding that the Mann Act extended to noncommercial immorality. He pointed out that *Bitty* was decided in 1908, prior to the 1910 enactment of the Mann Act. Congress presumably knew of the meaning given to the phrase "any other immoral purpose" in *Bitty*, and knowing of it, approved the Court's interpretation by using the exact language in the Mann Act, which prohibited transportation of women "for the purpose of prostitution or debauchery, or for any other immoral purpose."[35]

In the *Caminetti* dissent, McKenna claimed that *Bitty* did not apply because the immigration act "was a prohibition against the importation of alien women or girls, a statute, therefore, of broader purpose than the one under review. Besides, the statute finally passed upon was an amendment to a prior statute and the words construed were an addition to the prior statute and necessarily, therefore, had an added effect."[36]

McKenna's brief discussion of *Bitty* was not particularly apt. As we have seen before, Congress probably did not consider the implications of *Bitty* in enacting the language "any other immoral purpose." Beyond that, it seems the facts in *Bitty* are quite different than those in *Caminetti*. Concubinage is not a precise legal term, but it denotes an inferior sort of marriage, a living together, a stable and more or less

118   *Chapter Five*

long-term domestic relationship. Thus, a concubine is a woman who lives with a man without being married to him.

Concubinage, at least circa 1917, implied a woman's economic dependency on a man. He supported her and might pay additional compensation, and, following the termination of such a relationship, in those years, the woman often became a prostitute. This support and the common end results made the concubinage relationship much closer to prostitution than the freewill fornication engaged in by Marsha Warrington and Lola Norris. Marsha had an occupation as a stenographer, and Lola was employed in the State Library and had been learning the stenographer's trade in evening school. Whatever support was involved in their living with the two men in Reno, even had that extended several months, was designed to be temporary and limited. There is nothing in *Bitty*, a case involving a concubine, that forces the conclusion that the phrase "any other immoral purpose" also necessarily applies to an adulterous couple sharing a cottage for a short interval.

When Justice McKenna in his dissent pointed out a few cases in which the Court had departed from the plain meaning rule to give a liberal construction of a statute, he was being kind by his reticence. In the few years from 1911 until the *Caminetti* decision in January 1917, there were about a dozen cases in which the Supreme Court used congressional committee reports and debates, which sometimes were the decisive factor of decision. Justice Day was more reluctant than most justices to resort to legislative history, but even Day himself "was not altogether without an occasional guilty knowledge of a committee report."[37]

The willingness of the Court to use legislative reports *if it so desired*, plus the large minority of justices *who did desire*, suggest that the job of the historian is to look behind the rhetoric in *Caminetti*. The Court had a choice. It might have used the legislative history of the Mann Act to announce that Congress never intended the Act to apply to noncommercial sexual activities, and therefore such prosecutions would not be permitted unless Congress amended the statute. Since it had this option, rejected by the majority, the Court made a choice. It made a conscious decision to expand the application of the Act. Why did the Court include private immoralities within the Mann Act? What considerations induced the Court to choose that path?

Pieces of the *Caminetti* Puzzle

One hint to the reasoning of *Caminetti* may be found in the curious personal reaction of Congressman James R. Mann to the decision. The opinion was made public on January 15, 1917. Within two weeks, on January 29, Representative Mann wrote Justice Day congratulating him on the recent decision. He stated that the Court in *Caminetti* had:

> construed the law the way I intended when I very carefully considered and wrote it, and while I think there probably was no public statement to that effect, yet in private statements made on the floor of the House before the bill was passed, I explained to a good many Members the bill as going fully as far as is stated in your valuable opinion.[1]

This sentiment was not entirely new for Representative Mann. Just after the conviction of Diggs, in September of 1913, he was quoted in the *Sacramento Bee* as saying that Diggs and Caminetti were "typical cases. The law is a strong statute without a loophole. . . . A man might be prosecuted under the law for transporting a woman, when the question of money did not enter in it all. . . . Its purpose was to reach just such cases as [Diggs and Caminetti]."[2]

Justice Day sent back his thanks for Mann's 1917 note and expressed his appreciation of the congressman's views. "While of course we could not know, except from the language used, the purpose and intent of the framers of the Law, the confirmation which you give the construction of the act is very gratifying indeed."[3]

These statements of Mann regarding the scope of his law, different than what he told Congress in 1910, might be simple gratification for vindication as the Republican leader who had led the charge that the Democratic Wilson administration wrongfully delayed the trial of Diggs and Caminetti. Had the trial judge or the Supreme Court gone the other way and held their conduct not to be within the Act, then Mann might have been accused of politicizing a prosecution that ought never have been brought. But politicians are not necessarily insincere, especially not in their private letters, and Mann's letter to Day was purely private. An assumption that Mann was sincere in his statement that he thought the phrase "any other immoral purpose" did include noncommercial immorality leads to a line of inquiry that may be the primary reason for why the Court took the approach it did.

A key consideration in understanding the *Caminetti* Court's approach to private, noncommercial immoralities is that in the early twentieth century people did not have the same understanding of prostitution as we do today. There are lesser policy concerns that may have influenced the Court, which cannot be as well documented and are therefore somewhat speculative. One is the fear of social disintegration arising from the widespread ownership of automobiles; a second is the widely held fear of venereal disease and the clear understanding that it could be spread through irregular sexual contacts; and third, related to this, is apprehension of the state of readiness of American youth for what appeared in January 1917 as the likely entrance of the United States into the world war.

The balance of the chapter makes many references to "public understanding" and "social thought" concerning both prostitution and sexual permissiveness among working-class women. No claim for universality is made. The lower class may have thought differently about these matters, as may have women generally. But the middle-class, male reformers, who expressed the sentiments we are about to explore, published them in formats and under the sponsorship of groups that might have influenced the justices on the United States Supreme Court. Therefore, it is to this middle-class, male viewpoint we must turn to try to make sense of the *Caminetti* decision.

In our own day, we distinguish sharply between prostitutes and women who are sexually active, even promiscuous. The bright line of demarcation is the payment of money. But in the early part of this century that sense of clear distinction simply did not exist. We have seen

the Progressive reformers horrified at the sight of unchaperoned working-class women in the cities. Progressives viewed the women's open-
ness in manner and moral standards as the precursor to the breakdown
of civilization itself. Those women who were willing to exchange sexual
favors for entertainment or pleasure, the "charity girls" we have noted
before, were often labeled as actual prostitutes, even though no financial
transaction might be involved.

In the early nineteenth century, reformers interested in vice had
often also been religious leaders. In their schemes of classification they
had sought to separate the sinners from the saved, the stolid working-
man's family from the squalid urban poor. Thus they included within
the term "prostitution" many nonmarital sexual encounters that we
would not.[4] The Progressive reformers who studied urban conditions
in the early twentieth century were no longer particularly religious, but
they shared the earlier apocalyptic view of an impending breakdown in
moral standards.

Today we have a wide vocabulary to describe gradations in sexual
license, ranging from "promiscuous," "loose," "sexually active," to
"prostitution." One historian has noted that in the early twentieth century Progressives lacked the "vocabulary, or methodological apparatus,
which would have provided the means to distinguish prostitution from
permissiveness or promiscuity. . . . Thus, when confronted with what
appeared to be ominous shifts in sexual mores and behavior, progressives often categorized all of what they saw as 'prostitution,' a historically familiar phenomenon."[5]

The various vice commissions regularly juxtaposed discussion of
"charity girls," young urban women looking for men with only a good
time in mind, alongside more conventional prostitutes. Indeed, when
the vice reformers wanted specifically to refer to women who accepted
money for sexual services on a full-time basis, those we would today
label as prostitutes, they used the term "professional prostitute."
"Clandestine prostitute" often was a term that referred to women who
accepted money or a good time as the basis for sexual favors on a part-
time basis. The Syracuse, New York, report, for example, included
within the term "prostitute" those "girls, many in number, who go out
with men for an evening of pleasure and drink and intercourse where no
money is asked or offered." It included within its case histories, as "Girl
X247," an eighteen-year-old woman that the strictest of moralists
would never today label as a prostitute:

> She was born in Syracuse 18 years ago and has lived there all her life. A friend caused her downfall two years ago. She works every day at present, receiving $5 a week salary. She has never received money for prostitution, but likes to go out for a good supper and theatre with men. She is pretty, very foolish and easily led. She lives at home.[6]

Thus to many in the Progressive years, women such as Marsha Warrington and Lola Norris, willing lovers and sexually active, really *were* prostitutes, or something so close that the distinction was not important. As the brief for the United States before the Supreme Court in the *Caminetti* case put it, "The proposition that, though interstate commerce may be regulated when its purpose is *prostitution*, it may not be regulated when its purpose is merely *illicit sexual intercourse* is untenable, for obviously the two purposes differ not in principle but merely in degree"[7] (emphasis in original). The view that receipt of money was not required for a woman to be a prostitute was not merely a theoretical belief of Progressive reformers. There was confusion in the law as well and a solid body of precedent that money was not the touchstone of prostitution.

In the earlier English law prostitution was not an offense as such, because the church courts, not the secular courts, dealt with moral offenses. The common law secular courts were involved only indirectly, by defining prostitution as vagrancy and brothels as nuisances. Vagrancy, moreover, was a status offense. Its violation depended on who the person was, not the specific acts he or she had committed. A vagrant was a person who compromised the public order, affronted public morality, strayed aimlessly about public places, especially at night.[8] A consequence of this was that the term "prostitution" was never crisply defined, or indeed as one judge in Maine put it in 1915, the word "has no legal meaning at common law."[9]

This vagueness of who was a prostitute and what constituted prostitution carried over to American law. Until the early twentieth century, to the extent they were prosecuted, prostitutes were charged with having the status of vagrants. Because vagrancy referred to status and not specific acts, the law was very uncertain as to whether receipt of money was required for a woman to attain the status of prostitute. Vagrancy proceedings were summary in nature, imposed relatively low-level punishments, and therefore were not often appealed. But there were some appeals and also a few cases that raised the issue of the definition of prostitution for other purposes, such as in defamation cases where a defendant might be sued for damages for calling a woman a prostitute.

Prostitution increasingly became a statutorily defined crime after 1919. A study of appellate judicial decisions before that time shows no clear pattern as to whether pecuniary gain was an essential element of prostitution. Some cases said yes; others, no.[10] In 1889 the Iowa Supreme Court opined that a prostitute is a female who engages in indiscriminate sexual intercourse that she "invites or solicits by word or act. . . . Her avocation may be known from the manner in which she plys [*sic*] it, and not from pecuniary charges and compensation."[11] To an Alabama court in 1920 a prostitute was a woman given to indiscriminate lewdness, a strumpet.[12]

A more striking example is a 1910 case in Washington where the defendant was charged with the crime of living with a common prostitute. He defended on the basis that the woman he had been living with was not a prostitute, and this raised the definitional issue. The trial court instructed the jury that "whether a woman is a common prostitute is a question of fact which does not depend . . . upon the question of whether she submits herself for gain." This instruction was affirmed by a divided court. The majority was of the opinion that while "the sake of gain is probably the most usual motive, it is not the only one, and it is not necessarily essential to constitute a common prostitute. A woman who submits herself to indiscriminate sexual intercourse with men, without hire, is certainly as much a common prostitute as one who does so solely for hire."[13]

The Washington court used the term "common" prostitute. An earlier Texas case had drawn a distinction between an ordinary prostitute and a "common prostitute," a line drawn by few jurisdictions. For the Texas court a *common* prostitute had to exhibit a lewdness that was general and indiscriminate. However, for more ordinary prostitution, "a woman may be a prostitute, and yet have illicit connection with one man only." In either case, the payment of money was not essential.[14] In a still earlier Massachusetts case, the court was forced to consult a dictionary because it could not find a legal definition. The then-current (1846) Webster's dictionary told the court that prostitution consisted of "the act or practice of offering the body to an indiscriminate intercourse with men."[15]

The vagueness in definition of prostitution had some very practical consequences. A recent study of a woman's reformatory in the state of New York sampled 1,583 cases of young women confined at the Albion Reformatory during the years 1894 through 1931: 46.5 percent of the women had been convicted of vagrancy of which the specifics consisted

of being a "public nuisance" or "keeping bad company" and had overtones of sexual promiscuity and not professional prostitution. The study
concluded that "for at least half (and perhaps up to three-quarters) of
Albion's inmates, the act that led to incarceration had actually been sexual misconduct. . . . [The majority] were merely sexually active, engaging in flirtations and affairs for pleasure instead of money."[16]

As of 1917, there were contrary voices, espousing the modern position that payment and receipt of money was essential to prostitution.
The 1910 edition of *Black's Law Dictionary* concisely defined a prostitute as "a woman who indiscriminately consorts with men for hire."[17]
Even crisper was that great repository of Victorian knowledge, the
eleventh edition of the *Encyclopedia Britannica*. It defined prostitution
as "promiscuous unchastity for gain."[18] The Illinois Senate Vice Commission cautioned in 1916 that "the act of selling oneself, which is prostitution" should not be confused with "the act of giving oneself without pay."[19]

Prior to 1919 there was apparently only one statutory definition of
prostitution, that of Indiana. That law, although clearly directed toward
"adultery or fornication for hire," also included within the web of prostitution, "any female who . . . associates with women of bad character
for chastity."[20] In 1919 a model statute was proposed through the joint
efforts of three federal agencies, for adoption by the states.[21] In 1919
alone, eight states, pursuant to the model law, adopted the following
statutory definition of prostitution:

> The term "prostitution" shall be construed to include the offering or
> receiving of the body for sexual intercourse for hire, and shall also be
> construed to include the offering or receiving of the body for indis-
> criminate sexual intercourse without hire.

This statute expressly denied any need for compensation and also
achieved the old Progressive goal of eliminating the double standard by
criminalizing the conduct of the male customer as well the female. This
definition was adopted by the legislatures in states from all over the
country but with a concentration in New England: Vermont, Connecticut, New Hampshire, Maine, Ohio, North Dakota, North Carolina, and
Delaware.[22] However, in the following year Maryland adopted a statutory definition, "the offering or receiving of the body for sexual intercourse for hire," that expressly required payment.[23]

While there was considerable confusion, there was a body of thought that would have regarded Lola Norris's and Marsha Warrington's activities with Caminetti and Diggs to be within the legal definition of prostitution. Although the federal courts had less need to define the term prostitution, there was federal precedent that agreed with the more expansive meaning that money was not required. In the *Bitty* case, an important precedent for *Caminetti,* the United States Supreme Court had itself stated, although as dictum not necessary to its decision, that prostitution "refers to women who for hire or without hire offer their bodies to indiscriminate intercourse with men."[24] And in an early Mann Act prosecution, before *Caminetti* but involving a commercial prostitute, a trial court, with the appellate court's subsequent blessing, had instructed the jury that "prostitution . . . means that the woman is to offer her body to indiscriminate sexual intercourse with men, either for hire or without hire."[25]

To be sure, while many in 1917 might regard Lola and Marsha as prostitutes, many other persons would not. A married man's uncompensated mistress might be immoral, but many would think the lack of hire took her out of whoredom. Even those who rejected the need for compensation would think that the lack of indiscriminate sexual activities, the relative loyalty of the mistress to the single male of her affections, also removed her from the prostitute class. But there was yet another and different strand of social thought, circa 1917, that tied the sexually permissive woman into the category of prostitution. This was the notion that the sexually promiscuous woman, the charity girls especially, but even more moderately permissive women such as Lola Norris and Marsha Warrington, were very likely *to become* professional prostitutes, whether their immediate activities made them that or not.

There may have been an element of truth in this supposition. As we have already seen, a substantial number of urban young women were employed at less than $8 per week, regarded as the lowest possible living wage. For working-class women in New York around the turn of the century, "treating," the contemporary term, by better-paid males was their primary access to entertainment.[26] The same was true in other cities. In 1910 a Chicago hotel chambermaid told an investigator that "if the girls are good and refuse invitations to go out, they simply have no pleasure," and in 1912 a Chicago waitress said that "if I did not have a man, I could not get along on my wages."[27]

There does appear to have been a considerable element of exchange, even if not strictly monetary, in the dating relationships of working-class women in the early twentieth century. The following two notes are not untypical of the interviews made by the Chicago vice investigators of young working women at the public dance halls:

> Lillie, 19 years old, works in [a] department store, salary $5 per week. Will go out for a "good time"; but will not take any money. Her friend gave her a bracelet last week. . . . She will take presents from her men friends, but refuses the actual money. . . .
>   Rosie . . . said she had a friend who gave her a pair of gloves, and is going to give her an old-gold bracelet. He is an insurance agent. She works at [a] department store. Receives $11 per week. . . . Rosie said she would make a date and go out anytime.[28]

In New York, a sociologist reported conversations of waitresses "talking about their engagements which they had for the evening or for the night and quite frankly saying what they expected to get from this or that fellow in the line of money, amusement or clothes."[29] In Syracuse, a vice inspector observed two fifteen-year-old girls

> looking into a jewelry store window, admiring the paste display. I stopped and looked into the next window. They opened the conversation by asking me if I would not buy them "that" necklace. They said they would come with me to any room, etc., etc.[30]

And in Chicago a male in 1910 noted that many women "would not accept money from any man, but would let the man give them a present of anything from a pair of stockings to an automobile, and think they were lucky."[31] Two modern feminist historians of prostitution assume that the charity girls did more frequently turn to professional prostitution.[32] And there is anecdotal evidence of one famous madam of the period who first turned to professional prostitution when she began to question her "charity" and "decided to start merchandising sex instead of giving it away."[33]

But whether or not the charity girls were truly likely to become professional prostitutes is largely beside the point. To grasp the thinking that underlies the *Caminetti* Court's easy merger of noncommercial sexual permissiveness into the larger category of prostitution, what is essential to understand is that large numbers of Americans, circa 1917, thought it was true. Sexually active young women were definitely on the path to prostitution, whether they were there already or not. Such was the conventional wisdom of the age. Following the Diggs and

Caminetti convictions the Galesburg, Illinois, *Register* editorialized that there was practically no difference between professional procurers of prostitutes and men who "use their wealth to bedazzle young girls with pleasure and entice them into disgrace. . . . Too often the ready victim for the procuress is the one whom men of the Diggs and Caminetti type start with their rich allurements on the way to damnation." The Atchell, South Dakota, *Republican* noted "this much is certain, that, so far as his [Diggs] relations with Marsha Warrington were concerned, they were of the sort that often convert a whole life into one of prostitution."[34]

We can also see this attitude in the accounts of several of the vice commissions. The Massachusetts commission reported in 1914 on the "large numbers of young girls who habitually have immoral relations with boys and men without expecting or accepting financial reward or gain. . . . Most of them would resent a suggestion of direct pecuniary reward for their immorality, but they expect to be given a good time, to be taken to supper or to the theatre, etc. Some of them already are willing and anxious to begin a life of professional immorality."[35] The secretary of the Massachusetts Society for the Prevention of Cruelty to Children, writing in 1915, described an unidentified study in an unidentified middle-sized Massachusetts city. Several teenaged girls, engaged in sexual activities with boyfriends, were motivated not by money but a "desire for innocent amusement." Gradually, however, the older girls began to accept payment and "they were inevitably one by one slipping into conditions of disease and prostitution."[36] The New York vice investigation in 1912 reported that the sexual freedom young working women found in the city made it possible for them "to experiment with immorality without losing such social standing as they may have, thus many of them drift gradually into professional prostitution."[37]

Social loss is the chief key to this thinking. So much social loss was supposedly lost to a woman by her seduction that her inability to regain it eased the downward slide into prostitution. Henry J. Dannenbaum, Special Assistant to the Attorney General, explained this to his superior by private letter in 1911. "The fact is, and it is of vital importance in interpreting the law [Mann Act], that the girl is seldom thrown at once on the market. After she has been a private mistress, has lost her social standing and is well in the power of the trafficker, he persuades or compels her to sell her body publicly. It is sickening to hear these women tell of their gradual fall from wifehood or mistress to streetwalker. . . . It is manifest that to cope with the trafficker, the transportation of the mistress must be forbidden."[38]

The Minneapolis Vice Commission graphically told of "the large number of young girls in the streets at night in the downtown sections. . . . They may be found in numbers loitering about the fruit stores, drug stores and other popular locations, haunting hotel lobbies, crowding into the dance halls, the theaters and other amusement resorts; also in the saloon restaurants and the chop suey places and parading the streets and touring about in automobiles with men." Writing their report in 1911, the Minneapolis commission admitted that it was unfair "to charge that all or a large proportion of these girls are prostitutes." Nevertheless, it was "perfectly plain . . . that many . . . are on the direct road."[39]

Supporting the popular conception that sexual immorality was but a stepping-stone toward professional prostitution was the alarming fact that much of prostitution's subculture had entered the general culture of working-class women. These attitudes tie the vice commission reformers into the more general reform movements of the early twentieth century, including the prohibition movement. The criticism of looseness in style of young women's dress and dancing is similar to the criticism of the conviviality of beer garden amusements that so offended sabbatarians and other pietists. In the use of makeup and wigs, in the style of dress and dancing, prostitutes provided a model for working women and aided the working women's freedom of manner and morals. By the 1910s, some middle-class investigators found it difficult to distinguish respectable women from prostitutes at dances. In 1917 one waiter reported to an investigator that he had to be very careful handling customers, because "the way women dress today they all look like prostitutes."[40]

Again, there were contrary viewpoints. One of the most interesting was a report prepared under the direction of the Federal Commissioner of Labor. The portion of the 1911 report that deals with the relation between occupation and criminality of women was written by a woman, and her description of the sexually permissive working-class women seems to be a more rounded account:

> They do not consider themselves fallen women. . . . They simply take this means of securing more amusements, excitements, luxuries, and indulgences than their wages would afford them. . . . Of course, while a girl is living this kind of life an accident or miscalculation may send her over the dividing line into the class who are promiscuously

immoral, or she may find her taste for gay living developed to such an extent that she crosses the line intentionally. But more often she has her fling and then settles down to quiet living. Ordinarily, it is supposed, she marries, and the general impression is that in many cases she makes a rather unusually good wife.[41]

But this was a minority viewpoint. The more common sentiment was expressed by Walter Clarke, the Field Secretary of the American Social Hygiene Association, writing in the same month of January 1917 when *Caminetti* was decided by the Supreme Court. Clarke wrote that many a young working girl who frequents questionable dance halls, then acquires the "drink habit," and drifts from bad to worse associates. "From illicit relations with one man, she becomes what is known as a 'charity girl,' picking up a man here and there for an evening's excitement and dissipation. The step from 'charity girl' to common prostitute is a short one. . . . By commercializing her immoral conduct, which previously she had followed for pleasure and excitement, money can be earned."[42]

The relevance of this thinking to the *Caminetti* decision is clear. Even if Lola Norris and Marsha Warrington were not yet prostitutes, they had a direct relationship to prostitution. Women of their sort, sexually permissive and active, having affairs with married men and free in their conduct, were very likely to become professional prostitutes, or so it was thought. The point was even argued by the prosecutor to the jury, albeit indirectly. He pointed out how little money the girls had with them when they left for Reno and suggested that, while the men were free to return to Sacramento, "'neither of the two girls could ever go back and occupy the same social position they had before.'" What, the prosecutor asked ominously, did they have in mind for the girls?[43] An investigator, formerly with the Bureau of Investigation, just after the Diggs conviction asked those critical of the Act's application to noncommercial cases to consider: "'what would have happened to these girls if Diggs and Caminetti had been able to desert them? . . . What was the way out other than the red light?'"[44]

In the 1920s and thereafter, the cultural link between female sexual freedom and professional prostitution would grow increasingly attenuated. Sexual permissiveness and prostitution would uncouple as related concepts. Today few would think, regardless of their view of the morality of sexual permissiveness, that a woman who has a sexual relationship with her boyfriend is more likely because of that to become a prostitute.

Therefore the holding of *Caminetti* that private noncommercial sexual activity is within the phrase "prostitution or debauchery, or for any other immoral purpose," grew increasingly anachronistic. But Representative Mann's letter to Justice Day, in 1917, stating that when the law was passed representatives had thought private noncommercial immorality fell within their statute, may not have been the absolute hypocrisy that it appears to late twentieth-century eyes to be.

Nothing can make the reality of the 1917 mind, connecting private immorality with prostitution, more vivid, than a look at the brief filed by the government in *Caminetti*. Today no one would dare argue as the government did then that "a girl indulging even infrequently in illicit sexual intercourse, is a prostitute in the making" and that therefore "commercialized vice cannot be effectively excluded from channels of interstate commerce, unless its facilities be denied for transporting her for purposes such as here proven [that is, their affair with Diggs and Caminetti] *and having so strong and natural a tendency to make her an ultimate subject of commercialized vice*"[45] (emphasis added).

Three other policy factors, the growth of the automobile culture, venereal disease, and war preparedness, may have led the Supreme Court to act as it did in *Caminetti*, applying the Mann Act to private immorality. These are more elusive reasons, speculative by their nature, and insusceptible of definite proof.

One of these may have been the rise of the automobile in American society. In the years immediately preceding *Caminetti* automobile registrations were increasing at an ever incremental rate. There were 8,000 automobiles registered in the United States as of 1900; 32,950 in 1903; 458,377 in 1910; and 901,596 in 1912.[46] By three years later, in 1915, automobile registrations had jumped to 2,500,000.[47] Although even more dramatic increases in automobile registrations were to follow *Caminetti*, 6,771,000 in 1919 and 23,121,000 in 1929,[48] the shape of the automotive future was clear enough by January 1917. Well prior to *Caminetti*, in fact as early as 1903, there were widespread and public prophecies and newspaper editorials that automobiles would become a mass product, widely owned, and a major mode of American transportation.[49]

The automobile had a large impact on American morals. As Frederick Lewis Allen felicitously observed, "one of the cornerstones of American morality had been the difficulty of finding a suitable locale for misconduct."[50] This difficulty crumbled as young people were quick to discover the intimate uses to which the automobile could be put. The numerous articles on the sexual dangers of the automobile that appeared in popular newspapers and magazines beginning as early as 1903 justify one historian's conclusion that "from the earliest days of the car culture, automobiles had been expected to provide a new space for courtship and sex." This was not a thought (or a worry) that developed in the 1920s; the concern had existed for years prior to *Caminetti*.[51]

There was great impact on law enforcement as well. In January 1919, Bascom Johnson, counsel to the American Social Hygiene Association, wrote that "the automobile prostitute . . . is the bane of law enforcement officials. . . . Few city police departments, or country sheriffs . . . are sufficiently equipped with motorcycle police to patrol the city streets and country roads, and the prostitute may indefinitely vary the scene of her operations, or the car itself may be used if necessary." He urged federal legislation to combat these "new and elusive methods of operation."[52] And a juvenile court judge in the early 1920s, in the classic study of *Middletown*, charged that "'the automobile has become a house of prostitution on wheels.'"[53]

Some of the vice commission reports specifically mention the sexually permissive young women of their towns "touring about," in the words of the Minneapolis report, with their men. It is admittedly speculative but not unreasonable to surmise that the *Caminetti* court, or at least some members of the majority, may have reasoned that because of the increased privacy and especially mobility that the automobile afforded, the traditional police powers of the states were not entirely sufficient to prevent a breakdown of morality. Federal powers, arising from the crossing of a state line, had to be invoked or government on all levels might be impotent to forestall the collapse of the civilized morality that was of such importance to the adults of Progressive America.

Certain of the justices among the majority in *Caminetti* also may have been motivated on a policy level by the need to curb private, noncommercial immorality, then regarded as nearly as important as professional prostitution in spreading venereal disease. The fear of disease among the poor, amidst the "dangerous classes," was common to the early twentieth-century reformers. The Progressives feared germs as much as muggings.[54] Specifically, in this pre-penicillin age, venereal disease was regarded as ever so much an urban menace as socialist city councilmen. There was a lot of talk of epidemic levels of venereal disease in the medical literature between 1900 and 1915, and in 1904

Prince A. Morrow, an influential physician, predicted that one in every seven marriages would be sterile because of venereal disease.[55]

The year 1913 saw the Broadway production of Eugene Brieux's *Damaged Goods*. In this cheery play, an infected man ignores the advice of his physician not to marry. Syphilis then spreads to his wife, through her to their newborn child, and subsequently to a wet-nurse. The message was deemed so significant that a Progressive organization, called the Sociological Fund, commissioned a special showing of the French playwright's work in Washington, for the benefit of President Wilson, his cabinet, and members of Congress.[56]

The risk of venereal infection was thought to be almost as great among the sexually permissive working-class "charity girls" as among the professional prostitutes. Several of the vice commission reports commented on the problem, the Massachusetts report concluding expressly that "the vast majority of professional prostitutes, of clandestine prostitutes, *and of girls and women who are promiscuously immoral* are affected with these diseases sooner or later. The man who patronizes them risks his health and life at every exposure"[57] (emphasis added). Indeed, one commentator in 1918, asserted that the "so-called 'charity girl,' pursuing the avocation for erotic, not meretricious, reasons, is even more notably a disease carrier" than professional prostitutes.[58]

The general concern over venereal disease was heightened in 1917 by the federal government's gearing up of its military machine for the ultimate of Progressive follies, a "war to end all wars." There had been considerable military concern over venereal disease in the period from 1900 to 1916. In 1897 the rate of infected recruits was 84.59 per 1,000. By 1910 that had soared to 196.99 per 1,000 recruits, and this doubling of the venereal disease rate was much discussed in War Department memos. In 1909, one-third of all days lost from military duty were from venereal disease.[59] Naturally, the purity press railed against the high incidence of venereal disease in the American armed forces,[60] but so did the mainstream press. In 1913 *Current Opinion* presented an article pointing out that the incidence of venereal disease in the American army was almost three times as great as the British and ten times as great as the Prussian and concluded that this was a "reproach" to the American military.[61]

Then came the American military incursion into Mexico in 1916–17. Secretary of War Newton Baker appointed Raymond Fosdick, an experienced investigator of prostitution, to study the high rate of infection among American troops stationed along the border and in Mexico. Fosdick investigated and advocated a policy, adopted by Baker, of repression near the military camps in Douglas and El Paso. During the winter of 1916–17, Fosdick and Baker prepared a new American approach toward military morality, thought necessary by the probability of American entry into the European war.[62] That policy involved vigorous repression. It resulted later in the incarceration without trial or legal representation, not only of prostitutes, but of all sexually active women near military camps. Ultimately some thirty thousand sexually active young women, mostly not prostitutes, were incarcerated by the federal morals squads, usually without trial or legal representation.[63]

The publicity concerning the plans for the repression of prostitution and the associated purity campaign for the military conscripts did not begin to appear until the spring of 1917, just *after* the Court's decision. Nevertheless, these ideas were floating about, had been more or less successfully applied in the Mexican operations, and may have been known to several of the Supreme Court justices. Many Americans were certain the country would soon enter the war. Congress had established the Council of National Defense, a body to coordinate the social hygiene activities of voluntary agencies and government, as early as August of 1916. Thus, war preparedness may have been a factor in the *Caminetti* decision.

The automobile, venereal disease, and war preparedness, were all important aspects of American culture at this time. It is somewhat speculative, however, to attribute the *Caminetti* decision to their influence. There is no specific evidence for the justices having them in mind. Quite unlike the issues of who is a prostitute and who is likely to become a professional prostitute, there was no argument presented in the government's brief regarding them. Nevertheless, concerns about these three things were in the air at the time and may have played a role in the Court's decision.

The public reaction to the Supreme Court's decision in *Caminetti* was favorable yet guarded. Most newspaper editorials were persuaded that the plain meaning rule of statutory construction forced the Court's hand, yet also worried about the possibilities of blackmail inherent in the extension of the Mann Act to noncommercial immorality. The *Washington Post* took this position and urged Congress to promptly amend the act to "remedy the defect" by eliminating opportunities for blackmail.[64]

The *New York Times* wrote that "the language being clear, no extrinsic reference to the debates in Congress or to the misuse of the statute by blackmailers is pertinent. The intent of Congress is to be judged by what it said plainly in the act. The words 'or for any other immoral purpose' still seem final to the layman, as they seem to the majority of the court." Still, the *Times* hoped that Congress would amend the statute. "How much longer," it asked, "will Congress leave the blackmailers their boundless opportunity?"[65]

One journal of opinion, *The Outlook*, retorted that no danger of blackmail "threatens so many innocent people as to make it imperative to weaken the law . . . to the peril of hundreds and thousands of young women." To the contrary, the *Caminetti* decision was desirable since the effect "will be to make it impossible for the true white slave offenders to escape from the law's clutches by covering up evidence of money transactions."[66]

The *Literary Digest* editorialized that because of the plain meaning rule, the Court "could not act differently," but worried about blackmail and saw "the only way out in action by Congress." It reported several other papers' reactions. The Pittsburgh *Gazette-Times* opposed any change in the statute and dismissed the concern over blackmail by moralizing that "no tears need be wasted on those whose private peccadillos put them in a position to be plucked." The Boston *Journal* likewise opposed amendment, taking the stern puritanical position that while blackmail was possible, no "law-abiding citizen has reason to fear such blackmail, and the enforcement of such a law is a logical supplement to the enforcement of local laws."[67] However, the *Washington Post* thought that prompt amendment was "the natural verdict of the common sense of the people, who need no legal training to tell them that a law that offers opportunity for blackmailers of both sexes is a bad law unless its form is altered."[68]

Other New York papers beside the *Times* had reservations. The *World* asked whether by applying the White Slave Traffic Act "to individual escapades as well as to commercialized vice," the government was to become "permanently a party to organized blackmail?" *The Mail* opined that because of the language of the statute the Court was "constrained to uphold the conviction" even though it was also of the opinion that Congress had not intended that result. It urged a new law to expressly cover personal derelictions, even though it fretted over the "constant temptation to blackmailing women to lure men to travel with them across a State line and then extort money from them as the price of secrecy."

However, the New York *Tribune* asserted there was little likelihood of congressional action. It reported that leaders of both houses were in agreement on that. It quoted one leading Democratic senator as saying:

> No member of Congress ought to be expected to undergo the penalty that would surely follow the introduction of a bill which would restrict the present statute. Every purity league in the United States would crucify him. The trouble is, good people do not distinguish. They would mistake motives. No, the only chance of an amendment to the law would come from the Department of Justice. . . . Then, if there was not much howling about it, it might slide through. But there is no chance of that.[69]

The American Social Hygiene Association, the leading purity and social hygiene organization, was not nearly as stiffnecked as the good senator thought the purity folks might be. The association's journal editorialized that the *Caminetti* decision was correct, for the contrary would have been "judicial legislation." But on the merits of federal prosecution of noncommercial vice it opined that it was "not altogether clear that the inclusion within the act of cases of personal immorality where neither force or fraud nor money is involved, is desirable. . . . Personal immorality across interstate lines is not a matter which ought to concern the national government." It also felt there was little likelihood that any amendment would be passed by Congress excluding private immorality.[70]

Another purity publication, *Vigilance,* had supported the trial court's determination that the Act applied to noncommercial vice. In October 1913 it supported the conviction arguing that the defendants were simply two "fast young men" and that they did transport two girls for immoral purposes. The journal argued that the Mann Act did not mention "white slave traffic" in any of its sections, a poor argument since section 8, the title section, did so very clearly.[71]

The immediate reactions of the legal community to *Caminetti* were negative. Department of Justice officials were reported by the *New York Times* as worried whether juries would be less inclined to convict unless there was ample proof of the male's instigation. They were also concerned about blackmail prosecutions in which victims would now be reluctant to testify for fear of prosecution for Mann Act violation. One

Justice Department official, echoing the newspaper editorials, was quoted as saying that "under the construction of the law, the Mann act is a menace rather than a help to the public. . . . Unless it is amended, I expect to see the already big army of blackmailers largely increase."[72]

One New York lawyer declared that the result of *Caminetti* "is that the Mann Act offers to the crooks of the country the easiest means of unlimited graft in the history of our country." Unfortunately, he went on, "it is doubtful if there is a single member of Congress—Senate or House—who has the nerve to even introduce a bill to amend the law so as to limit its operation to cases of commercialized vice."[73] Another New York attorney maintained "that while he believed the Mann law had been enacted for a good purpose, it had been so construed that it would serve the blackmailer rather than the decent people."[74]

The dissent in *Caminetti* had pointed out the problem of blackmail, although that was far from its principal argument.[75] The majority had reasoned that even if its construction "opens the door to blackmailing operations upon a large scale, [that] is no reason why the courts should refuse to enforce it according to its terms. . . ." It cavalierly tossed "such considerations" to Congress, "which alone had authority to enact and may if it sees fit amend the law."[76]

As the power of the plain meaning rule of interpretation declined, legal analysis of *Caminetti v. United States* became increasingly hostile. Throughout the 1930s there were scholarly criticisms of the case.[77] A critic in 1947 charged that the Court's invocation of the plain meaning rule and refusal to recognize ambiguity in the statute's sources was "deviational" in that the Court "has frequently resorted to the legislative history of statutes whose apparent scope is alleged to belie Congressional intent. . . . For thirty years, however, the *Caminetti* construction of the Mann Act has been the law, breeding criticism of the Court and blackmail of the interstate traveler."[78] Another law review attack came in 1984.[79] In fact, the only modern defense of *Caminetti* was made in a 1969 article in which the author rather limply stated that the dissenters' "arguments cannot be regarded as conclusive. The composite intention of any large group of men, such as a legislative body, is always difficult to establish."[80]

The criticism of Alexander M. Bickel and Benno C. Schmidt, Jr., in 1984, is probably the most insightful. They acknowledged the profound influence of the plain meaning rule in that time. Therefore, "Day's absolute refusal to consider committee reports and debates was less extraordinary in 1917 than it would be today. . . . And yet it is easy enough to point to a sufficiency of cases decided before *Caminetti* in which use was made, sometimes decisively, of committee reports and debates." Their most pointed criticism involved the puritanical political context in which the decision was made:

> But judges are most to be censured when in a case like Caminetti there can be no . . . expectation of legislative revision of their decision . . . when therefore the only course open to the judges that is consistent with ultimate legislative responsibility is to construe the statute narrowly, and yet they construe it broadly . . . the least bit of insight would have revealed that while Congress could have freely decided whether or not to overrule the opposite result in Caminetti and extend the coverage of the Mann Act, no legislature in our society was then capable of affirmatively legalizing debauchery.

They concluded that "*Caminetti* has remained a much-discussed object lesson in how not to discharge the function of statutory construction."[81] This argument and the observations of contemporaries that we have reviewed all assume that Congress was unable to amend the statute. This again highlights one undesirable consequence of this repressive statute. However bad its enforcement turned out to be, Congress found it politically impossible to amend or repeal its work.

Over the years the Supreme Court has had many opportunities to overrule *Caminetti*. Regardless of the criticisms and the changing mores of the American people, it has refused to overturn its 1917 case. As we shall see in chapter 8, the Court expressly refused to do so in 1946. The only criticism of *Caminetti* from the pens of United States Supreme Court justices was to be in dissent.

Following the Supreme Court's decision, over a thousand persons petitioned President Wilson to grant Diggs and Caminetti pardons, including lawyers and judges in San Francisco, several Democratic senators, Caminetti's mother, and, most significantly, ten of the jurors who had convicted Caminetti and Diggs.[82] But Wilson, no doubt mindful of the political storm that had already broken over the case, refused. He did shed crocodile tears in a letter to Mrs. Caminetti. He wrote that were he to follow "the dictates of my heart or allowed myself to be influenced by my genuine friendship for yourself and your husband, I would of course do it."

Yet "imperative duty" to "look at the matter from the public point of view" led Wilson to conclude that he should deny a pardon. He said all the correct things in the letter, including a reference to his heart going out in sympathy to Mrs. Caminetti and that he could not tell her "what it costs me to write you this." Actually, it cost this federal politician very little, as a copy of his letter was promptly distributed to the press.[83]

Drew Caminetti and Maury Diggs began their prison service on April 2, 1917, and were released on parole in October and December 1917, each serving a little over one-third of their sentences. Many years later both men were granted pardons for the purposes of restoring their civil rights. Caminetti became a contractor and Diggs continued his career as an architect. Caminetti's wife divorced him in 1927, after four children and "'a long list of alleged infidelities.'" He died in 1945. Lola Norris married a superintendent of a construction company and continued to live in Sacramento.

Diggs and his wife had divorced in 1914, before the Supreme Court appeal, and, on December 15, 1915, he married Marsha Warrington. Diggs was married to Marsha at the time he entered prison for transporting her to Reno. This irony had meant nothing to the morals zealots. Their marriage remained intact until Diggs died in 1953 at the age of sixty-six. He had accrued a number of significant architectural accomplishments in the San Francisco Bay Area. His obituary in the *Sacramento Bee* suggested that "he will long be remembered for originality in race track design."[84] Historians remember him longer for other reasons.

When the Supreme Court affirmed the convictions of Caminetti and Diggs in 1917, all doubts vanished as to the applicability of the Mann Act to noncommercial, interstate travel by consenting adults. The only question that remained was how the federal government would use its great powers. That question is explored, for the years between 1917 and 1928, in the following chapter.

The Morals Crusade, 1917–1928

An extension of the logic of the *Caminetti* would have been truly revolutionary. The regulation of morality, traditionally a very local concern dealt with by the lowest level of tribunals, would have shifted to the federal courts. An immediate effort was made to avoid that result.

Less than two weeks after the Supreme Court handed down the decision in January 1917, the Department of Justice issued a circular to all U.S. Attorneys setting forth guidelines for the prosecution of noncommercial cases. Attorney General Gregory wrote that the case did not seem to require any change in the Department's policy. He quoted from a 1911 circular of Attorney General George W. Wickersham, warning United States Attorneys of the dangers of turning the federal courts into local tribunals by enforcement of morals regulation. Not every technical violation of the Mann Act should be prosecuted. The department, Wickersham said, relied upon the discretion of the local federal prosecutors who would have firsthand knowledge of the facts and witnesses and who could therefore ascertain "what circumstances of aggravation, if any, attend the offense; the age and relative interest of the parties; the motives of those urging prosecution," and why the ends of justice would be better served by federal rather than state prosecution.

Attorney General Gregory decided that more specific guidelines were required in light of *Caminetti*. He wrote his prosecutors that as a guide to their discretion the following types of noncommercial cases could properly receive consideration: "[1] cases involving a fraudulent overreaching, or [2] involving previously chaste, or [3] very young women or girls, or [4] (when State laws are inadequate) involving married women (with young children) then living with their husbands." He added that blackmail cases should be avoided so far as possible and that "whenever the woman herself voluntarily and without any overreaching, has consented to the criminal arrangement she, too, if the case shall seem to demand it, may be prosecuted as a conspirator."[1]

These guidelines left many blank spaces. What of adulterous couples who departed from one state for a romantic weekend with no intention of deserting their minor children? How about an unmarried couple, both of mature age, who sought the same romantic weekend in another state? And then, too, what of an unmarried couple living together who desired to travel? These guidelines were never significantly amended. In fact, they were reissued in exact form in 1919, 1929, and, with a small amendment, in 1935.[2]

Nevertheless, there was a significant shift in the interpretation of those guidelines and the actual policies of prosecution between the first guideline in 1917 and the final one in 1935. In the years 1917 through the late 1920s, there was such an ardent zeal among the United States Attorneys in their prosecution of noncommercial cases that the period may properly be called a morals crusade. There is no specific date or event by which one may date the close of this crusade, but the general trend and tendency of events suggests that by the late 1920s, for convenience we may date it 1928, the focus had shifted and the fervent prosecution of noncommercial cases had largely ceased. There were, however, important exceptions.

Before examining the sorts of noncommercial cases that the federal government prosecuted, we should look at their context. In retrospect, in our post–Sexual Revolution world, it is easy to scoff at the moralists of the 1910s and 1920s and to be angry at the virtual persecution of those persons whose sexual practices we would think nothing of today. But the United States Attorneys were often under pressure to prosecute noncommercial cases. The Department of Justice and the various local federal prosecutors received thousands of letters from neighbors, wives, husbands, fathers, and busybodies complaining of sexual irregularities.

It was not just those with specific grievances that wanted to climb onto the morals bandwagon. As we have seen, the arrests of Caminetti and Diggs in 1913 inspired a rumor that the Wilson administration intended to cease any prosecution of noncommercial violations of the Mann Act. We can recall the severe reaction of various church groups and other civic organizations.

It is difficult to know the actual extent of the American sentiment that was reflected in the morals crusade. There has always been a sharp divergence between the professed moralistic standards of Americans and their actual practice, for reasons varying from decorum, idealism, to simple hypocrisy. It is easy to find those with enthusiasm for morality. Regardless of their personal beliefs or practices, it is more difficult for people to stand up and be counted for venery and libertinism. For example, no matter what they thought or did, few people in the 1960s joined the Sexual Freedom League. Politicians, including United States Attorneys, respond to the squeaky wheel, and in the teens and twenties the forces of morality, emboldened with success in their imposition of Prohibition and the resurgence of the Klan, were out in force with their high-pitched shrill.

In the middle of the morals crusade, in 1926, the Attorney General wrote that "practically all of the [Mann Act] cases in which the persons investigated were indicted are cases which involved some feature of aggravation, such as commercialized vice, the breaking up of families with young children, or the debauchery of previously virtuous women or of young girls and children."[3] That is untrue, as will be seen by government records. More honest was the report of the United States Attorney in Centerville, Iowa, who advised the department at the end of January, 1917, that he was a "strong believer in the wisdom and justice of this law. Very few of the cases that I have prosecuted have been genuinely commercial but rather have been cases of what some are pleased to term 'private escapades.'"[4]

The Iowa federal prosecutor added that he limited prosecution of noncommercial cases to those with some aggravating features. Unfortunately, whatever standards, if any, of aggravating circumstances were applied by local prosecutors during this period had little relationship to the guidelines established by the department. It is evident that the noncommercial prosecutions during the years from 1917 through 1928 were not limited to the guidelines, but were far more general. A considerable amount of evidence, of various types, clearly demonstrates this.

There were thirty-two appellate opinions of appeals from Mann Act convictions for noncommercial violations issued during the period of 1919 to 1930. Appeals of convictions lag behind trials, and trials follow many months after prosecutorial decisions to initiate a case. Therefore this selection of time reflects what was happening in prosecutors' offices during the period between 1917 and 1928. Of the thirty-two appellate opinions, three have insufficient facts stated to judge the nature of the case.

Of the remaining twenty-nine appeals, seventeen, or just over half, met the departmental guidelines. Nine involved girls under eighteen years of age; three were women who had abandoned husband and children; and five situations involved some sense of overreaching (married doctor had a relationship with eighteen-year-old female patient; married pastor had affair with member of his church, aged eighteen; two transportations involved bigamous marriages; one secretary claimed she was hypnotized by her employer).

The other twelve cases had fully discussed facts, and no fact meeting the guidelines was disclosed. Why then were they prosecuted, in defiance of national policy? What features link them together? In two cases the man was married (although not in the original guidelines, that criterion would be added in 1935), and in four cases the woman became pregnant; there is little similarity between the twelve cases.

These appellate cases range from seduction and betrayal, to casual romantic trips, to serious relationships of living together. Most of the convictions were affirmed. A few examples will illustrate, and more are collected in a note.[5] H. W. Elrod and his girlfriend had already established a sexual relationship when she agreed to accompany him on a business trip he took from Nashville to Louisville in 1918. He paid all of the expenses, and while in Louisville they occupied a room together and had sexual relations. She returned to Louisville the next day unharmed in any way. "Whether or not defendant had a business engagement at Louisville," the appellate court intoned, "he violated the act if he took the girl there for the unlawful purpose alleged, and even though she were thought to be a willing participant in that purpose, and notwithstanding the relations between them were not commercial in character."[6]

C. W. Aplin and his lady friend began a trip at Salem, Oregon, in March 1928 and drove together down the Pacific Coast, stopping first at an auto camp in Chico, California. They lived together there for a few weeks and then went to Las Vegas, Nevada, where they continued to live together. She was twenty-two, but as the court said, "there were illicit relations in Oregon before their departure from that state, there were illicit relations in the course of the trip, and illicit relations after its termination . . . the jury might well infer that at least one purpose of the transportation was debauchery, or other immoral purpose."[7] In the late 1920s Reese Christian transported Lucy Hendrix from Tupelo, Mississippi, to Nixburg, Alabama. They lived together there for a few months, although Reese was already married. Then they moved to Monette, Arkansas. Throughout their travels they lived as husband and wife. She was not an unexperienced woman. She had been married three times, and her sixteen-year-old son accompanied them on their trip.[8]

Internal records of the Department of Justice provide additional information concerning the crusade against those whose morals differed from the majority and the zealous disregard of the departmental standards of aggravation by enthusiastic prosecutors. Once a case reached the indictment stage, the department's regulations apparently required approval from Washington before a local prosecutor could dismiss. There is a long series of letters from United States Attorneys requesting permission to dismiss, usually routinely granted. These letters contain considerable information about the facts of these cases, and from them we can see clearly that noncommercial cases were routinely prosecuted even in the absence of aggravating circumstances. The cases discussed from this source were all dismissed, but it is important to bear in mind that the reason they were dismissed had nothing to do with the fact that their very existence violated the guidelines in their lack of aggravating circumstances. The few cases described below are just a small sampling.

In the early 1920s Henry M. Delaney filed for a divorce in Florida. He was told by his attorney that it would become final by a certain date unless the attorney advised him otherwise. He did not hear further and assumed his divorce was final. Thereupon, he married his sweetheart, Ida Nelson, in Georgia, and they went to Florida to live. Shortly thereafter he discovered that the divorce was not final. He did what undoubtedly he regarded as the only honorable thing to do. Henry took Ida back to her parents in Georgia, obtained the final decree, remarried Ida, and all ended well, except with the federal prosecutor. That model of self-righteousness prosecuted Henry for the trip from Georgia to Florida with the woman he thought was his wife but turned out was not because the final decree had not been entered.

True, the case was dismissed. But because it was outrageous and no decent-minded federal prosecutor should have filed it? No. The federal prosecutor in Macon, Georgia, would have loved to imprison Henry for his error. He had even set the case for trial on several occasions. The problem was that it proved impossible to get Ida into court, and, as the prosecutor explained, "even if she should be present, in view of the fact that she is now the wife of the defendant, I am doubtful about whether she would be allowed to testify."[9]

In July 1920, Ola Mae Olson was twenty-one years old and unsuccessfully trying to get a job in Springfield, Missouri. She met Walter Nutting and liked him because he was kind to her. They drifted around together for over a year, living as man and wife, first to Eldorado, Kansas, for a couple of weeks, then to Wichita, to Denver, next to Cheyenne. Then they drifted through Nebraska to Colorado, to New Mexico, Arizona, back to Colorado and then to Eldorado, Kansas, again. They lived there for six weeks before they were arrested for violation of the Mann Act. Walter was married, but Ola Mae told the Bureau of Investigation that she had no desire to prosecute the defendant "as she has the utmost confidence and faith in him and believes he will marry her as soon as he secures a divorce."

An indictment was sought by the federal prosecutor, notwithstanding the "victim's" desire. However, the Denver-based prosecutor ultimately dismissed the indictment because investigation did not reveal any hotel in Colorado in which they stayed, Ola Mae had disappeared, and even if found he did not want to take "a chance of having the defendant acquitted on account of her attitude."[10]

Maude Crowles and Clarence Broom met in Roseburg, Oregon. He was married, but without children. She had been formerly married and likewise had no children. They were both of mature age. Following a summer affair, he planned to drive to Champaign, Illinois, his hometown. They reached an understanding that they would take the trip together as a vacation, he to furnish the automobile, and they both to share the expenses. They started off in September 1924 and had sexual relations along the way. Once in Champaign, Broom resided with his parents and Crowles lived in a rooming house. They entered into a partnership to operate a roadhouse and continued their affair in Champaign, apparently briefly.

Broom was prosecuted in Oregon, their point of departure, for violation of the Mann Act. Again the dismissal had nothing to do with the absurdity of the federal felony charge. Broom skipped bail and almost six years later when the case was dismissed he could not be found. Furthermore, Maude Crowles had remarried and was extremely reluctant to testify. As the prosecutor explained, "she had been married since the violation occurred and did not care to have her husband subjected to the embarrassment of a trial, wherein she would have to testify as to her relationship with the defendant."[11]

In 1984 a legal scholar published a study of the effect of Mann Act prosecutions on female defendants. Women were criminally liable for the transportation of *other* women in interstate commerce for immoral purposes and were also liable under the *Holte* doctrine for conspiracy to aid the male with *their own* transportation. This was the state of the law regarding women offenders under the Mann Act during the period of the morals crusade, namely, the years from 1917 to 1928. After 1927, female offenders were generally imprisoned at the Federal Industrial Institution for Women, in Alderson, West Virginia.

Marlene D. Beckman completed a study of female prisoners housed in Alderson for violations of the Mann Act, between 1927 and 1937, studying intake interview records. She found that thirty-six of the women committed to this federal prison, or 23 percent of the prison's total female incarcerations for violation of the Mann Act, had undertaken absolutely no prostitution activity. Only nine of the thirty-six had been living with husbands at the time of their offense, and none had previously been convicted of a felony. Beckman concluded that notwithstanding the Attorney General's circulars to the United States Attorneys, requiring aggravated circumstances for the prosecution of noncommercial cases, nonaggravated cases continued to be prosecuted. "U.S. Attorneys," she wrote, "continued to prosecute individuals engaged in strictly personal sexual escapades that in no way involved either commercial gain or exploitation of innocent victims. [This] cannot be explained by an occasional error on the part of federal prosecutors in judging the circumstances of a particular case to be 'aggravated.'"[12] Two of the many cases studies she relates, based on prison intake records, illustrate the extent to which the Mann Act had the consequence of confining the conduct of women and their expression of sexuality through interstate travel.

> Viola had known Blake since she was eight years old—he owned a tin shop and she worked in his office. . . . A friend of his came to the shop by the name of Thomas. He was 24 years old and married, also not living with his wife. Viola became infatuated with Thomas. Her family objected to her working for Blake and she finally had a quarrel with her mother. She left home. . . . Blake told her that he was going to close his shop and going away with a girl by the name of Loretta and sug-

gested that she go along with Thomas. She says she went willingly and that she has only herself to blame. . . . They left Pittsburgh on January 27, 1927, and went as far as Fredericksburg, Virginia. There they stayed all night, Loretta and Blake registering as man and wife and Viola and Thomas as man and wife. The fourth day they stopped in Charleston, South Carolina, and there they rented two rooms. Viola says they decided to separate, that she had had quite enough of the trip and she wanted to go home. While the two men were willing to send them home, the other girl didn't want to be discarded, so she went out and telephoned the police that they were being beaten by two men. When the police arrived they were all arrested and put in jail. Later the Mann Act charge was put against them.

When she was imprisoned in 1927, Viola was single, nineteen years old, with an eleventh-grade education. She was white with no children and no previous convictions. For her indiscretion in crossing a state line with her boyfriend, the federal morals judge in South Carolina sentenced her to one year in prison.

Even women who might be considered as genuine victims received substantial prison terms. For example, Elizabeth, who was probably only seventeen when she met Ezra:

He never told her that he was a married man, but proposed to her and would postpone the date of marriage until their arrest. He claimed that he had to make trips to Fairmont, W. Va. on business and asked her to accompany him. He delivered liquor, but never told her. She would stay with him at a hotel as his wife and they both used the alias of Miller. They made eleven trips back and forth to Fairmont [over a period of approximately eighteen months]. She always told her aunt she was staying with a girl friend. They were arrested on the road as they neared Fairmont on August 2, 1931. . . [and] remained in jail three months then were taken to Elkins, W. Va. . . . she received 18 months [at Alderson] and he received 2½ years at Atlanta [federal prison for men].

Elizabeth was committed in 1931. She was single, white, and nineteen years of age at the time of her imprisonment for one and one-half years. She had no children and no previous convictions.

These cases might make one suspect that the Mann Act was used as a lever to control the lower class. But the morals crusade was much broader in scope. The Progressives and religious zealots foolishly wished to force men and women to be good, whether they wanted to be or not, and regardless of their class. In the 1920s, influential people, ranging from high city officials to preachers, were arrested for non-commercial violations of the Mann Act.[13] The Vice Consul General of Guatemala was indicted, as was the Military Governor of Sonora, who made the mistake of briefly crossing over the borderline into Douglas, Arizona, with his girlfriend.[14]

Mature wives of middle-class businessmen were the basis of many Mann Act violations. They would come to feel, as the wife of a rich New York confectioner put it, "that her husband had neglected her for the past ten years." An affair with another man, travel outside the state, and complaint of the husband generated many "white slave" prosecutions.[15]

The crusading morality behind these noncommercial cases is seen in the many efforts of judges and prosecutors to force defendants to marry their "victims." In 1925 a defendant was sentenced to only one day in jail after he agreed to marry his girlfriend, whom he had brought to Baltimore from Philadelphia.[16] That same year another federal judge, this one in Detroit, forced a shotgun marriage. A student at the University of Michigan had taken his girlfriend on a trip out of state. The judge placed the hapless young man, a foreign student from Brazil, on probation for two years, but on the strict condition that he marry the girlfriend. "If you ever cast Margaret Bailey [girlfriend] off after you are married," the federal morals judge threatened the defendant, "I will have you brought before me again and you will be sentenced to Leavenworth Prison. This is the happiest solution to the situation. . . . Don't think, however, that you are evading the penalty of the law by marrying, because the marriage must last."[17]

These prosecutions were initiated in a variety of ways. Sometimes, local police would make an arrest for other reasons, discover an unmarried couple who had come in from another state and inform the federal authorities. For noncommercial cases, however, it was more typical that there would be a denunciation. Wives would complain when their husbands ran off with other women; husbands would complain when their wives ran off with other men; and fathers would complain when their daughters left. Sometimes busybody moralists with nothing better to do would denounce the conduct of the couple next door, down the hall, or around the block.

These citizen complaints would be directed toward the Bureau of Investigation or the local United States Attorney, and a considerable volume of mail also arrived at the Department of Justice in Washington complaining of people's moral conduct in towns spread across the country. Many complainants failed to understand the necessity of interstate movement as a basis of federal jurisdiction, another indication of the generally moralistic temperament of the federal efforts. They were generally turned politely away. Other complainants were vague, and they often would be asked to confer with the Bureau of Investigation with greater specificity. Occasionally, even during the morals crusade, individual United States Attorneys would decline to prosecute a noncommercial case on the principled basis that there were no elements of aggravation.[18] However, this would become much more common in the 1930s and 1940s.

However initiated, the agents of the Bureau of Investigation would work the case, gathering statements and tangible evidence, and present a formal report to the local United States Attorney for decision whether to prosecute. There were far more complaints than investigations made, and, in turn, the FBI investigated far more cases than were actually prosecuted. From June 30, 1922, through June 30, 1937, the FBI investigated 50,500 alleged violations of the Mann Act—3,396 of these within the twelve months preceding June 30, 1937.[19] During the 1920s, the large majority of these investigations would be for noncommercial violations.

Once an affirmative decision to prosecute was made by the local United States Attorney, an arrest would be made, unless the defendant were already in custody, and a hearing would be held before a United States Commissioner as to whether there was sufficient evidence to hold the defendant. This is a minimal legal standard, simply that a crime has been committed and it is probable that the defendant did it. Thereafter, the grand jury would consider the matter for indictment, and following that, the defendant would be held for formal trial.

The complaints received from the moralists, out to force their beliefs on the rest of the population, were usually the most colorful. In the fiscal year of 1921, alone, there were 9,949 such letters from citizens and reports from investigators.[20] One such was sent to the Department of Justice from West Palm Beach on October 31, 1927, reproduced here exactly as written:

> There is a J. S. Nouser liveing at 727 Kanuga drive with a woman that he not married to and they was on a trip this summer to california and new Yory they stoped at the pennsylvania Hotel in new york as man and wife i think this agants the man ack and should be looked in to
>
> yours very truly
> from a mother[21]

The director of the Bureau of Investigation passed along a copy of this communication to the agent stationed at Jacksonville, Florida, and requested him to investigate.[22]

Far more typical, however, of the origination of these noncommercial prosecutions, was the complaint of husband, wife, or father, as in this letter from a Corporal of the Michigan State Police sent to the Department of Justice on June 6, 1929:

> I have this date received a complaint from one Mr. Eugene Kavan of White Pigeon Michigan who states that his Wife is Continually stepping out with another man, which is breaking up his home. Mr. Kavan says that they go across the line into Indiana where they register as man and wife at hotels in Elkhart.[23]

Mr. Kavan asked to have the man prosecuted under the Mann Act, and Hoover ordered the Chicago office of the Bureau of Investigation to follow through. Similar complaints, from wives, husbands, and fathers were addressed to the federal government's local officials.

After indictment, the cases then went on to a finding of guilt, through trial or plea, an acquittal, conviction, or a dismissal. The Department of Justice kept meticulous records of the total numbers of convictions, acquittals, and dismissals, by years, but did not separate out the noncommercial from commercial cases, nor whether they were obtained through trial or plea of guilty. The total number of convictions for 1917 through 1928, together with the average prison sentence and fine is shown in the table below. It should be remembered that these are mere averages. Many convictions resulted only in imprisonment without fine and, in others, fines only were imposed. Further, most of these sentences were subject to parole after the service of one-third of the term.

Varying with the case and defendant, judges tend to emphasize fine *or* imprisonment, but usually not both in an individual case. Therefore, to combine these as averages tends to show an average imprisonment that is lower than that typically imposed in a prison sentence case and a fine that is actually lower than typically imposed in a case in which a fine was the major sentence. There is no other way to use the available data, but it would be more accurate to think of the average sentence as *either* a two-year prison term *or* a $250 fine, approximately $3,000 in 1994 dollars.

Year	Convictions	Acquittals	Dismissals	Imprisonment (average months)	Fine
1917	309	45	75	cannot be calculated	
1918	352	40	136	cannot be calculated	
1919	261	19	80	15.2	$134
1920	342	38	79	12.5	$ 88
1921	307	21	30	13.3	$116
1922	418	not reported		cannot be calculated	
1923	386	not reported		cannot be calculated	
1924	515	40	159	12.3	$123
1925	428	39	128	cannot be calculated	
1926	528	not reported		12.0	$ 69
1927	408	32	160	cannot be calculated	
1928	424	not reported		cannot be calculated	

These figures are for the fiscal years ending June 30th.[24] The several decreases in convictions are not explained in the Attorney General's *Annual Reports*, except the sharp decline for fiscal 1919 is attributed to wartime priorities that diverted immediate attention to "offenses against the war statutes."

Although the department did not break down the statistics into prostitution and noncommercial cases, some idea of the range of sentences can be seen by an examination of the Mann Act prosecutions for two specific federal court districts, Providence, Rhode Island, in the north, and Mobile, Alabama, in the south. It would not be meaningful to consider just the period, from 1917 to 1928, because too few cases would be measured and too much emphasis would be placed on the impact of particular judges. However, an analysis of the Mann Act prosecutions from the enactment of the statute through the end of 1944 yields some interesting information.[25]

In Providence, 56 percent of the Mann Act prosecutions were for noncommercial cases; in Mobile, 63 percent. In Providence, 42 percent of these noncommercial prosecutions led to some jail time. Removing acquittals and dismissals, 71 percent of those actually convicted of a noncommercial Mann Act violation received some jail time. The average noncommercial jail sentence was 9.8 months. In Mobile, 50 percent of the noncommercial prosecutions resulted in some jail time. Of those convicted of a noncommercial violation, 59 percent received some jail time. The average noncommercial jail sentence was 7.4 months. By contrast, the average commercial sentence in Providence was 29.1 months, and in Mobile, 13.2 months. These jail sentences would be subject, normally, to parole after service of one-third of the time.

This study of Mobile and Providence also shows that noncommercial prosecution of Mann Act cases was not in any way confined to the Southern Bible Belt. Mobile and Providence were deliberately selected to test this supposition, since they are both port cities, sandwiched between other states. Providence is Northern and Roman Catholic; Mobile is Southern and Baptist, although with a larger Roman Catholic population than most Southern cities. However, there is no significant difference in the prosecution rates and the average jail time given for noncommercial cases between the two areas. Interestingly, there is no evidence in either jurisdiction that Mann Act prosecutions were used to control racial minorities.

One striking feature of the national statistical table is the high number of dismissals. These were dismissals requested by the government, not those ordered after a hearing by the court. They were also dismissals *after* indictment, despite the Attorney General's claim that only aggravated cases led to indictment. Why such a large number? A sampling of the letters sent to the department by the United States Attorneys, seeking permission to dismiss noncommercial cases, suggests several reasons.

Some are simply practical reasons: the defendant cannot be found, the witnesses have scattered, the evidence is insufficient, or the "victim" in a noncommercial case is extremely hostile toward the government. A few dismissals were sought because the defendant had already been punished or was being punished by state authorities on charges stemming from the same facts. Very often, these requests for dismissals based on practicality added the information that the "victim" was, in any event, a woman of bad character.

Based on an admittedly unscientific sampling, the majority of the dismissals were based upon the fact that the woman had married or was contemplating marriage to another person, or, alternatively, that the defendant had married the "victim" himself. Where the woman had married another, the usual story was that "she is now happily married and fears it would cause trouble between herself and husband if she were to testify,"[26] or "her present husband knows nothing as to this episode which his wife was involved in and for that reason she is a very unfriendly and unwilling witness."[27] A variation of this theme was where the woman had returned to an existing husband, or the male defendant had returned to his wife.

The second largest category of dismissals came where the parties had married after their arrest. Sometimes local prosecutors sensed that there was no moral point in prosecuting such defendants. For example, in 1923 Madeline Irvin, a married woman, ran off with Carl Gray. They were charged with conspiracy to violate the Mann Act. Before trial she had divorced her husband and married her "co-conspirator." Aubrey Boyles, the United States Attorney in Mobile, Alabama wrote that "it would be impolitic and contrary to the true intent and purpose of the law to proceed in a prosecution of these defendants in the face of these facts."[28]

But usually the United States Attorneys had more practical things on their minds and thought it useless to prosecute since the "victim" would not be allowed to testify. The criminal defendant had a privilege, weakened during the 1940s and no longer available, to prevent his wife from taking the stand to testify against him. This applied to Mann Act prosecutions.[29] Curiously, the privilege did not apply when the defendant and woman were *already* married when they crossed the line for a prohibited purpose.[30] A pre-existing marriage would eliminate the noncommercial case, but there might well be a commercial violation of the Mann Act where a defendant took his wife to work in a brothel in another state.

The operation of this spousal immunity from testimony bothered the Department of Justice, probably more out of concern for commercial cases, where a pimp might marry the girl he transported, than marriage following a romantic elopement. "Numerous cases of merit have failed solely because of the inability to use the wife as a witness," the Attorney General wrote to the Chairman of the Senate Committee on the Judiciary in January 1916. He suggested that the Act be amended to provide that in Mann Act prosecutions "the wife shall be a competent and compellable witness against her husband."[31]

Legislation to that effect was introduced in the Senate, but not the House.[32] It went nowhere. The request was renewed by the Department of Justice the following year.[33] The chairman of the House Committee on the Judiciary advised the department that the year before when the matter was considered, some members had "expressed the fear that this amendment would probably produce greater evils than those we now bear."[34] The proposal died a quiet death.

The table also reveals that there were acquittals, and, of course, some cases shown as convictions were ultimately overturned on appeal. While there were several grounds of defense, one thing that failed to provide a clear defense was the testimony of both defendant and his "victim" that no sex had occurred. Even where the woman testified that she took the trip of her own accord, defendant had not induced her, and there was no sex, the jury would be allowed to disagree and convict.[35]

Where a charge was brought under the section enhancing punishment when the woman is under eighteen, it was a good defense under that count alone if the jury found the male had reason to believe she was eighteen, even though she was not.[36] Two of the transportation sections of the Mann Act required a common carrier, that outlawing the encouragement of a woman to undertake an interstate journey for immoral purposes and that dealing with minor females. Under a prosecution for these sections, it was a good defense that the prosecution failed to prove the travel was by common carrier—for example, if the trip were made by automobile.[37]

The interstate transportation had to be caused or induced by the defendant. If the woman were to follow the man, not at his request or expense, and thereafter resume a sexual relationship in a different state, the Mann Act would not be violated. It was reversible error for the trial court to instruct the jury that such a contention was "wholly unreasonable."[38] Even if a man and woman, having a sexual relationship, were to travel together into another state and continue their relationship, there was no violation where the woman paid her own way and went "entirely of her own accord and without the slightest persuasion on his part,"[39] or where she persuaded him.[40]

If the couple traveled for a lawful purpose and their sexual relations were merely "incidental" to their trip, the statute was not violated. These cases were always the most complicated. In *Sloan v. United States* (1923),[41] Martha Jerden, a single young adult, had been employed in a store in St. Louis. She lost her position and returned to Shafter, Illinois, her hometown. There she met and entered into a relationship with Selz Sloan, an apparently unmarried young man. Martha wanted to resume employment in St. Louis. When Selz was required to take a business trip to St. Louis, he telephoned her and asked if she would like to come along to visit her sister and check out the job opportunities. She agreed and they drove together to St. Louis in his car.

They arrived in St. Louis in the early evening. Selz took her to the sister's rooming house, where she expected to stay. Martha, Selz, the sister, and another gentlemen decided to drive out to a restaurant in the country. On the way back to the rooming house, a dispute of some sort arose between the other man, Martha's sister, and Selz. Eventually, Selz ordered them out of his car. Following this verbal altercation Selz suggested to Martha that the two of them might stay together at a hotel. They did so, and the following evening Martha returned to Shafter.

The appellate court reversed the defendant's conviction. It noted that "the intention to transport the woman for immoral purposes must have been formed by the parties before they reached the foreign state." The mere fact that there was an interstate journey followed by sex was not enough when the purpose of the trip was something else. The court said that it was clear that the purpose of taking Martha to St. Louis was for her to visit her sister and try to obtain employment. Selz and Martha frequently had sexual intercourse in Illinois, and "there is nothing in the evidence to show any possible reason why he should have gone to the trouble and expense of taking her to St. Louis, merely in order that he might have illicit intercourse with her, when he could have done so at home."[42]

A man could be persecuted by the federal government even for a sincere effort to be helpful to a woman. In 1923, Mrs. Panagoula Georgopoulos lived with an abusive husband and their three children in Salt Lake City. His assaults on her were severe. Harry Drossos formerly had been a boarder in their home. On June 23, 1923, matters came to a head when her husband told her that if she were still there when he returned, he would kill her. She fled from the house with the smallest of their children, a little girl, met with Harry Drossos, and poured out her troubles. He advised her to go back home, but she asked him to take her away. She would marry him if he did, and she suggested Montana. Drossos bought the railroad tickets and they left.

Drossos had the naive but apparently sincere belief that they could be married in Montana, notwithstanding that she was still married to Mr. Georgopoulos. He tried to obtain a wedding license at the courthouse in Anaconda and was advised by the clerk to see the County Attorney. That official advised Harry that he could not marry Panagoula until she was divorced. They could live in the same house, but he could not sleep with her. The appellate court later noted that "up to this time there is no evidence or circumstantial proof tending to show sexual relations. The proof is to the contrary." He rented a three-room house for the woman, her young child, and himself.

Eventually, but some time after the state line was crossed, a sexual relationship developed and the woman became known in the community as Mrs. Drossos. He was arrested, charged with a violation of the Mann Act, and given a two-year prison term in Leavenworth. The first conviction was reversed in 1924 because of error in the instructions. But the federal government was not finished with Mr. Drossos. It retried him. The trial judge mimicked Drossos's naive thought that he could marry the woman in another state without a divorce and, in the words of the second appellate court to review his convictions, "impressed the jury with the idea that no one with the slightest degree of intelligence above insanity could believe that the device was practicable."

The appellate court noted that in the end the woman did divorce her husband and did marry the defendant, but the federal persecution continued. The appeals panel rebuked the trial court, writing that while the defendant's story "may seem absurd to the [trial] court . . . it is not for the court to decide the point," but rather, for the jury. "Clearly, defendant was not guilty of the charge, if before going to Montana he had no intention of having sexual relations with the woman unless and until they might be lawfully married."[43]

Interstate transportations of prostitutes were also prosecuted during the morals crusade of 1917 to 1928, but noncommercial cases dominated the thoughts and activities of the federal morals police. In the 1924 *Annual Report* of the United States Attorney General, there is a very revealing breakdown of cases for that fiscal year. "There have been 515 convictions . . . [and] of offenders punished this year by the courts 65 of their victims were under the age of 18 years. . . . Thirty victims were induced to leave their homes under promise of marriage and 50 were commercialized. [FBI jargon for prostituted.] In 70 per cent of these cases there were families involved."[44]

In other words, of 515 persons branded as federal felons that year, only 10 percent (50) had been involved in commercial prostitution, about 7 percent (30) had seduced women under promise of marriage, and a full 70 percent had been merely interstate adulterers or boyfriends and girlfriends. Therefore, the Mann Act prosecutions for prostitution were relatively minor during the period of the morals crusade.

The last chapter briefly suggested the efforts of the federal government to eliminate sexual temptations facing the troops about to be shipped to Europe. Although these exertions had a heavy impact on the civil liberties of both prostitutes and sexually active women, these arrests and incarcerations did not see any parallel expansion of Mann Act arrests. Indeed, the *Annual Reports* for both 1917 and 1919 attribute a decrease in indictments and convictions to more pressing work related to the war effort.[45]

Most of the commercial cases were quite routine and require no elaboration. Two stand out for special comment. In *Rizzo v. United States* (1921), the appellate court stated that "the offense is complete when the interstate transportation takes place for the defined purpose, without regard to whether later the purpose is accomplished," although subsequent behavior might shed light on the earlier purpose.[46] This merely reaffirmed the earlier doctrine declared by the Supreme Court in *Wilson* that has been discussed before. It recommitted the federal courts to the Orwellian proposition that what was being punished was essentially bad thoughts plus transportation.

Simpson v. United States (1917) was an unusual situation. The male defendant transported a woman from San Francisco, California, to Tijuana, Mexico, not to be a prostitute, but to manage a Mexican brothel called "The Palace." One would think the morals squad would be happy the defendant had rid the United States of a madam and cheerfully concede jurisdiction to the Mexican and not the American *federales*. Not so. Being a madam in Mexico was still an immoral purpose, and a state line had been crossed while leaving California. The conviction was affirmed, the appellate court merely noting that it did "not think the scope of the statute is limited to cases of personal acts of sexual immorality upon the part of the woman transported."[47]

One theoretical problem concerning prostitution confronted the upholders of morality during the late teens and early 1920s. It was being discovered that the white slave gangs so feared during the white slavery hysteria of 1907 to 1914 had either never really existed or, alternatively, had been thoroughly suppressed. The federal government, to justify the Act it had passed and justify its persecutions thereunder, took the approach that there had been a problem but now it was all over. In his 1922 *Annual Report* the Attorney General wrote that the White Slave Traffic Act was more vigorously enforced than ever with the result that "the organized white-slave gangs which formerly existed have been very thoroughly broken up."[48]

Obviously this created a tension. Why have a White Slave Traffic Act if there were no more white slaves and gangs herding them about the country? In the years of 1907 to 1914 everyone knew who a white slave was: she was a helpless, pathetic young woman, forced into prostitution by drugs, alcohol, and kidnapping, kept in a brothel against her will, and shipped about the nation as demand and police crackdowns dictated. And everyone knew about the white slavers as well. They were unscrupulous young men, mostly swarthy-skinned foreigners, who lurked about the railroad stations, dance halls, and immigrants' docks looking for victims. These were clearly the victims and villains for whom the Mann Act was enacted.

With the acknowledgment that there were no more white slave gangs (if ever there were), the federal government might have celebrated its victory, kept the statute on the books to prevent their reappearance, and terminated its enforcement in voluntary and noncommercial cases— but that way the federal bureaucracy could not have justified its continued parasitic existence. What happened was that with the revelation that the white slave gangs never existed, or in the alternative, had been wiped out, the very terms "white slave" and "white slaver" were redefined to mean more simply, "prostitute" and "pimp." By changing the meaning of the words, the morals soldiers and their social worker civilian allies could continue to justify their existence and operations.

This process did not come about overnight, and obviously it was not accomplished by some vast conspiracy. It was an evolutionary process that took place over a number of years. The seeds of the shift in meaning were planted during the mid-teens, although its culmination was not achieved until the 1930s. The white slavery hysteria is generally regarded as having spent its force by the end of 1914. Even as early as the year before, the process of redefinition was underway. In April 1913, a probation officer of the New York City Night Court shifted the focus of the coercion that turned girls into slaves from force, as in the old stereotype, to *fear*:

> People have a curious idea about the "white slaves" anyway. They seem to think a girl is not in that class unless she is hidden away somewhere behind bolts and bars, and that the only reason she remains bound to a man is because she cannot get out into the supposed freedom of the streets. Of course some girls are in actual captivity of that sort, especially at first. But there are plenty of white slaves walking the streets in apparent freedom. . . . They are not held by bars or locked doors, but by fear! The unspeakable creatures who have these girls in their power have so completely terrorized them that the girls feel escape to be utterly impossible.[49]

By 1916 there was a further shift in meaning. Maude E. Miner, the secretary of the New York Probation and Protective Association, published a book that year, entitled *Slavery of Prostitution—A Plea for Emancipation.*[50] In it she acknowledged that women were rarely physically abducted into prostitution, but instead claimed that "through the loss of freedom and will of action, they have been bound to prostitution . . . their demoralization of character has constituted moral enslavement."[51]

No longer force, no longer fear, but moral slavery. As a review of Miner's book summarized it: "It is not a physical slavery, but one much more subtle and harder to break away from—moral slavery. It is the breaking down of moral fiber, the fear of facing the world from which she has stepped down, the hold that her distorted emotions have upon her. . . . To those who have questioned the validity of the term "White Slavery," Miss Miner's splendid analysis will present a new meaning."[52]

And indeed, it was a new meaning. A scholar, writing in 1921, noted the confusion in definition and the shift in meaning. Howard Woolston wrote:

> Ten years ago the newspapers were filled with startling accounts of the existence of a system of procuring women and girls for prostitution by means of fraud or violence, and of transporting and detaining them in vice resorts against their will. This is what is generally understood as "White Slavery." Sometimes the term has been loosely applied to cover all phases of the traffic in women and made to include cases where the girls remain in the business not unwillingly. . . . The latter meaning would extend the term white slavery to include practically the whole field of commercialized vice.[53]

And thus "white slavery" was extended to include all commercial vice, without any question of force, fear, or moral enslavement. In 1929 a United States Attorney was quoted about an investigation in "white slave traffic" operating in the Atlantic and southern New England states. In the same string of sentences in which he said "white slavery," he acknowledged that "there is no indication that there has been anything compulsory about the traffic . . . the girls used have gone willingly."[54] Increasingly, speakers and writers used the term white slavery as synonymous with prostitution, and white slaver for pimp, as in the remark of the Governor of New Jersey in 1930 that he did "not believe there are more crooks, gamblers, bootleggers and white slavers in Atlantic City than there are honest persons."[55]

In an interesting parallel, the international conventions, through which the worldwide traffic in women were studied, were similarly changed. In the 1910 convention, operating under the mental regime of the old-fashioned white slavery, the victims were defined as women under the age of twenty-two and all other women procured by force or fraud. For a study conducted during the years from 1924 to 1927 by the League of Nations the international traffic in women was redefined to be "the sexual exploitation abroad of females of any age with or without their consent."[56] The chief rationale for the change reflected the discomfort with the traditional definition of white slavery. Bascom Johnson, an American and the director of the League's investigations concerning traffic in women, wrote that "it was believed that no woman, even though she be an experienced prostitute, can possibly understand and therefore consent in advance to the sort of exploitation and *virtual slavery* to which she is often subjected in a foreign country of whose language and customs she is ignorant and where she is far from home and friends"[57] (emphasis added).

Although the shift in popular understanding of the term white slavery was very largely complete by the end of the 1920s, there were occasional reinforcements at later dates. In 1938, J. Edgar Hoover wrote that "it is true that the term 'white slave traffic' is at times misleading, as in many instances the victims willingly consent to the practices in which they are engaged. However, all too frequently they are led into the racket by lurid promises and kept there by threats."[58]

A year later in 1939 a writer close to Hoover wrote a book about vice conditions in the United States. The transformation in meaning of white slavery and white slave was so complete that he could parody the meaning traditional to the years of 1907 to 1914. "The average person," he wrote, implying that term ought certainly not include his readers, "looks upon a White Slave as an innocent little virgin who, some dark night, is seized by a vile villain, carried away in a lightless taxicab, stuffed into a house of prostitution, stripped of her clothes, and then introduced to a horrible beast known as a Passion-Mad Man."[59] In 1969, a writer discussing the Mann Act casually wrote that white slavery had always been simply a polite euphemism for prostitution.[60] The full accomplishment of a shift in a term's meaning comes when it is possible to assert there has never been any change.

It should be stressed again, however, that prostitution cases were not the true focus of the federal efforts during the morals crusade of 1917 to

1928. Instead, the targets were generally noncommercial adulterers and lovers. Noncommercial violations of the Mann Act, once thought to be only technical violations and a long distance away from the classic white slavers, were vigorously prosecuted. Because of this, Americans' ability to engage in interstate travel and also express their sexuality was curtailed, unless it conformed to the majoritarian norm of reserving sex only for marriage. Surprisingly, this prohibition fell with some force on women as well as men, and women were regularly prosecuted during this period for conspiring with their boyfriends to arrange a trip that took them across a state line. This prosecutorial focus on noncommercial violations would shift in the following fifteen years. Commercial cases would become much more prominent, and the targets of noncommercial prosecution would be much more narrowly focused. In turn, that highlighted yet another collateral consequence of the statute: the selective nature of prosecutions directed toward specific classes of persons.

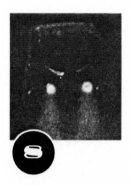

The Focus Shifts, 1929–1943

No bell rang, no memo can be quoted, and no precise date can be specified, but a definite shift in Mann Act prosecutions took place at the end of the 1920s. The morals crusade ended, and with it so did noncommercial prosecutions where no aggravating circumstances existed. A big exception was made where a specific defendant was politically unpopular with the federal government or where his activities were of a type despised by the federal authorities. For such a targeted defendant, any crime for which he could be convicted, including a nonaggravated Mann Act offense, was cheerfully seized upon by the government in an effort to get the man. But these were an exception to a general pattern of shifting away from noncommercial prosecutions.

From the late 1920s, local United States Attorneys repeatedly advised the Department of Justice of the difficulty or impossibility of obtaining convictions from local juries in nonaggravated noncommercial situations. Quite unlike the attitude of the prosecutors in the 1910s and 1920s, they expressed concern over whether the harm that might be caused the prosecuting witness was worth the punishment that might be extracted, and often this factor was thrown into the consideration.

Where a man and a woman had been having an affair, juries became increasingly disinclined to convict merely because they crossed over a state line. In one such case the federal prosecutor in Baltimore advised the department in 1927 that because sexual relations had occurred prior to the trip, it could be argued that sex was not the real object of the journey and an acquittal was likely. Beyond that, however, the prosecutor believed that because of the lapse of time and of the probable harm to the woman that a trial would be "productive of more social harm than good."[1] Even in an aggravated case, where the girl was only seventeen and the man thirty-six, the Grand Rapids, Michigan prosecutor recommended the case be dropped in 1932 after one trial led to a hung jury. "This girl was a willing witness," he wrote, "but at the present time is in the home of a good family, and we believe a retrial will be more injurious to her than any good that can be derived from retrying it. Of course, we shall have the same difficulty in securing a verdict as before due to the immoral relation before leaving Michigan."[2] Also in 1932, another Baltimore prosecutor wrote that because the couple in question had had sexual relations for an extended period prior to their travel, it would "be difficult to prove the purpose of the alleged transportation. . . . I do not believe a successful prosecution can be had."[3]

In 1931 the Montana federal prosecutor advised that it was practically impossible to obtain a conspiracy conviction against a woman in a Mann Act case,[4] and two years later the New Mexico United States Attorney wrote of a particular case that "the facts did not warrant a prosecution for the reason that there were no commercial features involved. The parties were both far beyond legal age, and further there was no evidence of abandonment of minors on the part of either party. . . . It is impossible to make a case in this part of the country under the Mann Act where the above mentioned elements or any one of them, are entirely lacking."[5]

The United States Attorney in Little Rock, Arkansas, was questioned in 1937 why he had not prosecuted a man who had asked an unmarried woman to travel from Memphis across the state line to West Memphis, Arkansas, for the purpose of a noncommercial assignation with him in a cheap hotel. He wrote that "it seems to be nothing but a place of clandestine meetings for immorality between two people of mature age, and there is no commercial vice involved. We could not successful[ly] prosecute in this District such a case."[6]

Earlier, the fact that the victim and defendant had become married was important chiefly because the victim, as defendant's wife, could not testify against him. Now it took on additional significance. "Local juries are strongly influenced by the domestic status of the victim and defendant at the time of trial," said the federal prosecutor in Florida in 1929. Therefore, he recommended the dismissal of a case of double adultery where both parties had returned to their spouses by time of trial.[7] Since the woman would have been testifying against another person's spouse the evidentiary privilege would not have applied. The settled domestic situation would not have prevented the prosecution, but instead it was the anticipated jury's reaction to such a noncommercial prosecution that deterred the prosecutor.

Even where the prosecution had sufficient other evidence to convict a defendant and did not need the testimony of the victim, prosecutors were reluctant to go forward if the man had subsequently married her. The Miami, Florida, federal prosecutor believed in 1936 that "despite the instructions and argument, a jury would have before it a picture of a man who has righted any wrong which he may have done to the victim and the wrong which he may have done in violating the laws of the United States would probably be overshadowed thereby."[8]

As a result of this change of thinking, there were some occasions where grand juries refused to indict for noncommercial violations, once in a case involving a high-school girl, aged sixteen, and a married man, and once in a case where two girls involved were only fifteen.[9] But more typically prosecutors just refused to present noncommercial cases to grand juries unless there were significant aggravating circumstances. Again, we must bear in mind that this is in the normal case, not that of a selected and targeted defendant.

Numerous FBI reports, thousands of them in the years between 1928 and 1943, from all parts of the country, conclude in substantially the language of one dated October 10, 1939, that "the facts in this case were presented to Assistant United States Attorney JOHN W. BAB-COCK, Detroit, Michigan, who declined prosecution for the reason that no commercialism or aggravating circumstances were involved."[10] Even in one situation where a wife had abandoned her husband and two minor children, aged four and six, the FBI reported that "U.S. Attorney advised unless commercialized prostitution can be proved, circumstance not sufficiently aggravated to warrant prosecution."[11] In a case involving Southern country folks of the lower class, federal prosecutors of two different states declined prosecution of a purely noncommercial case, both parties unmarried, where the man was twenty and the girl only fourteen at the time of transportation.[12]

Often other factors are cited in the refusal to prosecute. The woman's prior sexual relations with defendant, her good or poor repute, whether the defendant was or could be charged by the state for the conduct involved in the case, availability of witnesses and their level of cooperation, these were all factors, but towering above them all was simply whether or not it was a case involving commercial prostitution.

Likewise, cases that had been filed and indictments obtained were dismissed when it appeared that the case had no commercial features. A few snippets from letters of prosecutors seeking dismissals indicates how different the outlook was during those years from that of the time of the morals crusade just a short time before. Baltimore, Maryland, 1928: "Inasmuch as there was no commercial aspect to the matter, and also inasmuch as the alleged offense was in the nature of an escapade, we believe that all proceedings should be dropped."[13] Washington, D.C., 1933: "There was no commercialism at all connected with this case and the girl was of sufficient age to realize thoroughly what she was doing."[14] South Bend, Indiana, 1934: "[T]he victim was over 21 years of age at the time; there was no evidence of commercialized vice and nothing wherein a family with children was involved. It was merely a case of two men and a girl on an automobile trip and immoral relations by the men with the victim."[15] Of course, there were still exceptions. We must recall the misfortune of the poor young couple we met in the first chapter, down on their luck, camping on the outskirts of Mobile, Alabama, on Christmas, 1934, and thereafter absolutely persecuted by the local authorities.

When prosecutorial attitudes and practices are rapidly changing, as they were in the late 1920s and early 1930s, some people see the trend as completely accomplished and others view it as incomplete, a variant of the glass half empty or half full. In 1933 the FBI's Hoover wrote that, by following the prosecutorial guidelines for the Mann Act, "police court cases of escapades [that is, noncommercial affairs] . . . have been avoided."[16] In the following year Hoover's boss, the Attorney General, complained to a congressional committee that "many noncommercial cases of ordinary immorality, belonging in State tribunals, have been drawn into Federal jurisdiction."[17] But as a generalization, juries grew increasingly reluctant to convict in noncommercial cases in the years following 1928. Accordingly, local prosecutors generally declined to prosecute this type of case. It remains to be asked, why the shift in popular attitudes that prompted jurors to refuse to convict in cases that they probably would have only a few years before? To answer the question even partially we must take a closer look at the sexual mores of both the 1920s and the 1930s.

Beginning with the 1920 publication of F. Scott Fitzgerald's *This Side of Paradise,* the nation gained a new look at the sexual behavior of

American youth and learned to its great dismay of petting parties, all night automobile rides, "indecent" dancing and dress, and the participation by women in drinking parties, heretofore a largely male prerogative. As the incredibly insightful social critic Frederick Lewis Allen put it, "the book caused a shudder to run down the national spine. . . . It was incredible. It was abominable. What did it all mean? Was every decent standard being thrown over? . . . in due course other books . . . magazine articles and newspapers reiterated the scandal. . . . the forces of morality rallied to the attack."[18]

Actually the changes in mores were not that great in the 1920s. True, the rate of premarital sexual intercourse was twice as high among those women born after 1900 as among those born before. And two-thirds of American wives born between 1910 and 1919 had slept with a man at least once prior to marriage, compared with one-half of American wives born between 1900 and 1909. But it was still primarily their future husbands with whom, after engagement, they had premarital sex; throughout the 1920s those women who had premarital sexual relations with men other than their future husbands were still a distinct minority.[19]

What was so different about the late 1910s and 1920s was the atmosphere. There was a feeling of change, and experiment, and self-conscious rejection of puritanical restraint.[20] Campus life always generated the most publicity. On the campus, the men "reworked their code to incorporate into it sexual play and conquest," while the women "no longer had to pretend that females were non-sexual beings."[21] The spirit of sex, actual and playacted, was visible for all to see.

What has all this to do with the morals crusade and Mann Act prosecutions? The key is Allen's suggestion that "the forces of morality rallied to the attack." The *Literary Digest* weighed in with an article entitled "The Case against the Younger Generation," published in 1922. It quoted an article taken from the *Lutheran* magazine:

> There is such a thing as Bolshevism in the moral and spiritual spheres. . . . A spirit of libertinism is abroad among our young. There is little or no respect for parents and superiors in many of our homes and schools and churches. There is . . . a bold and brazen defiance of decency and modesty in dress and speech and conduct. Women paint and powder and drink and smoke, and become an easy prey to a certain class of well-groomed and well-fed high-livers whose chief business is "to pluck the blush of innocency from off the cheek of maidenhood and put a blister there."[22]

Then, as in our own day, self-righteous politicians and preachers blathered on about moral decay and degeneracy. The religious magazine *Lutheran Witness* claimed that modern dancing was "undeniably indulgence in fleshly lust" and a "training school for fornicating." The Methodists refused to admit dancing teachers into church membership unless they renounced their "teaching lasciviousness and adultery and of ruining homes and youth." The *Baptist* magazine bemoaned youthful access to automobiles and urged that more motorized police be appointed to curb the "carnival of lust."[23]

The men and women of this older generation were the jurors who convicted the poor wretches for the noncommercial violations of the Mann Act during the years of 1917 to 1928, while the men of this generation made up the United States Attorneys and FBI agents who persecuted them. While the defendants in these cases were seldom college men, that hardly mattered. Cracking down on prurience and unchanneled sexual expression was a way for this moral majority to send a message and reassure themselves that they were holding the line for God and decency. Sending poor lower-class fools to prison for expressing their sexuality simply made decent, middle-class, God-fearing Americans feel good. The morals crusade of the Mann Act essentially arose out of a spirit of angry vindictiveness.

This began to change by the end of the 1920s and rapidly became an entirely different mood by the 1930s. First, the youth of the 1920s had matured and had themselves become the prosecutors and jurors, perhaps not yet the judges. They lacked the fear of sexual expression that had so bedeviled the older generation of the 1920s and therefore felt no need to strike out in anger. Second, beginning with the Depression, most Americans worried about economic survival, a matter far more compelling than the morals of others. And third, the spirit of youth was different in the 1930s and less likely to inflame the passions of their elders.

The 1930s did not bring a return to the rigid conventions of the time prior to the 1920s. But the public display and preoccupation with sex was gone. Young people were "less conspicuously and self-consciously intent upon showing the world what advanced young devils they were."[24] On the campus "there was little of the rebellious talk about sex and marriage that had characterized the nineteen-twenties. . . . Whether there was less actual promiscuity is doubtful. . . . The striking thing was that there was less to-do about sex. One's personal affairs were one's personal affair."[25] This was not the flamboyant display that had angered the judges, jurors, and prosecutors during the morals crusade. They could now feel good enough about youth as to cease the persecution.

The Mann Act had definitely entered the American public consciousness by the 1930s. Almost everyone knew of its provisions and relationship to immorality. Fitzgerald had incorporated it into another of his novels, *Tender Is the Night* (1934). Americans, of both higher and lower class, were aware of the statute and showed that knowledge in their actions.

On the higher level is the amusing case of *Hart v. United States* (1926).[26] In June of 1922, Frank C. Hart, a married Portland physician, traveled by automobile with his young mistress and her sister from Portland to San Francisco. A little knowledge was a dangerous thing for this doctor. Before leaving Portland, he asked each of the women to sign an affidavit, attesting that she wanted of her own accord to travel to San Francisco and intended to pay her own expenses. When they arrived in southern Oregon, he asked each of them to buy train tickets from Ashland, Oregon, to the first stop across the line in California. Each of the women took the train with all of her luggage, while Hart drove over the line and picked them up at the California station. They then continued the journey in Hart's car. The stratagem failed to impress the courts.

At the other end of the social scale, the Mann Act may have played a role in the tragic 1931 case of the Scottsboro boys. The young female "victims" in that case may have been riding the rails with two white men with whom they were having sexual relations. The girls may have claimed they were raped by the Negro defendants to evade prosecution for the Mann Act violation.[27]

One sign of the public notoriety of the Mann Act was that it was bitterly attacked by the acerbic *American Mercury*. A 1936 article, "Adultery on Wheels," charged that "as a matter of federal law . . . the soul of Cotton Mather marches on. Under the famous Mann Act, as it has been judicially construed, the enforcement of the Seventh Commandment is still the special business of the national constabulary . . . the operation of this statute would have satisfied the pious ire of the most hardened witch-burning Puritan." It fussed that "for the first time in the history of law and morals, adultery is treated as a *geographical* offense: there is no crime unless the gentle passion combines with the wanderlust" (emphasis in original).[28]

The shift in focus in Mann Act prosecutions from enforcing morality to prosecuting pimps for interstate transportation of prostitutes came in large part because of a transformation of American attitudes, but it also was created by a great increase in the volume and flagrancy of prostitution in many American cities over the period of 1928 to 1933.[29]

This not only changed the character of the Mann Act prosecutions, it also increased them. While the national average number of prosecutions, between 1910 and 1921, was around three hundred cases annually, by the later decade of 1930 to 1941 the average number of prosecutions reached four hundred cases annually. Between the end of Prohibition and the mid-1940s, the Mann Act vied for second place in federal convictions, always trailing behind interstate transportation of stolen vehicles.[30] Some statistics will illustrate this. They are taken from the Attorney General's annual reports but must be looked at for trends rather than read with literalness for individual years. The figures released by the Attorney General in many years do not agree with those from the FBI, and in several years insufficient information is given to calculate averages. The sentences are of actual sentences, but before good time or parole, and do not consider probationary time or suspended sentences. Still, they are revealing when compared with those figures for the period of the morals crusade shown in the last chapter.

Year	Mann Act Convictions	Average Actual Sentence (in months)	Fine (in dollars)
1929	457	14.6	23
1930	516	14.0	36
1931	487	13.2	43
1932	431	16.7	64
1933	316	11.9	16
1934	213	cannot calculate	70
1935	203	15.8	66
1936	298	20.1	145
1937	479	18.3	274
1938	576	28.1	168
1939	524	37.9	62
1940	476	32.4	101
1941	443	30.6	56
1942	no information available		
1943	no information available		

It is striking that the average fines are significantly *lower* than those imposed during 1917 to 1928. To some extent that reflects the poverty and deflation of the Depression, but it also suggests that most of these were straight prison cases. The increased incarceration rate indicates the commercial character of these prosecutions as opposed to the earlier concentration on noncommercial violations.

These figures also reveal a great increase in average prison sentence in the late 1930s and early 1940s. During this time there was an increased FBI concentration on enforcement of the Mann Act that coincided with the uncovering of several large-scale and organized syndicates operating in prostitution. These rings supplied women to New England and Florida resorts and moved them in and out of Atlantic City, New Jersey.

The year 1936 saw the convictions of thirty-eight members of a gang that operated in five states, controlled hundreds of prostitutes, and enjoyed an annual income of over two and one-half million dollars.[31] Twenty-four indictments charging forty-four men and women were returned by the federal grand jury in Trenton, New Jersey, on October 25, 1937, involving another group.[32]

Prosecutions of these large organized groups tended to result in far greater sentences than the individual pimp taking his prostitute girlfriend over a state line. In 1938, for example, fifteen members of a Maryland gang were convicted. One member received a sentence of three years in prison, three received terms of five years and a $5,000 fine, and another was sentenced to four years. Ten others were sentenced to terms ranging from three to twelve years, with fines totaling $23,050.[33] Sentences like these, often handed down in cases involving organized crime, greatly increased the average sentence, and to a lesser extent, average fine, during the late 1930s and early 1940s.

J. Edgar Hoover, the director of the FBI since 1924, often personally led the raiding parties making these massive arrests. Although he was always a moralist, Hoover's sense of moral righteousness and his sense that the FBI stood as the moral guardian of the nation increased in the late 1930s and early 1940s.[34] Hoover thought of himself as the symbol for the entire FBI and believed that his own self-aggrandizement created a high profile of the organization and promoted public respect for law.[35] Accordingly, his "white slavery" raids were always made to the accompaniment of massive publicity.

"Hoover Seizes 137 in 16 Vice Resorts," heralded the headline on

9. J. Edgar Hoover, 1932. Photograph by Underwood and Underwood. Courtesy of the Library of Congress.

the front page of the *New York Times* for August 30, 1937. This was a simultaneous raid on sixteen different brothels in three states. The article informed its readers that "Mr. Hoover personally led the raiders in two of the Atlantic City places . . . where he declined with thanks the proffered aid of a city policeman."[36] Hoover personally conducted more raiding parties in Baltimore in May 1937[37] and in Connecticut in August 1936.[38] The Baltimore caper required ten months to prepare and yielded almost no one who had violated the Mann Act.[39] Hoover's raiding parties were always extensively reported, and in connection with the Connecticut raid readers were told that "the chief of the G-men had spent three days in that area personally guiding preparations."[40] These personally conducted massive raids continued at least as late as May 1940, when Hoover led a huge vice raid in Miami.[41]

These massive raids were a colorful side story of the enforcement of the Mann Act, but hardly its central plot. An important by-product of vice investigations was the possibility that Hoover could obtain some information he could use to buttress his political position. In July 1949 he advised his agents that during a vice investigation they might come across address books containing data concerning prominent public officials, presumably with names, addresses, and sexual preferences. He ordered that "unless the names appearing therein are material to the investigation, this type of information should be placed in the administrative section."[42] It was in this manner that Hoover gained access to information that he could use to strengthen his political position, by leaking or threatening to leak it to the press.

Hoover was personally interested in the prurient activities of public figures. He took a personal interest in the investigation of Charlie Chaplin's sex life and persuaded the Department of Justice to indict Chaplin for violation of the Mann Act.[43] Hoover also tracked Errol Flynn for years in a vain attempt to uncover a Mann Act charge.[44]

The zeal of their chief toward enforcement of the Mann Act was transmitted to the rank and file of FBI agents. But it was not the self-righteous zealousness of the older days when, as we have seen, volunteers were appointed as Special White Slave Agents and served in the war on vice for minimal compensation. As early as 1921 it was a rule of the department "of long standing" that no person could be commissioned a Special Agent unless they were prepared "to give its work his full time and attention."[45] Thus the worst of abuses was avoided by the increasing professionalism of the FBI.

However, the enforcement of the Mann Act by the FBI continued to be oppressive. The federal use of strong-arm tactics continues today and ought to be intolerable in a free society. It is tolerated because the middle and upper classes refuse to believe that these crude tactics could ever be used against them. Some examples of these tactics used by the FBI included the arrest of doctors who had done nothing more than practice medicine and in that practice had treated prostitutes. They were arrested for "withholding knowledge of a felony," that is the interstate travel of their patients, their names were publicized, and newspaper headlines proclaimed: "2 Doctors Seized as Vice Ring Aides: Atlantic City Physicians Are Linked by Federal Men to White Slave Traffic."[46] The message to doctors was plain: have nothing to do with prostitutes, do not treat them as patients, or we will hassle you. Another common technique, used where the FBI wanted to come down on a targeted defendant, was to put pressure on prostitutes he may have used. The prostitute would be threatened that unless she cooperated in the Mann Act prosecution, she would be arrested and locked up every time she appeared on the street.[47] Then there was the bugging of hotel rooms where targeted defendants stayed, with the hope that the FBI could listen in on some dirt. Charlie Chaplin was treated in this manner.[48]

The most common method of FBI oppression was to threaten the woman, the "victim" involved with an interstate travel. In the early days of Mann Act enforcement the women were routinely locked up to keep them as government witnesses.[49] In 1915 the *Holte* case permitted the victim to be charged with conspiracy, although *Gebardi*, in 1932, limited that prosecutorial option. Even though it was not lawful after 1932, FBI agents were advised in their policy memoranda as late as 1949 that complaints were "usually filed against victims charging conspiracy to keep them in custody." However, if the woman proved to be cooperative, usually because of the charge brought against her, then, in that event, "she is not prosecuted on a charge of conspiracy as United States Attorneys are of opinion she is a most valuable witness." The FBI policy memoranda further suggested, in appropriate cases, that agents threaten a charge of the interstate transportation of venereally infected persons against "subjects and victims with contagious disease . . . who, on interview, have been found to be uncooperative and hostile."[50]

The way this typically worked, especially in noncommercial cases, was that after the couple was arrested, they would be interrogated separately. The woman would be threatened with prosecution with conspiracy. Or perhaps she actually would be prosecuted, and then a sly suggestion of a better deal would be offered. In any event, the value of cooperation would be stressed, and then information would be obtained, such as the route of travel, the names and locations of hotels at which the couple had registered, the names and addresses of other witness, and so forth. Armed with this information, hard evidence could be subpoenaed and brought into court to convict the male offender.

A specific example of the pressure that could be put upon the woman by the FBI comes from a case brought in Mobile, Alabama. An adult man and woman had been living together for a number of years, although unmarried, when they were arrested in 1938. The man was thought to be a petty con man, and, as explained more fully later, that was why he was prosecuted. The woman came from a middle-class family in Mississippi, and the couple had visited there and represented themselves as married. The testimony of the FBI agent regarding his questioning of the woman following their arrest reveals a skillful manipulation, as the agent planted a hope in her anxious mind without making an actual promise:

> I did not talk to both of them in one another's presence. I would talk with one, and then with the other, and play one statement against the other.

> . . . she was anxious to keep from her family any information about being arrested. I subsequently noticed that that was the primary thing in her mind. . . . She said that her family thought that they were married and that she would rather do almost anything than have the true facts get back to them . . . she was concerned about the reaction of her family in Jackson. I did not use the knowledge of her concern in order to secure her signature to sign any statement. I did not tell her that, if she would sign this statement, I would make no further investigation in Jackson, Mississippi. [But] I told her that if she would make a statement and plead guilty to the charges here, that the chances were that the investigation would not be as complete, and [that] it would not be necessary to go into the details, than if she did not, and that was the way that those two signed statements were given.[51]

In 1932, the United States Supreme Court ruled in *Gebardi v. United States*,[52] that merely by consenting to her own transportation for immoral purposes, the woman was not a conspirator. She had to do more, such as purchase the tickets or plan the trip. A decision such as this, had it come twenty years earlier, might have even further encouraged blackmail and extortion, by leaving the woman in a position of impunity from prosecution. However by 1932, noncommercial prosecutions had largely ceased except for targeted defendants or cases of genuine aggravation. There is no evidence that the *Gebardi* decision resulted in an increase in extortion. However, it did decrease the opportunity of the FBI and the prosecutors to threaten the "victim" with conspiracy charges.

The Department of Justice continued to communicate with its local prosecutors through circulars. It circularized the *Gebardi* decision, with the result that it probably inhibited prosecutions for conspiracy more than was truly required by the language of the Court's opinion. Most United States Attorneys read the *Gebardi* case as effectively overruling *Holte* and foreclosing conspiracy prosecutions in the normal situation where only one couple had traveled,[53] although this was not actually demanded by the language of the opinion. If the woman, in a one couple situation, was not a conspirator, then that left no one for the male to conspire with. While he might be guilty of the Mann Act itself, neither would be guilty of conspiracy.

On September 5, 1935, the department issued another general set of guidelines for prosecutions under the Mann Act. Although based on the memorandum issued immediately after *Caminetti* in 1917, it made one interesting change in one of the circumstances regarded as aggravating and therefore encouraging prosecution. The prior circulars of 1917, 1919, and 1929 had referred to violations involving married women with young children and living with their husbands, and where state laws failed to provide adequate punishment. The 1935 re-issue eliminated that particular aspect of the double standard and specified "married persons deserting young children."[54] As a practical matter, the policy had for many years been read in this manner, as a door that swung both ways.

The 1940s brought the specialized problem of offenses committed by military personnel during the war. In early 1943 a policy decision was made that, "except for the most serious charges," federal offenses committed after entrance into the armed forces by military personnel should ordinarily be left to the military justice system. A listing of specific crimes, presumably less serious charges, that should be handled by military authorities, included Mann Act violations.[55]

There was still the occasional legal article decrying the application of the Mann Act to noncommercial interstate travel. "The evils which have grown out of such constructions," one legal writer opined in 1933, "might have been avoided, but now the situation seems to have gotten beyond control. The only way to relieve the situation is for Congress to declare that the act shall not be interpreted to apply to other than commercialized vice."[56] Actually, bills were introduced in both 1934 and 1937 to reduce the scope of the statute concerning noncommercial travel. Neither was reported out of committee.[57]

Politically, it is often far easier to adopt a new law than amend or repeal an old statute. One consequence of the enactment of the Mann Act was that it acquired a real constituency. The law became a symbolic statement of the preferred norm. Church groups and moralists approved the hegemonic statement of the superiority of their own values as shown in the repression of any other. We saw this clearly in the earlier campaign against the possible amendment of the statute to exclude noncommercial journeys. After that campaign and the creation of this constituency, what congressman would dare be counted as standing with the forces of immorality by supporting an amendment?

Even efforts to *toughen* the statute became difficult. There was a lackluster effort by the Attorney General in 1939 to amend the provision concerning the transportation of girls under eighteen. A bill was drafted and forwarded to Congress that would provide greater penalties and eliminate the requirement of that section that a common carrier be the means of transportation.[58] It is not clear whether a bill was actually introduced.

In the realm of noncommercial cases, we have seen the disinterest of United States Attorneys, beginning around 1928, to prosecute cases where there were no aggravating circumstances. That reluctance reappears in the reported appellate cases that are noncommercial for the period of 1928 to 1943. Most present aggravated circumstances, usually that the girl was under eighteen.[59] But occasionally there were also more unusual circumstances. In *United States v. Grace* (1934) a bishop of the "House of Prayer for all People," engaged in sex with a female member of his flock, sometimes at the unusual location of the floor of his chauffeured automobile while motoring through New Jersey. Whether or not this ministration was good for her soul is problematic, but it did result in her pregnancy.[60] In *King v. United States* (1932) a traveling salesman, so the prosecutor alleged, convinced a naive young woman of eighteen that she had a disease which if left uncured would result in her inability to have children. He took her out in the country in the evening, crossing over a state line, to demonstrate the "electrode" that would cure her. Whether he succeeded in alleviating a nonexistent disease is unclear, but he did succeed in seducing the young woman and giving her gonorrhea.[61] There was obviously an advantage taking in these two cases that came, in part, from the defendant's claiming a position of trust. It existed as well in the *Hart* case, seen earlier, involving the married doctor and his young female patient.

In 1933, J. Edgar Hoover wrote that noncommercial Mann Act cases were prosecuted only under aggravated circumstances.[62] This was true for ordinary defendants, and one sees relatively few noncommercial cases that smack of the moral vengeance of the days of the moral crusade.[63] But the federal government continued to use noncommercial Mann Act prosecutions as an instrument of terror to reach and punish defendants it specifically wanted to punish. In other words defendants that met certain categories were selected for harassment. If they could be convicted on tax evasion, that was good. If they could be gotten for the Mann Act, that was fine as well. In other words, noncommercial cases were still prosecuted, during the years of 1929 to 1943, but not at all in an evenhanded way. There were, in other words, some people the federal government simply went out of its way to get. Whatever dirt might stick, that is what the federal prosecutors threw. These selective prosecutions existed throughout the history of the Mann Act, but they became more noticeable from 1929 to 1943, when ordinary noncommercial prosecutions all but disappeared.

Who were these people that were targeted for prosecution? In the context of noncommercial Mann Act prosecutions, and in no particular order, they seemed to fit within four categories. First were gangsters. Second were black men who dared to travel with white girlfriends. Third were persons espousing political opinions obnoxious to the government. During the wars these included German sympathizers and men dating overseas servicemen's wives, and there was always room for radicals on the government's list of enemies. Fourth was a miscellaneous category that included con men, gamblers, brothel owners, and other classes of undesirables.

There is no hard evidence, no smoking gun, that proves that the federal government specifically selected these sorts for Mann Act prosecution, but we can analyze the facts involved in the noncommercial cases for which these types of people were prosecuted. That analysis will show that they were the nonaggravated sorts of noncommercial and "technical" violations that simply were not generally prosecuted during the period after 1928, unless, that is, the violator were among those types selected out for special treatment. Another way of seeing the selectivity of the targets for noncommercial Mann Act prosecution is by noting the glee in the statements of public officials describing the prosecutions and convictions of these gangsters, uppity blacks, political opponents, and other undesirables, as they were accused of committing acts for which others of a more favored class were no longer indicted. To understand this pattern we must look at the facts of several of these cases of selective prosecution. We can start with gangsters.

Jack Gebardi lived with his wife and child in Chicago until their separation in March 1928.[64] He had had an adulterous relationship with Louise Rolfe, an unmarried woman, for a period of several years. Beginning in late December 1928 and continuing for a month they undertook a series of railroad journeys to and from Florida and Mississippi. They resided as husband and wife in various hotels in Miami, Biloxi, and Chicago for periods of one day to three weeks.[65] At the time of these travels Louise Rolfe was divorced and approximately twenty-two years of age. Her lover was twenty-six. Subsequently, Gebardi divorced his wife and married Rolfe.[66]

For these railroad journeys Gebardi and Rolfe were each charged with three counts of conspiracy to violate the Mann Act. Foolishly trusting in the fairness of a federal judge, they waived a jury trial. The judge expressly found that "there was no commercial purpose involved in the transportation" and even that "there was no direct evidence of sexual intercourse." But there was considerable circumstantial evidence of sexual activities and the judge handed the couple a wedding present of two years on each count, or six years of which four were suspended, plus five years probation, for Gebardi, and four months for his wife, Louise.[67]

The effort mounted by the federal government to prosecute the couple was truly monumental. The trial was in Chicago and dozens of witnesses from out of town were subpoenaed and transported to Chicago at government expense. Among the transported witnesses were a motorcycle officer, police desk sergeant, hotel room clerk, and mail carrier from Miami. A railroad auditor came from Wilmington, North Carolina, a baggage agent from Jacksonville, Florida, and conductors from Albany, Georgia, and Cairo, Illinois. Biloxi produced a baggage clerk, baggage porter, truck driver, bell boy, and hotel manager. Two porters were summoned from New Orleans, a passenger agent from St. Augustine, Florida, a credit manager from Dubuque, Iowa, and two ticket agents from Gulfport, Mississippi. There were other prosecution witnesses, also summoned at great expense, including a compensated handwriting expert.[68]

As we have seen, this was not the sort of case that federal prosecutors were eager to file during this period. And the expense to which the government put itself was exceptional. Why? The answer is clear. Jack Gebardi was also known as "Machine Gun" Jack McGurn and in that capacity was a major killer for Al Capone. Hoover himself called Gebardi a "Capone gangster,"[69] and he was strongly suspected of engineering the St. Valentine's Day Massacre in February of 1929. He was charged with the multiple murders of that day's events but never brought to trial.[70]

The government persecuted Gebardi for the alleged Mann Act violation because it wanted to put him away and lacked sufficient evidence to charge a straightforward crime. In the end, the effort did not succeed. The couple was charged only with conspiracy, and Gebardi was not charged with a separate count of his personal violation of the Act. In a unanimous decision the United States Supreme Court reversed their convictions. It held that Louise Rolfe by merely consenting to her own transportation did not do enough to be guilty of conspiracy. Since she could not be a conspirator, there was no one else with whom Gebardi could conspire, as there was no evidence whatsoever of any third person's involvement in arranging for the transportation.[71]

Throughout the years the Attorney General's office continued to select gangsters for prosecution. The real crimes were ones which the government apparently could not prove. But having convicted them of those greater offenses to their own satisfactions, acting as both judge and jury, the prosecutors then turned to the lesser Mann Act violations, even though these lesser offenses went unprosecuted with citizens not on the government's hit list. For example, in September 1950 the Philadelphia United States Attorney went on a crusade and sought to charge gangsters with various federal crimes, including the White Slave Traffic Act.[72] The broad scope of the statute permitted this unintended consequence.

Minneapolis had a similar incident in 1959. Marilyn Ann Tollefson became a prostitute in 1953, and one of her best customers, not her pimp, was Isadore Blumenfield. In July 1954 Tollefson left Minneapolis and plied her trade in New York, Chicago, and other locales, but she would loyally return to Minneapolis from time to time to service her good customer Blumenfield. On May 8, 1956, she and the defendant Blumenfield held a telephone conversation, in which he urged her to come from Chicago to Minneapolis. She complied and, once she was in Minneapolis, engaged in sexual relations with Blumenfield and an associate of his. Blumenfield then paid her $200, presumably in addition to her transportation expenses.

The government prosecuted Blumenfield for a violation of the inducement and persuasion section of the Mann Act, together with conspiracy with another of his associates, not the man who joined him in the prostitute's sexual services. The acts of the other associate in furtherance of the conspiracy were primarily the transportation of Tollefson between the airport and the hotel. The prostitution involved in this case was entirely for the personal benefit of the defendant Blumenfield. He did not "commercialize" the woman, in the language of the FBI bureaucracy, for the purpose of profit.

Ordinarily this sort of "personal use" was not prosecuted in 1960, but the Blumenfield case was a big one. Jury selection alone consumed three days and 485 pages of transcript, and the trial itself lasted five and one-half days. Blumenfield was convicted and given a sentence of two years and a $2,500 fine for the transportation of a $200 prostitute for his own use.[73] But was that the real reason why Blumenfield was punished? It would seem not.

The annual report of the Attorney General for the year in which Blumenfield was convicted crowed loudly about the successful prosecution. It proclaimed that the conviction was the "most notorious" of the year since it "resulted in the conviction of a well-known Minneapolis, Minnesota, underworld figure. The defendant . . . [was] also known as Kid Cann and Fergie Bloom."[74] In other words, Blumenfield was prosecuted because of his status as a person the government regarded as a gangster and not because of what he had done in urging a prostitute to travel from Chicago to Minneapolis to sell him sexual favors. Blumenfield had been tried and acquitted for murder in 1936 and had been publicly accused by a gubernatorial candidate of being a racketeer engaged in selling liquor. He had also been tried in federal court, and acquitted, on charges of looting a local transit company.[75] This prosecution was merely an opportunity for the federal government to "get" someone they wanted to punish for other alleged crimes for which they could not obtain convictions by normal prosecutions.

Black men who dared to date white women were also on the government hit list. It is hard to definitely prove this, since defendants' racial status are generally not noted in the judicial records. But racial motivation can be clearly shown in two spectacular cases with black defendants, one the prosecutions of the heavyweight champion boxer, Jack Johnson, in the years immediately following the passage of the Mann Act, and the second the prosecutions of Chuck Berry, the famous rock and roll star, in 1960 and 1961.

Jack Johnson was a prototype of the independent black man who paid no deference whatsoever to white society or its sensibilities. He wore flashy clothes, drove fast automobiles recklessly, and had numerous brushes with the law. There were lurid tales of his drinking parties, and he constantly appeared with white women, sometimes wives but primarily prostitutes, with whom he traveled about the country. Johnson maintained a stable at his training camps as well, often with two or three favorites at a time, supplemented by local talent.

Prior to 1908 there was a color barrier in professional boxing. White boxers refused to engage blacks, who were thought to have less stamina and weaker stomachs. Boxing slumped economically in 1908, and the reigning heavyweight champion, a Canadian named Tommy Burns, agreed to accept Johnson's challenge. Johnson soundly beat him, and for the first time a black man became the heavyweight champion. There was an immediate outcry in the United States and a search for the Great White Hope, a white boxer who could beat Johnson. The problem, however, was that Johnson consistently won.

A clamor arose that former champion Jim Jeffries come out of retirement. As the sportswriter for the *New York Herald* put it, "Jim Jeffries must now emerge [from retirement] and remove that golden smile from Jack Johnson's face. Jeff, it's up to you. The White Man must be rescued."[76] Eventually Jeffries agreed to fight Johnson. The symbolism and significance of what was billed as the "fight of the century" was apparent to all. Just before the bout Jeffries told his anxious followers that "that portion of the white race that has been looking to me to defend its athletic superiority may feel assured that I am fit to do my very best."[77]

In Reno, Nevada, on July 4, 1910, Jack Johnson knocked out Jim Jeffries. White America was in shock, and rioting broke out among lower-class whites.

> A cartoon in Life magazine graphically portrayed white fears. In the middle of the page stands a large, apelike Johnson. He is smiling, and a halo circles his head. Beneath his right foot is Jeffries's head; he is pushing the white fighter's face into the dirt. No longer the respectful darky asking, hat in hand, for massa's permission, Johnson was seen as the prototype of the independent black who acted as he pleased and accepted no bar to his conduct. As such, Johnson was transformed into a racial symbol that threatened America's social order.[78]

Johnson was riding high for the moment, but was soon to fall. Lucille Cameron was an eighteen-year-old woman who ostensibly worked as a private secretary in Johnson's Chicago restaurant and bar, Cafe de Champion, but in reality was yet another of his mistresses. Before meeting Johnson she had come to Chicago from Minneapolis, where she had worked as a prostitute. Her mother followed her from Minneapolis, insisting that Johnson had some evil influence over the girl. The federal authorities were only too eager to agree with the mother, and in October 1912 they arrested Johnson on charges of abduction and violation of the Mann Act.

The reaction to Johnson's arrest clearly demonstrates the racial nature of the accusations and the federal government's efforts to prosecute the black boxer. Effigies of Johnson were burned in white sections of Chicago, and crowds followed him when he was released on bail, shouting "Lynch him! Lynch the nigger!"[79] The good Christians of the Bible Belt took that recommendation rather literally. The *Beaumont Journal* (Texas) editorialized that "the obnoxious stunts being featured by Jack Johnson are not only worthy of but demand an overgrown dose of Southern 'hospitality.'"[80] The popular journal *Police Gazette* deemed Johnson "the vilest, most despicable creature that lives . . . he has disgusted the American public by flaunting in their faces an alliance as bold as it was offensive."[81]

The federal prosecutors assumed that Lucille Cameron would cooperate, but nevertheless took the precaution of isolating her by confining her in the Rockford, Illinois, jail and not allowing her to communicate with friends or the press, let alone Johnson. On October 22, 1912, the United States prosecutors dragged her before the grand jury, but she sorely disappointed the government by the simple expedient of being honest. Cameron admitted she was a prostitute long before meeting Johnson and refused to implicate Johnson in any way regarding her move from Minneapolis. The federal prosecutors then remanded her back to the Rockford jail, probably as punishment for allowing the truth to come between them and a targeted defendant.

By late October 1912 the Bureau of Investigation had come to believe that it had acted too hastily and had unhelpfully excited the public. The Lucille Cameron charge simply was not sticking. However, Assistant U.S. Attorney Harry A. Parkin reasoned that with Johnson's immense sexual appetite and habit of traveling with a stable of white women, there had to be a Mann Act violation somewhere. He instructed the Bureau of Investigation to find it and to secure evidence of the "transportation by Johnson of any other woman" in violation of the Mann Act. Washington agreed and Attorney General Wickersham wrote the Chicago office of the Bureau that the Department of Justice would cooperate fully in the effort to target Johnson. The Bureau's agents

10. Belle Schreiber, 1910, Jack Johnson's alleged victim. Courtesy of the National Archives.

then roamed through America's black districts and Johnson's former haunts in an effort to come up with something. They eventually happened upon Belle Schreiber.[82]

Belle Schreiber was twenty-three and had been working as a prostitute for two years when she first met Johnson in 1909. After she began servicing Johnson, she was fired from the Everleigh Club, one of America's finest brothels and certainly the best in Chicago. Such a firing was a common fate for white prostitutes who took on black customers. For the next year and a half, she traveled around the country with Johnson sporadically, sometimes staying at his training camps, sometimes meeting him on the road. At times, she was a sort of first among equals, but she was never the only young white woman with whom Johnson was sleeping. When he traveled he had his women stay in different hotels, sometimes even having his wife reside in a separate hotel. He then visited them day or night as the mood struck him, and they were spared the indignity of seeing each other.

By the fall of 1910 Belle Schreiber was working in a Pittsburgh brothel but had just been ejected for robbing a customer. She contacted Johnson and asked him for help. Johnson was apparently in a generous mood. He wired Schreiber $75 and asked her to meet him in Chicago. That was only the beginning. He fronted several thousand dollars to enable her to open up her own establishment. Apparently, he did this gratuitously, with no expectation of reward from the operation of her brothel.

The federal agents were exuberant over finding Belle. The Acting Division Superintendent of the Chicago branch of the Bureau of Investigation exulted to his superior that "we are very much pleased with the prospects of making a case against Johnson."[83] They whisked her secretly before a grand jury in November 1912 and obtained an indictment against Johnson, primarily for his transportation of Schreiber from Pittsburgh to Chicago for personal sexual use and also for the purpose of prostitution. The Southern Christians brayed again. Governor Cole Blease of South Carolina, speaking before the nation's governors, lectured that "the black brute who lays his hands upon a white woman ought not to have any trial."[84]

After Johnson's indictment for the transportation of Belle Schreiber, journalists and others began to question and criticize the continued incarceration of Lucille Cameron. The charges against Johnson for that transportation were finally dismissed, and Lucille herself was released. She went straight to Johnson and in early December 1912 they were married, Johnson's previous white wife having committed suicide three months earlier. It would seem almost impossible for Johnson to further outrage white American opinion, but he succeeded in doing so by this marriage to Lucille Cameron while awaiting trial for the transportation of Belle Schreiber.

11. The boxer Jack Johnson and his wife Lucille Cameron, 1912. Courtesy of the National Archives.

While awaiting trial, the government had to contend with Belle Schreiber. She proved to be very erratic in temperament. She was not technically in custody, but the government moved her about the country, from city to city, pampered her, took her to the theater and to dinners—anything to keep her in the good graces of the government and also out of Johnson's contact. Twice Johnson offered to plead guilty and pay a substantial fine on the condition that he would not be sentenced to prison. The government, however, wanted to wreak its vengeance on this targeted defendant and twice refused.[85]

Johnson was tried in May 1913, and convicted of transporting Schreiber from Pittsburgh to Chicago for the purposes of prostitution, and also for "other immoral purposes," that is his own sexual use. The racial basis for the prosecution is shown once again by the reaction to the verdict. The *Boston Globe* reported "general rejoicing all over the city when the news of the finding of the jury became known."[86] After the verdict the federal prosecutor told the press that "this negro, in the eyes of many, has been persecuted. Perhaps as an individual he was. But it was his misfortune to be the foremost example of the evil in permitting the intermarriage of whites and blacks."[87] This is an incredible statement when it is recalled that the facts of this prosecution had absolutely nothing to do with either of Johnson's white wives. This racial motivation is also shown in the remarks of United States District Judge George Carpenter, at the time of his sentencing of Johnson, in explanation of why a fine would not be sufficient:

> The circumstances in this case have been aggravating. The life of the defendant by his own admissions has not been a moral one. The defendant is one of the best-known men of his race and his example has been far-reaching.[88]

In actuality, however, the federal judiciary, by the lights of the day, was quite fair to Johnson, far more so, certainly, than the federal prosecutor. The appellate court strongly criticized the prosecution for making contentions before the jury for which it had no evidence, overstepping the proper bounds of cross-examination, and creating "an atmosphere of prejudice that pervades the record." It reversed the "purpose of prostitution" charges and called the government's evidence that Johnson had a financial interest in Belle Schreiber's brothel "slight and dubious."

However, the appellate court affirmed the conviction for "other immoral purposes" on the basis that the Mann Act was violated merely "by evidence that transportation was furnished for the purpose of enabling the defendant to have sexual intercourse with the woman."[89] It remanded the case for resentencing in light of its reversal of the prostitution feature in April 1914. But by that time the matter was moot; Jack

Johnson had fled the country on a sojourn that took him throughout Europe and into Mexico. He lost his heavyweight title in a 1915 match he fought in Cuba. In 1920 he voluntarily surrendered to American authorities and served his original prison term of one year. Ultimately, he died in an automobile accident in 1946.

In the late 1950s Chuck Berry was probably the most creative song-writer in the rock and roll genre, responsible for such hits as "Maybellene" (1955), "Roll Over Beethoven" (1956), and "Johnny B. Goode" (1958), to name just a few. But, as was noted by a commentator on the MacNeil/Lehrer NewsHour in 1987, Berry's "fondness for women, women of all ages, women of all colors . . . proved his downfall in 1959 when he was twice charged with violation of the Mann Act. Many think Berry's two trials were blatantly racist and that he was railroaded into a three year prison sentence."[90]

Actually, there two different women and three trials. The first incident began on June 2, 1958, when Berry had a flat tire on a bridge in St. Charles, Missouri. A state patrol officer arrested him after discovering a gun and a large amount of money. Also arrested was Joan Mathis, a young lady of French descent, but not a minor. According to Berry they had met a year earlier at a concert and "she had traveled along with me to visit people she knew in the area and see the Topeka concert,"[91] from which he was returning to his home in St. Louis. Ms. Mathis later told Berry that when she was interrogated "she had insistently stated that she had not been molested although some officer encouraged her to declare that such was my intention."[92] No Mann Act charges were leveled immediately.

About a year later, in August 1959, there was a well-publicized incident in Meridian, Mississippi, when, following a show, several young people crowded onto the stage. "One of the girls threw her arms around me and hung a soul-searching kiss that I let hang a second too long." One of the men then drew a knife, while another clamored, "this nigger asked my sister for a date!" The promoter of the concert escorted Berry out of the building and delivered him to the local sheriff who relieved Berry of all the money found on his person, as an advance payment of a fine for disturbing the peace.[93]

In the first half of December 1959 Berry and a small band were engaged in a tour of the Southwest, including gigs in Texas, Arizona, New Mexico, and Colorado. Just before a concert in El Paso, Berry picked up a girl in Juárez, Mexico. Janice Norine Escalante was an

Apache Indian girl, perhaps as young as fourteen years old, who was already working as a prostitute in Juárez. Berry offered her a job, to join his tour and sell photographs at concerts, and once back in his base of St. Louis to serve as a hatcheck girl at the nightclub he owned. She accepted his offer. For the next two weeks as they traveled about, Berry and the girl occupied the same hotel rooms, and the evidence seems overwhelming that they engaged in sex.

The girl did work as Berry's hatcheck girl upon his return to St. Louis in mid-December, but within a few days there was a parting of the ways, the girl saying Berry in effect ditched her, Berry claiming she had reverted to her prior profession of prostitution. In any event, she called the police,[94] and Mann Act charges followed.

Because of the age of the girl the prosecution would appear at first as well within the guidelines for aggravation. But the racial motivation of the federal prosecutors to target Berry appears clear from the total context. Berry went to trial in March 1960. In January of 1960 the government secured an indictment for the transportation of Joan Mathis, a full year and one-half earlier. The motive for the Mathis indictment appears clearly to prejudice Berry before the pool of jurors who would be trying him in the Escalante case. When the prosecution came to trial, the trial judge made racial slurs toward Berry and acted with such an unfair attitude toward him that the appellate court reversed his conviction on that ground.[95]

When the Mathis case came to trial, the federal prosecutor riddled her with questions designed to prove Berry's immoral purpose, such as "How aggressive was he?" and "How did he approach you intimately?" But Mathis did not consider herself a victim, refused to perjure herself for the benefit of the federal prosecutors' racism, and the government's case made no headway. Finally, the prosecutor asked her, "Well, are you in love with him?" to which she answered "Well . . . yes I am." Thereupon, the case was dismissed by the government without submission to the jury. A few days later, according to Berry, Joan Mathis called Berry to congratulate him on the victory and wish him well with the Escalante trial. Berry explains:

> I never heard from or of her again, but I will always know of one girl who to my own estimation, and I should know, did not actually love me but was bold enough to conceive the injustice that was flowing in my direction, and chose to open herself to what was then considered indignity by declaring that she was in love with a Negro.[96]

On the second Escalante trial the racial slurs continued. Berry had a long-time business associate and secretary, a white woman named Francine Gillium. The federal prosecutor insulted her, using phrases such as, "This blonde claims to be a secretary" and demanding answers to questions such as, "What kind of secretarial duties do you perform?" and "Did you tell your people you work for a Negro?"[97] But Berry was convicted and sentenced to serve three years and pay a fine of $5,000.[98] He was released on parole after serving twenty months.[99]

Berry's two prosecutions were both for noncommercial violations. The Mathis prosecution, with a "victim" who was adult and willing, would never have been brought by 1960 but for a racial motive. Although the Escalante woman's transportation was clearly within the guidelines for aggravation, there is even some doubt as to it. Her age was apparently never definitely substantiated, and she looked more mature than fourteen. Additionally, she was a prostitute before Berry met her. The impact on Berry was great. Although he would later make a partial comeback, as one pop music critic wrote, Berry's "career was practically undone by sex when he was incarcerated on a questionable Mann Act conviction . . . at his creative peak."[100]

Political irritants to the federal government also were likely to find themselves prosecuted if occasion presented itself. There is a grave danger in a statute such as the Mann Act where the prosecutor enjoys such a wide freedom of prosecution. Supreme Court Justice Robert H. Jackson put the problem well in 1940, when serving as Attorney General:

> [It is when] the prosecutor picks some person whom he dislikes or desires to embarrass, or selects some group of unpopular persons and then looks for an offense, that the greatest danger of abuse of prosecuting power lies. It is here that law enforcement becomes personal, and the real crime becomes that of being unpopular with the predominant or governing group, being attached to the wrong political views, or being personally obnoxious to or in the way of the prosecutor himself.[101]

Most of the politically inspired charges revolved around men having affairs with women whose husbands were overseas with the American military in the World Wars. The reasons for the proposed prosecutions must be seen from the context. For example, when a University of Chicago sociology professor was arrested with his paramour in a Chicago hotel in April 1918, the *New York Times* noted in its lead paragraph that the woman was the wife of a Texas man then with the American army in France. The newspaper noted that the culprits were interrogated by the district attorney "in the presence of an assistant skilled in Mann act [*sic*] proceedings."[102] Likewise, during the Second World War, if defendants in noncommercial cases were involved with women whose husbands were overseas at war, that fact was prominently mentioned in the opinions on their appeal, suggesting that this is why the prosecutions likely were initiated.[103] Indeed, at the close of World War II a formal proposal was made in the Justice Department to make an exception to the general policy of not prosecuting "personal escapade," or noncommercial cases, under circumstances where the woman was a wife of an overseas serviceman.[104]

The March 1942 prosecution of John Tilley illustrates the political nature of some prosecutions. Tilley was a 43-year-old man, married with one child, but separated from his wife. He lived in Rock Island, Illinois; his wife and child lived in Chicago. He worked in the sensitive position of armament machinist in the Rock Island Arsenal. Tilley had a girlfriend and on a few occasions the couple would cross over the Mississippi River to Davenport or Clinton, Iowa, register at a hotel as man and wife, stay overnight, and have sexual relations. The woman was an adult and single. It was not an aggravated case according to the guidelines, since, because Tilley was already separated, the relationship did not result in abandonment of wife and child.

What really bothered the government was the suspicion that Tilley was gathering information for the Germans during this early stage of World War II. Indeed, the FBI report is much more concerned about Tilley's possible German sympathies and espionage activities than with the Mann Act violation. The FBI reported that the Military Intelligence Division had conducted an extensive investigation on suspicion of espionage, but had determined only that Tilley was strongly anti-British, had traveled in Europe in 1938, and was having information properly obtained through his position at the arsenal unnecessarily typed, but with "no evidence that this information is being furnished to outside sources."

The FBI tried its hand. It learned that a woman the suspect once dated, not the victim, and her mother "became suspicious of subject because he was very secretive concerning his associates, appeared to be extremely interested in anything pertaining to the Army or the Rock Island Arsenal, and spoke of traveling in Germany, France, Italy and

England." A personal surveillance revealed nothing of interest, and even a mail interdiction "produced nothing of significance." A police detective reported that he had learned that Tilley "talks German frequently," and even more alarming news came from a young woman he had once taken to a movie. Tilley had "appeared to be bored at the singing of the national anthem, remarking that 'Germany is not defeated yet' and 'Germany is a wonderful and powerful country.'"

These were dangerous sentiments to hold in an America at war. If the government could not prove espionage, it at least could suspend him from employment at the arsenal and charge him with the heinous crime of taking his girlfriend across the river for a romantic evening. But this politically motivated prosecution proved to be of no avail to the federal government; the jury acquitted Tilley.[105]

The most elaborate political prosecution was that of Charlie Chaplin, the "little guy" of the movies, selected for special treatment by J. Edgar Hoover personally on account of Chaplin's alleged radical political ideas.

In June 1941, Tim Durant, a friend of Chaplin's, brought Joan Barry to meet Charlie at a dinner at Perino's. Barry had furnished Durant with a letter of introduction from an associate of J. Paul Getty, the oilman. Barry had been and would continue to be a close friend of Getty. She wanted to become an actress and Getty arranged an introduction.

Chaplin was in his mid-fifties, separated from Paulette Goddard, his third wife, and vulnerable. Years after the event he described Barry as a "big handsome woman of twenty-two, well built, with upper regional domes immensely expansive."[106] Barry later claimed it was Chaplin who did the chasing, and Chaplin claimed the reverse. He wrote in his autobiography that "persistence is the road to accomplishment. Thus she achieved her object and I began to see her often."[107] She became his mistress, and during the summer and fall of 1941 she visited him five or six times a week, which diminished to three times a week by midwinter and thereafter.[108] Barry must have been a busy young lady since during her affair with Chaplin she continued to see other men, including a trip in May 1942 to Tulsa to see Getty.[109]

At some point Chaplin noticed that she read a script well. He did a screen test, put her on payroll with a contract and modest salary, and sent her to a well-regarded acting school. But by the spring of 1942 the affair unraveled. Chaplin complained that she showed up at his home without notice, at all hours of the night, and often drunk. Then he discovered that she had not been attending her classes. When he confronted her, Barry announced that she no longer wished to be an actress, and that if he would give her $5,000 and pay for her way (and that of her mother as well) to New York, she would release him from the filming contract. Chaplin claimed he did so and was "glad to be rid of her."[110] But if Barry left, she quickly returned to Hollywood.

Barry claimed that Chaplin asked her to go to New York in the fall of 1942. This was the trip that resulted in the Mann Act prosecution. Chaplin was to make a speech there in October and, according to Barry, he told her "'I'd like you to be near me.'"[111] Both Chaplin and Barry later were in agreement that Chaplin paid for her transportation to New York and back to Hollywood, and that Chaplin neither traveled with her, nor paid her hotel bills in New York, at a different hotel than where he stayed.[112] Chaplin claimed Barry came to his hotel room at her request, for one-half hour, there was no sex, and Tim Durant was present at all times. Barry claimed he summoned her to his hotel room, but only on one night of a 23-day stay, that she stayed three hours, and they had sex.

Their relationship was cool when they returned to Hollywood, and Barry admitted she broke into Chaplin's house with a gun in late December, forced her way into his bedroom and held him at gunpoint. Chaplin claimed she threatened his life; Barry said she intended to commit suicide. Chaplin said he calmed her down and persuaded her to sleep it off in another bedroom; Barry claimed he talked her out of the gun and into his bed for another round of sex. During the next few days at the end of December 1942, Barry was a pathetic figure. While drunk she tried several times to see Chaplin, but he refused her admittance. Her hotel evicted her over an unpaid bill. On January 1, 1943, she took an overdose of barbiturates and the Beverly Hills police arrested her for vagrancy. The local court placed her on probation with a condition she leave town. She left for New York on January 5, 1943, via Tulsa.

Barry returned in spring 1943, claiming she was destitute and pregnant. Chaplin said he could not be the father (blood tests later proved he was not) and would not see her. When she persisted, he had her arrested, and she was jailed for violating her probation. Then she contacted two leading Hollywood gossip columnists, Hedda Hopper and Florabel Muir, and planned her revenge.[113] Until then there had been little publicity about the affair. But that changed quickly. The federal authorities were alerted when, on June 3, 1943, Joan Barry filed a paternity suit, claiming Chaplin was the father of her unborn child.[114]

12. Charlie Chaplin being booked for violation of the Mann Act. Looking on, in rear, is his attorney, Jerry Giesler. From *New York Times*, February 15, 1944, p. 34. Courtesy, AP/Wide World Photos.

On June 24, 1943, the Los Angeles Special Agent in Charge sent J. Edgar Hoover a memo about Chaplin's activities, with a follow-up on August 20 that Chaplin had paid for Barry's tickets to New York. On this memo Hoover wrote, "Shouldn't we run this down? If a White Slave violation, we ought to go after it vigorously." On August 20, Hoover ordered his Los Angeles office to "expedite investigation."[115] A massive investigation was initiated into Chaplin's alleged Mann Act violation. By December Hoover was worried that Chaplin might try to flee the country, perhaps to the Soviet Union. He ordered the Los Angeles agents, "give immediate attention. Don't let this fellow do a run out," and the Los Angeles office dutifully alerted the West Coast border stations to put out a stop order.[116] The FBI bugged Chaplin's hotel rooms, conducted an intensive investigation into his sex life, and shared information with the gossip columnists, Florabel Muir and Hedda Hopper. In turn, the columnists cooperated by attacking Chaplin's politics in print during late 1943 and early 1944 and even testifying before the grand jury that indicted Chaplin. Once the four-month investigation was complete, Hoover persuaded the Justice Department to seek an indictment.[117] The indictments of Chaplin for Mann Act violations that were handed down on February 10, 1944, made headlines in the following day's editions of the *New York Times* and the *Chicago Tribune.*

Joan Barry was a pathetic woman, but certainly no victim of a classic sort. Nor, as we have seen, were noncommercial cases involving the consensual lust of two single individuals generally prosecuted in 1944. Most important, the case was very weak. The government would be urging the jury to believe that sexual intent motivated Chaplin to transport Barry and her mother to New York, when out of their 23-day stay the lovers met only once for a few hours, and with sharply divided testimony as to whether on that occasion they engaged in sex. There were a lot of things that did not add up. Why then the prosecution?

Chaplin first came to the Bureau's attention in 1922 when he held a reception for William Z. Foster, a leader of the American Communist Party, who was visiting Hollywood. A copy of the report was routed to Hoover. Throughout the early 1940s Chaplin flirted with "progressive" politics and was especially involved with visiting Soviet artists, diplomats, and various Soviet-American friendship groups. In April 1943, for example, he was a sponsor of the National Council of American-Soviet Friendship. After Hitler attacked the Soviet Union, he worked vigorously on Second Front activities, a movement to encourage an immediate invasion of Europe and thereby relieve Germany's military pressure on the Soviet Union.

Chaplin made several speeches supporting a Second Front and used language that could be interpreted as pro-Communist. He began one talk with "Dear Comrades" and went on to emphasize his pleasure to use that word. At another time he said, "after the war Communism may spread over [the] world."[118] A major purpose of Chaplin's trip to New York, during which he met with Joan Barry, was to speak at Carnegie Hall on October 16, 1942, at a rally in support of a Second Front.

This political involvement, of course, did not go unnoticed. On December 12, 1942, the conservative columnist Westbrook Pegler wrote "after years of sly pretending . . . [Chaplin] has frankly allied himself with the pro-Communist actors and writers of the theater and the movies."[119] The Los Angeles FBI office regularly reported on his Second Front activities and enthusiasm for entertaining visiting Soviet artists. On December 3, 1942, it reported that Chaplin said in a speech, "'I am not a Communist, but I am pretty pro-Communist.'" It was enough for J. Edgar Hoover's FBI to want to take on Chaplin, and if the Mann Act were the best method, so be it. Significantly, another FBI report stated "never did either BERRY[120] or her attorney request this investigation or express a desire for the Government to take action against CHAPLIN."[121] They hardly needed to, the federal government was already so eager.

Chaplin hired prominent attorney Jerry Giesler to defend him. The press coverage was almost entirely one-sided, against Chaplin.[122] The seven-woman, five-man jury[123] listened as Chaplin "almost shouted his denial" of sex after Barry broke into his house, as he also "denied emphatically" any sexual intimacy in New York with Barry.[124] Giesler wrote later that Chaplin was "the best witness I've ever seen in a law court. . . . He looked helpless, friendless and wistful, as he sat there with the weight of the whole United States Government against him."[125] The judge specifically instructed that commercial motive or pecuniary gain were unnecessary and that the Government's case would be proved if it believed Chaplin aided Barry's transportation for the purpose of her "having illicit sexual relations with him."[126]

The jury was out almost seven hours, eventually acquitting Chaplin.[127] As Chaplin was thanking the jury, one of the female jurors told him, "It's all right, Charlie. It's still a free country."[128] But only apparently if a targeted defendant had the wealth or wits to stay clear of the clutches of the federal government.

Yet another broad class of defendants was targeted for noncommercial prosecutions. It is hard to categorize this group other than to say they were persons of general undesirability. It included Joseph Conforte, the owner of the nation's largest, and legal, brothel, in Storey County, near Reno, Nevada. In 1968 he was indicted and tried in Reno for a violation of the Mann Act. The case was so weak that the trial judge granted a motion for acquittal at the conclusion of the government's case.[129]

It is a big jump from Joe Conforte to Edward Y. Clarke, in the early 1920s the Imperial Giant and sometime Imperial Wizard of the Ku Klux Klan. But they share in common the government's sense of their general undesirability. In the early 1920s, J. Edgar Hoover collected information about the sexual practices of this leader of the Klan.[130] This resulted in a March 1, 1923, indictment for the transportation of

13. Joan Barry, Charlie Chaplin's alleged victim, conferring with U.S. Attorney Charles H. Carr at Chaplin's Mann Act trial. Courtesy, AP/Wide World Photos.

a woman from Houston to New Orleans. The charges did not allege prostitution, only an immoral purpose, and the case was undoubtedly noncommercial in nature.[131] Clarke was apparently unmarried, and eventually pled guilty to the charge and was fined $5,000, a considerable sum in the 1920s.[132] This case probably would have been prosecuted in any event in 1923, the period of the morals crusade, but the fact that Hoover went out of his way to collect data about a particular individual indicates that Clarke was targeted because of his role as leader in the Klan.

Marco Reginelli is another example of the sort of defendant who was prosecuted because of his status as an undesirable person. He was hounded and persecuted, thrown into a federal jail for six months, deprived of naturalization, and would have been deported except for the reasonableness of a judge who prevented it, because of a ten-day sojourn he and his adult girlfriend spent together in a state other than their residence. Both were single and both were adult. The date was

1942, a time when noncommercial violations of the Mann Act were not generally prosecuted.

The real reason Reginelli was prosecuted had little to do with his invitation to his girlfriend to join him in Florida. This was an excuse. The motivation behind the prosecution was that Reginelli had gambling interests in New Jersey and was therefore deemed undesirable by the federal prosecutors. We have met Reginelli before in the first chapter and will meet him again in the last.

A final example of the selectivity of prosecutions for noncommercial violations is the case of Gerald Mackreth and Clemmie Rushing, tried for Mann Act offenses in Mobile, Alabama, in 1938. Rushing was thirty-three years old and her boyfriend was slightly older. They had both been married and were divorced when they began living together in 1934. They traveled around the country together and registered at various hotels as man and wife, sometimes under fictitious names. The boyfriend was engaged in buying and selling securities of questionable value. He supported the woman entirely, and there was no question that there was no prostitution activity at all. They were simply a couple who traveled about, acting as though married when they were not.

Why then were they picked on by a selective federal prosecution and the man sentenced to two years in prison, at a time when noncommercial offenses were no longer generally prosecuted? The answer is found in the nature of some of the evidence introduced by the prosecutor, designed to show the jury why this defendant ought to be punished:

> Over the objection of defendants, the government introduced evidence in chief tending to show the man had served a term in a penitentiary, had been indicted in Jackson, Mississippi, had engaged in swindling operations in connection with his business and that, to some extent, the woman had aided him in these swindling operations.

Apparently the government could not prove these allegations to the extent needed to sustain a conviction for fraud or any other crime, so the United States Attorney settled for the Mann Act on the theory that these were bad people and ought to be charged with something. Hence, the prosecution for something not ordinarily prosecuted. The appellate court reversed on the basis of *Gebardi*, as the couple had only been charged with a conspiracy to arrange the woman's transportation. However, the court also described the evidence of the man's imprisonment, indictment, and swindling as irrelevant to the Mann Act charge.

"Its admission was highly prejudicial and seriously affected the sub-stantial rights of the defendants," said the court.[133] That innuendo, the fobbing off onto the jury of the *real* reasons for this prosecution, was, of course, exactly what the federal prosecutors wished to accomplish.

In the years between 1929 and 1943, the focus of Mann Act prosecu-tion shifted from a morals crusade to prostitution violations, excepting the few categories of noncommercial violations that were still prose-cuted, namely, the aggravated cases and those cases where the defen-dants were within a selective and targeted class. But there was still the element of a crusade, as shown in Hoover's highly publicized raids. It was just a different target. Nonetheless, in the next fifteen years, from 1944 to 1959, the crusade itself, the enthusiasm behind the concept of the Mann Act, would begin to sputter.

The Crusade Sputters, 1944–1959

A person may take an interstate trip for multiple purposes, and sexual intercourse may be a large aspect of that journey or may be merely incidental. Prior to 1944 there was a welter of precedent regarding the relation of different purposes to the trip as a whole, and how much of an "immoral" purpose in a particular trip made the intent within the prohibited purposes of the Mann Act. This question arose almost exclusively in noncommercial cases; if a man intended to prostitute the woman transported or induced to travel, the purpose of the travel would be clearly within the statute. However, the vagueness of the phrase "or any other immoral purpose" left room for many questions in the noncommercial context.

Earlier precedent had established that the mere fact a man had sexual intercourse with a woman to whom he was not married, following an interstate trip with her, did not in itself violate the Mann Act. The *Fisher* case of 1920 is illustrative. The defendant lived near Wheeling, West Virginia, and became acquainted at a carnival with a sixteen-year-old girl who lived just across the river in Ohio. They began a casual affair, the activities of which were at first confined to Ohio. One day the girl showed up in Wheeling, packed suitcase in hand. There was some doubt, but apparently she came of her own accord and without his knowledge. Defendant installed his young paramour in a boarding house in Wheeling. He visited her nightly for some two weeks and enjoyed her favors. He frequently took her out for rides in his automobile, and one day they crossed over the Ohio River to call on the girl's mother and sister in Ohio. After a few hours they returned to Wheeling, and the defendant continued his nocturnal calls. He was prosecuted for the travel from Ohio to West Virginia when returning from the girl's relatives.

The trial judge instructed the jury that if the defendant brought the girl back from the visit to her mother and sister in Ohio with the purpose of continuing his intercourse with her, he violated the statute and it was the jury's duty to find him guilty. Not so, said the appellate court. The day's outing across the river was a "mere incident" of their association, and that travel did not in any way "contribute" to their immoral conduct. The defendant probably had in mind, while taking the day's excursion over the state line, that he would, after their return to Wheeling, "continue to do what he had been doing." But that does not amount to a violation of the Act.

The court reasoned that "the interstate transportation . . . must have for its object, or be a means of effecting, or at least of facilitating, the sexual intercourse . . . the mere fact that a journey from one state to another is followed by such intercourse, when the journey was not for that purpose, but wholly for other reasons [in this case, to visit the girl's relatives], to which intercourse was not related, cannot be regarded as a violation of the statute."[1] Of course, what is or is not a "mere incident" is a matter of fine interpretation, and the cases involving this principle seemed to go in every direction, sometimes leading to acquittal and at other times to conviction.

Another confusing line of cases held that if the sole purpose of the trip were legitimate, then a purely incidental intent to have intercourse was not a violation. In *Van Pelt v. United States* (1917), the defendant, Rinker Van Pelt, aged thirty-five and divorced, began a sexual relationship with a fourteen-year-old girl in Augusta County, Virginia. She permitted him to have sex with her whenever he wanted, which worked out to about twice a week, and this pattern continued for over three years. This may or may not have violated the Virginia statutory rape statute, depending on how it then read, but it clearly did not violate the Mann Act since the activities through 1913 all took place in Virginia.

In October 1913 the girl, then seventeen, realized that she was pregnant and asked Rinker to find a place of confinement for her before her condition became obvious. The relationship had been unknown in the community in which they both lived. He made arrangements with a midwife in Baltimore, reimbursed the girl for the cost of the train ticket, and she left her small town on January 30, 1914, ostensibly traveling alone. By prior arrangement he met her on the train. They stopped for the night in Washington, and in a hotel there he had sex with her. Continuing on together to Baltimore the next day, Rinker once again had intercourse with the girl, after which she remained with the midwife until the birth of their child, and without the defendant's further attentions.

Van Pelt was prosecuted and convicted on the basis of the trip to Baltimore and the sex that occurred in Washington and upon their arrival in Baltimore. Not enough, said the appellate court, reversing. There must be evidence that the defendant arranged the transportation so that he "might more surely, more readily, or more safely induce her to yield to his wishes." But there was no evidence that the defendant held any such purpose for their trip to Baltimore.

The appellate court concluded that there was no possible reason "why he should have gone to the trouble and expense of having her make such a trip . . . merely in order that he might twice more exercise a liberty which he had taken hundreds of times before, and could just as well have taken an indefinite number of times more, if she had remained at home . . . there can be no doubt that the girl was brought to Baltimore in order that she might go into seclusion during the later months of her pregnancy and have care. . . ." The court suggested that it would be a different case had *defendant* moved to Baltimore and induced her to join him so that sex could continue. But in this case, "the defendant may have anticipated that while on the journey he would gratify his desire, as he doubtless would have done, had the trip never been taken; but there is no evidence . . . that such anticipation played any part whatever in inducing him to arrange for her coming to Baltimore."[2]

Other cases excluded incidental sex from the Act if the sole purpose of the trip were legitimate,[3] but again there was ambiguity. If there were a dual purpose to the trip, one legitimate and one immoral, the man was guilty. Indeed, *Van Pelt* was a split decision and the dissenting judge in the 2–1 decision regarded the defendant's purposes as two, one of which was to continue his debauchery. Two early cases illustrate this principle.

George Carey was a dentist in Remsen, Iowa. In September 1914 he seduced his fiancée under promise of marriage and enjoyed a steady sexual relationship until February 1915, when he moved to Bancroft, Nebraska. They had a few more encounters in the fall of 1915, and in November the woman, an adult, discovered she was pregnant. Thereafter, there were two interstate trips and sojourns at hotels, during which, after "talking over what was to be done to relieve her condition," Carey, in the quaint language of the court, "again possessed her." The defendant insisted that the purpose of the trips was to talk over her condition. Indeed, following the trips, Carey arranged for the expenses of her confinement and the birth. The appellate court was willing to concede that discussion of her pregnancy was "one object, possibly the main object" of Carey inducing her into interstate travel. But it was enough for conviction if intercourse was one of his purposes, and there was an ample basis for "a conclusion by the jury that he had the old motive also in mind."[4]

In *Ghadiali v. United States,*[5] defendant Dinshah Ghadiali employed a nineteen-year-old woman as his secretary. They began an affair in September 1924 which continued on "intermittently" until April 1925. Toward the end of their relationship defendant Ghadiali transported her from New Jersey to Los Angeles and then to Portland, continuing to enjoy, en route, the same combined benefit of her secretarial skills and sexual favors as he had even before the trip began. The girl testified that while she was in his employ he exercised an influence over her which she "could not throw off." She stated: "I had no will power of my own, and somehow or other, whenever I had the desire to go away, I felt something that was drawing me back. I did not have any will power to act and stand on my own feet." Defendant acknowledged he was a master hypnotist and a mesmerist and it was the prosecution's theory that he had mesmeric control over the young woman. That may be true, but the skeptic may be forgiven the thought that the story offered a convenient way for the woman to avoid any personal responsibility for her conduct.

The appellate court stated that the evidence was such that the jury could conclude that one purpose of the transportation was to continue the girl's sexual favors and reasoned that "if, in addition to the secretarial duties, it was also his purpose to have sexual intercourse with her . . . he would be guilty. It was lawful to transport her in interstate commerce as his secretary, but unlawful to have her as his mistress as well."

Carey and Ghadiali received very different sentences, even though their affairs continued for about the same length of time. Their paramours both became pregnant, Carey's mistress carrying her baby and Ghadiali's being aborted. Carey was married to a different woman at time of trial, which might possibly have justified a stiffer sentence. But

Carey, a white dentist, received a punishment of three *months* in jail. Ghadiali, doubtlessly a dark-skinned foreigner and a "mesmerist" by trade, received a sentence of five *years* in prison and a fine of $5,000. Carey was tried in Nebraska and Ghadiali in Oregon, states not dissimilar in legal and social cultures. Neither was tried in the South. The racism and class bias thus displayed reflects the general, and not regional, prejudices of the federal judiciary.

It is clear from these cases that while the law might be easy to state, it was difficult to apply to interstate journeys where multiple purposes existed. It was not until 1944 that the United States Supreme Court attempted to clarify this murky situation. Almost all of the multiple purpose cases had occurred in noncommercial contexts. Ironically, it was a prostitution case in which the Supreme Court first laid down its views in this area of Mann Act law.

In 1940 Hans Pete Mortensen and his wife Lorraine owned and operated a small family business in Grand Island, Nebraska. They occupied a fifteen-room second story of a building located on the edge of the business district and operated it as a rooming house and brothel under the suggestive, if understated, name of "Nifty Rooms." In August 1940 the couple planned a trip from Nebraska to Salt Lake City, Utah, in order to visit Mrs. Mortensen's relatives. Two of the women who had worked about a year as prostitutes in the Mortensens' brothel asked to be taken along for a vacation.

The couple, Hans Pete and Lorraine Mortensen plus Margaret Smith and Doris McMahon, the two employees, set out on August 22, 1940. In good middle-class form, Mr. Mortensen drove the family car. They motored westward, visited Yellowstone National Park, and then drove on to Salt Lake City. At Salt Lake they stayed in a tourist camp for five or six days. All four visited Mrs. Mortensen's parents, and, in addition, Margaret and Doris went to various shows, visited the Salt Lake parks, and took in other local sights. No acts of prostitution occurred during the entire trip, nor was there any discussion of their business. The two employees paid their own living expenses during the trip, and their employers paid for the transportation. In short, it was a *bona fide* vacation.

The four vacationers returned by way of Colorado and, once back in Grand Island, the two women resumed their work as prostitutes.[6] The federal government prosecuted the Mortensens for the return trip, alleging that the purpose of the interstate journey, that is the return portion from Salt Lake, Utah, to Grand Island, Nebraska, was for the two women to engage in prostitution. Doubtless in an effort to prejudice the defendants before the jury, the federal prosecutor introduced considerable evidence concerning the irrelevant details of the brothel's operation for two years before the journey and a year afterward. The jury convicted, and the federal judge handed the defendants what he deemed a suitable reward for their kindness in providing vacations to their employees: three years in prison and a $1,000 fine for the husband and three years in prison for the wife.[7]

The Eighth Circuit Court of Appeal affirmed in a 2–1 decision. The dissenting judge wrote that "splitting the round trip up into two transportations, innocent while outward bound but criminal on the homeward lap, seems to me a mental operation that reflects ingenuity of the prosecutor rather than fair application of the Act . . . I can discern only one intent . . . and that was to take a vacation. They went away with that intent and held to it till they got back."[8]

The Supreme Court agreed to review the conviction and by a 5–4 margin agreed with previous dissent. The Court, Justice Frank Murphy writing for the bare majority, held that "to constitute a violation of the Act, it is essential that the interstate transportation have for its object or be the means of effecting or facilitating the proscribed activities. . . . An intention that the women or girls shall engage in [prostitution, debauchery, or other immoral purpose] . . . *must be the dominant motive of such interstate movement* [emphasis supplied]. And the transportation must be designed to bring about such result. Without that necessary intention and motivation, immoral conduct during or following the journey is insufficient."

Murphy then applied his legal reasoning to the facts of the *Mortensen* case. He wrote that "the sole purpose of the journey from beginning to end was to provide innocent recreation and a holiday for petitioners and the two girls. It was a complete break or interlude in the operation of petitioners' house of ill fame and was entirely disassociated therefrom. . . . The return journey under the circumstances of this case cannot be considered apart from its integral relation with the innocent round trip as a whole."[9]

The federal courts then began to apply this new test of "dominant motive" to ambiguous cases. The reaction of the lower federal courts throughout the 1940s was hostile toward *Mortensen*. When faced with an issue of dual motives for a trip, courts were quick to distinguish the

Supreme Court's ruling on the basis that the *sole* purpose for the journey in *Mortensen* had been a vacation.

In October 1944 the Fourth Circuit considered *Simon v. United States*.[10] A married defendant, separated from his wife, moved in with the wife and six children of a soldier who was off to war. Obviously, all of the patriotic instincts of jurors and judges were stacked against such a defendant, and a state judge in Virginia ordered Simon to leave the woman's home. His response was to move to Tennessee, taking along the woman and some of her children. That led to the Mann Act indictment.

Simon claimed he moved to look for employment, and that was the trip's dominant purpose, citing *Mortensen*. The judges doubted that was the purpose since he left an area where "there was an abundance of work." Even if it were true, they pointed out that purpose provided no reason to take the woman along. Clearly, sexual intercourse with the soldier's wife was one purpose for *her* coming along, and "the Mann Act does not require that the interstate transportation need be solely for immoral purposes, if such purpose constitute one of the reasons." *Mortensen* did not apply since there "the whole purpose . . . was the taking of a vacation."[11]

Another example of judicial narrowing of *Mortensen* began on August 8, 1944, when Ralph B. Mellor and Charles J. Ford, both in their late thirties, were driving down a highway near O'Neill, Nebraska. They noticed two girls hitchhiking and picked them up. The girls were both young adolescents, sexually experienced, hitchhiking to California. They drove to Mellor's ranch house near Atkinson, went to a nearby dance, and stayed at Mellor's house for two days. The men attempted to have sex with the girls, were turned down, and the girls slept in a separate bedroom.

While at the ranch, Mellor mentioned that he and Charles were about to leave for a fishing trip in Wyoming and invited the girls to join them. They accepted; it was in their line of travel. The foursome motored westward on August 10. The car stopped just short of the state line, and the girls got out and walked across the line. The men then drove the car forward and picked them up on the Wyoming side. It was unclear who suggested this futile device to evade the Mann Act, but it certainly shows their awareness of the statute. The federal trial judge later characterized it as "puerile," and a "pitiful device [that] was in its very nature the act of guilty men—and probably guilty girls—with lewd, obscene, and illegal designs."[12]

They rented a two-bedroom cabin at Signal Mountain Lodge, near Moran, Wyoming. They stayed together a week, fishing by day, and pairing up by night, one girl sleeping with Mellor and the other with Ford. The men paid for the expenses of the trip and some slight clothing for the girls, presumably appropriate for fishing. After a week's sojourn, they parted company; the girls resumed their hitchhiking to California and the men returned home, all concerned unharmed by the experience.

However, the federal government thought differently and threw the girls into a federal reformatory and the men into prison. Typical of the emotional hyperbole federal prosecutors employed to induce convictions, the United States Attorney harangued the jury in closing argument that if they acquitted "we might as well tear up this law, throw it into the ashcan and send notice to all the playboys that henceforth they can transport a female from one state to another for the purpose of debauchery and defile the womanhood of America."[13]

At trial and on appeal, the men relied on *Mortensen*, arguing that the "dominant purpose" for the trip, using the language of the Supreme Court decision, was fishing for the men and advancing their progress toward California for the women. The trial court refused to give a "dominant purpose" instruction to the jury, instead charging the jury only that the immorality had to be "not a mere incident but rather an efficient purpose prompting and impelling" the transportation of the women. This may seem an arcane and academic dispute, but it is not. Were sex required to be the "dominant purpose," the prosecutor would have a higher burden in a case like this, where the men clearly had another reason for the trip.

Furthermore, the trial court virtually dismissed the *Mortensen* defense, saying "it is unnecessary that in the charge to a jury a trial court adopt as a fetish the exact verbiage, however striking, of an appellate court [namely, the United States Supreme Court] in an earlier opinion in a case arising under the same statute."[14] On appeal the Circuit Court affirmed. The instruction of "not a mere incident but rather *an* efficient purpose" [emphasis added] was sufficient; "it was not necessary to incorporate therein the exact language of the Supreme Court. . . . The Mortensen case was totally different on the facts . . . [because] the transportation involved no immoral purpose."

In an additional noncommercial case,[15] the trial court instructed the jury that it could convict if it found that *one* of the purposes underlying defendant's transportation of the female was to have sexual intercourse with her. The appellate court acknowledged that a new trial ought to be ordered if a conviction had to rest upon a finding that an immorality had to be the "dominant purpose," since the jury had not been so instructed. However, the appellate court concluded that "it is enough if one of the purposes of his transportation of her was within the ban of the statute."

As for *Mortensen*, the court simply brushed aside the Supreme Court's language as to "dominant purpose" and stated that it was "not . . . to be taken literally. . . . We incline to think that if the Supreme Court had intended . . . to invalidate a respectable line of authority, [here citing *Van Pelt, Carey, and Ghadiali*] and for the future to establish the rule . . . not merely that one of the purposes of the interstate trip was to do some forbidden act, but that its 'dominant' purpose was to do such an act, it would have given the matter more detailed consideration and stated its conclusion in more explicit terms."[16]

The possibility that the Supreme Court could review and reverse the appellate courts' decisions inhibited them from totally ignoring *Mortensen*. In two cases, the United States Supreme Court did summarily reverse the decisions of the appellate courts, without written opinion, on the express basis of *Mortensen*, thereby stating that the appellate courts had not properly applied their precedent. In *United States v. Oriolo*,[17] a young adult woman worked as a prostitute for defendant Oriolo in Philadelphia. On July 19, 1942, the couple, prostitute and pimp, traveled by Oriolo's car to Atlantic City, New Jersey, "for a day's outing," with no professional motive. For reasons that are unclear, they were arrested in Atlantic City and their car was held by the authorities.

That delayed their return to Philadelphia until the following day, and then by train. During that journey the defendant told the woman, who was already working for him as a prostitute, that she would have to work so that he could pay the fine imposed on him in Atlantic City and recover the car. Upon their return to Philadelphia, the woman resumed her profession as prostitute, and the defendant was arrested for a Mann Act violation based upon his return trip with the woman from Atlantic City to Philadelphia.

The Circuit Court of Appeal thought that *Mortensen* did not control the case. In *Mortensen* the purpose had been a vacation and that purpose never changed throughout the trip. But in the *Oriolo* case, the appellate court thought in a 2–1 opinion, the fact that the trip to New Jersey had been interrupted by the arrest and the seizure of the car, together with defendant's discussion that the woman must prostitute herself to pay off his fine and recover his car, gave a new intent to the return trip to Philadelphia than had existed on the outgoing portion of the trip. The Supreme Court disagreed and summarily reversed the conviction on the basis of *Mortensen,* but without opinion.

The second case where the Supreme Court intervened and summarily reversed was in 1955 with *Becker v. United States.*[18] The defendant, Ralph Becker, owned and operated a nightclub in Medford, Wisconsin. He hired Lila Lane through a Minneapolis booking agent to work in his place as a stripper. She started her act on November 2, 1953, and at some point thereafter began an affair with Ralph. There was no suggestion of prostitution or of his payment for any sexual services. Both were adults; Ralph was married with two children and Lila was apparently single with a daughter who lived with Lila's mother in Minneapolis. Lila danced in the club and cavorted with Ralph until a few days before Thanksgiving, when she returned to Minneapolis to be home for the holiday with her mother and daughter.

The evidence was undisputed that at the time Lila left Medford she intended to return to Medford. In fact, she did return shortly after Thanksgiving, and Ralph paid her fare. So far it seems exactly like the vacation in *Mortensen,* excepting only the irrelevant detail that the defendant aided the transportation by money and not personal accompaniment. But a difference that the appellate court thought significant was that there was some evidence of Lila's change of heart during her stay in Minneapolis.

Lila left her dancing equipment in Medford, but apparently she did not have a return ticket nor any definite date in mind as to when she was coming back. Once back in Minneapolis, she informed her booking agent that she did not know whether she wanted to return to Medford. Ralph called the agent, asked whether Lila was returning, and was told he did not know. Thereupon, Ralph asked the agent to supply another dancer, but he was apparently not content to leave things alone with Lila personally. He called her and "begged her to come back and said he couldn't live without her, and all that, and that she just had to come back." He even promised to support both Lila and her mother.

It was this change of heart on Lila's part that influenced the appellate court to find that the return trip stood on a different footing than the return in *Mortensen.* It was not an implausible argument. The defendant was not charged with transporting Lila from Minnesota to Wisconsin for immoral purposes, that is, to be his mistress. He was instead charged with the second transportation section of the Mann Act, through his *inducing* Lila to return, when she was wavering and might not have traveled back to Wisconsin but for his persuasions. In any event, the Supreme Court thought the Circuit Court had made a distinction between these facts and *Mortensen* without there being any real difference and summarily reversed the conviction without opinion. Although the lower courts' reception of *Mortensen*, in general, was not enthusiastic, appellate courts did apply the case where the facts were clearly analogous.[19]

Justice Murphy's opinion in *Mortensen* directed a rather definite, albeit indirect, slap at *Caminetti*. Indeed, it was a general expectation among the legal community that *Caminetti* might soon be overruled. One appellate judge wrote that the Supreme Court "has not yet over-ruled that decision [*Caminetti*], although it has intimated that it may do so," citing *Mortensen*.[20] At least one law review commentator likewise thought the days of *Caminetti* were numbered.[21]

But *Mortensen* had been decided by a 5–4 division, and almost immediately the Court reversed direction, heading back toward an expansive construction of the Mann Act. *Mortensen* turned out to be a mere sputter in the morals crusade. The change of heart first appeared in the following year of 1945. Carmen Beach was a Washington, D.C., dress shop operator, who doubled as a procurer for her young female employee. The girl met customers in Carmen's apartment and in various hotel rooms to which her employer sent her. It was an entirely voluntary arrangement, and there was no element of compulsion or enticement of the prostitute by her employer.

One day Carmen accompanied the girl to a hotel four blocks away from the apartment for the purposes of prostitution. The trip was made by taxi and Beach paid the fare. For this four-block trip, wholly within the District of Columbia, Beach was prosecuted under the Mann Act. The literal language of the statute forbade transportation of a woman "in the District of Columbia" for the purpose of prostitution, debauchery, or any other immoral purpose. She was convicted.

The Circuit Court of Appeal for the District of Columbia reversed by a 2–1 decision. It acknowledged that the literal language would compel affirmance of the conviction, but it reasoned that the Mann Act could not reasonably be so interpreted. On the very day in 1910 when the Mann Act was passed, Congress also enacted a pandering ordinance for the District of Columbia. Following the passage of the Mann Act, Congress continued to pass other legislation suppressing various aspects of local prostitution. Clearly, the appellate court reasoned, Congress did not regard the Mann Act as regulating local transportation of prostitutes within the District, and did not intend that result, regardless of the literal application of the language of the statute. It quoted from Murphy's opinion in *Mortensen*:

> We do not here question or reconsider any previous construction placed on the Act which may have led the federal government into areas of regulation not originally contemplated by Congress [that is, *Caminetti*]. But experience with the administration of the law admonishes us against adding another chapter of statutory construction and application which would have a similar effect and which would make possible even further justification of the fear . . . [of] blackmail and make unnecessary trouble, without any corresponding benefits to society.

The appellate court then stated that "it is difficult to think that this language was inadvertent, when it so plainly admonishes us not to impose on the Mann Act a new phase of construction which, with no corresponding benefits to society, will open wider than it is the door to blackmailing."[22]

However, the 2–1 majority in *Beach* had overlooked the fact that *Mortensen* was a 5–4 decision. The Supreme Court reviewed the *Beach* conviction and reinstated it. In an unsigned *per curiam* decision, it held that the literal language of the Mann Act should stand, unaided by second-guessing of congressional intent. "[N]one of these enactments of local application speak of 'transportation' for immoral purposes. . . . Whether the District was already adequately protected from the evils of prostitution without the added prohibition of transportation for that purpose, was for Congress, not the courts, to decide. The prohibition was deliberately adopted by Congress, and it conflicts with no other legislation applicable in the District."[23] The American Social Hygiene Association praised the decision, calling it a powerful anti-prostitution weapon for the District and for Puerto Rico. It added the dubious proposition that the decision "reaffirms and upholds" the original congressional intent to punish intraterritorial transportation even if it also be punishable under local laws.[24]

Justices Murphy and Black dissented. "The Congressional debates and committee reports on the legislation make it plain that . . . it should not be applied to the situation present in this case. . . . That courts in the past have ignored the plain Congressional purpose and have applied these statutory words in a literal sense, so as to punish anyone transporting a woman for immoral purposes quite apart from any connection with white-slavery, does not command us to continue such an erroneous construction and application of the Act."[25]

One of the reasons the lower federal courts did not seize the opportunity presented by *Mortensen* to liberalize their constructions of the Mann Act was that the Supreme Court seemed to be polarized. Although *Mortensen* was never reversed, the Court seemed to change direction immediately afterwards. While Murphy referred to the *Beach* decision as "adding another instance of tortured and grotesque application to [the Mann Act's] already unhappy history,"[26] others saw the change of direction as an affirmation that the "respectable line of authority"[27] broadly interpreting the Act, including its application to noncommercial sexual purposes, had never been abandoned.

Contributing to the view that *Mortensen* might be an aberration was an understanding that the author of the opinion, Justice Frank Murphy, held curious views, out of the mainstream of legal thought, on the enforcement of morality by repressive legislation. His biographer has noted that "observers attributed [these views] to temperamental quirks. The most revealing was his campaign to restrict prosecutions under the Mann and Kidnapping statutes for acts of general immorality. This effort . . . led to endless jokes about his priestly sympathies for a sinful flock, which the Justice himself enjoyed."[28]

Murphy had a viewpoint more in accord with our contemporary understandings about the limitations of law to deal with issues of morality. Sexuality, or "sin" from Murphy's strong Roman Catholic perspective, was as inevitable as life itself. Therefore, repression could not be successful. As he once wrote in a private letter, "Someone must speak for sinners and reality. The law is for all."[29] But that viewpoint was deviational in 1945, and that fact helps explain why *Mortensen* was so poorly followed.

If the low estate of *Mortensen* was not already clear in 1945 with the *Beach* decision, it became obvious in 1946 with the *Cleveland* case. The defendants were members of a Mormon sect, known as Fundamentalists. They not only believed in polygamy but practiced it. The defendants had plural wives and transported them across state lines in order to live with them. In a 6–3 decision the Supreme Court found that this transportation violated the Mann Act.[30]

Justice William Douglas wrote the majority opinion. He found that polygamous practices were immoral, and "they are in the same genus as the other immoral practices covered by the Act." The appellants made a direct assault on *Caminetti* and asked the Court to overrule the precedent. That would have determined the case, as there was no hint of commercial motive among these sincere religious practitioners. The majority just as directly refused to overturn the earlier case:

> We do not stop to reexamine the Caminetti case to determine whether the Act was properly applied to the facts there presented. But we adhere to its holding, which has been in force for almost thirty years, that the Act, while primarily aimed at the use of interstate commerce for the purposes of commercialized sex, is not restricted to that end.[31]

Behind the smokescreen of polygamy, all concerned understood that the case was a review of *Caminetti*. The decision was really closer than the 6–3 vote would indicate. Justice Rutledge, who voted with the majority, gave a separate concurring opinion. He wrote that much could be said for the view that "*Caminetti* was wrongly decided and should be overruled. . . . In my opinion that case and subsequent ones following it extended the Mann Act's coverage beyond the Congressional intent and purpose." Rutledge viewed *Caminetti* as an error of the Supreme Court, but to overturn the convictions before them in *Cleveland*, the Court would have to overrule *Caminetti*. "The *Caminetti* case, however, has not been overruled and has the force of law until a majority of this Court may concur in the view that this should be done and take action to that effect." Reluctantly, Rutledge joined the majority decision.[32]

Justices Black and Jackson voted to reverse. They were of the opinion that "affirmance requires extension of the rule announced in the *Caminetti* case and that the correctness of that rule is so dubious that it should at least be restricted to its particular facts."[33] To restrict a case to its particular facts is a way of saying a case is no longer a viable precedent without actually overruling it. As could be anticipated, Frank Murphy wrote the most elaborate dissent. He began with the observation that "today another unfortunate chapter is added to the troubled history of the White Slave Traffic Act. It is a chapter written in terms that misapply the statutory language and that disregard the intention of the legislative framers. It results in the imprisonment of individuals whose actions have none of the earmarks of white slavery."[34]

He went on to argue that polygamy was not "in the same genus" as "any other immoral purpose," arguing that "marriage, even when it occurs in a form of which we disapprove, is not to be compared with prostitution or debauchery or other immoralities of that character."[35] But Murphy's real quarrel was with the inclusion of noncommercial immorality within the proscriptions of the Mann Act. He made a ringing denunciation of the Court's refusal to reconsider *Caminetti*:

> The result here reached is but another consequence of this Court's long-continued failure to recognize that the White Slave Traffic Act, as its title indicates, is aimed solely at the diabolical interstate and international trade in white slaves. . . . [T]his Court in Caminetti . . . closed its eyes to the obvious and interpreted the broad words of the statute without regard to the express wishes of Congress. . . . [T]he principle of the Caminetti case is still with us today, the principle of interpreting and applying the White Slave Traffic Act in disregard of the specific problem with which Congress was concerned. I believe the issue should be met squarely and the Caminetti case overruled. It has been on the books for nearly 30 years and its age does not justify its continued existence. Stare decisis certainly does not require a court to perpetuate a wrong for which it was responsible, especially when no rights have accrued in reliance on the error. . . . Otherwise the error is accentuated; and individuals, whatever may be said of their morality, are fined and imprisoned contrary to the wishes of Congress. I shall not be a party to that process. . . . The consequence of prolonging the Caminetti principle is to make the federal courts the arbiters of the morality of those who cross state lines in the company of women and girls. They must decide what is meant by "any other immoral purpose" without regard to the standards plainly set forth by Congress. I do not believe that this falls within the legitimate scope of the judicial function.[36]

The *Cleveland* decision was not well-received by the legal community. Several law review comments and notes criticized it.[37] The lead counsel for the defendants wrote a small booklet attacking the decision by way of an extensive analysis of the history of the Act's origins.[38] Probably the keenest analysis of *Cleveland* was the laconic statement in a student comment that "the case indicates that the intimation in the

Mortensen case, that the court might overrule the *Caminetti* case, was not well founded."[39]

The hope that *Caminetti* would someday be overruled was never to be realized. However, almost all of the cases that questioned the extent of the Mann Act's reach in consensual, noncommercial situations were decided by divided courts, both on the Supreme Court and the circuit courts. That *Caminetti* was constantly challenged and that precedent in noncommercial cases was so divided were significant facts. Doubtless the constant assaults, the splits in viewpoints, and the legal community's criticisms, all rendered aid to the more courageous federal judges who soon thereafter, faced with the Sexual Revolution of the 1960s, simply defied earlier appellate rulings.

The usual Mann Act case did not present these philosophical difficulties. The average prosecution throughout the period of 1944 through 1959 continued to be for transportation with a commercial purpose of prostitution. For many years before 1944, as we have seen, most noncommercial cases were not prosecuted. Conviction figures were not reported throughout the war years and the Attorney General's Annual Reports did not resume their coverage of the Mann Act until the mid-1950s. The numbers of convictions reported for the mid to late 1950s were certainly much lower than in the 1920s and 1930s. For the fiscal year ending June 30, 1954, 266 convictions were reported; for fiscal 1955, 332; fiscal 1957, 230; and fiscal 1959, 184. As can be seen, they had already slipped downward significantly; yet the huge slide of the 1960s and 1970s was still to come.

Most of the prostitution cases throughout the years between 1944 and 1959 were routine, seldom stirring up dissent or controversy. Yet here and there a few cases are interesting for their particular facts. One such was the 1945 case of *La Page v. United States*.[40] The defendant was a madam in a Fargo, North Dakota, brothel. One of her girls had gone to Minneapolis for a vacation. The madam telephoned her and urged her to return because another of her girls was leaving. The woman returned from Minneapolis the next day, by train and at her own expense. The madam was charged with a violation of the first transportation section, that of transporting, aiding, or causing the transportation of a woman in interstate commerce for the purpose of prostitution.

The appellate court reversed her conviction. The defendant may have *induced* or *persuaded* the woman to travel by a common carrier in interstate commerce for prostitution. That would be a violation of the *second* transportation section, but she was not charged with that, only with the first section. Inducing and persuading cannot be the same as causing, the court declared, or all distinction between the two sections would be lost.

Another interesting case was *Batsell v. United States.*[41] The defendant transported a willing prostitute from Minneapolis, Minnesota, to Duluth, Minnesota. The idea was to see if work were available for her in a brothel in Superior, Wisconsin, a short distance away from Duluth. It was proposed that if work were available, apparently someone else, or the girl herself, would travel across the state line to Superior. En route to Duluth, they ran into road difficulties and to avoid those turned eastward into Wisconsin. They continued traveling within Wisconsin, passed through Superior without pause, back into Minnesota and on to Duluth. There, defendant made a telephone call to the brothel and was advised that there was no work available for his girl.

Batsell was prosecuted for transporting the girl from Minneapolis, Minnesota, to the state of Wisconsin, for the purposes prohibited by the Mann Act. He contended that the detour from Minnesota into Wisconsin was merely a necessity caused by the road conditions and there was no immoral purpose whatsoever in going into Wisconsin. He relied on *Mortensen,* but the appellate court turned that case back on his argument. The ultimate purpose of the trip was to obtain work for the girl in Superior, Wisconsin, as a prostitute, said the court. That was within the Act, and it was well established by case precedent that the purpose did not have to be accomplished.

Although the number of annual convictions declined by the 1940s from their earlier peaks, the punishments imposed were greater. In the early periods of the Act's enforcement sentences had varied widely but averaged under two years; by 1947 they averaged nearly three years. Perhaps it was for this reason Bascom Johnson, the associate director of the American Social Hygiene Association, noted at the end of 1946 that the Mann Act had been so effective as to make control of commercial prostitution almost entirely a local problem.[42]

Just a few years later, in 1952, the executive director of that same association announced that "America is winning the long fight against commercialized prostitution." He noted that the association's surveys of 228 cities showed that "there were fewer communities with open . . . prostitution in 1951 than at any time since 1940, with the single exception of 1944."[43] The venerable Chicago Committee of Fifteen, formed in 1907 to combat white slavery, disbanded in 1951. Once one of the original boosters of the Mann Act, the committee closed its doors on March 31, 1951, because "public support had waned" while prostitution had "dwindled to its lowest ebb." Reportedly, "the old-fashioned disorderly house in this city [Chicago] has disappeared."[44]

It is difficult to generalize about the noncommercial cases during the period of 1944 through 1959. The easy availability of the trial records stops in the mid-1940s, as does the Department of Justice correspondence accessible in the National Archives. One must rely on the cases that were appealed, and therefore published, or on prosecutions so notorious that they generated newspaper accounts. Neither of these categories are necessarily representative of the much larger mass of noncommercial cases.

There were seventeen appellate cases during the period of 1944 to 1959, in which neither prostitution or any other sort of commercial sexual activity nor forcible rape were involved. These are the cases of consensual, noncommercial sex. The Department of Justice did not issue any new general circulars during this period, but a look backward to the last circular issued, that of September 5, 1935, indicates that many of these noncommercial cases that appeared in 1944 through 1959 fit within the categories specified. The 1935 circular indicated that factors to be considered as favoring prosecution included (1) "very young women or girls," and (2) "when State laws are inadequate . . . married persons deserting young children."[45]

By this time period, the authorities were concerned that local federal prosecutors might embarrass law enforcement by untoward prosecution of noncommercial cases. Eventually, in 1962, the Department of Justice would put a direct control over the initiation of noncommercial prosecutions. But in 1949 significant indirect controls, beyond the guidelines, were in place. A 1949 FBI policy memorandum concerning enforcement of the Mann Act advises all agents that "care must be taken, however, lest by the improper handling of what may be termed 'borderline' cases, the Bureau discredit the excellent results otherwise achieved and bring the White Slave Traffic Act into public disrepute."

How was this to be done? First, there should be no "active investigation" of a complaint "failing to indicate commercial prostitution" unless specifically authorized by the local United States Attorney with whom the agent worked. But that was not enough, and agents were called upon to blow the whistle on local federal prosecutors who were overzealous and acted as though they were still back in the days of the morals crusade. "In the event," the FBI agents were told, "the United States Attorney authorizes that an investigation be conducted in a matter which appears to be a technical violation, or contemplates prosecution in such a case, the Bureau should immediately be advised of his decision."[46]

In nine of these seventeen noncommercial cases, in the years of 1944 to 1959, the women involved were clearly stated as under the age of eighteen. Of the remaining eight, the ages of two of the women involved are unclear. For the women who were almost assuredly over eighteen, three out of six were situations where one of the parties was married and had left young children. In two of these three, however, the spouse left before the transportation that was prosecuted. Taken as a whole, the appealed cases fit the patterns suggested for prosecution by the earlier circulars.

But the cases involving young girls do not necessarily imply that the men involved were all older. The *Toronto Star* ran a column asking readers to share their most unforgettable dates. One of the responses demonstrates how all so easily young people could be swept up in the Mann Act hysteria. It involved a man who grew up in Pittsburgh, Pennsylvania, received his driver's license on his sixteenth birthday, and borrowed his father's car that night:

> I invited my friend Ellen to a hayride, and we had a great time. We were supposed to be home by midnight, but lost our bearings. While looking for a pay phone to call home when we were pulled over by an Ohio State trooper. Omigosh! We'd crossed the state line! Since Ellen was just short of her 16th birthday, this was considered a violation of the Mann Act—the federal law that forbids transporting a minor [*sic!*—a common misunderstanding] across a state line "for immoral purposes." Next thing we knew, we were in custody, being questioned by an FBI agent. I was allowed one phone call, and when I reached my father it was 3 a.m. Our parents were frantic with worry. Finally, all four parents came to fetch us and we got home around dawn. I didn't get the car again until my 17th birthday.[47]

It must be recalled in these noncommercial cases that the crime was complete upon crossing the state line with the guilty purpose; the completed seduction need never happen. A good example of this is *Qualls v. United States.*[48] Edward Qualls was a married man with children. In

1945 while in North Carolina he persuaded an uneducated, sixteen-year-old girl, her mother, and stepfather that he was working for the Navy in Atlanta. He needed more help immediately, he told them, and he would drive the daughter there.

The two had not left North Carolina before Qualls asked her for sex. She refused. They went into Georgia, and at Cornelia he left the car to obtain, as he said, two hotel rooms. He returned with the news that only one was available. At first the girl refused to share it, but then relented when he promised to leave her alone, which he did. In Atlanta he again tried to maneuver her into a hotel for sex, but she refused. Then he told her he really was working in Florida and asked her to go on to that state. She refused and demanded her job. He said her job depended on his having intercourse with her.

At that point a policewoman overheard the conversation and arrested them. The Mann Act conviction was upheld on appeal. It did not matter that nothing happened. The jury was warranted in thinking that the purpose of his transportation was "having her engage in debauchery with him. This is within the very language of the Act, and the fact that she . . . successfully evaded it afterwards [that is, after crossing the line] does not erase appellant's offense."[49]

During the 1940s and 1950s the Supreme Court made law in other Mann Act cases that involved collateral policy issues, not issues going to the heart of the Act. They can be stated briefly. In 1949 the Court considered an alleged conspiracy of a man and woman to transport another woman from New York to Miami to work as a prostitute. The case determined that the statements made by a co-conspirator after the conspiracy has ended were inadmissible against the other conspirator.[50] In the 1955 case of *Bell v. United States*,[51] the defendant transported two prostitutes on the same trip and in the same vehicle. The issue was whether he could be sentenced for two *separate* offenses, or whether the single nature of his act permitted only a single punishment. The Court said the Mann Act was unclear as to multiple offenses and that the ambiguity ought be resolved in favor of leniency. If a defendant transported more than one woman in a single act, he could be given only one sentence, with the maximum of five years. In so ruling the Court resolved conflicts between the different circuit courts which had split in their views.[52]

In the 1960 case of *Wyatt v. United States*,[53] the defendant transported a woman across a state line for her to work as a prostitute and then married her. The Supreme Court found the spousal privilege inapplicable because the facts brought it within an exception where the defendant's wife is his victim. Not only was the defendant powerless to prevent his wife from testifying, she could be *compelled* to testify against him.

In *Hawkins v. United States*,[54] the defendant was convicted of transporting a seventeen-year-old girl from Arkansas to Oklahoma to work as a prostitute along with his wife. Unlike *Wyatt*, the wife in this case was already in Oklahoma and hence not a "victim" of the illegal transportation. She was willing be a government witness and testified against her husband over his objection. The Supreme Court reversed the conviction that resulted, holding that the testimonial privilege was the defendant's right and not a privilege that belonged to the witness. Within two decades of this 1958 case the Supreme Court would change its mind on this issue.

In the late 1940s and 1950s there was a high public awareness of the Mann Act. We have already seen in the *Mellor* case the crude effort of the men to evade the Act by having the girls walk across the Nebraska-Wyoming line. That sort of behavior was frequent.[55] In *Lawrence v. United States*[56] (1947), a pimp transported one of his girls from San Francisco to Battle Mountain, Nevada. The defendant steered the car up to the state line but then informed the girl that he was not supposed to drive across. Some other person then drove over the line and defendant resumed driving.

This sort of behavior did not help the defendants. Generally, it hurt them by clearly showing their guilty intent. In *Holder v. United States*[57] (1959), two pimps sent prostitutes from Des Moines, Iowa, to Fort Leonard Wood, Missouri, to solicit the soldiers there. They made the girls take the train by themselves. As the appellate court noted, "sending the women by train to conceal defendants' transportation of them for fear of penalty was a circumstance to be considered."

Even more amusing is the 1956 case of *Bennett v. United States*.[58] The appellate court noted with rye amusement:

> It is interesting that at the time the party crossed into Canada from the State of Washington, Bennett [male defendant] alone crosses in the Cadillac. Kehert is by himself in his Buick and Mrs. Bennett, Miss Casey, Miss Ward and Miss Crosby motor across in Mrs. Bennett's Mercury. There was evidence, the business of crossing the line having been negotiated, the parties stopped the cars a few miles down the road and rearranged themselves in the cars. It was possible that

all such doings were a mere coincidence. On the other hand, neither the jury nor this court needs the help of Professor Wigmore [a noted authority on trial evidence] to draw legitimate inferences of certain illegitimacy in the event.

In *Long v. United States*[59] (1947), two men were taking several children across a state line under questionable circumstances. One was making advances on a twelve-year-old girl. She recalled at trial that one man said to the other before reaching the line, "'You know the Mann Act charge against carrying someone across the line. You better marry her when you get across.'" We even find evidence of Mann Act awareness in divorce cases. Sometime between 1954 and 1958 an adulterous husband in Iowa was with his paramour, the wife of a neighbor. She suggested a cozy late supper together in Prairie du Chien, a town just across the Mississippi River, in Wisconsin. He replied to his loved one: "I don't dare to take you across the state line."[60]

Up through the 1950s, the public not only was aware of the Mann Act, it still respected the statute. The Act's strictures might not be in conformity with behavior. Fornication and adultery might occur and state lines crossed in connection therewith. Still, the Mann Act set the standard and the norm; there was not yet a general outcry of rebellion and wholesale disregard for the statute that would come with the Sexual Revolution of the 1960s.

However, there were harbingers in the 1950s of things yet to come in the 1960s. And these signs appeared in both the popular and scholastic arenas. As early as 1944 that bellwether of popular sentiment, *Time Magazine*,[61] observed that the Mann Act "was aimed at traffickers in commercial prostitution. But many a U.S. philanderer has discovered to his unhappy surprise that, amateur though he be, the law makes him a criminal." It called the Act a "wide-open invitation to blackmail and feminine revenge," cited some examples of "Mann Act miscarriages," and quoted with approval from Turano's earlier attack on the statute in the *American Mercury.*

At the opposite end of the cultural continuum, the 1955 annual meeting of the American Law Institute was held at the Mayflower Hotel in Washington, D.C. At the time the distinguished lawyers and judges met, forty-three states still retained some sort of adultery statute. They gathered, in part, to consider a comment to a draft of a new Model Penal Code that proclaimed that it "does not attempt to use the power of the state to enforce purely moral or religious standards. We deem it inappropriate for the Government to attempt to control behavior that has no substantial significance except as to the morality of the actor."

A heavy majority of the assembly agreed that adultery should not be a statutory crime. By a closer vote, 35–24, the Institute went on to recommend that sodomy be decriminalized.[62] These were merely recommendations of a high-level advisory group. They changed no law. Yet, already, as early as these events in 1955, profound change was in the air, change that would so revolutionize this country during the following decade that it would be called a revolution—the Sexual Revolution.

The Mann Act and the Sexual Revolution of the 1960s and 1970s

his is not the place to describe the Sexual Revolution of the 1960s and 1970s in detail. Our focus necessarily must be the impact of that revolution on the enforcement of the Mann Act. Yet the changes in the American sexual culture in the 1960s and 1970s were so extreme that it would be well to review them. Although there have been other periods of sexual liberalism, such as the 1920s, no earlier unloosening of traditional restraints had such a profound impact. Notwithstanding the AIDS crisis and tendency towards more conservative practices in the 1980s and 1990s, much of the sexual liberalism of the 1960s will probably be permanent.

The changed sexual mores were most acutely sensed in the colleges. The revolution destroyed, as one commentator put it, "the older dating codes that had persisted since the 1920s, codes that had insisted upon male courtship, focused upon petting as an end, not just as foreplay, and limited, at least theoretically, sexual intercourse to the committed." Women's access to the birth control pill meant that "sex could be casual, divorced from commitment, out in the open, and initiated by women."[1] These attitudes and behaviors intensified during the 1970s.

Surveys of college students showed that whereas, at the beginning of the 1960s 40 percent believed that it was all right for women as well as men to engage in premarital intercourse, by the end of the 1960s 70 percent believed so. That would rise to 80 percent in the 1970s. In the early 1950s, 80 percent of the nation's coeds remained virgins throughout college. By the 1970s that figure had reversed as 80 percent *did not* retain their virginity throughout their collegiate experience.[2] A study of Cornell University students in the late 1970s found that 31 percent of the student body had cohabited with a member of the opposite sex without marriage.[3]

Nor was the Sexual Revolution confined to the campus. Everywhere, as Peter G. Filene has written, "eros seemed to be running loose: hair bouncing on male as well as female shoulders; women's breasts swaying braless under sweaters; miniskirts and see-through blouses and topless dance clubs; rock singers pleading 'let's spend the night together' and 'c'mon, baby, light my fire' . . . down at the corner newsstand *Playgirl* cohabited with *Playboy*, and *Cosmopolitan* opened its centerfold to Burt Reynolds smiling in blissful nudity. Once there had been *The Joy of Cooking;* now there was the *Joy of Sex*. Chateau Martin wines asked 'Had any lately?' and Noxzema shaving cream's woman said, 'Take it off, take it all off.' There were no rules, no roles, nothing but self-indulgence."[4]

It also appeared that people were having sex at a much younger age, and that it had invaded the high schools. The percentage of single seventeen-year-old girls who had experienced sex rose from 27 percent in 1971 to 41 percent in 1976.[5] That figure would rise to 51 percent by 1988, in which year the percentage of single women aged nineteen who had had sexual intercourse reached 75 percent.[6]

Quite obviously these sexually liberated Americans traveled. College boys took their girlfriends to Daytona Beach, Florida, for spring break. Older dating couples, emulating and perhaps envious of their juniors' new freedom, likewise felt free to travel about the country, enjoying vacations together or attending business meetings. They registered in motels and hotels as husband and wife, though they were not, or increasingly, defiantly registered in their own individual names while asking for a room with a king-sized bed, tossing aside all pretense of marriage.

The "establishment" might well remain "uptight" about all this immorality, to borrow two words prominent in the 1960s, yet faced with an upheaval of this magnitude, the authorities had to make some sort of accommodation. No government can imprison, or even threaten to imprison, a significant number of its population for activities the overwhelming majority think are legitimate or at least harmless. The government attempted a massive crackdown and imprisonment of youth with a felony status for marijuana use, but ultimately failed as the sanctions for marijuana possession were lowered almost everywhere. With sexual activity the government was simply overwhelmed by changed attitudes, and surrendered almost immediately.

The liberalizing tendencies that led to freer sexual attitudes among college students also led to looser, more accommodating views of prostitution. This would likewise have an impact on Mann Act enforcement. Throughout the 1960s, individual judges[7], prosecutors[8], police officers[9], and corrections officials[10] called for the decriminalization of prostitution. Organizations, including the American Bar Association's committee on Individual Rights and Responsibilities[11] and the American Civil Liberties Union,[12] also called for legalization. A prostitutes' union organized[13] and feminists protested the legal system's treatment of prostitutes and demanded legalization.[14] These voices made no real headway. Majoritarian politics still called for a statement of the illegitimate nature of the prostitute's business, and that statement could most easily be made through its continued criminalization. But this stirring of ideas weakened any remaining will to vigorously enforce sexual laws concerning prostitution and with that lessening of vigor, the much lesser vice of fornication.

What was the impact of all these new freedoms and new ideas on the Mann Act? We have seen the failure of attempts to amend the Mann Act in Congress. Throughout the period of the Sexual Revolution the federal politicians remained paralyzed, fearful of alienating the still significant hordes of puritanical voters. The body politic would not taste the bitter medicine of reality, not if these elected officials had to do the doctoring.

But while the elected branch could dither and delay, the judiciary could not. Prosecutors continued to bring some noncommercial Mann Act cases. Judges were forced to face and reconcile the social fact of the Sexual Revolution and hard precedent that placed boyfriend-girlfriend travel and numerous other sexual "immoralities," now deemed harmless by most of American society, within the proscriptions of the Mann Act. How did they do it?

One technique was to redefine the meaning of "immoral purpose" so as to exclude activities, such as nude photography, erotic dancing, and B-girl hustling for drinks, that once had been clearly within the felonious "immoral purpose." There is no single year in which these changes took place, but the liberalizing tendency over time is clear.

In the area of nude photography, for example, the 1946 case of *Jarabo v. United States*[15] affirmed a conviction for several counts of violating the Mann Act. The defendant, a student at the University of Puerto Rico, transported a female, probably a fellow student, to his apartment. Since this was Puerto Rico and under direct federal control, only an "immoral purpose" would be required for the Act's violation; no state line need be crossed. Once in his apartment, the evidence was that he "attempted to take pictures of her at least partially undressed, but that she refused to permit him to do so, whereupon he struck her several times and tore some of her clothes off but that she escaped." There was a separate charge for another incident in which he took pornographic photographs of himself and two other women having intercourse. That may have colored the jury's appraisal of the clothes tearing count, but so far as the evidence went, the immoral purpose that sustained the conviction was simply that of taking pictures of a woman "partially undressed."

Let us move forward to 1956. Raymond S. Mathison was the advertising salesman for the radio and television station in Marinette, Wisconsin. Myrna Lee was a naive sixteen-year-old who dreamed of becoming a model and lived just across the state line in Menominee, Michigan. Raymond assisted her in obtaining some commissions for advertising and commercial pictures that were shown on local television. He also brought her across the state line for intercourse on many occasions and exploited her shamelessly, even to the point of insisting that she also have sex with his friends.

On one occasion Raymond took Myrna Lee from Michigan to a Marinette motel, but this trip had an unusual sequel. They were met by the professional photographer who had previously taken the pictures that were used on television. She disrobed and in the presence of the two men the photographer took several nude and semi-nude pictures for the purpose, he later testified, of determining whether she had the figure that would justify the pursuit of a modeling career. There was no sexual activity during the session, nor were any sexual suggestions made. The photographs were not pornographic, but of the type, according to the photographer, that would have been acceptable to the camera magazines that use that sort of nude study.

The defendant Mathison was convicted of multiple violations. However the appellate court felt constrained to reverse the conviction of the count arising out of the nude photographic session, "unless the mere taking of a picture in the nude is an 'immoral purpose' as that phrase is used in the Act." The court would not go that far and reversed that count, reasoning that this nude photographic session "might be considered by some as immoral but to others as entirely legitimate."[16]

Curiously enough, there has been only one appeal of a conviction under the Mann Act for the making of an X-rated movie. In *United States v. Roeder*[17] (1975), the defendant transported Bobbie Lynn, the star of the show, in interstate commerce, for her to engage in various sexual acts with him in front of a camera in the production of a commercial pornographic motion picture.

The trial court instructed the jury that the term "other immoral purposes" had "no broader meaning than the term 'prostitution.'" Of course, that misstated the law as established in *Caminetti* and hundreds of other cases, but was misstated favorably to the defendant. The appellate court emphasized the commercial nature of the project, the fact that the woman was paid for her sexual performances, and that spectators paid money to watch the production of the film. Both trial and appellate courts apparently wanted the case considered as a *prostitution* case, perhaps to prevent it from criminalizing interstate travel for sexually explicit, but noncommercial, home film productions.

The appellate court stated the issue as "whether the fact that a movie was made and that payment was at least in part for this activity detracts from the fact that sexual acts were performed" and money paid for the sex. It concluded that "the performance of the [sexual] acts was absolutely essential to the production of the movie; the acts could not be divorced from the movie making." In other words, the making of a pornographic movie was not an immoral purpose within the Act. But the engaging in sexual acts for compensation, which formed the basis of the movie's production, was an immoral purpose if they were the purpose of the interstate transportation.

There is an entire genre of Mann Act cases involving transportation of women for erotic dancing. The legal issues are either whether the dancing is itself an immoral purpose, or whether the environment where the erotic dancing is performed is such that the woman is so likely to become "debauched" that "debauchery" was one of the purposes of the transportation. There is substantial overlap of the strip situations with the B-girl cases, but one may distinguish and consider the pure strip cases, those without drink hustling, separately.

Athanasaw, the classic 1913 case that made its way to the Supreme

Court, involved dancing. But the nature of the dancing was not clear, and the case involved drink hustling and probable sexual activity as well. *United States v. Long*[18] was, in 1936, the first reported case clearly involving nude dancing by itself. Sam Long owned a strip show that he operated out of a carnival in Hymera, Indiana. He was in need of more girls and he and his associate, Davis, went over to Paris, Illinois, to recruit fresh talent. He falsely represented to two young girls that their employment at the show would consist of taking tickets and, on that basis, persuaded them to come to the carnival in Indiana.

The two girls slept by themselves in a trailer. They did not collect tickets but were informed that they were to participate with Sam Long's wife as dancers in "muscle or 'hootchie-coochie' dances." The two girls and Mrs. Long dressed in brassieres, skirts that reached their knees, and shorts underneath the skirts. The Long couple also told the girls to join Mrs. Long in an "after-show" during which "Mrs. Long removed her shorts and, at a certain time in the dance, drew open her skirt so that she stood nude before the audience." The girls refused to take part in the "after-show," which struggled on with Mrs. Long alone. One of the two girls had intercourse with Davis; neither had sex with the defendant Long. The sex was not in itself charged as an "immoral purpose," probably because of difficulty in proving that the intention for that activity had been formed before the state line was crossed. The two girls stayed with the carnival for three days, then rebelled and returned to their homes.

Sam Long was charged with violation of the Mann Act under the theory of debauchery. He waived a jury trial, and the court found him guilty. Drawing on the precedent of *Athanasaw*, the trial judge found the issue to be "whether or not the influences and environment by which the girls were surrounded in their employment tended to induce them to give themselves up to a condition of debauchery, which eventually would lead to a course of sexual immorality." Of course, said the court. Long "contemplated from the beginning that they should do lewd dancing and eventually become dancers in the nude . . . the show in which these dances were exhibited was for men." These circumstances "under natural trends and tendencies would lead them from chastity to unchastity and so into a life of debauchery." Guilty!

Four years later another transportation between Illinois and Indiana for nude dancing resulted in a conviction. In 1940 a husband and wife operated what they described as an educational show, designed to demonstrate the disastrous effects of immoral conduct. They displayed their edifying performances as part of a traveling carnival. Act one concerned a female procurer who was looking for a girl to take to a house of prostitution, and the second act portrayed an "over sexed girl." The third act was labeled "White Slavery Act," probably an unfortunate word choice from the vantage of the defendants. "The theme of the exhibition," as the court gravely intoned, "was essentially sex, and its medium of expression was nudity accompanied by words and pantomime which emphasized sexual action."

These married defendants brought three young girls, in their midteens, from Indiana to Illinois to participate in this show. They also urged the girls to accept prostitution dates they would arrange. The girls refused the monetary dates, but did sleep casually with some of the boys who worked at the carnival. In *United States v. Lewis*[19] the husband and wife were convicted of Mann Act violations. It was not necessary, the court decided, that they intended that the girls participate in sexual acts with themselves or anyone else. But, relying on *Athanasaw*, it was enough if they intentionally brought them to circumstances, surroundings, and influences that would tend to induce the girls to "give themselves up" to a condition of debauchery that would eventually lead to sexual immorality.

These two cases fairly represent the older view that nude dancing, even without responsibility for hustling drinks, represented an environment that so tended toward immorality that it constituted debauchery. Therefore interstate transportation for these purposes violated the Act. Now let us move forward in time once again.

We have already seen the *Becker* case of 1954 in the preceding chapter. There, the immoral purpose of the woman's return from Minneapolis to Medford, Wisconsin, was allegedly to resume her sexual relationship with her married employer. Yet her employment was that of an "exotic dancer." Had that itself been an immoral purpose, or if the engagement in defendant's nightclub had been the "efficient school of debauchery" contemplated by the *Athanasaw* opinion, defendant's *original* transportation of the woman from Minneapolis to Medford, Wisconsin, would have been a Mann Act violation. The roundtrip nature of the Thanksgiving holiday in Minneapolis would have been irrelevant. But there is no suggestion of this in the circuit court's opinion. It is simply assumed that exotic dancing is a legitimate employment and the nightclub not a place of debauchery.

United States v. Prater[20] displays the changed attitudes even more clearly. On March 21, 1974, about seventy-five members of the Fireman's Association of Washington Park, Illinois, attended a stag party at their Fireman's Hall. The organizers of the party wanted some sexual entertainment and hired four girls to perform a strip act to begin about 7:30 P.M. Efficient in their preparation for the party, the organizers also hired backup strippers for 10:30 P.M., in case the first group did not show. The defendant, Della Marie Prater, was one of the backup strippers, and she transported a second backup stripper, Vivian Deering, from St. Louis, Missouri, to Washington Park, Illinois, to perform. The testimony of the organizers was clear that they were hired to perform a strip tease and not to render any other sexual services.

As it turned out, the original four strippers did appear and performed their acts, the finale of which was a public fornication between one of the dancers and a member of the audience. They then left without further sexual activities. By the time the backup women arrived at 10:30 there was no need for further strip acts. Nevertheless, the men were glad to see them, and Della Marie and Vivian quickly seized the commercial possibilities the moment offered. Two law enforcement officers were present, a deputy sheriff and an agent of the FBI, and they offered a detailed picture of the activities of the two backup women.

Both women allowed the men to fondle their breasts, and defendant Prater walked about and talked with several of the men, giving out her telephone number and talking about the possibilities of future prostitution dates. The law enforcement officers were clear, as were other witnesses, that the defendant did not engage in sex with any of the men. They did observe Vivian Deering engage in fellatio and sexual intercourse with three men, and she herself testified that she had earned $60 from sexual activities that evening with three of the firemen.

Della Marie Prater was convicted of transporting, Vivian Deering across the Illinois state line for prostitution, debauchery, and other immoral purposes. The appellate court reversed. They were hired as strippers and there was no evidence that anything else was contemplated when they traveled from St. Louis to Illinois. That Vivian Deering did in fact engage in prostitution once there did not establish Prater's earlier purpose as they were driving over in her car. As to what *was* contemplated, the court declared unequivocally that "a strip tease act is not prostitution or debauchery or other immoral act within the meaning of the Mann Act."

Of course the women in *Long* and *Lewis* were young and therefore susceptible of being lead to a place at which they could be debauched by bad influences from a supposed, but never established, previous chastity. The women in *Becker* and *Prater* were all sexually experienced adults. However, the change in judicial attitude is more fundamental than this distinction. In *United States v. Le Amous*[21] (1985), a man was charged with transporting a young girl, fourteen years old and just as young as the girls in *Long* and *Lewis*, for the purpose of prostitution. The defendant described himself as "a friend to young girls, trying to protect them from getting involved in prostitution by finding other employment for them." And what was that other employment? It was erotic dancing. Although there was ample evidence that the defendant was a pimp and the purpose of the transportation was prostitution, his defense was seriously considered. In the 1930s and 1940s—the days of *Long* and *Lewis*, it would have been an admission of guilt.

Athanasaw (1913) was the first Mann Act case involving B-drink solicitation. The conviction there was for bringing a naive seventeen-year-old girl to circumstances that would probably lead to debauchery. But the principle that B-girl operations were an "other immoral purpose" or a place of probable debauchery was soon extended to cover adult women as well.

In *Beyer v. United States*[22] (1918), defendant Frank Beyer owned and operated a business in Mexicali, Mexico, that consisted of a bar, casino, dance hall, and brothel. Beyer hired adult women in Los Angeles to come to his establishment as entertainers. Their duties were to sing and dance on stage and to dance with the male customers. They also solicited the men to buy them drinks, from which they earned a 40 to 50 percent commission. Beyond the dance floor was a hall, at the end of which were rooms occupied by prostitutes. These women were also permitted on the dance floor, bar, and eating areas.

The defendant took care to differentiate the entertainers from the prostitutes. "The entertainers were bound by contracts not to engage in prostitution, and they were instructed that, if men should approach them and make improper suggestions to them, they were to say that they were not there for that purpose, but that there were others there." The defendant was tried and convicted for violation of the Mann Act for the transportation of these entertainers from Los Angeles to Mexicali.

The appellate court acknowledged that there was no proof "that any of the girls was actually solicited to engage in sexual debauchery, and that there is no charge that such debauchery was contemplated by the accused in transporting the girls to Mexicali." Nevertheless, to this 1918 court, their mere presence in a brothel, aiding the purpose of prostitution and rubbing shoulders, as it were, with actual prostitutes was enough. The defendant "intended to and did place the girls in a house of prostitution . . . subjected them to all the evil influences of such surroundings . . . [and] required them to dance on the same floor with prostitutes."

"They were to be in the dance hall for the purpose of luring men to dance with them, and to induce men to purchase intoxicating liquors, and thereby to aid in maintaining the business of prostitution in which . . . [the defendant] was engaged." The requirement that the entertainers spurn propositions and inform customers of the availability of other women was "thus to advertise the prostitutes."

The two cases of *Athanasaw* and *Beyer* established quite early that B-girl activity was an immoral purpose or a place of debauchery. This interpretation continued until the 1950s. In *United States v. Amadio*[23] (1954) defendant transported two women, apparently one a minor and another an adult, from Indiana to Calumet City, Illinois, to work in his nightclub, the Derby Club, as B-girls. The court paints a graphic picture of their activities.

> They were engaged in soliciting drinks from men customers. These drinks were bought and consumed on the premises and the "B girls" received a commission upon the sales. They sat on the laps of men customers and exposed various parts of their bodies, all parts of which were fondled by men customers, who embraced these girls.

The two-block neighborhood of the nightclub was crowded with bars featuring strip shows and prostitutes. The two women were encouraged to prostitute themselves by their female bartender and various men, but not by the defendant. They did not engage in prostitution and left after about a month. The defendant was charged and convicted under the debauchery theory of *Athanasaw*. The majority of the appellate court, over a dissent deploring the misconduct of the federal prosecutor, sustained the conviction:

> Employment of these girls by defendant in his tavern required them to work nearly all night, seven days a week, in a bar room where gross lewdness and sexual immorality were not only tolerated, but . . . the

predominating motif was sexual over-indulgence. . . . The businesses in the area . . . were operated to the accompaniment of a blatant emphasis on sexual activity. Nearly the entire area of two blocks was devoted to taverns and nightclubs which, both inside and outside, featured lewdness. . . . Life as a "B girl" in defendant's tavern, with its surrounding conditions, would not only tend to cause a girl to give herself up to a condition of debauchery, which would eventually and naturally lead to a course of sexual immorality, but any other result could not reasonably be expected.[24]

But then a curious thing: the United States Supreme Court reversed the judgment in an unanimous *per curiam* decision. It ordered that the indictment be discussed "on the ground that it does not come within the purview of the statute."[25] The effect of this terse statement was to repudiate the *Athanasaw* doctrine of "leading into temptation" as a form of debauchery. Although this was never a widely followed theory of Mann Act liability, still some defendants had been ensnared by it, as in the *Long* and *Lewis* cases, just examined.

This nightclub owned by Amos Amadio, the Derby Club, would continue in its notoriety. In three cases in the early 1960s Amadio's manager, William Austrew, and a B-girl, Anne Sapperstein, together with her husband, Harold Sapperstein, were convicted of multiple Mann Act violations.[26] The intent behind the transportation of the four women involved in these cases was pretty clearly prostitution, although the indictment was pled in the language of the statute and included debauchery and other immoral purposes. Although it was merely *dicta* because of the solid evidence of the purpose of prostitution, in *United States v. Austrew*[27] (1962), the trial court did suggest, apparently heedless of the *Amadio* outcome, that employment in the "degenerate character of the Derby Club, with its B-drinkers, pick pockets, strip-dancers, and one-bed brothel in the rear room" might constitute debauchery within the Mann Act.

One senses in these Derby Club cases from the 1960s the beginning of changed attitudes. The women lured from Maryland to Calumet City had been told that they would be strippers and B-girls, and in one case a barmaid. The trial judge in one of the cases noted his conclusion that "all B-girls are not prostitutes, but the terms are not mutually exclusive. It appears from the evidence that B-girls and dancers in some places are paid a salary and a commission on the drinks they persuade the men to take, without engaging in prostitution."[28] The Attorney

General in his next annual report specifically commented on these convictions. "The girls were recruited by the *Sappersteins* in Baltimore, allegedly for employment as B-Girls and strip dancers at the Club in Calumet City managed by *Austrew.* In fact, upon arrival in Calumet City it turned out that they were expected and encouraged to prostitute themselves, as well as to engage in activities for which they were ostensibly employed."[29]

The implication of the judicial observation and the comment in the Attorney General's report is clear enough. Had the girls been asked only to perform as strippers and B-girls, probably there would be no violation of the Mann Act, notwithstanding it was the same old degenerate Derby Club. Throughout the 1960s and 1970s there were more cases in which women were transported for the multiple purposes of prostitution, stripping, and B-drinking. Probably this reflects the changed nature of prostitution itself and the demise of the old-fashioned brothel. The defenses became the *Mortensen* style defense of dominant purpose, with the dominant purpose alleged by defendants to have been erotic dancing and B-girl activities. The fact that these activities were raised as *defenses* reflects the collapse of an earlier understanding that these activities themselves would be immoral purposes and just as fully violative of the Act as prostitution.

In *Nunnally v. United States*[30] (1961), the defendant, a madam, operated a house of prostitution in Montgomery, Alabama, and induced a prostitute to travel from Athens, Georgia, to work in her brothel. The defense was that the madam had merely "promised to put in a good word to obtain employment as a strip dancer in a local club in Montgomery." The evidence showed to the contrary, but the court made no mention that strip dancing might itself be immoral.

Even stronger was the 1974 matter of *United States v. Snow.*[31] A male defendant transported a woman from Covington, Kentucky, to Hurley, Wisconsin. There she engaged in strip dancing and B-drinking, and also prostituted herself "on an average of two or three times per week." There was substantial evidence that the defendant knew of the employment possibilities for prostitutes at the Hurley bar before they left Kentucky and had already talked the girl into joining that profession. The defense was that he had other motives for taking her to Wisconsin. The court assumed that these other motives were "substantial legitimate reasons." Those substantial and legitimate reasons included the fact that the owner of the bar "needed women solely to dance and solicit drinks during the busy hunting season." Again, there was no thought that this itself might violate the Mann Act.

Thus, there was a shift in judicial reaction to nude photography, erotic dancing, and B-drinking as immoral purposes in response to the Sexual Revolution and the sharp changes in American mores and sexual practices from the 1960s onward. But these cases must have been easier for judges than the occasional prosecution involving interstate travels of unmarried couples living together or weekend travels of girlfriends to see boyfriends for purposes that included sex. These were more classically "immoral purposes," and there was a solid wall of precedent denouncing interstate travel to facilitate them.

An unmarried couple living together were in a state of concubinage, to use the older, pejorative term. As early as 1913 a court had considered the case of a man who persuaded a woman with whom he lived "to go from one state to another for the purpose of engaging in illicit intercourse, cohabitation, and concubinage" with the defendant only. There was no element of prostitution nor of a temporary affair. He was guilty, without doubt. "Certainly illicit cohabitation and concubinage are immoral acts analogous to prostitution, and come well within the letter of the statute."[32]

Concubinage, or living together, was thereafter quite regularly regarded as well within the forbidden purposes of interstate travel. In an earlier chapter we considered the *Mackreth* prosecution as an example of Southern moralistic bigotry. Four years before trial, the defendants "began living together as man and wife . . . The woman was 33 years old and the man older. Both had been married and divorced. They held themselves out as married and the man supported the woman entirely. She never engaged in public prostitution. They travelled around the country together . . . and registered at various hotels in different states as man and wife."

The conviction of the Mackreth couple was reversed because they were charged only with conspiracy. After *Gebardi* the woman could not be guilty of conspiracy by simply consenting to the travel, and the man could not conspire by himself. However, the appellate court that reversed the conviction was prepared to concede, in 1939, that "the man was guilty of the substantive offense denounced by the statute."[33] Had he been charged simply with the Mann Act violation, rather than a conspiracy, the transportation in interstate commerce of his common law wife would have been enough to render him guilty.

All of this had changed by the 1970s. In part, men simply were no longer prosecuted for traveling with women with whom they lived. But even in prostitution cases, there is plenty of judicial expression in dicta that living together, or concubinage, would no longer be a sufficient immoral purpose to violate the Mann Act. In *United States v. Tobin*[34] (1970), defendant Daniel Tobin lived with Janice Tressa, a prostitute in Peoria, Illinois, and lived off her earnings. A second prostitute, Venus Wright, independently planned a trip to Topeka, Kansas, to work as a prostitute in a hotel there.

The defendant denied any role in asking Janice to go to Kansas, and there was some evidence that indicated she had an independent family reason to go. The three traveled to Kansas, and Janice continued working as a prostitute. It was undisputed that in Topeka Venus handled all the financial arrangements for both herself and Janice. Tobin played no role in the prostitution arrangements, although he did continue to live with Janice and was supported by her.

His defense would have been unthinkable in the old days where prosecutions were routine for traveling to facilitate concubinage. He claimed, as the appellate court stated it, that "his dominant motive in transporting Janice Tressa to Topeka was not for immoral purposes but rather was for accommodation in that he had been living with her as her common law husband and desired to continue to do so." The court fully accepted that were this established it would be a good defense and reversed the conviction and sentence of five years in prison because of overly eager cross-examination conducted by the judge himself who had lost his position of neutrality in the trial.

We have already looked at the *Snow* case, wherein the appellate court considered erotic dancing and B-drinking as "substantial legitimate reasons" for a man's interstate transportation of a woman. Another one of those "substantial legitimate reasons" that court listed as a motive for the transportation was that the male defendant lived with the woman.[35]

What about interstate transportation of women for casual sexual relations, with no pretense of a stable relationship? Surely that is a classic "immoral" purpose. In 1960 Clarence McClung was indicted for transporting two different women, both having the same surname and very possibly sisters, on two different occasions, from Huntington, West Virginia, to LaPlace, Louisiana, "for an immoral purpose, to-wit, for the purpose of engaging in sexual intercourse . . . with her." A courageous judge, J. Skelly Wright, who later almost singlehandedly

created the implied warranty of habitability in residential rental hous-
ing, granted a defense motion to dismiss the indictment.

As he analyzed the indictment, it alleged only "a single, isolated
instance of intercourse. . . . The inference is left open that all there was
to the affair, and all that was ever contemplated, was the single act."
Wright summarized the charges as being only that "on two occasions
the defendant brought an unattached and willing woman across state
lines for a casual affair and she did not suffer from the experience." He
asked rhetorically whether he was "the evil 'trafficker' the Mann Act
condemns or she the 'white slave' it was designed to protect?"

Wright acknowledged, as he had to, the numerous cases extending
the Act to noncommercial, consensual affairs. But he wrote that neither
Caminetti nor "any other case" had gone as far as the bare facts of this
indictment, and that in the "absence of compelling precedent this court
must refuse to violate both the letter and the spirit of the enactment." It
would violate this letter and spirit for two reasons. First, "other
immoral purpose" had to have some of the same character as prostitution and debauchery and therefore could include "only the more notorious or vicious sexual immoralities." A single act of intercourse could
not qualify.

But even if mere sexual intercourse did qualify as an immoral purpose, the Act could only be violated by an immorality which is "habit-
ual . . . an immoral *status* of some duration" (emphasis in original).
Wright concluded on a tone of moralism and righteousness: "Let no
one read here an apology for the conduct charged. . . . Nor yet do judges
make the law. Approve or not, the court must apply the statutes which
others have written." The decision itself was approved by many legal
commentators.[36]

How reasonable Wright makes it seem. He is merely compelled by
the statute Congress wrote to find that the Act does not condemn the
acts alleged. Therefore, he must dismiss the indictment. It is a superb
example of a common law judge making new law even while denying
that he is making law at all. The Supreme Court itself had done no less
in *Caminetti* by ignoring obvious legislative intent.

Clearly Wright changed the law because he ignored obvious precedent by denying that it existed. In *Elrod v. United States*[37] (1920), the
defendant took a woman from Nashville, Tennessee, to Louisville,
Kentucky. They registered at a hotel, stayed there one night, enjoyed
sexual relations, and returned. For all that appears, as in the McClung

indictment, they were both single and the woman was of age. That evidence was deemed sufficient in 1920 to support the conviction.

In 1927 an appellate court considered an indictment nearly identical to that deemed insufficient by Judge Wright in *McClung*. An indictment was held good in *Blain v. United States*[38] that alleged the immoral purpose to be that "Lovel A. Blain [defendant] and Willie Bragg ["victim"] to have unlawful sexual intercourse, the said Lovel A. Blain and Willie Bragg being not married." A single act of consensual intercourse was likewise judicially deemed a sufficient immoral purpose in *Neff v. United States*[39] (1939).

In *Jarabo v. United States*[40] (1946), a male student at the University of Puerto Rico attended a party with a female student. After the party the couple went to a cafe where they danced and drank until about 10:00 P.M. The defendant drove his date home, but on the way they stopped and had intercourse, which may or may not have been consensual.

The appellate court held that the evidence was sufficient to convict. The jury could have found "that at some point on the trip, either on the way from the party to the cafe or after leaving the cafe to go home, the purpose developed in the appellant's mind . . . of having sexual intercourse with her. . . . [T]hat is enough to sustain the conviction . . . [even though he] also intended eventually to take the woman home. It is enough if one of the purposes of his transportation of her was within the ban of the statute."

Brown v. United States[41] (1956), although a case of forced sex, specifically rejected the argument that the Act was not applicable to "a noncommercial, isolated, single immoral transaction." It is clear enough that there was an abundance of precedent that isolated acts of intercourse were an immoral purpose for Mann Act convictions. The real driving force beyond Judge Wright's opinion was simply that the times had changed. To *change* the law while wrapping the opinion within a guise of reluctantly *following* the law, is an old and useful trick of the common law judge. It permits flexibility while preserving the socially useful sense of continuity.

After *McClung*, judges became increasingly hostile to allegations of Mann Act violation for consensual, noncommercial sexual activities, in what few circumstances they had to pass on such issues. *United States v. Wolf*[42] (1986) was a Mann Act prosecution of a man who clearly sexually exploited female immigrants from Thailand, perhaps even by force. His conviction was reversed for trial errors, but not without a clear expression of skepticism being first sounded by the majority of the Court of Appeals. "This country's sexual mores have changed in the last thirty years and it may be questioned whether today a purpose to engage in adultery or fornication, when these acts are committed without aggravating circumstances, such as force, misrepresentation, or taking advantage of a minor, is immoral within the meaning of the Mann Act."

The court expressly "left the question open," providing a hint to the prosecutor to do some screening, to make sure before retrying the case that such aggravating circumstances existed or run the risk in a later appeal that the law would simply be changed.

Also in 1986 a trial court in Kansas had opportunity to pass on a motion to dismiss a civil complaint of a RICO or racketeering violation. To constitute a RICO violation it is necessary that the defendant have committed a prior "crime" within specified categories before and in addition to the specific crime charged. A Mann Act violation could qualify as such a prior crime. In *NL Industries, Inc. v. Gulf & Western Industries, Inc.*[43] plaintiff NL Industries claimed that the crime of defendant Gulf & Western Industries was a violation of the Mann Act. A low-level female employee of Gulf & Western was having an affair with the Houston plant manager of NL, and NL alleged she was hired by Gulf & Western for the reason of exploiting that connection. The couple traveled together to a business meeting across state boundaries and there continued their affair. The court simply brushed this aside, stating that an "on-going affair between two consenting adults in the 1980s was not 'any other immoral purpose' as intended to be prohibited and punished by the Mann Act."

It was not just the judiciary that responded to the changed sexual culture in America. The Department of Justice issued many guidelines over the years, urging restraint in the prosecution of noncommercial cases. That restraint was not uniformly exercised in the various regions of the country. In 1962 the Department of Justice went much farther and prohibited United States Attorneys from prosecuting noncommercial Mann Act cases without express approval of the Criminal Division. The FBI responded in like fashion and relied on local authorities to handle routine cases, concentrating its efforts on what it described as "organized commercialized prostitution."[44]

The only way to analyze the circumstances under which the Criminal Division gave permission for prosecution is to assess appeals from

Mann Act convictions. Since the 1962 prohibition there have been only four appeals from convictions involving consensual and noncommercial sexual activities. One was the 1986 *Wolf* case, and that may have involved elements of force. In any event, as we have seen, *Wolf* was reversed for a new trial with strong hints that the prosecutor ought to reconsider. The two *Hattaway* appeals of 1968 and 1969[45] were from Mann Act prosecutions that followed acquittals of kidnapping charges involving the same fifteen-year-old girl. Even though the Hattaways were acquitted of the kidnapping charges, there is reason to suspect that force was used for the sexual activities involving the girl.

In the years after 1962, when the Department of Justice began to require advance clearance for noncommercial prosecutions, there has been only one appellate case involving a clearly consensual and non-commercial Mann Act violation. From what appears in that case, *United States v. Auterson*,[46] there were only two single incidents of for-nication. But the two girls, sisters, were only fourteen and fifteen years old.

Although there may be other convictions that were never appealed, it would seem from the appellate record that Mann Act prosecutions for consensual, noncommercial sexual activities virtually ceased after 1962. In 1966 the Attorney General stated flatly, in sharp contradiction of past practices, that the Mann Act "is designed to deprive those engaged in commercialized prostitution of the use of the facilities of interstate commerce."[47] However, Washington continued to approve noncom-mercial prosecutions involving rape and kidnapping.

Mann Act prosecutions for forcible sex following interstate trans-portation had been made from the earliest days of enforcement. There are at least two from 1918 and 1926.[48] But only in the 1960s, 1970s, and 1980s did they become quite common and routine. Mann Act charges sometimes were simply added onto kidnapping charges if sexual activi-ties were involved. At other times they were brought where the actual transportation was consensual and therefore kidnapping could not be established, but the intention to have sex with the woman, *nolens volens*, could be inferred at the time of the crossing of the state line.[49] Still another circumstance prompting Mann Act prosecution was where state charges of rape were dismissed or had resulted in an acquittal.[50]

Several defendants in these prosecutions for forced sex attempted to use the *McClung* precedent for the assertion that the Mann Act did not apply to rape, since that activity, whatever else it might be, is noncommercial. This led the 8th Circuit to gently disapprove *McClung*,[51] and the 7th Circuit to hold that rape was within the *McClung* court's definition of immoral purpose as "a limited category, encompassing only the more notorious or vicious sexual immoralities."[52] *McClung* was raised in the pornographic movie prosecution, but the *Roeder* court distinguished it on the basis that *McClung* involved uncompensated and private sexual activities.[53]

The optimism of the social hygienists in the 1950s that the corner had finally been turned in the control of prostitution was dashed by the experience of the 1960s and 1970s. In the late 1970s the federal government estimated that there were approximately two million prostitutes in the United States, and of those 600 thousand were teenagers. Indeed, it calculated that the number of teenage girls entering prostitution jumped 242 percent between 1967 and 1976.[54] It was the time of the "Minnesota connection" between Minneapolis and New York, and a Minneapolis policeman testified before a New York legislative committee in November 1977 that pimps were taking three hundred to four hundred women annually to New York from Minneapolis alone.[55]

In fact, there was a revival of discussion of forced prostitution. Throughout the 1970s and into the early 1980s articles appeared from time to time in the *New York Times* wherein women claimed they had been forcibly held as prostitutes in the New York City area.[56] In 1979 two men transported two fourteen-year-old girls from Missouri to Chicago. One of the men drugged the girls, forced them to engage in prostitution, and held them in a condition as closely approximating the original conception of "white slavery" as any case that has ever made its way to the appellate courts. The Mann Act conviction was affirmed.[57] 1983 saw a federal conviction for forcible prostitution in Florida.[58] On one hand, one reputable study in the late 1960s claimed that most prostitutes became such out of individual choice, not force or trickery, that the current surveys of prostitution were devoid of references to seduction, procurers, or white-slavers, and that organized crime rings were much less active in prostitution than formerly.[59] However, there were other studies that found considerable organization and extent to coerced prostitution.[60]

Gangs or no, forced or free, it was clear that the 1960s and 1970s saw a sharp increase in the number of teenaged prostitutes and that many of these young prostitutes were transported into New York from other areas of the country. Occasionally there would be a crackdown, as in

1978 when the Washington, D.C., police began an investigation of California pimps bringing teenage prostitutes into the District.[61] But the reality was that total Mann Act convictions, and therefore prosecutions, crashed during the 1960s and 1970s. It must be remembered that the conviction figures, shown in tabular form below, reflect *all* Mann Act convictions—for prostitution, rape, and the rare noncommercial and consensual prosecution. Most of these were very serious cases; the average prison sentences for the convictions in fiscal years 1973 and 1974 were 43.5 months and 47.0 months, respectively. These were considerably longer than in the days of the morals crusade and even stiffer than the period of the vice rings attacked by Hoover in the late 1930s.

Year (fiscal years)	Convictions[62]
1959	184
1960	153
1961	169
1962	170
1963	146
1964	115
1965	96
1966	75
1967	81
1968	80
1969–72*	
1973	58
1974	48
1975	45
1976	36
1977–79	
1980	14
1981	16

* Mann Act conviction figures were not published in the Annual Reports after fiscal year 1968, with the exceptions of 1973–76. They were available through another source for 1980–81.

A commentator writing in 1969 claimed that the Mann Act was in its twilight.[63] Even though it might be in twilight, there was still a considerable amount of awareness of the Act, at least by those within the business of prostitution. A madam of a small house in the early 1970s reported to an interviewer that she had a rule of refusing to hire women from outside her state and even went so far as to check the telephone numbers of employees for possible residence out-of-state. She reportedly told the FBI that "if any girls are coming in here from across state lines, they're getting over on me as well as you, so I would appreciate knowing about it."[64] In 1960 two pimps and a prostitute concocted a story that the woman was picked up *after* crossing the line, in the event of a subsequent arrest,[65] and in 1976 a prostitute about to travel from Portland to Alaska was told she must purchase the airline ticket herself. "We have to do that . . . this way because there is a legal hassle."[66]

Law was still being made involving the Mann Act, notwithstanding its "twilight" appearance. Congress had made Mann Act violations one of the necessary prior, or predicate crimes, in cases brought under the RICO statute, the Racketeer Influenced and Corrupt Organizations Act. Where the defendant had assets, this statute offered the prosecution the additional sanction of forfeiture. Prosecutors used the RICO tool in both prostitution[67] and child sexual molestation cases.[68] Civil litigants attempted to use the Mann Act in private RICO litigation, with much less success.[69]

Indeed, the *Mortensen* defense was still being litigated. Most of the circuit courts agreed on the test of "dominant purpose," with the refinement that prostitution, debauchery, or other immoral purpose had to be *one* of the dominant purposes, not necessarily *the* dominant purpose.[70] And there were acquittals and reversals on appeal[71] due to a failure of the evidence to pass the dominant purpose standard in commercial cases.

Although it may have been in twilight, as of the late 1970s there was still considerable heat and light cast by the Mann Act. But changes were soon to come.

The Collapse of Federal Standards of Morality

After the dawn of the Sexual Revolution in the 1960s the Mann Act entered into a gathering darkness. Following the 1962 order of the Department of Justice, it was virtually unenforced in non-commercial settings, except for rape. Even in cases of actual prostitution, enforcement fell to a minimum. Convictions under the Mann Act plummeted, totaling for the entire country, only forty-eight in fiscal year 1974, thirty-six in 1976, and dropping to fourteen in 1980.[1]

But Congress still remained paralyzed, unable to repeal the statute, or even to amend the act to eliminate the "other immoral purpose" that had facilitated the repressive activity of the morals crusade in earlier decades. Indeed in 1970, in a minor way, Congress actually toughened the obscure section of the Act that required the filing of a statement of an alien female maintained for prostitution or any other immoral purpose.[2]

The more familiar transportation provisions of the Mann Act remained essentially as they had been in 1910. Prior to 1978, notably in the late 1940s, there had been some few amendments to the more familiar provisions of the statute. These were merely language simplifications, and the only modification of any interest was the deletion of the title "White-slave traffic Act."[3]

Congressmen were as unwilling to be viewed as standing up for immorality as they had been in the wake of the *Caminetti* case. Doubtless they sensed that the church and civic groups could still mount the letter campaigns they had in the past and protest any weakening of this monument to morality. But in 1978 and then again in 1986, congressmen amended the archaic act in a somewhat cowardly fashion by sweeping the amendments within related bills that commanded great popularity.

A major public concern of the mid-1970s was an explosion in the sexual exploitation of juveniles. First, there was a startling rise in prostitution among juvenile girls. FBI statistics indicated that the numbers of teenage girls becoming prostitutes boomed by 242 percent between 1967 and 1976.[4] In the years 1975 through 1977 many articles analyzed and appraised prostitution among teenaged girls, particularly the movement of these girls from the upper Midwest to New York.[5]

Second, there was great public apprehension about the increasing use of juveniles in pornography. Typical of the current political comments and reminiscent of the old white slavery allegations was that of State Senator Ralph J. Marino, Chairman of the State [New York] Select Committee on Crime. He claimed that his committee had "information which indicates that there are organized rings involved in 'kiddie pornography'"—that is, using children for obscene films.[6] Many, many articles were written about the perceived problem, generating political pressure for Congress to act.[7]

A third public concern in the mid-1970s, and directly related to the Mann Act, was the growth of male prostitution, a phenomenon which almost invariably involved juvenile males. One of the earliest American histories of prostitution, published in 1858, had observed that in the early Roman empire the male prostitutes had probably been as numerous as the female. But in speaking of the United States with a good deal of self-satisfaction, the male author of this text noted that "fortunately the progress of good morals has divested this repulsive theme [male prostitution] of its importance; [it is] a branch of the subject which in this country is not likely to require fresh legislative notice."[8]

The phenomenon of male prostitution, or at least the notice of it, grew very slowly. A scholarly study in 1968 concluded that "it is very difficult to judge how numerous male prostitutes are,"[9] whereas a 1971 observer thought that "though it is difficult for them to make a living at it, male homosexual prostitutes are increasing."[10] By the mid-1970s there was the same explosion in newspaper coverage of male prostitution, almost always involving juveniles, that existed on parallel tracks with articles concerning female juvenile prostitution. Lurid headlines from 1976 and 1977 tell the story: "At Night, Block Belongs to the Male Prostitutes"; "'Chicken-Hawk' Trade Found Attracting More Young

Boys to Times Square Area"; "Chicago Jury to Probe Pornography and Prostitution Involving Boys"; and "3 Arrested in Raid on Alleged Male Prostitution Ring."[11]

These concerns and the political pressures resulting from their vast publicity led to several hearings before various subcommittees of the United States House and Senate during the spring and summer of 1977. The result of a rather complicated course of legislative maneuvering was the passage of the Protection of Children Against Sexual Exploitation Act of 1977, unanimously approved by the House, with only one dissenting vote in the Senate.[12] It was signed into law by President Carter in January 1978.[13]

The major theme of the bill was to prohibit the use of minors in pornography and the sale or distribution of materials depicting juveniles engaged in sexually explicit acts, whether or not legally obscene. However, during the course of its hearings the Senate Subcommittee to Investigate Juvenile Delinquency had heard considerable testimony concerning the interstate traffic in young boys for prostitution, was made to understand that the existing Mann Act applied only to females, and resolved to amend the Mann Act by an amendment to the pending bill dealing with child pornography.

The 1978 amendment to the Mann Act involved only the third of the three transportation sections. This section, as originally written, doubled the maximum punishment, from five years or $5,000, or both, to ten years or $10,000, or both, in the case of a female under the age of eighteen years. It was patterned after the second of the transportation sections in that it required persuasion, inducement, enticement, or coercion of the transportation, interstate, foreign, or within a federal territory, of a girl under eighteen for the purpose that she engage in prostitution, debauchery, or any other immoral purpose.

Like the second transportation section, and unlike the crime of actually transporting the woman, the third section had required that the girl travel "upon the line or route of any common carrier." Common carrier does not include automobile, and we may recall this had led to a major anomaly in the law. If a man transported a woman across a state line for a prohibited purpose by private automobile he violated the Mann Act, as the first section did not require travel along the line of a common carrier. If a man induced or persuaded a woman (the second section) or a girl under eighteen (the third transportation section) to cross a state line by private automobile to come to *him*, the Act was not violated.

The 1978 amendment recast the Mann Act's section on minors to begin with language applying its sanctions to "any person who transports, finances in whole or in part the transportation of, or otherwise causes or facilitates the movement of, any minor" within interstate or foreign commerce or within a federal district or possession for a prohibited purpose. This part of the amended statute eliminated the requirement that the transportation be by common carrier; transportation by automobile would do. It also eliminated the requirement of inducement, persuasion, and so forth, in favor of doing the transporting or otherwise causing or facilitating—a much broader provision. Finally, this introductory language used gender neutral language of "any minor," hence making the prohibition equally applicable to male juveniles as females.

The prohibited purpose was also changed in the 1978 amendment. No longer was it that the defendant intended that the juvenile engage in prostitution, debauchery, or any other immoral purpose. Rather, the 1978 amendment required the intent that the minor either engage in "prostitution" or, alternatively, engage in "prohibited sexual conduct," if the person transporting the minor or facilitating the transportation "knows or has reason to know" that the sexual conduct "will be commercially exploited by any person."

The enhanced punishment of the original section, ten years or $10,000, or both, was retained. Prohibited sexual conduct was defined in great detail as including either: "(A) sexual intercourse, including genital-genital, oral-genital, anal-genital, or oral-anal, whether between persons of the same or opposite sex; (B) bestiality; (C) masturbation; (D) sado-masochistic abuse (for the purpose of sexual stimulation); or (E) lewd exhibition of the genitals or pubic area of any person."[14]

The FBI utilized the 1978 amendment in a crackdown on male prostitution in the District of Columbia in 1983,[15] but the new law's more general effectiveness was questioned because male prostitutes tend not to have pimps. If a male juvenile crosses a state line for purposes of prostitution, he usually does so by his own resources and under no one's persuasion but his own.[16] Therefore, he would not be within the Act, which has never prohibited persons from transporting *themselves* for purposes of prostitution, debauchery, other immoral purposes, or even the new "prohibited sexual conduct." Quite aside from these theoretical concerns, the total numbers of Mann Act convictions were in sharp decline in the years before and after 1978. It is clear that the amendments of that year had no particular impact.

In the early 1980s congressional attention turned to the removal of sexism from federal statutes. These changes were more than cosmetic and were an effort to eliminate sex discrimination by changing the substance of various laws as well as to recast statutes into gender neutral language. As a part of this process of examining unfairly differing treatment for men and women, the Mann Act came under fire in Congress, as reported by United Press International, "for putting the onus of the law on the male partner of a couple who drive from one jurisdiction to another and have consenting sexual relations."[17]

There had been attacks on the one-way street aspect of the Mann Act in the courts. In the 1975 case of *United States v. Garrett*,[18] a pimp lived with his girl in St. Louis and took her to Las Vegas, Nevada, because there was more money to be made there. It was a classic commercial case. He raised the interesting defense that the Mann Act was unconstitutional because it was only illegal to transport females for immoral purposes, and this denied him the equal protection of the law. The appellate court said not so. First, Garrett, the defendant-pimp, was not the proper person to raise the claim because he was not an unprotected male victim of such interstate transportation. Second, "though novel, defendant's equal protection argument is untenable." The court reasoned that the persons affected by a criminal statute are the defendants, and the Mann Act defendants could be either men or women, and therefore it was sexually neutral. It was only that the *victims* had to be female, and that did not give the defendant a ground to attack the statute's constitutionality.[19] This logic may be of questionable vitality in current 1994 constitutional adjudication but is nevertheless significant in analyzing the congressional motivation behind the 1978 and 1986 amendments of the Mann Act.

Garrett was decided in the 8th judicial circuit. However, its holding was quickly adopted, in 1977 and 1979, by the 9th Circuit and 5th Circuit as well.[20] Therefore, it was not the compulsion of court cases that motivated Congress to further amend the Mann Act in 1986. It was rather, as reported in September 1983, that congressmen felt the essential unfairness of a law, in the post–Sexual Revolution world, that punished only men for consensual sexual activity of couples.[21] At the same time, other congressional critics criticized the harshness of a law that could make federal felons of teenagers who engaged in sex on a date and happened to cross a state line.[22]

The public expression of these views would have been censurable prior to the Sexual Revolution. Privately, some senators and represen-tatives may have held these thoughts long before 1982, but the sugges-tions of amendment in the past had been blocked by fear of political reactions by American puritans. Now, however, amendment could be described as an elimination of sexism and double standards and could ride on the crest of that tidal wave of the 1980s. It must have caught the attention of some congressmen that the 1978 amendments to the Mann Act, although described in newspaper articles, were generally in the fine print of columns headlined by the theme of child pornography.[23]

Furthermore, it was becoming clearer and clearer that people were just forgetting about the Mann Act. In Vladimir Nabokov's *Lolita* (1955), the aging protagonist, Humbert Humbert, reads in the newspa-per of a middle-aged man convicted of a Mann Act violation with a young girl. In light of his own situation with Lolita, Humbert under-standably "deplore[s] the Mann Act as lending itself to a dreadful pun, the revenge that the Gods of Semantics take against tight-zippered Philistines."[24] In the early 1960s, Frank Sinatra cracked jokes about the Mann Act,[25] and his reference was still clear. However, the public lost touch with that understanding in the 1970s, as Hollywood's treatment of the Mann Act illustrates.

The Great White Hope was a much-fictionalized account of the career of Jack Johnson, the black boxer whose 1912 prosecution was sensational. Directed by Martin Ritt, 20th Century Fox issued the film in 1970. Although primarily concerned with the racial discrimination levied against Johnson in a more general sense, the treatment of his prosecution for the Mann Act violation is significant. The film briefly ran through what was required for the statute's violation, but assumed that viewers would have some familiarity with the Act. Not so with the fact that noncommercial sexual conduct could violate the law. There, it used a plot development to make it very clear to the audience that non-commercial sexual purpose was also included within the Mann Act.

The plot of a 1975 movie, *The Fortune*, released by Columbia Pic-tures and directed by Mike Nichols, was driven in part by an effort to evade the Mann Act in a cross-country journey of a married man and his girlfriend. The filmmakers thought it necessary, as the movie began, to screen a legend, explaining the Mann Act to the audience and how it struck terror into the hearts of men in the 1920s.

To the extent the American people did remember the Mann Act, it was becoming an object of parody or bemusement. In June of 1980 the

Washington Post Magazine ran a story about a newly married couple in the mid-1950s who went to Mexico. When they re-entered the United States the authorities discovered guns, and the couple was arrested and put in jail. "After several hours penned up . . . the captain summoned them and announced that all [the guns were] clean, and that the newlyweds were free to go—providing they could prove they were really married. 'The Mann Act, you know,' he explained. In those days that meant something."[26] In 1980 the writer for the *Post* felt it necessary to remind readers that this law, now violated by lovers with impunity on a routine basis, once was enforced.

A month later in July 1980, *Fortune* spoofed some bungling bureaucratic efforts to protect the poppy mallow flowers. Making sarcastic references to Fish and Wildlife Service regulations, it analogized them to the Mann Act: "The Feds are proposing to protect it in their usual perfectly reasonable way. First, there would be regulations making it illegal to transport the poppy mallow in interstate commerce—sort of like the Mann Act."[27]

Only one major newspaper commemorated the 75th birthday of the Mann Act. The *Boston Globe* recounted the "I am a white slave" note exploited by Clifford G. Roe in Chicago so many years ago. It speculated that the prostitute who wrote the note "quickly forgot her anger at her pimp and went back to work. But she had ignited a holy war. For the next five years, the halls of Congress resounded with the cries of legislators . . . denouncing the perfidious purveyors of shame. The outcome of this national outrage was the Mann Act, which . . . salved America's social conscience. The practice persists because even Congress cannot legislate morality, nor limit its boundaries."[28]

By 1986 congressmen must have felt the political climate for amendment of the Mann Act was not as dangerous as before. Furthermore, they were able to disguise a significant amendment by a twin device. First, it was promoted as an amendment making the law gender neutral and, second, they buried it within the Child Sexual Abuse and Pornography Act of 1986. This Act was prompted, in part, by the Final Report of the Attorney General's Panel on Pornography, issued in July 1986. This Report recommended the amendment of the Mann Act to make all of its provisions gender neutral.[29] There had been some earlier effort to extend the Mann Act to cover the transportation of males. As early as October 1944 the Department of Justice had considered the desirability of securing an amendment to the Act for this purpose, and a bill was introduced in 1962 to extend its provisions to males.[30] It had not been accomplished, however, except for the amendment of the third section alone in 1978.

The major part of the 1986 statute was an amendment to the 1978 legislation regarding juvenile pornography to close a "loophole." The Child Sexual Abuse and Pornography Act of 1986, as its major theme, dispensed with the requirement that the pornography for which juveniles were transported in interstate commerce had to have a commercial purpose. Under the 1986 legislation the interstate transportation of a child to produce pornography even for noncommercial personal gratification was declared illegal.[31]

As a less-publicized part of that statute the Mann Act was significantly amended and weakened. The section requiring the reporting of an alien held for the purposes of prostitution was amended to make it gender neutral. The transportation sections were completely amended and simplified, including the third section which had been amended, as we have seen, as recently as 1978. The three transportation sections, after the 1986 amendments, were and still are as follows, all being a part of Title 18, United States Code:

Section 2421. Transportation generally
    Whoever knowingly transports any individual in interstate or foreign commerce, or in any Territory or Possession of the United States, with intent that such individual engage in prostitution, or in any sexual activity for which any person can be charged with a criminal offense, shall be fined under this title or imprisoned not more than five years, or both.

Section 2422. Coercion and enticement
    Whoever knowingly persuades, induces, entices, or coerces any individual to travel in interstate or* foreign commerce, or in any Territory or Possession of the United States, to engage in prostitution, or in any sexual activity for which any person can be charged with a criminal offense, shall be fined under this title or imprisoned not more than five years, or both.

Section 2423. Transportation of minors
    Whoever knowingly transports any individual under the age of 18 years in interstate or foreign commerce, or in any Territory or Possession of the United States, with intent that such individual engage

* Originally "of" in the 1986 amendment, the typographical error was corrected in 1988.

in prostitution, or in any sexual activity for which any person can be charged with a criminal offense, shall be fined under this title or imprisoned not more than ten years, or both.

All references to a common carrier are gone, all three transportation sections are gender neutral, and "debauchery or any other immoral purpose" have been replaced by "any sexual activity for which any person can be charged with a criminal offense." When President Reagan signed the bill into law in November 1986, the United Press International characterized the Mann Act as "a relic of the early part of this century." It said the new legislation would "eliminate anachronistic features" as well as making it gender neutral. Billed as an antipornography act to give children extra protection "from the slimy underworld," as one congressman put it, these significant amendments to the Mann Act escaped serious scrutiny and sailed through both houses by unanimous votes.[32]

The legislative history of the 1986 law, contained in House Report No. 99-910,[33] made a clear identification of a need for the gender neutral language when it said, "the problem of the sexual exploitation of young males is equally as serious" as that of females. It was somewhat more opaque when it explained the substitution of the new language, "any sexual activity for which any person can be charged with a criminal offense" for the older "debauchery or any other immoral purpose." The House Judiciary Committee wrote:

> Under this language, the offense is transporting any person for illegal sexual activity under any applicable law—Federal, State or local. This is a more appropriate standard for a Federal offense than the current vague standard of "immoral purpose," under which the transportation can be an offense even when the conduct for which the transportation takes place (such as non-commercial sex between consenting unmarried adults) violates no law in any of the jurisdictions involved in the travel. This change reflects a proper recognition of community standards regarding acceptable sexual behavior, in that Federal law would, in effect, apply those standards.[34]

The 1986 amendments took the federal government entirely out of the business of defining "immoral." Except for military and Indian reservations, direct federal possessions such as the District of Columbia, and some few federal enclaves, there are no federal laws on what is an illegal sexual activity. Likewise, there are relatively few municipalities or counties that have ordinances specifying sexual offenses within their boundaries. In many states, such ordinances would probably be void as preempted by state legislative action.

Thus the new Mann Act phrase "any sexual activity for which any person can be charged with a criminal offense" depends almost entirely on the law of the state into which the transported individual travels in order to undertake the sexual activity. Almost all American states have repealed their fornication statutes, and many have likewise decriminalized adultery.

The number of jurisdictions that have retained criminal sanctions against oral sex, anal intercourse, and other sexual practices regarded as deviant, is somewhat larger. However, it would be very difficult to establish that such a specific practice is the motivating intent behind interstate transportation. It might be relatively easy to infer that a man intends sex when he takes his girlfriend from Atlanta, Georgia, to Birmingham, Alabama, for a romantic weekend, but it is considerably more difficult to infer that he specifically intends, when crossing the state line, that she engage in oral sex with him—a Class A misdemeanor in Alabama.

Of course, the Mann Act is still available for an interstate transportation where the sexual activity is nonconsensual and clearly illegal. There continue to be prosecutions under the Mann Act in situations where women are consensually transported or induced to travel of their own will to another state by defendants who rape them once they have finished their interstate journey. An example following the 1986 amendments is *United States v. Howard*.[35] In this 1988 case, the male defendants allegedly lured sixteen different women, at varying times, to travel to Florida at their own expense, ostensibly to try out for a television show. Once they were there, defendants raped them.

Kidnapping would not apply here since the travel was consensual. But the Mann Act does fit, since rape is a crime punishable under Florida law and with this pattern the defendants clearly intended that the women travel in order to engage in a sexual activity (forcible intercourse) for which any person (the defendants themselves) could be charged with a criminal offense (rape under Florida state law). Likewise, the Mann Act is still fully applicable to transportation for prostitution or statutory rape. In 1987, for example, a 36-year-old man was charged with violations of the Mann Act for transporting two girls, on several occasions, from Brooklyn, New York, to New Jersey for fully consensual sexual intercourse. The girls were only twelve and thirteen years old.[36]

But in the area of adult, consensual, noncommercial sexual activity the Mann Act is now severely limited, both by law and social attitudes. There are only a limited number of states that criminalize adultery or fornication, and if the conduct is not punishable by state law there is no Mann Act violation. Except for very unusual situations, it would be practically impossible to prove the motivating intent to engage in a specific consensual sexual activity, such as oral or anal sex, that happened to be taboo in the state into which the transportation occurred.

Beyond this, however, the most significant barrier is that the vast majority of the American public is far more tolerant of extramarital sexuality than it was in the early part of the century. It would be extremely difficult today, anywhere in the United States, for a federal prosecutor to obtain a jury verdict convicting a man or woman for interstate travel involving noncommercial sexual activity between consenting adults. Therefore, as a practical matter, the Mann Act is now limited to prostitution, forced sex, and perhaps the creation of pornography.

Throughout this book, the focus has been on the direct effects of the Mann Act on individuals, either through prosecution or blackmail. It is important to understand that there were indirect effects as well and to briefly sketch those. For example, an attorney could be disbarred for a conviction under the Mann Act, even though he was guilty of no professional misconduct at all.[37] A Mann Act charge, even short of conviction, could bar an applicant from admission to practice law, especially if the applicant failed to disclose the fact that he had been accused.[38]

Often criminal statutes provide that a sentence can be increased if the defendant has suffered previous conviction. Mann Act convictions served as prior felony convictions for purposes of enhancing sentences on later, completely unrelated crimes.[39] Also, there are some crimes that require as an element of their offense that the defendant has previously been convicted of a felony. For these purposes a Mann Act conviction counted as a prior felony.[40]

Convictions could be used in subsequent proceedings as impeachment. A witness in an unrelated trial could be asked about a previous conviction of the Mann Act in order to persuade the jury that the witness was unreliable.[41] Or, if a criminal defendant called character witnesses to the defendant's good character, the prosecution could ask whether those witnesses had heard of the defendant's previous Mann

Act conviction.[42] These impeachment procedures are consistent with ordinary evidence law, and there is nothing special about the fact that the previous conviction was of the Mann Act.

Factual situations which amounted to a violation of the Mann Act undoubtedly were the legal bases of thousands of divorces, although they passed under the rubric of adultery, a standard ground for marital dissolution. In one interesting variation of that, a husband successfully urged "cruel and inhumane treatment" as a ground for divorce, based upon his wife having caused the Department of Justice to investigate her claim that he had violated the Mann Act.[43] Because violation of the Mann Act was a crime, the privilege against self-incrimination was fully applicable. The privilege applied not only in criminal investigations,[44] but to civil cases such as paternity,[45] divorce,[46] and breach of contract.[47]

Still another indirect use of Mann Act convictions was for naturalization and deportation. We will recall Marco Reginelli was the gambler in New Jersey hounded by the federal government for the transportation of his adult girlfriend to Florida in 1942 for a vacation. He remained single throughout this litigation, was a native of Italy, and had lived in the United States since 1914. Reginelli sought naturalization in 1944 and again in 1955. The federal government opposed it successfully, on the basis of the 1942 Mann Act conviction, his gambling activities, and, curiously, on the additional basis that he was still seeing the girlfriend, also single, that he had transported to Florida in 1942.[48]

But with the cruelty of a cat, the federal government was not through toying with Marco Reginelli. The government could not find evidence to convict him of a crime but tried to deport him instead. The Immigration Service began deportation proceedings in 1952 and urged as one ground the 1942 consensual, noncommercial violation of the Mann Act. The special inquiry officer found that Reginelli was not deportable on the grounds alleged by the government. Not content with that answer, the Immigration Service appealed the finding. The Board of Immigration Appeals found that the Mann Act conviction arising out of the transportation and sexual activity between two consenting, unmarried adults, did not amount to moral turpitude, and denied the deportation.[49]

The Mann Act touched surprisingly many aspects and institutions of American life during its tortured history. Its passage was rooted in the turn-of-the-century anxiety over urbanization, changing sexual mores, and the dangers thought to be threatened by the New Immigration. Early enforcement of the Act provided a tremendous impetus to the growth of the FBI and prepared it for an even greater role during the days of Prohibition. It not only became the stuff of blackmail and extortion, but also entered the American culture through literature, pop culture, and jokes. Unfortunately, the Mann Act also became an instrument of racism and a weapon to use on targeted defendants such as radicals and gangsters.

We might pause to ask a larger question. What is wrong with this prosecutorial discretion? Suppose that the U.S. Attorney in New Jersey knew terrible things about Marco Reginelli, for example, but the prosecution could not prove it. Why should not the prosecutor use any tool available to deal with such a person? Why not the Mann Act?

The prosecutorial discretion to refuse prosecution of a probable crime, perhaps because a case is too petty or the acts too justified by public opinion regardless of illegality, is an essential part of the justice system. It allows the cold commands of stern law to be moderated by feeling and by sentiment. But the discretion involved in targeting a German sympathizer or a gambler for a Mann Act violation is quite a different matter. The latter is an affirmative discretion to prosecute for acts—the noncommercial Mann Act violation—that in a more "normal" defendant the prosecutor would ignore and not even seek to indict.

This affirmative use of discretion to prosecute where ordinarily the prosecutor would not, perverts the legal system. It hands to the prosecutor the functions of both judge and jury. Suppose in the "ordinary" open-and-shut, consensual and noncommercial Mann Act violation, a certain local prosecutor would not seek an indictment. Now comes a possible defendant, whom the prosecutor "knows" to be a bad person, deserving of punishment or imprisonment. About this person there is also an open-and-shut, consensual and noncommercial Mann Act violation. If the prosecutor seeks an indictment, he is doing so for reasons entirely extraneous to the Mann Act offense; he is doing so because he "knows" the defendant to be a "bad man" and deserving of punishment. But since he is not required to prove the "bad man" status of the defendant in the white slavery prosecution, indeed would ordinarily be prevented from doing so, it is the prosecutor who is acting as judge and jury as to this defendant's real offense: whatever the prosecutor thinks it is that makes this person "bad."

That sort of affirmative discretion, as distinct from the negative variety, is a threat to the judicial system. It distorts the appropriate functions of the players, the proper roles of the prosecutor, judge, and finder of fact or jury. It also has the additional vice of being entirely free from any review and therefore totally unsupervised. Once the prosecutor has made the determination to go ahead with the prosecution, the focus then shifts to the acts that might constitute a violation of the Mann Act and not to the reasons why the prosecutor decided to go ahead with this case rather than the 99.9 percent of the cases he has declined to prosecute.

The danger involved in the exercise of this sort of discretion is exacerbated when the offense deals with sexuality, as natural and normal an aspect of life as eating and drinking. The danger can be illustrated by an exaggeration. Suppose there were a statute that made it a felony to eat any food before noon. Almost everyone would violate that law, and therefore it would give prosecutors the ability to punish anyone they did not like and the ability to do so for reasons having nothing to do with the morning consumption of food.

Occasionally, the probabilities for abuse of this prosecutorial discretion have been recognized by federal prosecutors, usually *after* they have left office. A former Special Assistant to the Attorney General wrote in 1945, after leaving the department:

> Though the public generally may applaud such unintended applications of the White Slave Traffic Act [noncommercial prosecutions, unintended by Congress] it can be easily seen that such wide latitude of discretion allowed to the prosecutor by the loose wording of the act leaves ample room for persecution and unequal enforcement of criminal law.[50]

The White Slave Traffic Act serves as a wonderful example of a political fact of life: it is far easier to enact a statute than it is to repeal one. The Act lingered on, long after its utility had passed. When the original "white slavers" had been crushed, the statute remained. When, by the 1930s, local U.S. Attorneys often refused to prosecute noncommercial cases, the Act was not amended. After 1962, when noncommercial prosecutions generally ceased, the Act was still not amended. No congressman had the courage to support the repeal or amendment of a statute that appeared to be a tool against prostitution, debauchery, or other immorality. No congressman wished to risk appearing to stand up and be counted in favor of sex and sin. Even after decades of virtual nonenforcement, and an entire revolution in American attitudes toward sexuality, Congress resorted to a trick to amend the Mann Act—by sweeping the change under the rug of a new and popular statute, itself promising to crack down on vice.

The Mann Act was born of hysteria over a crisis that was more myth than fact, more smoke than fire. But there *was* smoke, and the genuineness of the public's belief in the actuality of the white slavery fire of coerced prostitution justified some narrowly crafted legislative response. Unfortunately, Congress used overly general language, going far beyond the problem it purported to address. Congress itself crossed over the line by enacting a repressive statute, doomed to failure, that was antithetical to the traditions of maximization of freedom within a liberal state.

The language actually employed almost required the judiciary to apply the Act to voluntary as well as to coerced prostitution. However, by applying the Act to noncommercial sexual relations, *Caminetti* represented a significant turning point that was not at all required by the statute itself. The Court itself went too far.

The application of the Mann Act to consensual, noncommercial "immorality," regardless of whether it be an inspiring example of statutory interpretation, was, nevertheless, what the American people wanted. That real "moral majority" was perfectly prepared to brutally crush any who did not agree with its precepts. We can see these public majoritarian norms if we look once again at the *Caminetti* case. Maury Diggs and Drew Caminetti were not treated by the public as errant rascals. There was no boys-will-be-boys attitude toward what might seem today as rather ordinary seduction and adultery. The national journal *Current Opinion* stated in August 1913 that "Sacramento was shocked at the gravity of the allegations made against the two young men," and Hearst's newspaper, the sensational New York *American*, editorialized that "for deliberate, cold-blooded plotting at the ruin of two innocent young girls there is nothing in the annals of crime surpassing it."[51]

Upon their return from Reno, Caminetti was dismissed from his National Guard unit and Diggs lost architectural contracts through client cancellation. They were publicly ostracized and Caminetti could not find employment in Sacramento and was forced to resort to manual labor in the California oil fields. The prosecutor stated that public opinion throughout California was "burning a white heat."[52] Their hometown newspaper, the *Sacramento Bee,* headlined its editorial following the conviction of Diggs, "A Verdict Which Is Approved By All Good Men And All Decent Women."[53]

Nationally, the newspaper coverage of their trials was overwhelmingly condemnatory of the two, with only a few editorials raising reservations. The citation of just a few of the small-town newspapers editorializing about the convictions demonstrates the extent of American interest in the San Francisco trials. The Sharon, Pennsylvania, *Herald* wrote: "That the Mann Act has proved thoroughly effective should be a matter of rejoicing in every Christian American home." From the Des Moines, Iowa, *Capital*: "It is difficult to see where any other outcome could be expected in the case of Diggs. The evidence was so direct as to be startling." The El Reno, Oklahoma, *American*: "Diggs and Caminetti behind the bars will be a lesson that will have its effects in every hamlet in the land." Tacoma, Washington, *Tribune*: "Its proper enforcement [Mann Act] will rid society of leeches of the Diggs type."[54] Senator Tillman of South Carolina remarked in a public address that if California men had the Southern customs, Caminetti and Diggs "would have been shot like dogs."[55]

Morally repressive public opinion revealed itself again in the aftermath of the trials when a rumor was afloat in the fall of 1913 that the Department of Justice would no longer prosecute noncommercial cases. The Democrats were forced by public opinion to deny the rumor and insist that their policies would be the same as the previous Republican administration's policy. Washington did issue guidelines to local prosecutors, urging them to avoid nonaggravated cases, but, as we have seen, not all prosecutors followed these guidelines. Some, more moralistic themselves or finding themselves in communities of tightened standards, prosecuted just about every noncommercial case they could find.

By the end of the 1920s most local prosecutors had ceased any effort to enforce morality through the Mann Act. This abandonment of the statute was largely because juries refused to convict where there was no element of force or commercialism. After 1928, prosecutions were generally limited to aggravated cases, but the extended legal interpretation given through many precedents had made the Mann Act a powerful prosecutorial tool for other purposes.

Prosecutors used this weapon to target radicals, blacks who dared to have sexual relations with white women, and gangsters, although sometimes juries, to their credit, acquitted even unpopular defendants.

Many local prosecutors also used the Mann Act to persecute individuals they just did not like. These petty targets included political oddballs, out of the American mainstream, such as German sympathizers during the War. Sometimes they were con artists or gamblers, people the United States Attorneys "knew" were bad, but could not convict on any more straightforward basis.

Of course, localized tyranny was foreclosed by the directive in 1962 requiring approval from Washington before the initiation of any prosecution for a noncommercial violation. That simply shifted the possibility of unregulated prosecutorial vindictiveness from the local arena to Washington. However, it did make less likely actual abuse of discretion because its exercise was more controlled, exercised by far fewer persons, and subject to more direct scrutiny. But the history of even Washington's own application of the White Slave Traffic Act has not been encouraging, since it supported the use of the Act to oppress political dissidents and others the federal government found undesirable.

The Mann Act is a splendid example of the failure of American democracy and the federal government, at least so far as the politicization of morality is concerned. The statute was enacted by federal politicians in response to their constituents' hysteria over white slavery. These same bumptious congressmen thereafter lacked all courage to tame their Frankenstein's monster by amendment. The statute was interpreted by federal judges wearing blinders, not acknowledging the real concerns the Congress had addressed, and staying aloof from the collateral consequences caused by the Act's enforcement, and the cowardice of elected politicians to address those evils in a straightforward manner. The statute was enforced by hundreds of local prosecutors, guided until 1962 by national guidelines that were often ignored. Some United States Attorneys approached their task with compassion and understanding of humanity's foibles. All too many used their power to vent their spleen against "immorality," at least until the 1930s when juries ceased to cooperate and began acquitting noncommercial defendants. Other prosecutors, less concerned about moral judgments, saw the Act as a weapon to crush unpopular defendants deemed undesirable for reasons having nothing to do with the Mann Act.

But we should be clear that the Mann Act was not unwanted by Americans; it was nothing "slipped over" on the public when nobody was looking. At least until the 1930s, and perhaps even later, the statute and its enforcement accorded with general American standards of morality. The Mann Act is also, therefore, an equally splendid example of another collateral consequence of this sort of repressive legislation. It permits the exercise of a tyranny of the majority. In the area of non-commercial sexual expression, and particularly as regards women, the intended beneficiaries of the Act, this majoritarian morality profoundly oppressed those whose harmless conduct did not conform.

The Mann Act did not put a halt to interstate immorality. Such repressive legislation will not and did not work. Instead, it set in motion collateral consequences, such as blackmail, selective prosecution, the repression of female sexuality, and the forced imposition of majoritarian controls over harmless conduct. These evils far outweighed any benefits of combating the largely mythical white slavery. In addition, such a repressive statute proved almost impossible to undo and repeal.

In legislative reaction to panic, rigidity of judicial interpretation, and oppressive moralism of enforcement, the Mann Act serves as a model of the sort of statute that ill-serves the country. In future incarnations, not necessarily concerning only interstate sexual activity, any such statute laden with presumptuous moralism will once again ill-serve the nation.

Appendix

White Slave Traffic Act [Mann Act] of 1910

CHAP. 395.—An Act To further regulate interstate and foreign commerce by prohibiting the transportation therein for immoral purposes of women and girls, and for other purposes.

Be it enacted by the Senate and House of Representatives of the United States of America in Congress assembled, That the term "interstate commerce," as used in this Act, shall include transportation from any State or Territory or the District of Columbia to any other State or Territory or the District of Columbia, and the term "foreign commerce," as used in this Act, shall include transportation from any State or Territory or the District of Columbia to any foreign country and from any foreign country to any State or Territory or the District of Columbia.

SEC. 2. That any person who shall knowingly transport or cause to be transported, or aid or assist in obtaining transportation for, or in transporting, in interstate or foreign commerce, or in any Territory or in the District of Columbia, any woman or girl for the purpose of prostitution or debauchery, or for any other immoral purpose, or with the intent and purpose to induce, entice, or compel such woman or girl to become a prostitute or to give herself up to debauchery, or to engage in any other immoral practice; or who shall knowingly procure or obtain, or cause to be procured or obtained, or aid or assist in procuring or obtaining, any ticket or tickets, or any form of transportation or evidence of the right thereto, to be used by any woman or girl in interstate or foreign commerce, or in any Territory or the District of Columbia, in going to any place for the purpose of prostitution or debauchery, or for any other immoral purpose, or with the intent or purpose on the part of such person to induce, entice, or compel her to give herself up to the practice of prostitution, or to give herself up to debauchery, or any other immoral practice, whereby any such woman or girl shall be transported in interstate or foreign commerce, or in any Territory or the District of Columbia, shall be deemed guilty of a felony, and upon conviction thereof shall be punished by a fine not exceeding five thousand dollars, or by imprisonment of not more than five years, or by both such fine and imprisonment, in the discretion of the court.

SEC. 3.   That any person who shall knowingly persuade, induce, entice, or coerce, or cause to be persuaded, induced, enticed, or coerced, or aid or assist in persuading, inducing, enticing, or coercing any woman or girl to go from one place to another in interstate or foreign commerce, or in any Territory or the District of Columbia, for the purpose of prostitution or debauchery, or for any other immoral purpose, or with the intent and purpose on the part of such person that such woman or girl shall engage in the practice of prostitution or debauchery, or any other immoral practice, whether with or without her consent, and who shall thereby knowingly cause or aid or assist in causing such woman or girl to go and to be carried or transported as a passenger upon the line or route of any common carrier or carriers in interstate or foreign commerce, or any Territory or The District of Columbia, shall be deemed guilty of a felony and on conviction thereof shall be punished by a fine of not more than five thousand dollars, or by imprisonment for a term not exceeding five years, or by both such fine and imprisonment, in the discretion of the court.

SEC. 4.   That any person who shall knowingly persuade, induce, entice, or coerce any woman or girl under the age of eighteen years from any State or Territory or the District of Columbia to any other State or Territory or the District of Columbia, with the purpose and intent to induce or coerce her, or that she shall be induced or coerced to engage in prostitution or debauchery, or any other immoral practice, and shall in furtherance of such purpose knowingly induce or cause her to go and to be carried or transported as a passenger in interstate commerce upon the line or route of any common carrier or carriers, shall be deemed guilty of a felony, and on conviction thereof shall be punished by a fine of not more than ten thousand dollars, or by imprisonment for a term not exceeding ten years, or by both such fine and imprisonment, in the discretion of the court.

SEC. 5.   That any violation of any of the above sections two, three, and four shall be prosecuted in any court having jurisdiction of crimes within the district in which said violation was committed, or from, through, or into which any such woman or girl may have been carried or transported as a passenger in interstate or foreign commerce, or in any Territory or the

District of Columbia, contrary to the provisions of any of said sections.

SEC. 6.   That for the purpose of regulating and preventing the transportation in foreign commerce of alien women and girls for purposes of prostitution and debauchery, and in pursuance of and for the purpose of carrying out the terms of the agreement or project of arrangement for the suppression of the white-slave traffic, adopted July twenty-fifth, nineteen hundred and two, for submission to their respective governments by the delegates of various powers represented at the Paris conference and confirmed by a formal agreement signed at Paris on May eighteenth, nineteen hundred and four, and adhered to by the United States on June sixth, nineteen hundred and eight, as shown by the proclamation of the President of the United States, dated June fifteenth, nineteen hundred and eight, the Commissioner-General of Immigration is hereby designated as the authority of the United States to receive and centralize information concerning the procuration of alien women and girls with a view to their debauchery, and to exercise supervision over such alien women and girls, receive their declarations, establish their identity, and ascertain from them who induced them to leave their native countries, respectively; and it shall be the duty of said Commissioner-General of Immigration to receive and keep on file in his office the statements and declarations which may be made by such alien women and girls, and those which are hereinafter required pertaining to such alien women and girls engaged in prostitution or debauchery in this country, and to furnish receipts for such statements and declarations provided for in this act to the persons, respectively, making and filing them.

Every person who shall keep, maintain, control, support, or harbor in any house or place for the purpose of prostitution, or for any other immoral purpose, any alien woman or girl within three years after she shall have entered the United States from any country, party to the said arrangement for the suppression of the white-slave traffic, shall file with the Commissioner-General of Immigration a statement in writing setting forth the name of such alien woman or girl, the place at which she is kept, and all facts as to the date of her entry into the United States, the port through which she entered, her age, nationality, and parentage, and concerning her procuration to come to this country within the knowledge of such person, and any person who shall fail within thirty days after such person shall commence to keep, maintain, control, support, or harbor in any house or place for the purpose of prostitution, or for any other immoral purpose, any alien woman or girl within three years after she shall have entered the United States from any of the countries, party to the said arrangement for the suppression of the white-slave traffic, to file such statement concerning such alien woman or girl with the Commissioner-General of Immigration, or who shall knowingly and willfully state falsely or fail to disclose in such statement any fact within his knowledge or belief with reference to the age, nationality, or parentage of any such alien woman or girl, or concerning her procuration to come to this country, shall be deemed guilty of a misdemeanor, and on conviction shall be punished by a fine of not more than two thousand dollars, or by imprisonment for a term not exceeding two years, or by both such fine and imprisonment, in the discretion of the court.

In any prosecution brought under this section, if it appear that any such statement required is not on file in the office of the Commissioner-General of Immigration, the person whose duty it shall be to file such statement shall be presumed to have failed to file said statement, as herein required, unless such person or persons shall prove otherwise. No person shall be excused from furnishing the statement, as required by this section, on the ground or for the reason that the statement so required by him, or the information therein contained, might tend to criminate him or subject him to a penalty or forfeiture, but no person shall be prosecuted or subjected to any penalty or forfeiture under any law of the United States for or on account of any transaction, matter, or thing, concerning which he may truthfully report in such statement, as required by the provisions of this section.

SEC. 7.   That the term "Territory," as used in this Act, shall include the district of Alaska, the insular possessions of the United States, and the Canal Zone. The word "person," as used in this Act, shall be construed to import both the plural and the singular, as the case demands, and shall include corporations, companies, societies, and associations. When construing and enforcing the provisions of this Act, the act, omission, or failure of any officer, agent, or other person, acting for or employed by any other person or by any corporation, company, society, or association within the scope of his employment or office, shall in every case be also deemed to be the act, omission, or failure of such other person, or of such company, corporation, society, or association, as well as that of the person himself.

SEC. 8.   That this Act shall be known and referred to as the "White-slave traffic Act."

Approved, June 25, 1910.

Notes

CHAPTER ONE

1. Facts together with probable inferences taken from *United States v. Maurice Lorenzo Shannon and Eleanor Whilamea Becker,* No. 9362 and No. 9363, United States District Court, Southern District of Alabama, Record Group 21, Mobile Criminal Dockets, Book S-101, and No. 9362 and 9363, United States District Court, Southern District of Alabama, Southern Division, Record Group 21, Mobile Criminal Cases, Box 188, National Archives—Southeast Region, East Point, Georgia.

2. Facts together with probable inferences taken from *United States v. Reginelli,* 133 F.2d 595 (3d Cir.), *cert. denied,* 318 U.S. 783, *reh'g denied,* 319 U.S. 780 (1943); *Petition of Reginelli,* 86 F. Supp. 599 (D. N.J. 1949); *Petition of Reginelli,* 20 N.J. 266, 119 A.2d 454 (1956); *In the Matter of R——,* 6 I. & N. Dec. 444; 1954 BIA LEXIS 129 (1954).

3. Joseph R. Gusfield, *Symbolic Crusade: Status Politics and the American Temperance Movement* (Urbana: University of Illinois Press, 1963).

4. Robert H. Wiebe, *The Search for Order, 1877–1920* (New York: Hill & Wang, 1967).

5. David B. Danbom, *"The World of Hope": Progressives and the Struggle for an Ethical Public Life* (Philadelphia: Temple University Press, 1987), p. vii.

6. Vice Commission of Chicago, *The Social Evil in Chicago* (Chicago: n.p., 1911), p. 25. However, the commission was not naive. Two pages later its report admitted that "until the hearts of men are changed we can hope for no absolute annihilation of the Social Evil [i.e., prostitution]." On this Progressive belief in social control and human perfectibility, in the context of prostitution, see also, Leslie Fishbein, "Harlot or Heroine? Changing Views of Prostitution, 1870–1920," *Historian* 43 (November 1980): 28.

7. Danbom, *"The World of Hope,"* p. viii.

8. Walter Lippmann, *A Preface to Politics* (New York: Mitchell Kennerly, 1913; reprint, New York: Henry Holt & Co., 1917), pp. 36, 40, 45–46.

9. Ibid., p. 43.

10. *United States v. Williams,* 55 F. Supp. 375, 380 (D. Minn. 1944), paraphras-

ing *Denning v. United States*, 247 F. 463, 465 (5th Cir. 1918), ("A primary purpose of the Mann Act was to protect women who were weak from men who were bad").

CHAPTER TWO

1. Egal Feldman, "Prostitution, the Alien Woman and the Progressive Imagination, 1910–1915," *American Quarterly* 19 (1967): 192–206; Roy Lubove, "The Progressives and the Prostitute," *Historian* 24 (May 1962): 308–30.

2. Feldman, "Prostitution, the Alien Woman and the Progressive Imagination," p. 192n.1.

3. Brand Whitlock, "The White Slave," *Forum* 51 (February 1914): 195.

4. The best discussion of this is in Mark Thomas Connelly, *The Response to Prostitution in the Progressive Era* (Chapel Hill: University of North Carolina Press, 1980), a very perceptive study. See also, Frederick K. Grittner, *White Slavery: Myth, Ideology, and American Law* (New York: Garland Publishing, 1990); Mary de Young, "Help, I'm Being Held Captive! The White Slave Fairy Tale of the Progressive Era," *Journal of American Culture* 6 (1983): 96–99.

5. Neil Larry Shumsky, "Tacit Acceptance: Respectable Americans and Segregated Prostitution, 1870–1910," *Journal of Social History* 19 (September 1986): 673–74, 678n.34.

6. Francis E. Hamilton, "Restriction of Immigration," *Forum* 42 (December 1908): 553–54.

7. Jane Addams, *A New Conscience and an Ancient Evil* (New York: Macmillan Co., 1913), pp. 104–5.

8. Beth L. Bailey, *From Front Porch to Back Seat: Courtship in Twentieth-Century America* (Baltimore: Johns Hopkins University Press, 1988), pp. 79–80; John Milton Cooper, Jr., *Pivotal Decades: The United States 1900–1920* (New York: W. W. Norton & Co., 1990), pp. 204–7; John C. Burnham, "The Progressive Era Revolution in American Attitudes Toward Sex," *Journal of American History* 59 (March 1973): 885–908; James R. McGovern, "The American Woman's Pre–World War I Freedom in Manners and Morals," *Journal of American History* 55 (September 1968): 315–33; Daniel Scott Smith, "The Dating of the American Sexual Revolution: Evidence and Interpretation," in *The American Family in Social-Historical Perspective*, 2d ed., Michael Gordon, ed. (New York: St. Martin's Press, 1978), pp. 426–38; Nicole Hahn Rafter, *Partial Justice: Women, Prisons, and Social Control*, 2d ed. (New Brunswick: Transaction Publishers, 1990), p. 160.

9. Dean Briggs (educator), "Remarks," *Smith College Quarter Centennial Anniversary Proceedings* (Northampton, Massachusetts, 1900), quoted in Sheila M. Rothman, *Woman's Proper Place: A History of Changing Ideals and Practices, 1870 to the Present* (New York: Basic Books, 1978), p. 23.

10. Peter G. Filene, *Him/Her/Self: Sex Roles in Modern America*, 2d ed. (New York: Harcourt Brace Jovanovich, 1974; reprint, Baltimore: Johns Hopkins University Press, 1986), p. 91.

11. John D'Emilio and Estelle B. Freedman, *Intimate Matters: A History of Sexuality in America* (New York: Harper & Row, 1988), pp. 171–201; Henry F. May, *The End of American Innocence: A Study of the First Years of Our Own Time, 1912–1917* (New York: Alfred A. Knopf, 1959), pp. 340–47; Joanne J. Meyerowitz, *Women*

Adrift: Independent Wage Earners in Chicago, 1880–1930 (Chicago: University of Chicago Press, 1988), pp. 140–41.

12. Jane Addams, *The Spirit of Youth and the City Streets* (New York: Macmillan Co., 1909), p. 5.

13. Bailey, *From Front Porch to Back Seat*, pp. 13, 17–20, 23–24.

14. "Traffic in 'White Slaves,'" *New York Times*, July 18, 1909, p. 18.

15. Alice C. Smith, quoted in "Good Women Can Help Solve the White Slave Problem," *New York Times*, April 20, 1913, pt. 3, p. 10.

16. George J. Kneeland, *Commercialized Prostitution in New York City* (New York: Century Co., 1913; reprint, Montclair, New Jersey: Patterson Smith, 1969), p. 79.

17. S. Doc. No. 196, 61st Cong., 2d Sess. 23 (1909); George Kibbe Turner, "The Daughters of the Poor," *McClure's Magazine* 34 (November 1909): 57.

18. Accounts of protests by individual Jews and Jewish organizations may be found in "Congress Knew of 'White Slave' Trade," *New York Times*, October 27, 1909, p. 4; "White Slave Story False, Says Guide," *New York Times*, October 28, 1909, p. 3; "Mulry Says Turner Slandered the City," *New York Times*, October 29, 1909, p. 2; and "Report on White Slavery," *New York Times*, February 27, 1910, p. 16.

19. Edward J. Bristow, *Prostitution and Prejudice: The Jewish Fight Against White Slavery, 1870–1939* (New York: Schocken Books, 1983).

20. "Jews Plan to Fight White Slave Trade," *New York Times*, April 10, 1910, pt. 3, p. 4.

21. "To Uplift White Slaves," *New York Times*, May 15, 1910, p. 9.

22. "To Divert Emigrant Jews From America," *New York Times*, April 21, 1912, pt. 3, p. 3.

23. Arthur A. Goren, *New York Jews and the Quest for Community: The Kehillah Experiment, 1908–1922* (New York: Columbia University Press, 1970), p. 159.

24. S. Doc. No. 196, 61st Cong., 2d Sess. 10, 32 (1909).

25. Stanley W. Finch, "White Slavery in America," *Light* (January–February 1914): 67.

26. F. Mabel Dedrick, "What Are the Dangers of City Life for a Country Girl?" *Light* (September 1909): 45–50; Eleanor L. Burns, "Commercialized Vice and the Farm: Are Our Farm Girls in Imminent Danger from This Foe," *Light* (May–June 1914): 31–33; Willis Ray Wilson, "The Assault of Society upon the Country Boy," *Light* (September 1911): 21–24.

27. Addams, *A New Conscience*, pp. ix, 72–73.

28. Ibid., p. 216.

29. Kneeland, *Commercialized Prostitution in New York City*, pp. 70, 72; Kathy Peiss, *Cheap Amusements: Working Women and Leisure in Turn-of-the-Century New York* (Philadelphia: Temple University Press, 1986), pp. 50, 62, 98–107.

30. Quoted in Meyerowitz, *Women Adrift*, p. 62.

31. Vice Commission of Chicago, *The Social Evil in Chicago* (Chicago: n.p., 1911), pp. 95, 185, 191–94 (examples of charity girls); Kneeland, *Commercialized Prostitution in New York City*, pp. 70–72; Peiss, *Cheap Amusements*, pp. 110–13; Kathy Peiss, "'Charity Girls' and City Pleasures: Historical Notes on Working-

Class Sexuality, 1880–1920," in *Powers of Desire: The Politics of Sexuality*, edited by Ann Snitow, Christine Stansell, and Sharon Thompson (New York: Monthly Review Press, 1983), pp. 74–87.

32. Vice Commission of Chicago, *Social Evil in Chicago*, pp. 187–88 (examples); Addams, *A New Conscience*, p. 216.

33. B. S. Steadwell, "Some of the Causes of Present-Day Immorality," *Light* (September–October 1913): 29.

34. Leslie Fishbein, "Harlot or Heroine? Changing Views of Prostitution, 1870–1920," *Historian* 43 (November 1980): 24–28, 30; John W. Johnson, *American Legal Culture, 1908–1940* (Westport, CT: Greenwood Press, 1981), p. 130.

35. Shumsky, "Tacit Acceptance: Respectable Americans and Segregated Prostitution," pp. 665–79.

36. Joseph R. Gusfield, *Symbolic Crusade: Status Politics and the American Temperance Movement* (Urbana: University of Illinois Press, 1963).

37. Thomas C. Mackey, *Red Lights Out: A Legal History of Prostitution, Disorderly Houses, and Vice Districts, 1870–1917* (New York: Garland Publishing, 1987), pp. 213–14, 238–62; John C. Burnham, "The Social Evil Ordinance: A Social Experiment in Nineteenth Century St. Louis," *Bulletin of the Missouri Historical Society* 27 (April 1971): 203–17; John C. Burnham, "Medical Inspection of Prostitutes in America in the Nineteenth Century: The St. Louis Experiment and Its Sequel," *Bulletin of the History of Medicine* 45 (May 1971): 203–18; James Wunsch, "The Social Evil Ordinance," *American Heritage* 33 (February 1982): 50–55.

38. A good general history of the purity movement is David J. Pivar, *Purity Crusade: Sexual Morality and Social Control, 1868–1900* (Westport, CT: Greenwood Press, 1973).

39. William Lloyd Garrison, quoted in ibid., p. 67.

40. Allan M. Brandt, *No Magic Bullet: A Social History of Venereal Disease in the United States Since 1880* (New York: Oxford University Press, 1985), pp. 7–51; Burnham, "The Progressive Era Revolution in American Attitudes Toward Sex," pp. 885–908.

41. Lubove, "The Progressives and the Prostitute," pp. 326–27n.33.

42. See generally, Brandt, *No Magic Bullet;* Lubove, "The Progressives and the Prostitute,"; Lavinia L. Dock, *Hygiene and Morality* (New York: G. P. Putnam's Sons, 1910).

43. Howard I. Kushner, "Nineteenth-Century Sexuality and the 'Sexual Revolution' of the Progressive Era," *Canadian Review of American Studies* 9 (Spring 1978): 34–49.

44. Accounts of the various international conferences and agreements may be found in Bascom Johnson, "International Efforts for the Prevention of Traffic in Women and Children," *Journal of Social Hygiene* 9 (April 1923): 206–15; James Bronson Reynolds, "International Agreements in Relation to the Suppression of Vice," *Journal of Social Hygiene* 2 (April 1916): 233–44; and "The White Slave Trade," *Contemporary Review* 82 (1902): 735–40.

45. "Politics and the White Slave Trade," *Current Literature* 47 (October 1909): 597.

46. "Five 'White Slave' Trade Investigations," *McClure's Magazine* 35 (July 1910): 348.

47. Mackey, *Red Lights Out,* pp. 119, 125–27, 183–200.

48. Committee of Fifteen, *The Social Evil: With Special Reference to Conditions Existing in the City of New York* (New York: G. P. Putnam's Sons, 1902).

49. Turner, "The Daughters of the Poor," pp. 45–61.

50. "Murphy and Gaynor Answer Vice Charge," *New York Times,* October 25, 1909, p. 2.

51. "Rockefeller, Jr., Takes Hold," *New York Times,* January 5, 1910, p. 7.

52. Connelly, *The Response to Prostitution,* pp. 195–96n.2.

53. Joseph Mayer, *The Regulation of Commercialized Vice: An Analysis of the Transition from Segregation to Repression in the United States* (New York: Klebold Press, 1922), pp. 11, 24–25.

54. Examples are Kneeland, *Commercialized Prostitution in New York City,* pp. 105–6, and Vice Commission of Chicago, *The Social Evil in Chicago,* pp. 280–81. The chairman of the Illinois state commission, Lieutenant-Governor Barratt O'Hara, wrote flatly that "low wages are to blame for most of the immorality among young girls," quoted in "Wages and Sin," *Literary Digest* 46 (March 22, 1913): 621–24.

55. Ibid., p. 621; "Are Low Wages Responsible for Women's Immorality?" *Current Opinion* 54 (1913): 402; "Wages and Immorality," *Vigilance* 27 (June 1913): 18–19; "Economic Necessity," *Vigilance* 26 (April 1913): 1–2.

56. "A Living Wage for Women Clerks Demanded," *Light* (January 1909): 9–12; modern studies include Barbara Meil Hobson, *Uneasy Virtue: The Politics of Prostitution and the American Reform Tradition* (New York: Basic Books, 1987), which concludes that the structures of the economic and social systems created a dependence for women that often led to prostitution, and Joseph F. Tripp, "Toward an Efficient and Moral Society: Washington State Minimum-Wage Law, 1913–1925," *Pacific Northwest Quarterly* (July 1976): 97–112.

57. Henry Woods, S. J., "Sociology: Vice Commissions," *America* (May 31, 1913): 190, quoted in Eric Anderson, "Prostitution and Social Justice: Chicago, 1910–15," *Social Service Review* 48 (June 1974): 222.

58. Judge Daniel F. Murphy, quoted in "'Let Good Women Bestir Themselves,' Says Judge Murphy of the Night Court," *New York Times,* April 20, 1913, pt. 3, p. 10.

59. S. Doc. No. 645, 61st Cong., 2d Sess. 82, 108–10 (1910).

60. Addams, *A New Conscience,* pp. 5, 57, 59.

61. Daniel J. Leab, "Women and the Mann Act," *Amerikastuden/American Studies* 21 (1976): 58.

62. Alfreda Eva Bell, *Boadicea; The Mormon Wife, Life Scenes in Utah* (Philadelphia, 1855), 54. I am indebted to Sarah Barringer Gordon, University of Pennsylvania Law School, for this reference.

63. Anderson, "Prostitution and Social Justice," pp. 203–28.

64. George Kibbe Turner, "The City of Chicago: A Study of the Great Immoralities," *McClure's Magazine* 28 (1907): 581–82.

65. "Chicago's Civic Revolution That Shall Free The White Slaves," *Chicago Tribune,* October 17, 1909, pt. 7, p. 4.

66. Contemporary accounts of these rumors, for example, are in "Popular Gullibility as Exhibited in the New White Slavery Hysteria," *Current Opinion* 56

(1914): 129; Whitlock, "The White Slave," pp. 197–98; see secondary treatment in Connelly, *The Response to Prostitution*, pp. 114–35; Filene, *Him/Her/Self*, pp. 86–87; and Leab, "Women and the Mann Act," p. 61.

67. Congress, House, Committee on Appropriation, *Hearing before Subcommittee of Committee on Appropriation in Charge of Sundry Civil Appropriation Bill for 1914*, 62d Cong., 3d Sess., February 4, 1913, 877 (testimony of Stanley W. Finch).

68. M. Madeline Southard, *The White Slave Traffic Versus the American Home* (Louisville, KY, 1914), pp. 9–11, quoted in Walter C. Reckless, *Vice in Chicago* (Chicago: University of Chicago Press, 1933): pp. 34–35; Anna Garlin Spencer, "The Age of Consent and Its Significance," *Forum* 49 (April 1913): 409, 419; Ernest A. Bell, ed., *War on the White Slave Trade* (Chicago: Charles C. Thompson Co., 1909), p. 58.

69. J. W. Jenks, quoted in "Plan to Wipe Out White Slave Evil," *New York Times*, January 25, 1910, p. 16.

70. Superintendent Ophelia Amigh, quoted by Representative Russell of Texas, 45 Congressional Record 821 (1910).

71. "The Slave Traffic in America," *Outlook* 93 (November 6, 1909): 529; "The Social Evil: The Immediate Remedies," *Outlook* 103 (February 8, 1913): 298.

72. "There Is a White Slave Trade," *New York Times*, December 9, 1909, p. 10.

73. "Slavers Kidnap 60,000 Women Each Year," *San Francisco Examiner*, March 16, 1913, p. 84.

74. S. Doc. No. 196, 61st Cong., 2d Sess. 22–23 (1909). For a similar expression of sympathy, see editorial, "Traffic in 'White Slaves,'" 18.

75. Turner, "The Daughters of the Poor," p. 58.

76. Stanley W. Finch, "The White Slave Traffic," *Light* (July 1912): 18.

77. Edwin W. Sims, "Menace of the White Slave Trade," in Bell, *War on the White Slave Trade*, pp. 70–71.

78. "White Slave Traffic Shown to Be Real," *New York Times*, April 30, 1910, p. 1.

79. "More White Slave Arrests Coming," *New York Times*, May 1, 1910, p. 20.

80. "Facts That Cannot Be Denied," *New York Times*, May 2, 1910, p. 8.

81. "Four White Slaves Were Sold for $160," *New York Times*, May 3, 1910, p. 20; "'White Slave' Sales Described in Court," *New York Times*, May 19, 1910, p. 5.

82. "Belle Moore Guilty of Selling Girls," *New York Times*, May 20, 1910, p. 18.

83. "Ill-Chosen Agents of Reform," *New York Times*, May 21, 1910, p. 8.

84. "White Slavery Buncombe?" *New York Times*, May 24, 1910, p. 8.

85. "Does Not Fit the Crime," *New York Times*, July 19, 1914, pt. 3, p. 4.

86. "The Blackmail Act," *New York Times*, September 20, 1916, p. 8.

87. A general treatment of the white slave novels is in Grittner, *White Slavery*, pp. 107–13.

88. "Dramatizing Vice," *Literary Digest* 47 (October 4, 1913): 577.

89. Mrs. Barclay Hazard, in charge of New York branch of Florence Crittenton Foundation, quoted in "Lectures in Lent to Check Hysteria," *New York Times*, January 2, 1914, p. 5.

90. Connelly, *The Response to Prostitution*, pp. 117–18; Grittner, *White Slavery*, pp. 15–37, 61–81.

91. Leab, "Women and the Mann Act," p. 64.

92. Marjorie Rosen, *Popcorn Venus: Women, Movies & the American Dream* (New York: Coward, McCann & Geoghegan, 1973), p. 28.

93. Kevin Brownlow, *Behind the Mask of Innocence* (New York: Alfred A. Knopf, 1990), pp. 70–93.

94. "The White Slave Films," *Outlook* 106 (January 17, 1914): 120; "The White Slave Films: A Review," *Outlook* 106 (February 14, 1914): 345.

95. Leab, "Women and the Mann Act," p. 57; Lubove, "The Progressives and the Prostitute," pp. 314–15.

96. Vice Commission of Chicago, *The Social Evil in Chicago*, p. 41; "The Slave Traffic in America," *Outlook*, p. 528.

97. Berkeley Davids, "Construction of the 'Mann Act,'" *Law Notes* 17 (March 1914): 225; George Kibbe Turner, quoted in "Defends White Slave Story," *New York Times*, July 2, 1910, p. 2; *Vigilance* 26 (October 1912): 10–11.

98. Editorial, "Public Hysteria and the White Slave Traffic," *Medico-Legal Journal* 33 (September 1916): 1–4; Philadelphia Vice Commission, "Vice in Philadelphia," *Light* (July–August 1913): 49.

99. "Disagreement in White Slave Debate," *New York Times*, January 20, 1910, p. 4.

100. Whitlock, "The White Slave," pp. 201, 200.

101. Ibid., pp. 197, 201.

102. Jane Addams, "The Sheltered Woman and the Magdalen," *Ladies' Home Journal* 30 (November 1913): 25.

103. "License They Mean," *New York Times*, February 6, 1914, p. 8.

104. A. W. Elliott, quoted in, "Is White Slavery Nothing More than a Myth?" *Current Opinion* 55 (November 1913): 348.

105. For example, Connelly, *The Response to Prostitution*, and Grittner, *White Slavery*.

106. See Kathleen Barry, *Female Sexual Slavery* (New York: New York University Press, 1979), and Janet Eileen Mickish, "Legal Control of Socio-Sexual Relationships: Creation of the Mann White Slave Traffic Act of 1910" (Ph.D. diss., Southern Illinois University, 1980).

107. Ruth Rosen, *The Lost Sisterhood: Prostitution in America, 1900–1918* (Baltimore: Johns Hopkins University Press, 1982), p. 133.

108. Reckless, *Vice in Chicago*, pp. 42, 45.

109. S. Doc. No. 196, 61st Cong., 2d Sess. 14, 29 (1909). Similar expressions may be found at ibid., pp. 6–7, 8.

110. Ibid., pp. 25, 29, 9.

111. Ibid., pp. 23–24.

112. Graham Taylor, "Recent Advances Against the Social Evil in New York: The Committee of Fourteen and the Additional Grand Jury," *Survey* 24 (September 17, 1910): 862.

113. Vice Commission of Chicago, *The Social Evil in Chicago*, p. 41.

114. William Burgess, "A Wave of Sex Hysteria?" *Vigilance* 27 (September 1913): 8.

115. A. Bruce Bielaski, "The United States Government and the White Slave Traffic," *Light* (January–February 1915): 23.

116. Finch, "The White Slave Traffic," p. 17.

117. Edwin W. Sims, "The White Slave Trade of Today," in Bell, *War on the White Slave Trade,* pp. 56–57.

118. H.R. Rep. No. 47, 61st Cong., 2d Sess. 10 (1909).

119. S. Doc. No. 196, 61st Cong., 2d Sess. 36 (1909).

120. 45 Congressional Record 805–6 (1910).

121. "Attorney Sims on National Legislation," *Vigilance* 23 (January 1910): 12–13.

122. Letter, James R. Mann to B. S. Steadwell, March 31, 1913, published as "Origin of the White Slave Traffic Act," *Light* (May–June 1913): 17–19.

123. Ernest A. Bell, "New and Pending Laws," *Light* (May 1910): 27.

124. "To Curb White Slavery," *New York Times,* November 25, 1909, p. 7.

125. Compare, H.R. Rep. No. 47, 61st Cong., 2d Sess. 10–11 (1909), with the same statements Sims published much earlier, in *New York Times,* October 26, 1909, p. 3.

126. S. Rep. No. 886, 61st Cong., 2d Sess. (1909).

127. H.R. 12315, 61st Cong., 2d Sess. (1909); "Mann's White Slave Bill," *New York Times,* December 7, 1909, p. 3. A detailed study of the legislative history is in Grittner, *White Slavery,* pp. 83–105.

128. *New York Times,* December 8, 1909, p. 6.

129. James H. Patten, "National Legislation Against White Slavery," *Light* (March 1910): 15–16; James H. Patten, "The Passage of the White Slave Traffic Bill," *Light* (September 1910): 15–20; "Attorney Sims on National Legislation," *Vigilance,* pp. 12–13.

130. "Second White Slave Bill," *New York Times,* December 19, 1909, p. 3.

131. H.R. Rep. No. 47, 61st Cong., 2d Sess. 9–10 (1909).

132. Ibid., p. 10.

133. Ibid., p. 11.

134. Ibid.

135. Ibid. (Part 2, Views of the Minority), p. 1.

136. Ibid. (Part 1, Majority Report), p. 7.

137. 45 Congressional Record 1035 (1910).

138. 45 Congressional Record 810, 823 (1910).

139. 45 Congressional Record 548, 547, 1037 (1910).

140. 45 Congressional Record 811–12 (1910).

141. 45 Congressional Record 821 (1910).

142. White-Slave Traffic (Mann) Act, ch. 395, 36 Stat. 825–27 (1910).

143. "The Blackmail Act," *New York Times,* p. 8.

CHAPTER THREE

1. "First Arrest Under White Slave Act," *New York Times,* July 10, 1910, p. 14.

2. Circular No. 174 to U.S. Attorneys, October 31, 1910. Records of the Department of Justice, General Correspondence, Record Group 60, Class 31-0, Box 2620, National Archives, Washington National Records Center, Suitland, Maryland [hereinafter identified only by box number, unless a different record group or classification is intended].

3. Don Whitehead, *The FBI Story: A Report to the People* (New York: Random House, 1956), pp. 20–21; Arthur C. Millspaugh, *Crime Control by the National Government* (Washington, D.C.: Brookings Institution, 1937), pp. 73–78.

4. Athan G. Theoharis and John Stuart Cox, *The Boss: J. Edgar Hoover and the Great American Inquisition* (Philadelphia: Temple University Press, 1988), pp. 6, 43.

5. Max Lowenthal, *The Federal Bureau of Investigation* (New York: Harcourt Brace Jovanovich, 1950), pp. 12–13; Richard Gid Powers, *G-Men: Hoover's FBI in American Popular Culture* (Carbondale: Southern Illinois University Press, 1983), p. 26; Pat Watters and Stephen Gillers, eds., *Investigating the FBI* (Garden City, NY: Doubleday & Co., 1973), pp. 37–38.

6. Theoharis and Cox, *The Boss*, p. 43, state flatly that "the first Bureau field office was opened in Baltimore in 1911." However, early correspondence of the Bureau of Investigation indicates that there were "special agents" assigned to Chicago as early as the summer of 1908; that an individual in Chicago was designated as "Special Agent in Charge," the usual title given to special agents who run field offices, at least as early as July 1910; and that there were seven agents "more or less permanently engaged" working under a supervisor in Chicago by November 1910. Letters are in Records of the Bureau of Investigation, Letters Sent by the Chief Examiner, October 1907–June 1911, Record Group 65, National Archives, Washington, D.C., Chief Examiner to Edwin W. Sims, May 22, 1909, vol. 6, p. 297; Chief Examiner to Marshall Eberstein, July 19, 1910, vol. 13, p. 258; Chief Examiner to Charles DeWoody, November 23, 1910, vol. 17, p. 387. I am indebted to John A. Noakes, Wellesley College, for reference to this correspondence. All of this considered, it would seem the Chicago operation was much smaller and more marginal than that established by Finch in Baltimore in 1911.

7. Lowenthal, *The Federal Bureau of Investigation*, p. 14.

8. Richard Gid Powers, *Secrecy and Power: The Life of J. Edgar Hoover* (New York: Free Press, 1987), p. 134; Sanford J. Ungar, *FBI* (Boston: Little, Brown & Co., 1975), p. 41; Whitehead, *The FBI Story*, p. 23.

9. Congress, House, Committee on Appropriation, *Hearing before Subcommittee of Committee on Appropriation in Charge of Sundry Civil Appropriation Bill for 1914*, 62d Cong., 3d Sess., February 4, 1913, 872 (testimony of Stanley W. Finch) (hereinafter, *Sundry Appropriation Bill*, 1914).

10. Letter, Attorney General to Henry J, Dannenbaum, April 1, 1911, Box 2620.

11. Letter, Attorney General to Secretary of Commerce and Labor, February 2, 1912, Box 2620.

12. Letter, Henry J. Dannenbaum to S. W. Finch, May 18, 1911, Box 2620.

13. Illinois Central Railroad Company, Circular No. 1767 to Ticket Agents, September 15, 1910, accompanying letter, President, Illinois Central Railroad Company to George W. Wickersham, May 27, 1911, Box 2620.

14. Quoted in "Railroads Are Getting Right," *Vigilance* 23 (October 1910): 3–4.

15. Letter, President, Southern Railway Company to George W. Wickersham, June 1, 1911, Box 2620.

16. Letter, Stanley W. Finch to J. R. Knowland, June 3, 1912, Box 2620; Finch testimony, *Sundry Appropriation Bill, 1914*, p. 886; Joseph R. Knowland, "Early Efforts in the Suppression of the White Slave Traffic," *Light* (November 1912): 27;

Annual Report of the Attorney General of the United States for the Year 1913 (Washington, D.C.: Government Printing Office, 1913), p. 50.

17. Letters, W. R. Harr to B. S. Steadwell, January 3, 1912, and Attorney General to James Bronson Reynolds, January 24, 1912, Box 2620.

18. Letter, George W. Wickersham to John J. Fitzgerald, March 4, 1912, Box 2620.

19. Speech of Stanley W. Finch, "The White Slave Traffic," *Light* (July 1912): 24; "The Work of the United States Department of Justice," *Vigilance* 25 (April 1912): 13; B. S. Steadwell, "Suppressing the White Slave Traffic," *Light* (November 1912): 6; Stanley W. Finch, "Government Fails to Provide Funds," *Vigilance* 26 (April 1913): 20.

20. Finch testimony, *Sundry Appropriation Bill, 1914*, pp. 878–79.

21. *Annual Report of the Attorney General of the United States for the Year 1912* (Washington, D.C.: Government Printing Office, 1912), p. 48.

22. Finch testimony, *Sundry Appropriation Bill, 1914*, pp. 872–74.

23. Ibid., pp. 872, 878.

24. *Annual Report of the Attorney General, 1912*, p. 48; *Sundry Appropriation Bill, 1914*, pp. 868–69 (testimony of A. B. Bielaski, Chief of the Bureau of Investigation); "White Slave Law Deficient," *New York Times*, December 14, 1912, p. 3.

25. Finch, "Government Fails to Provide Funds," p. 20.

26. Letter, W. R. Harr to B. S. Steadwell, January 3, 1912, Box 2620.

27. "Editor's Note," in Stanley W. Finch, "The United States Government in the Fight Against the White Slave Traffic," *Light* (January 1913): 16.

28. B. S. Steadwell, "The Appropriation for Fighting White Slavery," *Light* (September 1912): 9–10.

29. Letters, Joseph R. Knowland to George W. Wickersham, March 16, 1912, and May 31, 1912, Box 2620.

30. Miriam Michelson, "Vice and the Woman's Vote," *Sunset* 30 (April 1913): 346.

31. Letter, Attorney General to Joseph R. Knowland, March 20, 1912, Box 2620.

32. Steadwell, "The Appropriation for Fighting White Slavery," *Light*, p. 10.

33. James Bronson Reynolds, "The Association's Department of Legislation and Law Enforcement," *Vigilance* 25 (May 1912): 6.

34. *Annual Report of the Attorney General, 1912*, p. 48.

35. *Annual Report of the Attorney General, 1913*, p. 50.

36. Letter, Stanley W. Finch to Clifford G. Roe, May 21, 1912, Box 2620.

37. Finch testimony, *Sundry Appropriation Bill, 1914*, p. 883.

38. Letters, Postmaster General to Attorney General, July 17, 1912; Special Commissioner Finch to Attorney General, July 23, 1912; Attorney General to Postmaster General, July 24, 1912; Box 2620.

39. Letter, Postmaster General to Attorney General, November 25, 1914, Box 2621.

40. Finch testimony, *Sundry Appropriation Bill, 1914*, pp. 880–81.

41. "Registration of Prostitutes," *Vigilance* 25 (June 1912): 17–18.

42. Finch testimony, *Sundry Appropriation Bill, 1914*, pp. 881–82.

43. Ibid., pp. 874, 887.

44. Ibid., p. 876; A. Bruce Bielaski, "The United States Fighting White Slavery," *Light* (November–December 1915): 56.

45. "Registration of Prostitutes," *Vigilance*, pp. 17–18.

46. Steadwell, "The Appropriation for Fighting White Slavery," *Light*, pp. 9–10.

47. "White Slave Law Deficient," *New York Times*, p. 3; Stanley W. Finch, "The United States Government in the Fight Against the White Slave Traffic," *Light* (January 1913): 19–20.

48. Finch testimony, *Sundry Appropriation Bill, 1914*, pp. 874, 886.

49. Ibid., pp. 873–74, 878, 880.

50. Leonard A. Watson, "Work of the Cincinnati Vigilance Society," *Vigilance* 24 (May 1911): 25.

51. Letter, Department of Justice to George H. West, President, Secret Law and Order League, March 13, 1911, Box 2620.

52. Letter, Acting Attorney General to George H. West, September 6, 1912, Box 2620.

53. *Annual Report of the Attorney General of the United States for the year 1914* (Washington, D.C.: Government Printing Office, 1914), p. 45.

54. "To Reclaim White Slaves," *New York Times*, January 13, 1913, p. 1.

55. Peter Y. Sonnenthal, "The Origins and Early Enforcement of the White Slave Traffic Act, 1910–1917" (M.A. thesis, Columbia University, 1977), p. 20.

56. John Edgar Hoover, "Organized Protection Against Organized Predatory Crimes," *Journal of the American Institute of Criminal Law and Criminology* 24 (July–August 1933): 476–77.

57. *National Municipal Review* 5 (October 1916): 698–702; Joseph Mayer, "The Passing of the Red Light District—Vice Investigations and Results," *Journal of Social Hygiene* 4 (April 1918): 197–209.

58. Raymond B. Fosdick, "Prostitution and the Police," *Journal of Social Hygiene* 2 (January 1916): 11, 14.

59. Bureau of Social Hygiene (New York City), *Commercialized Prostitution in New York City in 1916* (1916), quoted in "Note and Comment," *Journal of Social Hygiene* 3 (April 1917): 282.

60. Abraham Flexner, "Next Steps in Dealing with Prostitution," *Journal of Social Hygiene* 1 (January 1917): 532–33.

61. Finch testimony, *Sundry Appropriation Bill, 1914*, p. 877.

62. "White Slave Law Deficient," *New York Times*, p. 3.

63. Howard B. Woolston, *Prostitution in the United States Prior to the Entrance of the United States into the World War* (n.p.: The Century Co., 1921; reprint, Montclair, NJ: Patterson Smith, 1969), p. 175.

64. *Annual Report of the Attorney General, 1913*, p. 51; *Annual Report of the Attorney General, 1914*, p. 46.

65. A. Bruce Bielaski, "The United States Government and the White Slave Traffic," *Light* (January–February 1915): 19.

66. Finch testimony, *Sundry Appropriation Bill, 1914*, p. 884.

67. For examples, see letter, Henry J. Dannenbaum, Special Assistant to Attor-

ney General, to George W. Wickersham, Attorney General, May 11, 1911, Box 2620; "White Slavers Get Varying Penalties," *New York Times*, February 22, 1913, p. 8; *Survey* 29 (March 8, 1913): 801.

68. "Supreme Court Upholds the 'White Slave' Law," *Survey* 29 (March 8, 1913): 801.

69. Bielaski, "The United States Fighting White Slavery," *Light*, p. 58.

70. Computed from figures in *Annual Report of the Attorney General, 1913*, p. 362, and *Annual Report of the Attorney General of the United States for the Year 1916* (Washington, D.C.: Government Printing Office, 1916), p. 52.

71. Computed from *Annual Report of the Attorney General*, 1911–1916.

72. Finch urged these in various forms and combinations in "White Slave Law Deficient," p. 3; "The White Slave Traffic," pp. 22–24; "The United States Government in the Fight Against the White Slave Traffic," pp. 21–22; and in Stanley W. Finch, "White Slavery in America," *Light* (January–February 1914): 73–75.

73. Bielaski, "The United States Government and the White Slave Traffic," *Light*, pp. 21–22; Bielaski, "The United States Fighting White Slavery," *Light*, p. 59; *Annual Report of the Attorney General of the United States for the Year 1915* (Washington, D.C.: Government Printing Office, 1915), pp. 43–44; *Annual Report of the Attorney General, 1916*, p. 52.

74. Bielaski, "The United States Government and the White Slave Traffic," *Light*, p. 23.

75. *United States v. Westman*, 182 F. 1017 (D. Or. 1910).

76. For example, *United States v. Warner*, 188 F. 682 (C.C. S.D.N.Y. 1911).

77. 227 U.S. 308 (1913).

78. 227 U.S. at 320–23.

79. "The White-Slave Decision," *Literary Digest* 46 (March 8, 1913): 500–502; "White Slavers Routed," *Outlook* 103 (March 15, 1913): 569–71; "Supreme Court Upholds the 'White Slave' Law," *Survey*, p. 799.

80. "The Meaning of the White Slave Act as Shown by Federal Decision," *Central Law Journal* 77 (October 10, 1913): 261–62; "The White Slave Decision," *Law Student's Helper* 21 (April 1913): 4–5.

81. *New York Tribune*, quoted in "The White-Slave Decision," *Literary Digest* 46 (March 8, 1913): 501; "Supreme Court Upholds the 'White Slave' Law," *Survey*, p. 799; "White Slavers Routed," *Outlook*, p. 569.

82. 247 U.S. 251 (1918).

83. 227 U.S. at 322.

84. 247 U.S. at 275.

85. *United States v. Lombardo*, 241 U.S. 73 (1916).

86. 232 U.S. 563 (1914).

87. 232 U.S. at 571.

88. *Neff v. United States*, 105 F.2d 688, 691 (8th Cir. 1939).

89. *United States v. Marks*, 274 F.2d 15, 18–19 (7th Cir. 1959).

90. Letter, Attorney General to Henry J. Dannenbaum, July 28, 1911, Box 2620.

91. Motion for Rehearing at 2–3, Transcript of Record, *Caminetti v. United States*, 242 U.S. 470 (1917) (Docket No. 1008); 242 U.S. at 498–99 (McKenna, J., dissenting).

92. Letters, John I. Worthington to Attorney General, December 11, 1911; Stanley W. Finch and A. Bruce Bielaski to William R. Harr, December 15, 1911; Department of Justice to John I. Worthington, December 21, 1911, Box 2620.

93. Letter, William R. Harr to United States Attorney (Mississippi), February 10, 1913, Box 2620.

94. Memorandum, William R. Harr to Attorney General, August 4, 1913, Box 2620.

95. Finch, "The United States Government in the Fight Against the White Slave Traffic," *Light*, p. 18.

96. Finch testimony, *Sundry Appropriation Bill, 1914*, p. 875.

97. Finch, "The United States Government in the Fight Against the White Slave Trade," *Light*, p. 18.

98. A letter from William Wallace, Jr., Assistant Attorney General to John F. A. Merrill, United States Attorney for the District of Maine, September 8, 1915, Box 2621, in reply to an inquiry is typical. Another example is letter, Solicitor General to Walter Guion, United States Attorney, New Orleans, September 16, 1913, Box 2620.

99. Letter, William Wallace, Jr., to Senator Wesley L. Jones, December 16, 1913, Box 2620, quoting letter, William A. Harr, Assistant Attorney General, to United States Attorney, Milwaukee, May 3, 1913.

100. *Annual Report of the Attorney General, 1912*, p. 48.

101. For example, letter, United States Attorney for the District of Maine to Attorney General, September 3, 1915, Box 2621.

102. Guy D. Goff, "The White Slaver," *Light* (July–August 1915): 55.

103. "Construction of White Slave Act," *Law Notes* 16 (November 1913): 141; Letter, Solicitor General to Walter Guion, United States Attorney, New Orleans, September 16, 1913, Box 2620.

104. "Girl of 15 Runs Away," *New York Times*, April 4, 1914, p. 24 (fifteen-year-old); "Eloper Accused of White Slavery," *New York Times*, January 9, 1914, p. 3 (seventeen-year-old). See also, *Welsch v. United States*, 220 F. 764 (4th Cir. 1915).

105. "Accused of White Slavery," *New York Times*, September 29, 1913, p. 4; "Two White Slave Cases," *New York Times*, June 19, 1914, p. 15. See also, *York v. United States*, 224 F. 88 (8th Cir. 1915).

106. *Hays v. United States*, 231 F. 106 (8th Cir. 1916), *aff'd*, 242 U.S. 470 (1917); *Johnson v. United States*, 215 F. 679 (7th Cir. 1914).

107. *United States v. Flaspoller*, 205 F. 1006, 1007 (D. La. 1913).

108. "May Restrict Mann Law," *St. Paul Pioneer Press* (Minnesota), July 29, 1913, enclosed in letter, Mrs. Albert R. Hall to Woodrow Wilson, July 29, 1913, Box 2620.

109. "White Slave Debate Stirs Row in House," *New York Times*, July 30, 1913, p. 2.

110. Letter, Mrs. Albert R. Hall to Woodrow Wilson, July 29, 1913, Box 2620.

111. Letter, William B. Millard to James McReynolds, February 11, 1914, Box 2620.

112. "The Diggs-Caminetti Cases," *Vigilance* 27 (November 1913): 19; Ernest A. Bell, "The Struggle Against White Slavery in America," *Light* (September–October 1914): 60–61.

113. Letter, D. O. Hopkins to Woodrow Wilson, October 29, 1913, Box 2620.

114. Letter, John Timothy Stone to Woodrow Wilson, April 2, 1914, Box 2620.

115. Letter, Rev. Wilbur F. Crafts to Attorney General, January 3, 1914, Box 2620.

116. "No White Slave Order," *New York Times*, December 13, 1913, p. 14.

117. *Portland Telegram* (Oregon), quoted in "Repeal the Mann Act? Never!" *Light* (September–October 1913): 60–61; William Seagle, "The Twilight of the Mann Act," *American Bar Association Journal* 55 (July 1969): 645–46.

118. *Bennett v. United States*, 227 U.S. 333 (1913); *Harris v. United States*, 227 U.S. 340 (1913).

119. 227 U.S. 326 (1913).

120. 227 U.S. at 328.

121. Transcript of Record at 26–27, *Athanasaw v. United States*, 227 U.S. 326 (1913) (Docket No. 588).

122. 227 U.S. at 329.

123. Transcript of Record at 26, 29, *Athanasaw* (Docket No. 588).

124. 227 U.S. at 329.

125. Transcript of Record at 24–25, *Athanasaw* (Docket No. 588).

126. 227 U.S. at 330–31.

127. 227 U.S. at 332–33.

128. "White Slave Act," *Virginia Law Register* 19 (October 1913): 471–73.

129. "The Meaning of the White Slave Act as Shown by Federal Decision," 261–62.

130. Contained in letter, Attorney General to J. R. Knowland, March 20, 1912, Box 2620.

131. Transcript of Record at 24–25, *Athanasaw* (Docket No. 588).

132. Bielaski, "The United States Fighting White Slavery," *Light*, pp. 57–58.

133. *Annual Report of the Attorney General, 1915*, p. 44.

134. *Atlanta Constitution*, quoted in "The Chaotic Mann Law," *Light* (September–October 1913): 59.

CHAPTER FOUR

1. 45 Congressional Record 1033 (1910).

2. Letter, Attorney General to Henry J. Dannenbaum, July 28, 1911, quoted in Circular No. 647, T. W. Gregory, Attorney General, to United States Attorneys, January 26, 1917. Department of Justice File 145825-65.

3. "Girl Accuses J. P. Whitney," *New York Times*, February 26, 1914, p. 1.

4. "Alexander Gives Bail," *New York Times*, February 7, 1915, p. 4.

5. Berkeley Davids, "Construction of the 'Mann Act,'" *Law Notes* 18 (March 1914): 225.

6. "Uncle Sam, Blackmailer," *New York Times*, July 27, 1914, p. 6.

7. A. Bruce Bielaski, "The United States Government and the White Slave Traffic," *Light* (January–February 1915): 21.

8. Clifford G. Roe, "Federal Morals Commission," *Light* (March–April 1915): 60.

9. A. Bruce Bielaski, "Interpretation of the White Slave Act," *Light* (May–June

1915): 23; A. Bruce Bielaski, "The United States Fighting White Slavery," *Light* (November–December 1915): 58.

10. 236 U.S. 140 (1915).

11. Guy D. Goff, "New Interpretation of the White Slave Traffic Act," *Light* (September–October 1914): 29, 31; Bielaski, "The United States Government and the White Slave Traffic," *Light*, p. 21.

12. Transcript of Record at 1–4, *United States v. Holte*, 236 U.S. 140 (1915) (Docket No. 628).

13. Transcript of Record at 6, *Holte* (Docket No. 628).

14. 236 U.S. at 145.

15. 236 U.S. at 147 (Lamar and Day, JJ., dissenting).

16. 236 U.S. at 148 (Lamar and Day, JJ., dissenting).

17. Bielaski, "The United States Government and the White Slave Traffic," *Light*, p. 21; "Editor's Note," in Goff, "New Interpretation of the White Slave Traffic Act," p. 29.

18. 236 U.S. at 150 (Lamar and Day, JJ., dissenting).

19. "A Blow to Blackmail," *New York Times*, February 4, 1915, p. 8.

20. Harvey D. Jacob, "White Slavery," *Case and Comment* 23 (1916): 21.

21. Bielaski, "Interpretation of the White Slave Traffic Act," *Light*, p. 24; Bielaski, "The United States Fighting White Slavery," *Light*, p. 59.

22. Letter, T. W. Gregory to Charles A. Culberson, January 8, 1916. Records of the Department of Justice, General Correspondence, Record Group 60, Class 31-0, Box 2621, National Archives, Washington National Records Center, Suitland, Maryland [hereinafter identified only by box number, unless a different record group or classification is intended].

23. Ibid.

24. *Annual Report of the Attorney General of the United States for the year 1915* (Washington, D.C.: Government Printing Office, 1915), p. 44; *Annual Report of the Attorney General of the United States for the Year 1916* (Washington, D.C.: Government Printing Office, 1916), p. 52; Bielaski, "The United States Fighting White Slavery," *Light*, pp. 58–59.

25. H.R. 9044, 64th Cong., 1st Sess. (1916); S. 3597, 64th Cong., 1st Sess. (1916).

26. Letter, Assistant Attorney General to William G. Barnhart, March 30, 1915, Box 2621; Bielaski, "Interpretation of the White Slave Traffic Act," *Light*, p. 24.

27. "Blackmail Rich Men by White Slave Act," *New York Times*, January 13, 1916, sec. B, p. 1; "Another Blackmail Arrest," *New York Times*, January 14, 1916, p. 20; "Held in $50,000 Bail in Slave Extortion," *New York Times*, January 15, 1916, sec. B, p. 6.

28. "Blackmail Rich Men by White Slave Act," p. 1.

29. "Gang Uses Women in Blackmail Plots," *New York Times*, April 28, 1916, sec. B, p. 22.

30. Letter, W. D. Riter to Henry McAllister, Jr., May 19, 1916, Denver and Rio Grande Collection, Collection 513, Box 15, Folder 3304, Colorado Historical Society, Denver, Colorado. I am indebted to Nancy Taniguchi, California State University, Stanislaus, for this reference.

31. "Arrest 7 of Gang in Blackmail Trust," *New York Times*, September 18, 1916, p. 8; "Blackmail Gang Got a Million in a Year," *New York Times*, September 19, 1916, p. 5; "Woman Picks Three in Blackmail Case," *New York Times*, September 20, 1916, sec. B, p. 7; "May Call Victims of Blackmail Gang," *New York Times*, September 21, 1916, sec. B, p. 24; "Blackmailers Send Threat to Witness," *New York Times*, September 22, 1916, sec. B, p. 11; "Arrest Two More in Blackmail Plot," *New York Times*, September 25, 1916, p. 7; "Blackmail Snare Got Rich Merchant," *New York Times*, September 27, 1916, sec. B, p. 7; "Find New Gang Victim," *New York Times*, September 29, 1916, p. 9; "4 More Blackmail Arrests," *New York Times*, October 1, 1916, p. 21; "New Blackmail Charges," *New York Times*, October 7, 1916, p. 5; "Arrest Brown as a Blackmail Chief," *New York Times*, October 22, 1916, p. 1; "Blackmailers Sentenced," *New York Times*, October 24, 1916, p. 8; "Held as a Blackmailer," *New York Times*, November 1, 1916, p. 10; "Buda Godman Surrenders," *New York Times*, November 8, 1916, p. 11; "Two Admit Blackmail," *New York Times*, November 9, 1916, p. 8; "18 Months for Blackmail," *New York Times*, November 23, 1916, p. 8; "Sentence Blackmail Chief," *New York Times*, November 28, 1916, p. 8; "Mann Act Conspirator Sentenced," *New York Times*, March 12, 1918, p. 4.

32. "May Call Victims of Blackmail Gang," p. 24.

33. "Find New Gang Victim," p. 9.

34. Circular No. 647, T. W. Gregory, Attorney General, to United States Attorneys, January 26, 1917. Department of Justice File 145825-65.

35. Oscar J. Smith, "The Mann White Slave Law," *Medico-Legal Journal* 33 (1917): 6–7.

36. Berkeley Davids, "Application of Mann Act to Noncommercial Vice," *Law Notes* 20 (November 1916): 144–45.

37. Letter, Illinois Vigilance Association to Woodrow Wilson, with accompanying resolution, March 30, 1915, Box 2621.

38. "Government Aid to Blackmailers," *New York Times*, January 14, 1916, p. 8.

39. "The Blackmail Act," *New York Times*, September 20, 1916, p. 8.

40. "Government and Blackmail," *New York Times*, September 24, 1916, pt. 7, p. 2.

41. "Revise the Mann Act," *Washington Post*, January 19, 1917, p. 4.

42. "Say that Mann Act Should Be Amended," *New York Times*, January 17, 1917, p. 20.

43. Letter, Guy D. Goff to A. Bruce Bielaski, November 11, 1914, Box 2621.

44. Letter, Claude R. Rooter to Attorney General, January 31, 1917, Box 2621.

45. *Johnson v. United States*, 215 F. 679, 682 (7th Cir. 1914).

46. *Caminetti v. United States*, 242 U.S. 470, 502 (1917) (McKenna, J., dissenting).

47. 242 U.S. at 490–91.

48. Anthony M. Turano, "Adultery on Wheels," *American Mercury* 39 (December 1936): 447.

49. Berto Rogers, "The Mann Act and Noncommercial Vice," *Law Notes* 37 (July 1933): 108.

50. Courtney Ryley Cooper, *Designs in Scarlet* (Boston: Little, Brown & Co., 1939), pp. 152–55.

51. W. Lloyd Warner, Robert J. Havighurst, and Martin B. Loeb, *Who Shall Be Educated? The Challenge of Unequal Opportunities* (New York: Harper & Bros., 1944), p. 38.

52. Claude T. Barnes, *The White Slave Act: History and Analysis of Its Words "Other Immoral Purpose"* (Salt Lake City, UT: Sugar House Press, 1946), p. 30.

53. "Mann & Woman," *Time* 43 (April 3, 1944): 25.

54. *Beach v. United States,* 144 F.2d 533, 535 (D.C. Cir. 1944), *rev'd,* 324 U.S. 193 (1945).

55. 324 U.S. at 199–200 (Murphy, J., dissenting).

56. Letter, Edward J. Bowman to Attorney General, February 8, 1928 and letter, L. E. Wyman to Attorney General, April 30, 1930, Box 2627.

57. *Carey v. United States,* 265 F. 515, 518 (8th Cir. 1920).

58. *Parker v. United States,* 2 F.2d 710, 710 (6th Cir. 1924).

59. *Yoder v. United States,* 71 F.2d 85, 88 (10th Cir. 1934).

60. *English v. English,* 9 Cal. 2d 358, 70 P.2d 625 (1937).

61. *Oyama v. Oyama,* 138 Fla. 422, 189 So. 418 (1939).

62. Robert C. Twombly, *Frank Lloyd Wright: His Life and His Architecture* (New York: John Wiley & Sons, 1979), pp. 183–92; Frank Lloyd Wright, *An Autobiography: Frank Lloyd Wright* (New York: Horizon Press, 1932; reprint, 1977), pp. 303–20. See also, the most recent biography, Meryle Secrest, *Frank Lloyd Wright* (New York: Alfred A. Knopf, 1992).

63. Discussion drawn primarily from Twombly, *Frank Lloyd Wright,* pp. 185–92.

64. Quotations from Wright, *An Autobiography,* pp. 304–10.

65. Secrest, *Frank Lloyd Wright,* p. 245.

CHAPTER FIVE

1. Reported together as *Caminetti v. United States, Diggs v. United States,* and *Hays v. United States,* 242 U.S. 470 (1917).

2. The discussion of the facts of the *Caminetti* and *Diggs* cases are taken from the following sources: Record, *Caminetti v. United States,* 242 U.S. 470 (1917) (Docket Nos. 139, 163, & 464); recital of facts in both the majority and dissenting opinions of the Ninth Circuit Court of Appeals, issued March 18, 1915, reported at 220 F. 545 (9th Cir. 1915); Robert L. Anderson, *The Diggs-Caminetti Case 1913–1917: For Any Other Immoral Purpose,* 2 vols. (Lewiston, NY: Edwin Mellen Press, 1990) (quoting California newspapers and the trial transcripts); and the following newspaper articles: "Saw Diggs at Reno," *New York Times,* August 9, 1913, p. 8; "Diggs's Threats Made Her Elope," *New York Times,* August 13, 1913, p. 6; "Diggs Defense Scores a Point," *New York Times,* August 14, 1913, p. 5; "Lola Norris Frank Before Diggs Jury," *New York Times,* August 15, 1913, p. 5; "Wife Will Testify in Diggs Defense," *New York Times,* August 16, 1913, p. 3; "Diggs Tells Flight Story as 'Escapade,'" *New York Times,* August 20, 1913, p. 3; "Caminetti Trial Gets Quick Start," *New York Times,* August 28, 1913, p. 3; "Mrs. Diggs Hears the 'Other Woman,'" *New York Times,* August 29, 1913, p. 7; "Caminetti Not Passive," *New York Times,* August 30, 1913, p. 3; "Mrs. Caminetti Aids Defense of Husband," *New York Times,* September 4, 1913, p. 7; "Caminetti Brother Appeals to Jury," *New York Times,* September 5, 1913, p. 5.

3. The discussion of this short scandal is drawn from the following articles: "Political Influence Charged," *New York Times*, June 22, 1913, p. 1; "Won't Keep Office Under M'Reynolds," *New York Times*, June 22, 1913, p. 1; "Secretary Wilson Takes M'Nab Blame," *New York Times*, June 23, 1913, p. 7; "Demand an Inquiry on M'Nab Charges," *New York Times*, June 24, 1913, p. 3; "Wilson to Push California Cases," *New York Times*, June 25, 1913, p. 1; "M'Nab's Associate Suspended by Wire," *New York Times*, June 26, 1913, p. 1; "M'Nab Did Warn M'Reynolds Early," *New York Times*, June 27, 1913, p. 1.

4. Paul A. Freund and Stanley N. Katz, eds., *History of the Supreme Court of the United States* (New York: Macmillan Publishing Co., 1984), vol. 9, *The Judiciary and Responsible Government, 1910–21*, by Alexander M. Bickel and Benno C. Schmidt, Jr., pp. 347–48 (cited hereafter as Bickel and Schmidt, *The Judiciary and Responsible Government, 1910–21*); Stephen Tyree Early, Jr., "James Clark McReynolds and the Judicial Process" (Ph.D. diss., University of Virginia, 1954), pp. 73–74. The most recent analysis, also exonerating McReynolds, is James E. Bond, *I Dissent: The Legacy of Chief Justice James Clark McReynolds* (Fairfax, VA: George Mason University Press, 1992), pp. 44–47.

5. "Halts Attack on Wilson," *New York Times*, July 9, 1913, p. 1.

6. "M'Nab's Associate Suspended by Wire," p. 1; "McNab's Colleague Ousted," *New York Times*, July 2, 1913, p. 10.

7. "M'Nab Did Warn M'Reynolds Early," *New York Times*, pp. 1–2.

8. House Committee on Judiciary. *United States v. Farley Drew Caminetti and Maury Diggs*, H.R. Rep. No. 32 to accompany H.R. Res. 181, 63d Cong., 1st Sess. (1913).

9. "To Try Caminetti Aug. 5," *New York Times*, July 16, 1913, p. 3; "Hayden Retires from Case," *New York Times*, July 23, 1913, p. 6.

10. "McNab Row Won't Down," *New York Times*, July 26, 1913, p. 2; "White Slave Debate Stirs Row in House," *New York Times*, July 30, 1913, p. 2; *New York Times*, August 2, 1913, p. 1.

11. 50 Congressional Record 2532–3, 2874–900, 2906, 3006–23 (1913).

12. Accounts for the Diggs trial are from the *New York Times*, except where indicated by separate endnote: "Diggs to be Tried To-Day," *New York Times*, August 5, 1913, p. 1; "Blow for Defense Opens Diggs Trial," *New York Times*, August 6, 1913, p. 1; "Bachelors Barred from Diggs Jury," *New York Times*, August 7, 1913, p. 16; "Court Undermines Defense of Diggs," *New York Times*, August 8, 1913, p. 14; "Saw Diggs at Reno," p. 8; "Diggs Threats Made Her Elope," p. 6; "Diggs Defense Scores a Point," p. 5; "Lola Norris Frank Before Diggs Jury," p. 5; "Wife Will Testify in Diggs Defense," p. 3; "Diggs Held for Assault," *New York Times*, August 17, 1913, p. 1; "Diggs Tells Flight Story as 'Escapade,'" p. 3; "Diggs Found Guilty in Slavery Case," *New York Times*, August 21, 1913, p. 1; and, generally, Anderson, *The Diggs-Caminetti Case 1913–1917*.

13. The account of this trial is based on the following sources: "Caminetti Trial Gets Quick Start," p. 3; "Mrs. Diggs Hears the 'Other Woman,'" p. 7; "Caminetti Not Passive," p. 3; "Mrs. Caminetti Aids Defense of Husband," p. 7; "Caminetti Brother Appeals to Jury," p. 5; "Caminetti Guilty on Only One Count," *New York Times*, September 6, 1913, p. 1; and, generally, Anderson, *The Diggs-Caminetti Case 1913–1917*.

14. Account of the subornation of perjury trial is drawn from the following: "Diggs Again on Trial," *New York Times*, September 11, 1913, p. 4; "Diggs on Stand Again," *New York Times*, September 13, 1913, p. 4; "Diggs Perjury Case Fails," *New York Times*, September 17, 1913, p. 1; and, generally, Anderson, *The Diggs-Caminetti Case 1913–1917*.

15. "Prison for Diggs and Caminetti," *New York Times*, September 18, 1913, p. 9.

16. "Attack Mann Law's Scope," *New York Times*, December 14, 1913, p. 13.

17. *Diggs v. United States*, 220 F. 545 (9th Cir. 1915).

18. Bickel and Schmidt, *The Judiciary and Responsible Government, 1910–21*, pp. 429, 429n.63.

19. *Caminetti v. United States*, 238 U.S. 636, (1915); *Diggs v. United States*, 238 U.S. 637 (1915).

20. Motion for a Rehearing at 4, *Caminetti*, (Docket No. 1008).

21. Petition for a Writ of Certiorari, *Caminetti* (Docket No. 139).

22. 242 U.S. at 474, 478 (Argument for Petitioner).

23. Petition for a Writ of Certiorari at 6–7, *Caminetti* (Docket No. 139).

24. 242 U.S. at 484–85.

25. 242 U.S. at 485–86.

26. 242 U.S. at 489–90.

27. John W. Johnson, *American Legal Culture, 1908–1940* (Westport, CT: Greenwood Press, 1981), pp. 73–78.

28. See generally, John C. Grabow, "Congressional Silence and the Search for Legislative Intent: A Venture into 'Speculative Unrealities,'" *Boston University Law Review* 64 (July 1984): 737–65.

29. 242 U.S. at 497 (McKenna, J., dissenting).

30. 242 U.S. at 500–501.

31. 242 U.S. at 502.

32. Act of February 20, 1907, ch. 1134, 34 stat. 898 (act to regulate the immigration of aliens into the United States).

33. *United States v. Bitty*, 208 U.S. 393 (1908).

34. 208 U.S. at 402–403.

35. 242 U.S. at 486–88.

36. 242 U.S. at 502–503 (McKenna, J., dissenting).

37. Bickel and Schmidt, *The Judiciary and Responsible Government, 1910–21*, pp. 431, 431–32nn.73 & 74.

CHAPTER SIX

1. Letter, James R. Mann to William R. Day, January 29, 1917, Wm. R. Day Papers, Box 32, Manuscript Division, Library of Congress.

2. "Law Designed for Just Such Cases, Says Author Mann," *Sacramento Bee*, September 8, 1913, p. 3, as quoted in Robert L. Anderson, *The Diggs-Caminetti Case 1913–1917: For Any Other Immoral Purpose* (Lewiston, NY: Edwin Mellen Press, 1990), vol. 1:16.

3. Letter, William R. Day to James R. Mann, January 30, 1917, Wm. R. Day Papers, Box 4, Manuscript Division, Library of Congress.

4. Barbara Meil Hobson, *Uneasy Virtue: The Politics of Prostitution and the American Reform Tradition* (New York: Basic Books, 1987), pp. 21–22.

5. Mark Thomas Connelly, *The Response to Prostitution in the Progressive Era* (Chapel Hill: University of North Carolina Press, 1980), p. 19.

6. *The Social Evil in Syracuse* (Syracuse, NY: n.p., 1913), pp. 67, 76; reprinted in *Prostitution in America: Three Investigations, 1902–1914* (New York: Arno Press, 1976).

7. Brief for the United States at 7, *Caminetti v. United States*, 242 U.S. 470 (1917) (Docket Nos. 139, 163, 464).

8. See generally, Thomas C. Mackey, *Red Lights Out: A Legal History of Prostitution, Disorderly Houses, and Vice Districts, 1870–1917* (New York: Garland Publishing, 1987).

9. *State v. Cavalluzzi*, 113 Me. 41, 92 A. 937, 938 (1915).

10. Howard B. Woolston, *Prostitution in the United States: Prior to the Entrance of the United States into the World War* (New York: Century Co., 1921; reprint, Montclair, NJ: Patterson Smith, 1969), p. 35n.1.

11. *State v. Clark*, 78 Iowa 492, 494, 43 N.W. 273, 273 (1889).

12. *Wilson v. State*, 17 Ala. App. 307, 84 So. 783 (1920).

13. *State v. Thuna*, 59 Wash. 689, 690, 109 P. 331, 331, *aff'd per curiam*, (1910), 111 P. 768 (1910).

14. *Springer v. State*, 16 Tex. Crim. 591, 593 (1884).

15. *Commonwealth v. Cook*, 53 Mass. (12 Met.) 93, 97 (1846).

16. Nicole Hahn Rafter, *Partial Justice: Women, Prisons, and Social Control*, 2d ed. (New Brunswick: Transaction Publishers, 1990), pp. 117, 160.

17. *Black's Law Dictionary*, 2d ed. (1910), s.v. "Prostitute," quoted in Connelly, *The Response to Prostitution in the Progressive Era*, p. 161n.13.

18. *Encyclopaedia Britannica*, 11th ed., s.v. "Prostitution," quoted in Connelly, *The Response to Prostitution in the Progressive Era*, p. 17.

19. Illinois General Assembly, Senate Vice Committee, *Report of the Senate Vice Committee* (1916), p. 24, quoted in Connelly, *The Response to Prostitution in the Progressive Era*, p. 17.

20. *Indiana Statutes Annotated* (Burns 1914), sec. 2372.

21. The model legislation was sponsored by the Commissions on Training Camp Activities, Interdepartmental Social Hygiene Board, and United States Public Health Service. *Journal of Social Hygiene* 5 (October 1919): 625–28.

22. *Laws of Vermont* (1919), 25th Biennial Session No. 199, sec. 2 (S.107), approved April 8, 1919; *Laws of Ohio* (1919), 108–Part I, House Bill No. 350, sec. 13031-14, approved June 21, 1919; *Public Laws of North Dakota* (1919), ch. 190, sec. 2 (S.B. No. 61), approved March 7, 1919; *Public Laws of North Carolina* (1919), ch. 215, sec. 2, ratified March 10, 1919; *New Hampshire Laws* (1919), ch. 163, sec. 2, approved March 28, 1919; *Laws of Maine* (1919), ch. 112, sec. 2, approved March 27, 1919; *Laws of Delaware* (1919), ch. 233, sec. 2, approved April 2, 1919: *Public Acts of the State of Connecticut* (1919), ch. 77, sec. 2, approved April 2, 1919.

23. *Laws of Maryland* (1920), ch. 737, sec. 19-A.

24. *United States v. Bitty*, 208 U.S. 393, 401 (1908).

25. *Suslak v. United States*, 213 F. 913, 917 (9th Cir. 1914).

26. Kathy Peiss, *Cheap Amusements: Working Women and Leisure in Turn-of-the-Century New York* (Philadelphia: Temple University Press, 1986), pp. 51–55.

27. Quoted in Joanne J. Meyerowitz, *Women Adrift: Independent Wage Earners in Chicago, 1880–1930* (Chicago: University of Chicago Press, 1988), p. 102.

28. Vice Commission of Chicago, *The Social Evil in Chicago* (Chicago: n.p., 1911), pp. 187, 189, 211.

29. Peiss, *Cheap Amusements*, p. 112.

30. *The Social Evil in Syracuse*, p. 56.

31. Quoted in, Meyerowitz, *Women Adrift*, p. 124.

32. Hobson, *Uneasy Virtue*, pp. 101–2, 106; Ruth Rosen, *The Lost Sisterhood: Prostitution in America, 1900–1918* (Baltimore: Johns Hopkins University Press, 1982), p. 144.

33. Quoted in Rosen, *The Lost Sisterhood*, p. 144.

34. *Register*, August 28, 1913, *Republican*, August 22, 1913, as quoted in "Press Comments on the Diggs-Caminetti Cases," *Vigilance* 27 (October 1913): 13, 15.

35. *Report of the Commission for the Investigation of the White Slave Traffic, So Called*, [Massachusetts] House [Document] No. 2281 (Boston: Wright & Potter Printing Co, 1914), pp. 43–44; reprinted in *Prostitution in America*.

36. C. C. Carstens, "The Rural Community and Prostitution," *Journal of Social Hygiene* 1 (June 1915): 539–40.

37. Edwin Seligman, *The Social Evil, with Special Reference to Conditions Existing in the City of New York: A Report under the Direction of the Committee of Fifteen*, 2d ed. (New York: Putnam, 1912), p. 11, quoted in Rosen, *The Lost Sisterhood*, p. 43.

38. Letter, Henry J. Dannenbaum to Attorney General, July 29, 1911, Records of the Department of Justice, General Correspondence, Record Group 60, Class 31-0, Box 2620, National Archives, Washington National Records Center, Suitland, Maryland.

39. Minneapolis Vice Commission, *Report of the Vice Commission of Minneapolis* (1911), pp. 76–77, quoted in Connelly, *The Response to Prostitution in the Progressive Era*, p. 38.

40. Peiss, *Cheap Amusements*, pp. 66, 98; Rosen, *The Lost Sisterhood*, p. 107.

41. S. Doc. No. 645, 61st Cong., 2d Sess. 94, also printed as Mary Conyngton, *Relation Between Occupation and Criminality of Women*, vol. 15, *Report on Condition of Woman and Child Wage-Earners in the United States* (Washington, D.C.: Government Printing Office, 1911), p. 94.

42. Walter Clarke, "Prostitution and Alcohol," *Journal of Social Hygiene* 3 (January 1917): 81.

43. "Wife with Tears Pleads For Diggs," *San Francisco Call*, August 20, 1913, p. 1, as quoted in Anderson, *Diggs-Caminetti Case 1913–1917*, 2:580.

44. "White Slave Trials a Check to Lure of Girls to Ruin, Says Harrington," *San Francisco Call*, September 8, 1913, p. 2, as quoted in Anderson, *Diggs-Caminetti Case 1913–1917*, 2:741–42.

45. Brief for the United States at 17, *Caminetti* (Docket Nos. 139, 163, 464).

46. United States Department of Commerce, *Highway Statistics, Summary to 1955* (Washington, D.C.: Government Printing Office, 1957), p. 28, quoted in

James J. Flink, *America Adopts the Automobile, 1895–1910* (Cambridge: MIT Press, 1970), p. 58.

47. Harvey Wish, *Society and Thought in Modern America: A Social and Intellectual History of the American People from 1865*, vol. 2, *Society and Thought in America* (New York: Longmans, Green & Co., 1952), p. 276.

48. Frederick Lewis Allen, *Only Yesterday: An Informal History of the 1920s* (New York: Harper & Bros., 1931; reprint, Harper & Row, 1964), p. 136.

49. Flink, *America Adopts the Automobile*, pp. 35–36, 65, 136–37.

50. Frederick Lewis Allen, *The Big Change: America Transforms Itself 1900–1950* (New York: Harper & Bros., 1952; reprint, Bantam Books, 1961), p. 109.

51. Quotation from Virginia Scharff, *Taking the Wheel: Women and the Coming of the Motor Age* (New York: Free Press, 1991), p. 138. For contemporary articles concerning courtship, sex, and the automobile, prior to 1917, see, Scharff, *Taking the Wheel*, p. 204n.10, and James R. McGovern, "The American Woman's Pre–World War I Freedom in Manners and Morals," *Journal of American History* 55 (September 1968): 316, 319n.26, 320–26, 331–32. See also, David L. Lewis, "Sex and the Automobile: From Rumble Seats to Rockin' Vans," in *The Automobile and American Culture*, edited by David L. Lewis and Laurence Goldstein (Ann Arbor: University of Michigan Press, 1983), pp. 123–33.

52. Bascom Johnson, "Next Steps," *Journal of Social Hygiene* 4 (January 1919): 10, quoted in Allan M. Brandt, *No Magic Bullet: A Social Study of Venereal Disease in the United States Since 1880* (New York: Oxford University Press, 1985), p. 76.

53. Robert S. Lynd and Helen Merrell Lynd, *Middletown: A Study in Contemporary American Culture* (New York: Harcourt, Brace & Co., 1929), p. 114.

54. Otis L. Graham, Jr., *The Great Campaigns: Reform and War in America, 1900–1928* (Englewood Cliffs, NJ: Prentice-Hall, 1971), p. 6.

55. Brandt, *No Magic Bullet*, p. 16.

56. Ibid., p. 47.

57. *Report of the Commission* [Massachusetts], p. 45.

58. John G. Buchanon, "War Legislation Against Alcoholic Liquor and Prostitution," *Journal of Criminal Law, Criminology and Police Science* 9 (February 1919): 526 (formerly *Journal of the American Institute of Criminal Law and Criminology*) (speech of August 26, 1918).

59. Brandt, *No Magic Bullet*, pp. 97–98, 13.

60. "The Effect of Prostitution on our Army and Navy," *Vigilance* 26 (April 1913): 13.

61. "The Social Evil in the American Army," *Current Opinion* 54 (1913): 273–74.

62. Connelly, *The Response to Prostitution in the Progressive Era*, pp. 136–39. For a different view of antiprostitution activities along the border, see James A. Sandos, "Prostitution and Drugs: The United States Army on the Mexican-American Border, 1916–1917," *Pacific Historical Review* 49 (November 1980): 621–45. A general contemporary view of the World War I response to vice by an officer in the Army's Sanitary Corps is found in Buchanon, "War Legislation Against Alcoholic Liquor and Prostitution," p. 520.

63. Connelly, *The Response to Prostitution in the Progressive Era*, p. 143; Brandt, *No Magic Bullet*, pp. 80–84. See, more generally, David J. Pivar, "Cleansing the Nation: The War on Prostitution, 1917–21," *Prologue* 30 (Spring 1980): 29.

64. "Revise the Mann Act," *Washington Post,* January 19, 1917, p. 4.

65. "The Mann Act Upheld," *New York Times,* January 17, 1917, p. 8.

66. "The Mann Law Upheld," *Outlook* 115 (January 31, 1917): 179–80.

67. "'White-Slave' Law and Blackmail," *Literary Digest* 54 (January 27, 1917): 178.

68. "Revise the Mann Act," *Washington Post,* p. 4.

69. The quotations from newspapers subsequent to the prior note are from "'White-Slave' Law and Blackmail," *Literary Digest,* p. 178.

70. "Note and Comment," *Journal of Social Hygiene* 3 (April 1917): 279–80.

71. *Vigilance* 26 (October 1913): 13, quoted in Peter Y. Sonnenthal, "The Origins and Early Enforcement of the White Slave Traffic Act, 1910–1917" (M.A. thesis, Columbia University, 1977), p. 25.

72. "Say that Mann Act Should Be Amended," *New York Times,* January 17, 1917, p. 20.

73. Oscar J. Smith, "The Mann White Slave Law," *Medico-Legal Journal* 33 (1917): 6–7.

74. Abraham Levy, cited in "Say that Mann Act Should Be Amended," *New York Times,* p. 20.

75. 242 U.S. at 502 (McKenna, J., dissenting).

76. 242 U.S. at 490–91.

77. Berto Rogers, "The Mann Act and Noncommercial Vice," *Law Notes* 37 (July 1933): 107; Harry Willmer Jones, "The Plain Meaning Rule and Extrinsic Aids in the Interpretation of Federal Statutes," *Washington University Law Quarterly* 25 (December 1939): 7–8; Harry Willmer Jones, "Statutory Doubts and Legislative Intention," *Columbia Law Review* 40 (June 1940): 961.

78. Note, "Interstate Immorality: The Mann Act and the Supreme Court," *Yale Law Journal* 56 (April 1947): 719–20.

79. Marlene D. Beckman, "The White Slave Traffic Act: The Historical Impact of a Criminal Law Policy on Women," *Georgetown Law Journal* 72 (February 1984): 1118–19.

80. William Seagle, "The Twilight of the Mann Act," *American Bar Association Journal* 55 (July 1969): 642.

81. Paul A. Freund and Stanley N. Katz, eds., *History of the Supreme Court of the United States* (New York: Macmillan Publishing Co., 1984), vol. 9, *The Judiciary and Responsible Government, 1910–1921,* by Alexander M. Bickel and Benno C. Schmidt, Jr., pp. 431–34.

82. Ibid., p. 430.

83. "Explains to Mrs. Caminetti," *New York Times,* March 31, 1917, p. 6.

84. Anderson, *The Diggs-Caminetti Case 1913–1917,* 2:905, 913–19; Norbert MacDonald, "The Diggs-Caminetti Case of 1913 and Subsequent Interpretation of the White Slave Trade Act," *Pacific Historian* 29 (Spring 1985): 38.

CHAPTER SEVEN

1. Circular No. 647, T. W. Gregory, Attorney General, to United States Attorneys, January 26, 1917.

2. Circulars Nos. 986, 2027, and 2751, Attorney General to United States Attorneys, dated, respectively, August 5, 1919, April 19, 1929, and September 5, 1935.

3. *Annual Report of the Attorney General of the United States for the Fiscal Year 1926* (Washington, D.C.: Government Printing Office, 1926), p. 112.

4. Letter, Claude R. Rooter to Attorney General, January 31, 1917. Records of the Department of Justice, General Correspondence, Record Group 60, Class 31-0, Box 2621, National Archives, Washington National Records Center, Suitland, Maryland [hereafter identified only by box number, unless a different record group or classification is intended].

5. See also, *Tobias v. United States*, 2 F.2d 361 (9th Cir. 1924), *cert. denied*, 267 U.S. 593 (1925); *Bonness v. United States*, 20 F.2d 754 (9th Cir. 1927); *Hunter v. United States*, 45 F.2d 55 (4th Cir. 1930).

6. *Elrod v. United States*, 266 F. 55, 57 (6th Cir. 1920).

7. *Aplin v. United States*, 41 F.2d 495, 496 (9th Cir. 1930).

8. *Christian v. United States*, 28 F.2d 114 (8th Cir. 1928).

9. Letter, Charles L. Redding to Attorney General, April 19, 1922, Box 2627. I have altered the surnames of those accused of Mann Act incidents but never indicted, as well as those whose prosecutions were dismissed before trial. I have not changed the dates or location of any document and will be happy to supply the correct surname to any researcher who wishes to follow my tracks through the archives.

10. Letter, George Stephan to Attorney General, October 27, 1925, Box 2627.

11. Letter, George Neuner to Attorney General, March 14, 1930, Box 2621.

12. Marlene D. Beckman, "The White Slave Traffic Act: The Historical Impact of a Criminal Law Policy on Women," *Georgetown Law Journal* 72 (February 1984): 1111–42 (reprinted with minor alternations in Claudine SchWeber and Clarice Feinman, eds., *Criminal Justice Politics and Women: The Aftermath of Legally Mandated Change* (New York: Haworth Press, 1985), pp. 85–101).

13. "City Official Accused Under Mann Act," *New York Times*, September 20, 1921, p. 17 (President of the Board of Aldermen of Woonsocket, Rhode Island); "Runaway Pastor Fined $500," *New York Times*, April 5, 1922, p. 5 (pastor); "Accused Under Mann Act," *New York Times*, February 26, 1926, p. 8 (pastor).

14. "Indict Guatemalan Agent," *New York Times*, August 14, 1920, p. 18 (vice consul); "Arrest New Sonora Governor," *New York Times*, April 24, 1920, p. 15 (military governor).

15. "New York Woman Held in Baltimore," *New York Times*, October 31, 1921, p. 17 (rich confectioner); "Guilty Under Mann Act," *New York Times*, June 19, 1921, p. 6.

16. Letter, A. W. W. Woodcock to Attorney General, July 3, 1926, Box 2627.

17. "Avoids Jail By Marriage," *New York Times*, December 4, 1925, p. 2.

18. Letter, Arthur Butler Graham to Department of Justice, February 15, 1921, Box 2621.

19. *Annual Report of the Attorney General of the United States for the Fiscal Year 1937* (Washington, D.C.: Government Printing Office, 1937), p. 140.

20. *Annual Report of the Attorney General of the United States for the Fiscal Year 1921* (Washington, D.C.: Government Printing Office, 1921), p. 137.

21. Letter, Mother to Department of Justice, October 31, 1927, Box 2622.

22. Letter, Director to J. V. Blake, November 5, 1927, Box 2622.

23. Letter, Arlo Bailor to Department of Justice, June 6, 1929, Box 2622.

24. From the yearly *Annual Report of the Attorney General of the United States,* for 1917 through and including 1928, supplemented by letter, O. John Rogge to Julian D. Rosenberg, October 18, 1939, Box 2626. The average fine and prison sentence are calculated from information in certain of these annual documents. The average fine and prison sentences have been calculated from indirect information in some few of these annual documents which are not in the same format as most. It could not be reported or calculated for some years due to the absence of data.

25. Based on the author's personal examination of the case files for these two courts. Providence records are not available for the period June 1910–May 1912.

26. Letter, Ross R. Mowry to Attorney General, February 15, 1928, Box 2627.

27. Letter, James P. Dillie to Attorney General, October 9, 1929, Box 2627.

28. Letter, Aubrey Boyles to Attorney General, February 27, 1925, Box 2627.

29. *United States v. Gwynne,* 209 F. 993 (E.D. Pa. 1914), applied the common law privilege to Mann Act cases and held the exception for injuries to the wife did not apply where the marriage took place *after* the transportation. This doctrine was weakened subsequently by *United States v. Williams,* 55 F. Supp. 375 (D. Minn. 1944), and abrogated by the United States Supreme Court in *Wyatt v. United States,* 362 U.S. 525 (1960) (Mann Act case with marriage following alleged transportation; wife may both be called by prosecutor and also compelled to testify).

30. *Denning v. United States,* 247 F. 463 (5th Cir. 1918); *Pappas v. United States,* 241 F. 665 (9th Cir. 1917); *Cohen v. United States,* 214 F. 23 (9th Cir.), *cert. denied,* 235 U.S. 696 (1914); *United States v. Rispoli,* 189 F. 271 (E.D. Pa. 1911).

31. Letter, T. W. Gregory, Attorney General, to Charles A. Culberson, January 8, 1916, Box 2621.

32. Compare S. 3597, 64th Cong., 1st Sess. (1916) with H.R. 9044, 64th Cong., 1st Sess. (1916).

33. Letter, William Wallace, Jr., to E. Y. Webb, February 4, 1917, Box 2621.

34. Letter, E. Y. Webb to William Wallace, Jr., January 8, 1917, Box 2621.

35. *Nokis v. United States,* 257 F. 413 (8th Cir. 1919).

36. *Alpert v. United States,* 12 F.2d 352 (2d Cir. 1926).

37. *Coltabellotta v. United States,* 45 F.2d 117 (2d Cir. 1930); *Alpert v. United States,* 12 F.2d 352 (2d Cir. 1926).

38. *Parker v. United States,* 2 F.2d 710 (6th Cir. 1924).

39. *England v. United States,* 272 F. 102, 104 (4th Cir. 1921).

40. *Thorn v. United States,* 278 F. 932 (8th Cir. 1922).

41. 287 F. 91 (8th Cir. 1923).

42. 287 F. at 92.

43. *Drossos v. United States,* 16 F.2d 833, 834–35 (8th Cir. 1927); *Drossos v. United States,* 2 F.2d 538 (8th Cir. 1924). Other cases in a similar vein during this period include *Fisher v. United States,* 266 F. 667 (4th Cir. 1920) and *Van Pelt v. United States,* 240 F. 346 (4th Cir. 1917).

44. *Annual Report of the Attorney General of the United States for the Fiscal Year 1924* (Washington, D.C.: Government Printing Office, 1924), pp. 68–69.

45. *Annual Report of the Attorney General of the United States for the Fiscal Year 1917* (Washington, D.C.: Government Printing Office, 1917), p. 80; *Annual Report*

of the Attorney General of the United States for the Fiscal Year 1919 (Washington, D.C.: Government Printing Office, 1919), p. 79.

46. *Rizzo v. United States*, 275 F. 51, 52 (3d Cir. 1921).

47. 245 F. 278, 279–80 (9th Cir.), *cert. denied*, 245 U.S. 667 (1917).

48. *Annual Report of the Attorney General of the United States for the Fiscal Year 1922* (Washington, D.C.: Government Printing Office, 1922), p. 71.

49. Alice C. Smith, quoted in "Good Women Can Help Solve the White Slave Problem," *New York Times*, April 20, 1913, pt. 3, p. 10.

50. Maude E. Miner, *Slavery of Prostitution—A Plea for Emancipation* (New York: Macmillan Co., 1916).

51. Quoted in Allan M. Brandt, *No Magic Bullet: A Social History of Venereal Disease in the United States Since 1880* (New York: Oxford University Press, 1985), p. 34.

52. Review of *Slavery of Prostitution—A Plea for Emancipation*, by Maude E. Miner, in *Journal of Social Hygiene* 3 (April 1917): 263.

53. Howard B. Woolston, *Prostitution in the United States Prior to the Entrance of the United States into the World War*, (New York: Century Co., 1921; reprint, Montclair, NJ: Patterson Smith, 1969), pp. 159–60.

54. United States Attorney Tuttle, quoted in "Twelve Indicted as White Slavers," *New York Times*, November 14, 1929, p. 11.

55. Morgan F. Larson, quoted in "Larson Minimizes Atlantic City Vice," *New York Times*, February 2, 1930, p. 3. Compare "'G Men' Center upon White Slavery," *Literary Digest* 122 (August 29, 1936): 26–27, using "white slavery" as synonymous with prostitution.

56. "Trade Routes of White Slavers," *Survey* 59 (January 15, 1928): 486–88.

57. Bascom Johnson, "International Traffic in Women and Children," *Journal of Social Hygiene* 14 (February 1928): 68–69.

58. J. Edgar Hoover, *Some Legal Aspects of Interstate Crime* (Washington, D.C.: Government Printing Office, 1938), p. 12.

59. Courtney Ryley Cooper, *Designs in Scarlet* (Boston: Little, Brown & Co., 1939), p. 66.

60. William Seagle, "The Twilight of the Mann Act," *American Bar Association Journal* 55 (July 1969): 641.

CHAPTER EIGHT

1. Letter, A. W. W. Woodcock to Attorney General, September 7, 1927, Records of the Department of Justice, General Correspondence, Record Group 60, Class 31-0, Box 2627, National Archives, Washington National Records Center, Suitland, Maryland [hereafter identified only by box number, unless a different record group or classification is intended].

2. Letter, L. H. Grettenberger to Attorney General, April 19, 1932, Box 2627.

3. Letter, Simon E. Sobeloff to Nugent Dodds, October 13, 1932, Box 2623.

4. Letter, D. H. Dickason to Director, Bureau of Investigation, March 7, 1931, Box 2623, referring to comments of United States Attorney Arthur P. Acher.

5. Letter, William J. Barker to Attorney General, October 16, 1933, Box 2624.

6. Letter, Fred A. Isgrig to Attorney General, January 20, 1937, Box 2625.

7. Letter, Louis S. Joel to Attorney General, January 7, 1929, Box 2627.

8. Letter, W. Sanders Gramling to Attorney General, January 13, 1936, Box 2627.

9. For three examples, see, letters, Paul F. Jones to Attorney General, May 24, 1932 (high school girl), and Robert Van Pelt to Attorney General, November 10, 1931 (forty-year-old "victim"), Box 2623; Report of M. D. Traub, June 27, 1931, FBI file 31-2105, attached to cover letter, J. E. Hoover to Assistant Attorney General Dodds, August 5, 1931 (two fifteen-year-old girls), Box 2627.

10. Report of Ross K. Prescott, October 10, 1939, FBI file 31-4835, Detroit, Michigan, Box 2626.

11. Report of M. N. Roberts, February 11, 1942, FBI file 31-1283, Louisville, Kentucky, Box 2991.

12. Memo, J. E. Hoover to Nugent Dodds, March 10, 1931, with FBI report of R. N. Johnson, January 26, 1931, FBI file 31-1129, attached, Box 2623.

13. Letter, A. W. W. Woodcock to Attorney General, November 9, 1928, Box 2627.

14. Letter, Leo A. Rover to Attorney General, March 14, 1933, Box 2627.

15. Letter, James R. Fleming to Attorney General, October 25, 1934, Box 2627.

16. John Edgar Hoover, "Organized Protection Against Organized Predatory Crimes," *Journal of the American Institute of Criminal Law and Criminology* 24 (July–August 1933): 478.

17. Attorney General William D. Mitchell, quoted in Max Lowenthal, *The Federal Bureau of Investigation* (New York: Harcourt Brace Jovanovich, 1950), p. 19.

18. Frederick Lewis Allen, *Only Yesterday: An Informal History of the 1920s* (New York: Harper & Bros, 1931; reprint, Harper & Row, 1964), pp. 75–76.

19. Peter G. Filene, *Him/Her/Self: Sex Roles in Modern America*, 2d ed. (New York: Harcourt Brace Jovanovich, 1974; reprint, Baltimore: Johns Hopkins University Press, 1986), p. 131.

20. Frederick Lewis Allen, *The Big Change: America Transforms Itself, 1900–1950* (New York: Harper & Bros, 1952; reprint, Bantam Books, 1961), p. 120.

21. Helen Lefkowitz Horowitz, *Campus Life: Undergraduate Cultures from the End of the Eighteenth Century to the Present* (New York: Knopf, 1987; reprint, Chicago: University of Chicago Press, 1988), pp. 125–27.

22. George W. Sandt, The *Lutheran* (original citation not specified), quoted in "The Case against the Younger Generation," *Literary Digest* 73 (June 17, 1922): 40.

23. Quoted in Dorothy M. Brown, *Setting a Course: American Women in the 1920s* (Boston: G. K. Hall & Co., Twayne Publishers, 1987), p. 183.

24. Allen, *Only Yesterday*, p. 291.

25. Frederick Lewis Allen, *Since Yesterday: The 1930s in America, September 3, 1929–September 3, 1939* (New York: Harper & Row, 1939; reprint, Harper & Row, 1972), p. 109.

26. 11 F.2d 499 (9th Cir.), *cert. denied*, 273 U.S. 694 (1926).

27. Dan T. Carter, *Scottsboro: A Tragedy of the American South* (Baton Rouge: Louisiana State University Press, 1969), pp. 208–9, 228–32.

28. Anthony M. Turano, "Adultery on Wheels," *American Mercury* 39 (December 1936): 441, 443.

29. Bascom Johnson and Paul M. Kinsie, "Prostitution in the United States," *Journal of Social Hygiene* 19 (December 1933): 467–68, 478.

30. Note, "Interstate Immorality: The Mann Act and the Supreme Court," *Yale Law Journal* 56 (April 1947): 725–26n.48.

31. J. Edgar Hoover, *Some Legal Aspects of Interstate Crime* (Washington, D.C.: Government Printing Office, 1938), pp. 11–12.

32. "44 More Are Indicted in Jersey Vice Drive," *New York Times*, October 26, 1937, p. 18.

33. *Annual Report of the Attorney General of the United States for the Fiscal Year Ended June 30, 1938* (Washington, D.C.: Government Printing Office, 1938), pp. 84–85.

34. Richard Gid Powers, *Secrecy and Power: The Life of J. Edgar Hoover* (New York: Free Press, 1987), p. 214; Athan G. Theoharis and John Stuart Cox, *The Boss: J. Edgar Hoover and the Great American Inquisition* (Philadelphia: Temple University Press, 1988), p. 156.

35. Richard Gid Powers, "J. Edgar Hoover and the Detective Hero," *Journal of Popular Culture* 9 (Fall 1975): 257–78.

36. "Hoover Seizes 137 in 16 Vice Resorts," *New York Times*, August 30, 1937, p. 1.

37. "Hoover Leads Raids on Baltimore Vice," *New York Times*, May 16, 1937, p. 35.

38. "Three Seized Here in Vice Syndicate," *New York Times*, August 22, 1936, p. 28.

39. Lowenthal, *The Federal Bureau of Investigation*, p. 19.

40. "White Slave Hunt Widened by G-Men," *New York Times*, August 23, 1936, p. 26.

41. Theoharis and Cox, *The Boss*, p. 160.

42. Ibid., p. 258.

43. Ibid., pp. 96–97.

44. Tony Thomas (biographer of Errol Flynn), quoted in "Our Man Flynn," *Los Angeles Times*, July 24, 1988, Calendar Section, p. 95.

45. Letter, Chief (of Correspondence Section) to C. F. Knapp, January 27, 1921, Box 2621.

46. "2 Doctors Seized as Vice Ring Aides," *New York Times*, September 2, 1937, p. 22.

47. An example is in *United States v. Thomas*, 49 F. Supp. 547 (W.D. Ky. 1943).

48. Theoharis and Cox, *The Boss*, pp. 96–97.

49. Stanley W. Finch, "White Slavery in America," *Light* (January–February 1914): 76.

50. FBI Policy Memorandum, "Policy and Procedure, White Slave Traffic Act," September 15, 1949, FBI Policy File 66-6200-31, serial 85, pp. I-41, I-29.

51. Reporter's Transcript on Bill of Exceptions at 30, 32, *United States v. Mackreth*, No. 10166, United States District Court, Southern District of Alabama, Southern Division, Record Group 21, Mobile Criminal Cases, Box 211, National Archives—Southeast Region, East Point, Georgia.

52. 287 U.S. 112 (1932).

53. Marlene D. Beckman, "The White Slave Traffic Act: The Historical Impact of a Criminal Law Policy on Women," *Georgetown Law Journal* 72 (February 1984): 1127–28.

54. Circular No. 2751, Stanley Reed, Acting Attorney General, to United States Attorneys, September 5, 1935.

55. Circular No. 3785, Tom C. Clark, Attorney General, to United States Attorneys, February 23, 1943, and Supplement No. 4, December 1, 1943.

56. Berto Rogers, "The Mann Act and Noncommercial Vice," *Law Notes* 37 (July 1933): 107.

57. S. 2438, 73rd Cong., 2d Sess., 1934; S. 101, 75th Cong., 1st. Sess., 1937; see also *Cleveland v. United States*, 329 U.S. 14, 24n.10 (1946) (Rutledge, J., concurring).

58. Entry under "White Slavery," January 6, 1939, Records of the Department of Justice, New Subject Index, 1930–1981, Record Group 60, National Archives, Washington National Records Center, Suitland, Maryland; "Murphy Asks for a Law," *New York Times*, January 18, 1939, p. 7.

59. *Ellis v. United States*, 138 F.2d 612 (8th Cir. 1943); *Sedam v. United States*, 116 F.2d 80 (10th Cir. 1940); *Neff v. United States*, 105 F.2d 688 (8th Cir. 1939); *Coltabellotta v. United States*, 45 F.2d 117 (2d Cir. 1930).

60. 73 F.2d 294 (2d Cir. 1934).

61. 55 F.2d 1058 (10th Cir. 1932).

62. Hoover, "Organized Protection Against Organized Predatory Crimes," pp. 477–78.

63. *United States ex rel. Povlin v. Hecht*, 48 F.2d 90 (2d Cir. 1931), appears to be one such, but it was an appeal on an extradition request, and the facts are not delineated in detail.

64. Brief for the United States at 12, *Gebardi v. United States*, 287 U.S. 112 (1932)(Docket No. 97).

65. *Gebardi v. United States*, 57 F.2d 617, 617–19 (7th Cir. 1932).

66. Transcript of Record at 16, 114, *Gebardi* (Docket No. 97).

67. Ibid., pp. 8–9, 14–16.

68. Ibid., pp. 22–82.

69. Hoover, *Some Legal Aspects of Interstate Crime*, p. 13.

70. Jay Robert Nash, *Bloodletters and Badmen: A Narrative Encyclopedia of American Criminals from the Pilgrims to the Present* (New York: M. Evans & Co., 1973), pp. 347–50.

71. 287 U.S. at 123.

72. *Hoffman v. United States*, 341 U.S. 479 (1951).

73. *Blumenfield v. United States*, 284 F.2d 46 (8th Cir. 1960), *cert. denied*, 365 U.S. 812 (1961).

74. *Annual Report of the Attorney General of the United States for the Fiscal Year Ended June 30, 1961* (Washington, D.C.: Government Printing Office, 1961), p. 234.

75. 284 F.2d at 51 & 51.n5.

76. Quoted in Randy Roberts, *Papa Jack: Jack Johnson and the Era of White Hopes* (New York: Free Press, 1983), p. 68. Unless otherwise indicated, the discussion of Jack Johnson is drawn from this account.

77. Ibid., pp. 103–4.

78. Cartoon in *Life* (July 28, 1910): 137, as described in Roberts, *Papa Jack*, 110–11.

79. As to "Lynch him!," see *Chicago Tribune*, October 20, 1912, p. 3, quoted in Roberts, *Papa Jack*, 146, and *Chicago Daily News*, October 19, 1912, p. 1, quoted in Al-Tony Gilmore, "Jack Johnson and White Women: The National Impact," *Journal of Negro History* 58 (January 1973): 20.

80. Reported in *Fort Worth Citizen-Star*, October 24, 1912, p. 4, as quoted in Gilmore, "Jack Johnson and White Women," p. 19.

81. Quoted in Roberts, *Papa Jack*, p. 146.

82. Ibid., pp. 148–51.

83. Letter, Lins to Bielaski, November 4, 1912, as quoted in Roberts, *Papa Jack*, p. 153.

84. *Proceedings of the Fifth Meeting of the Governors of the States of the Union*, Richmond, Virginia, December 3–7, 1912 (Richmond: Virginia State Library, 1912), p. 52, as quoted in Gilmore, "Jack Johnson and White Women," p. 31.

85. Roberts, *Papa Jack*, pp. 157, 167.

86. *Boston Globe*, May 14, 1913, as quoted in Al-Tony Gilmore, *Bad Nigger!: The National Impact of Jack Johnson* (Port Washington, NY: Kennikat Press, 1975), p. 121.

87. "U.S. Jury Finds Johnson Guilty; May Go to Prison," *Chicago Tribune*, May 14, 1913, p. 1.

88. "Year in Cell for Johnson," *New York Times*, June 5, 1913, p. 1.

89. *Johnson v. United States*, 215 F. 679, 684–86 (7th Cir. 1914).

90. Penny Stallings, *MacNeil/Lehrer NewsHour* (network television broadcast, November 27, 1987) (Friday Transcript No. 3175).

91. Chuck Berry, *Chuck Berry: The Autobiography* (New York: Simon & Schuster, 1987), p. 195.

92. Ibid., p. 196.

93. Ibid., pp. 197–98.

94. Facts taken from Berry, *Chuck Berry: The Autobiography*, pp. 199–205, and *Berry v. United States*, 295 F.2d 192, 193–94 (8th Cir. 1961), *cert. denied*, 368 U.S. 955 (1962).

95. *Berry v. United States*, 283 F.2d 465 (8th Cir. 1960), *cert. denied*, 364 U.S. 934 (1961).

96. Berry, *Chuck Berry: The Autobiography*, p. 206.

97. Ibid., p. 207.

98. 295 F.2d at 193.

99. Berry, *Check Berry: The Autobiography*, pp. 212, 218.

100. Don McLeese, "The Spirit of a Rocker," *New York Times*, October 18, 1987, sec. 7, p. 13.

101. Robert H. Jackson, "The Federal Prosecutor," *Journal of the American Judicature Society*, 24 (June 1940): 19 (address before the Conference of United States Attorneys, April 1, 1940).

102. "Couple Arrested in Hotel," *New York Times*, April 13, 1918, p. 18.

103. For example, *Simon v. United States*, 145 F.2d 345 (4th Cir. 1944).

104. June 14, 1945, notation, "white slave" entries, New Subject Index, 1930–81, Box 97.

105. Report of W. G. Maupin re: John Francis Tilley, June 19, 1942, and investigative attachments, FBI file No. 31-1028, Department of Justice Case No. 31-12521, Box 2991.

106. Charles Chaplin, *My Autobiography* (New York: Simon & Schuster, 1964), pp. 413–14.

107. Ibid., p. 414.

108. Her trial testimony, reported in "Mann & Woman," *Time*, 43 (April 3, 1944): 24.

109. Charles J. Maland, *Chaplin and American Culture: The Evolution of a Star Image* (Princeton, NJ: Princeton University Press, 1989), p. 200.

110. Chaplin, *My Autobiography*, pp. 414–15.

111. Barry testimony, reported in "Joan Berry Tells of New York Visit," *New York Times*, March 24, 1944, p. 17.

112. "Mann & Woman," *Time*, p. 24.

113. Material on stay in New York and later developments upon their return to Hollywood is based on the books by Maland and Chaplin and article in *Time*, all previously cited.

114. "Names Chaplin as Father," *New York Times*, June 4, 1943, p. 16.

115. Maland, *Chaplin and American Culture*, p. 202.

116. Ibid., pp. 203–4.

117. Ibid., pp. 207–13; David Robinson, *Chaplin: His Life and Art* (New York: McGraw-Hill, 1985), p. 753; Theoharis and Cox, *The Boss*, pp. 96–97.

118. Maland, *Chaplin and American Culture*, pp. 186–94, 253–54, 265.

119. Ibid., p. 194.

120. Her name is sometimes spelled as Berry, and at other times Barry. I have used the Barry form since it appears at least half the time and Chaplin himself spelled it that way in his autobiography.

121. Robinson, *Chaplin: His Life and Art*, pp. 751, 753.

122. Maland, *Chaplin and American Culture*, pp. 215–20. An example of a slanted account is "Mann & Woman," pp. 24–25.

123. "Jury Is Completed for Chaplin Trial," *New York Times*, March 23, 1944, p. 17.

124. "Chaplin on Stand, Denies Girl's Story," *New York Times*, March 31, 1944, p. 38.

125. Jerry Giesler, *The Jerry Giesler Story* (New York: Simon and Schuster, 1960), pp. 187–88, as quoted in Maland, *Chaplin and American Culture*, p. 205.

126. *United States v. Chaplin*, 54 F. Supp. 682, 686 (S.D. Cal. 1944).

127. "Chaplin Acquitted in Mann Act Case," *New York Times*, April 5, 1944, p. 1.

128. Chaplin, *My Autobiography*, p. 429.

129. *United States v. Conforte*, 457 F. Supp. 641, 645 (D. Nev. 1978) (reporting earlier history in subsequent non-Mann Act prosecution), *modified*, 624 F.2d 869 (9th Cir.), *cert. denied*, 449 U.S. 1012 (1980).

130. Powers, *Secrecy and Power*, p. 140.

131. "Ex-Wizard Indicted Under Mann Law," *New York Times*, March 2, 1923, p. 6.

132. "Fines Ex-Wizard $5,000," *New York Times*, March 11, 1924, p. 21.

133. *Mackreth v. United States*, 103 F.2d 495, 496 (5th Cir. 1939).

CHAPTER NINE

1. *Fisher v. United States*, 266 F. 667, 670 (4th Cir. 1920).

2. *Van Pelt v. United States*, 240 F. 346, 348–49 (4th Cir. 1917).

3. For example, *Yoder v. United States*, 80 F.2d 665 (10th Cir. 1935) and *Welsch v. United States*, 220 F. 764 (4th Cir. 1915).

4. *Carey v. United States*, 265 F. 515, 517 (8th Cir. 1920).

5. 17 F.2d 236 (9th Cir.), *cert. denied*, 274 U.S. 747 (1927).

6. Facts are taken from the Brief for the United States at 6–8, *United States v. Mortensen*, 322 U.S. 369 (1944) (Docket No. 559).

7. Transcript of Record at 13–14, *Mortensen* (Docket No. 559).

8. *Mortensen v. United States*, 139 F.2d 967, 970 (8th Cir. 1943).

9. 322 U.S. at 374–76.

10. 145 F.2d 345 (4th Cir. 1944).

11. 145 F.2d at 346–47.

12. *United States v. Mellor*, 71 F. Supp. 53, 61 (D. Neb. 1946).

13. *Mellor v. United States*, 160 F.2d 757, 765 (8th Cir.), *cert. denied*, 331 U.S. 848 (1947).

14. 71 F. Supp. at 62.

15. *Daigle v. United States*, 181 F.2d 311 (1st Cir. 1950).

16. 181 F.2d at 314.

17. 49 F. Supp. 226 (E.D. Pa. 1943), *affirmed*, 146 F.2d 152 (3d Cir. 1944), *rev'd per curiam*, 324 U.S. 824 (1945).

18. 217 F.2d 555 (8th Cir. 1954), *rev'd per curiam*, 348 U.S. 957 (1955).

19. *United States v. Ross*, 257 F.2d 292 (2d Cir. 1958) (weekend trips of call girl and pimp from New York to New Jersey solely for "recreation and refreshment"; return trips to New York not violations of the Mann Act).

20. *Beach v. United States*, 144 F.2d 533, 536n.1 (D.C. Cir. 1944), *rev'd*, 324 U.S. 193 (1945).

21. Robert L. Heald, "Recent Decisions: Statutes," *Georgetown Law Journal* 33 (November 1944): 114.

22. 144 F.2d at 535.

23. *United States v. Beach*, 324 U.S. 193, 195–96 (1945).

24. "U.S. Supreme Court Rules that Mann Act Applies in District of Columbia," *Journal of Social Hygiene* 31 (May 1945): 313.

25. 324 U.S. at 196, 198 (Murphy and Black, J. J., dissenting).

26. 324 U.S. at 198 (Murphy and Black, J. J., dissenting).

27. 181 F.2d at 314.

28. J. Woodford Howard, Jr., *Mr. Justice Murphy: A Political Biography* (Princeton, NJ: Princeton University Press, 1968), p. 341.

29. Letter, Frank Murphy to John R. Watkins, March 1, 1945, cited and quoted in Howard, *Mr. Justice Murphy*, p. 341.

30. *Cleveland v. United States,* 329 U.S. 14 (1946).

31. 329 U.S. at 18–19.

32. 329 U.S. at 21–24 (Rutledge, J., concurring).

33. 329 U.S. at 20–21 (Black and Jackson, J.J., dissenting).

34. 329 U.S. at 24–25 (Murphy, J., dissenting).

35. 329 U.S. at 25–26 (Murphy, J., dissenting).

36. 329 U.S. at 27–29 (Murphy, J., dissenting).

37. Herman Leroy Taylor, "Manhandling the Mann Act?" *National Bar Journal* 5 (March 1947): 39; Lewis C. Nelson, "A Re-Examination of the Purpose of the White Slave Traffic Act," *George Washington Law Review* 15 (February 1947): 214; Note, "Interstate Immorality: The Mann Act and the Supreme Court," *Yale Law Journal* 56 (April 1947): 718.

38. Claude T. Barnes, *The White Slave Act: History and Analysis of Its Words "Other Immoral Purpose"* (Salt Lake City, UT: Sugar House Press, 1946).

39. Robert W. Barker, "Recent Decisions: Statutes," *Georgetown Law Journal* 35 (April 1947): 410.

40. 146 F.2d 536 (8th Cir. 1945).

41. 217 F.2d 257 (8th Cir. 1954).

42. "Interstate Immorality: The Mann Act and the Supreme Court," *Yale Law Journal,* p. 726n.48.

43. Walter Clarke, quoted in "Vice Racketeers Lose Ground," *Journal of Social Hygiene* 38 (April 1952): 186.

44. "Mann Act Sponsor Unit Disbands," *New York Times,* April 1, 1951, p. 67.

45. Circular No. 2751, Stanley Reed, Acting Attorney General, to United States Attorneys, September 5, 1935.

46. FBI Policy Memorandum, "Policy and Procedure, White Slave Traffic Act," September 15, 1949, FBI Policy File 66-6200-31, serial 85, p. I-27.

47. George Gamester, "These Were Dates to Forget," *Toronto Star,* August 3, 1990, p. A4.

48. 149 F.2d 891 (5th Cir. 1945).

49. 149 F.2d at 892.

50. *Krulewitch v. United States,* 336 U.S. 440 (1949).

51. 349 U.S. 81 (1955).

52. *St. Clair v. Hiatt,* 83 F. Supp. 585, 587–88 (N.D. Ga.), *aff'd per curiam,* 177 F.2d 374 (5th Cir. 1949), *cert. denied,* 339 U.S. 967 (1950), explores the conflict between the circuits.

53. 362 U.S. 525 (1960).

54. 358 U.S. 74 (1958).

55. In addition to the cases referred to in text, see also, *Wright v. United States,* 175 F.2d 384 (8th Cir.), *cert. denied,* 338 U.S. 873 (1949), and *United States v. Jamerson,* 60 F. Supp. 281 (N.D. Iowa 1944), involving prostitutes walking over the line under directions of defendants; *Helwig v. United States,* 162 F.2d 837 (6th Cir. 1947) and *Simon v. United States,* 145 F.2d 345 (4th Cir. 1944), noncommercial cases.

56. 162 F.2d 156 (9th Cir. 1947).

57. 271 F.2d 214 (8th Cir. 1959), *cert. denied,* 361 U.S. 933 (1960).

58. 234 F.2d 675 (9th Cir. 1956).

59. 160 F.2d 706 (10th Cir. 1947).

60. *Lane v. Lane*, 253 Iowa 92, 111 N.W.2d 286, 287 (1961).

61. "Mann & Woman," *Time* 43 (April 3, 1944): 25.

62. *Time*, 54 (May 30, 1955): 13.

CHAPTER TEN

1. Helen Lefkowitz Horowitz, *Campus Life: Undergraduate Cultures from the End of the Eighteenth Century to the Present* (New York: Knopf, 1987; reprint, Chicago: University of Chicago Press, 1988), p. 228.

2. Peter G. Filene, *Him/Her/Self: Sex Roles in Modern America*, 2d ed. (New York: Harcourt Brace Jovanovich, 1974; reprint, Baltimore: Johns Hopkins University Press, 1986), pp. 202–3.

3. Horowitz, *Campus Life*, p. 248.

4. Filene, *Him/Her/Self*, p. 203.

5. Francesca M. Cancian, *Love in America: Gender and Self-Development* (Cambridge: Cambridge University Press, 1987), p. 38.

6. Associated Press, "Sexual Activity Soars Among Young Women," *Birmingham News*, January 5, 1991, p. 4A.

7. For example, see, "Society Is Called Misguided on Vice," *New York Times*, February 9, 1964, p. 64.

8. For example, see, James P. Sterba, "Prostitution Is Flourishing in Rich Exurban Market," *New York Times*, June 9, 1974, p. 55; "Easy Stand on Marijuana Favored," *New York Times*, January 20, 1976, p. 67.

9. For example, see, Ralph Blumenthal, "'Peep-Show King' and 5 Others Are Seized as Bribers," *New York Times*, December 1, 1972, p. 43; United Press International, "Council Chief in Duluth, Minn., Would Decriminalize Prostitution," *New York Times*, December 18, 1977, p. 28; "Prostitution Plan Upsets Atlantic City," *New York Times*, November 26, 1981, pt. B, p. 2.

10. For example, see, Peter Kihss, "Repeal of Laws on Morals Urged," *New York Times*, February 13, 1968, p. 28.

11. United Press International, "A.B.A. Panel Seeks Repeal of Laws on Prostitution," *New York Times*, July 26, 1974, p. 39.

12. "A.C.L.U. on Prostitution," *New York Times*, July 5, 1976, p. 14 (letter to editor from Executive Director, American Civil Liberties Union).

13. "Decriminalizing of Prostitution Urged," *New York Times*, June 23, 1975, p. 28.

14. "Women's Liberationist Hails the Prostitute," *New York Times*, May 29, 1970, p. 30; "Feminists Protest Arrest of Prostitutes in the City," *New York Times*, March 30, 1971, p. 26; Martin Arnold, "Most Times Square Prostitutes Staying Off Street to Avoid Arrest," *New York Times*, July 9, 1971, p. 11; Eric Pace, "Feminists Halt Session on Prostitution, Demanding to Be Heard," *New York Times*, September 15, 1971, p. 43; Eileen Shanahan, "Women's Group Vows Poverty Fight," *New York Times*, February 20, 1973, p. 38.

15. 158 F.2d 509 (1st Cir. 1946).

16. *United States v. Mathison*, 239 F.2d 358, 360 (7th Cir. 1956).

17. 526 F.2d 736 (10th Cir. 1975), *cert. denied*, 426 U.S. 905 (1976).

18. 16 F. Supp. 231 (E.D. Ill. 1936)

19. 110 F.2d 460 (7th Cir.), *cert. denied*, 310 U.S. 634 (1940).

20. 518 F.2d 817 (7th Cir. 1975).

21. 754 F.2d 795 (8th Cir.), *cert. denied*, 471 U.S. 1139 (1985).

22. 251 F. 39 (9th Cir. 1918).

23. 215 F.2d 605 (7th Cir.), *rev'd per curiam*, 348 U.S. 892 (1954).

24. 215 F.2d at 609, 611–12.

25. *Amadio v. United States*, 348 U.S. 892 (1954).

26. *United States v. Austrew*, 190 F. Supp. 632 (D. Md. 1961); *United States v. Austrew*, 202 F. Supp. 816 (D. Md. 1962), *aff'd per curiam*, 317 F.2d 926 (4th Cir. 1963); *United States v. Sapperstein*, 198 F. Supp. 147 (D. Md. 1961), *aff'd*, 312 F.2d 694 (4th Cir. 1963).

27. 202 F. Supp. 816 (D. Md. 1962), *aff'd per curiam*, 317 F.2d 926 (4th Cir. 1963).

28. 198 F. Supp. at 149.

29. *Annual Report of the Attorney General of the United States for the Fiscal Year Ended June 30, 1962* (Washington, D.C.: Government Printing Office, 1962), p. 207.

30. 291 F.2d 205 (5th Cir. 1961).

31. 507 F.2d 22 (7th Cir. 1974).

32. *United States v. Flaspoller*, 205 F. 1006 (E.D. La. 1913).

33. *Mackreth v. United States*, 103 F.2d 495 (5th Cir. 1939).

34. 426 F.2d 1279 (7th Cir. 1970).

35. 507 F.2d at 24n.10.

36. *United States v. McClung*, 187 F. Supp. 254 (E.D. La. 1960). Favorable comments on *McClung* include: Sholom D. Comay, "Criminal Law—White Slave Traffic Act—An Indictment Alleging the Transportation of a Woman Across a State Line for a Single Act of Intercourse Does Not Allege a Mann Act Violation," *University of Pittsburgh Law Review* 22 (March 1961): 626–29; Charles Griffin, "Criminal Law—White Slave Traffic Act—Single Act of Intercourse Not Sufficient to Constitute Violation of the Mann Act," *Notre Dame Lawyer* 36 (May 1961): 423–26; Thomas D. Herlocker, "Criminal Law—White Slave Traffic Act," *University of Kansas Law Review* 10 (October 1961): 91–92; Edward L. Morgan, "Criminal Law—White-Slave Traffic Act—Transportation of a Willing Female for a Single Nonpecuniary Act of Sexual Intercourse Not a Violation," *Arizona Law Review* 4 (Fall 1962): 112–16.

37. 266 F. 55 (6th Cir. 1920).

38. 22 F.2d 393 (8th Cir. 1927).

39. 105 F.2d 688 (8th Cir. 1939).

40. 158 F.2d 509 (1st Cir. 1946).

41. 237 F.2d 281 (8th Cir. 1956).

42. 787 F.2d 1094 (7th Cir. 1986).

43. 650 F. Supp. 1115 (D. Kan. 1986).

44. "Appraisal of the Records of the Federal Bureau of Investigation," a report to the United States District Court, dated November 9, 1981, submitted by the National Archives and Records Service and the Federal Bureau of Investigation, a

copy of which is in the possession of the author, at p. 31, also quoted and cited in Marlene D. Beckman, "The White Slave Traffic Act: The Historical Impact of a Criminal Law Policy on Women," *Georgetown Law Review*, 72 (February 1984): 1134.

45. *Hattaway* (Virginia) *v. United States*, 416 F.2d 1178 (5th Cir. 1969); *Hattaway* (James) *v. United States*, 399 F.2d 431 (5th Cir. 1968).

46. 347 F.2d 503 (7th Cir. 1965).

47. *Annual Report of the Attorney General of the United States for the Fiscal Year Ended June 30, 1966* (Washington, D.C.: Government Printing Office, 1966), p. 251.

48. *Alpert v. United States*, 12 F.2d 352 (2d Cir. 1926); *Yeates v. United States*, 254 F. 60 (5th Cir. 1918), *cert. denied*, 248 U.S. 583 (1919).

49. For example, *United States v. Howard*, 691 F. Supp. 1398 (S.D. Fla. 1988); *Reamer v. United States*, 318 F.2d 43 (8th Cir.), *cert. denied*, 375 U.S. 869 (1963).

50. For example, *United States v. Howard*, 691 F. Supp. 1398 (S.D. Fla. 1988); *United States v. Jones*, 808 F.2d 561 (7th Cir. 1986); *United States v. Mitchell*, 778 F.2d 1271 (7th Cir. 1985); "FBI Arrests Pair in Sex Scheme," United Press International, May 20, 1988 (Howard case).

51. *Reamer v. United States*, 318 F.2d 43, 48 (8th Cir.), *cert. denied*, 375 U.S. 869 (1963).

52. *United States v. Mitchell*, 778 F.2d 1271, 1275 (7th Cir. 1985) (quoting *McClung*, 187 F. Supp. at 257).

53. *United States v. Roeder*, 526 F.2d 736, 739n.2 (10th Cir. 1975), *cert. denied*, 426 U.S. 905 (1976).

54. Robert Sam Anson, "Bodies for Sale: End of the Road for Runaways," *Mademoiselle* 87 (August 1981): 216.

55. Kathleen Barry, "The Underground Economic System of Pimping," *Journal of International Affairs* 35 (Spring/Summer 1981): 118.

56. Rudy Johnson, "Police Seize 10 and Charge Vice-Ring Kidnapping," *New York Times*, March 21, 1971, p. 47; Martin Arnold, "13 Accused Here of Torturing Girls to Force Them Into Prostitution Ring," *New York Times*, April 6, 1971, p. 78; "Two Women Seized in Alleged Kidnap Tied to Prostitution," *New York Times*, December 15, 1971, p. 106; Murray Schumach, "'Massage Parlor' Raided; Girls and $17,000 Seized," *New York Times*, August 27, 1972, p. 1; "3 Men Are Charged in Assault on Girls," *New York Times*, September 11, 1972, p. 28; Edward Hudson, "Suspect Is Charged With Kidnapping In Rape of Girl," *New York Times*, December 30, 1976, p. 27; United Press International, "14 Held in Forcing 3 Women Into Jobs," *New York Times*, June 10, 1983, pt. 2, p. 4.

57. *United States v. Vik*, 655 F.2d 878 (8th Cir. 1981).

58. "Motorcyclists Convicted as a Drug and Vice Ring," *New York Times*, April 2, 1983, p. 5.

59. T. C. Esselstyn, "Prostitution in the United States," *Annals of the American Academy of Political and Social Science* 376 (March 1968): 123–35.

60. See Kathleen Barry, *Female Sexual Slavery* (New York: New York University Press, 1979); Lan Cao, "Illegal Traffic in Women: A Civil RICO Proposal," *Yale Law Journal* 96 (May 1987): 1297.

61. Ron Shaffer, "Pimp Ring in District is Probed," *Washington Post*, August 25, 1978, sec. 2, p. 1.

62. *Annual Report of the Attorney General of the United States*, for fiscal years 1959 through 1968 and 1974 through 1976; D. Kelly Weisberg, *Children of the Night: A Study of Adolescent Prostitution* (Lexington, MA: D. C. Heath & Co., 1985), p. 208, for 1980 and 1981.

63. William Seagle, "The Twilight of the Mann Act," *American Bar Association Journal* 55 (July 1969): 641.

64. Barbara Sherman Heyl, *The Madam as Entrepreneur: Career Management in House Prostitution* (New Brunswick: Transaction Books, 1979), pp. 146–47.

65. *Stewart v. United States*, 311 F.2d 109, 111 (9th Cir. 1962).

66. *United States v. Price*, 577 F.2d 1356, 1360n.2 (9th Cir. 1978), *cert. denied sub nom. Mitchell v. United States*, 439 U.S. 1068 (1979).

67. "Motorcyclists Convicted as a Drug and Vice Ring," p. 5; "Woman Gets a 12-Year Term for Promoting Prostitution," *New York Times*, August 7, 1986, p. 24.

68. "Novel Laundering Forfeiture Sought in Mann Act Case," *Money Laundering Alert* 2 (March 1991): 2.

69. "Civil RICO Claim Against Bank Dismissed for Lack of Continuity," (*First New York Bank for Business v. Selzer*), *New York Law Journal*, July 11, 1990, p. 21; *NL Industries, Inc. v. Gulf & Western Industries, Inc.*, 650 F. Supp. 1115 (D. Kan. 1986). See also, Cao, "Illegal Traffic in Women: A Civil RICO Proposal."

70. *United States v. Drury*, 582 F.2d 1181 (8th Cir. 1978); *United States v. Snow*, 507 F.2d 22 (7th Cir. 1974); *Nunnally v. United States*, 291 F.2d 205 (5th Cir. 1961). See also *United States v. Sapperstein*, 198 F. Supp. 147 (D. Md. 1961), *aff'd*, 312 F.2d 694 (4th Cir. 1963), and cases cited at 150.

71. *Twitchell v. United States*, 330 F.2d 759 (9th Cir. 1964); *United States v. Reese*, 248 F. Supp. 688 (N.D. Ohio 1966).

CHAPTER ELEVEN

1. *Annual Report of the Attorney General of the United States, 1974* (Washington, D.C.: Government Printing Office, 1974), p. 201; *Annual Report of the Attorney General of the United States, 1976* (Washington, D.C.: Government Printing Office, 1976), p. 165; D. Kelly Weisberg, *Children of the Night: A Study of Adolescent Prostitution* (Lexington, MA: D. C. Heath & Co., 1985), p. 208.

2. Organized Crime Control Act of 1970, Pub. L. No. 91-452, sec. 226, 84 Stat. 930 (changing immunity offered for filing the statement from transaction to use immunity).

3. Act of May 24, 1949, ch. 139, sec. 47, 63 Stat. 96; Act of June 25, 1948, ch. 645, 62 Stat. 812.

4. Robert Sam Anson, "Bodies for Sale: End of the Road for Runaways," *Mademoiselle* 87 (August 1981): 216.

5. Examples of these articles, taken from just one source, the *New York Times*, include: Ted Morgan, "Little Ladies of the Night," *New York Times*, November 16, 1975, pt. 6, p. 34; Nathaniel Sheppard, Jr., "More Teen-Aged Girls Are Turning to Prostitution, Youth Agencies Say," *New York Times*, May 4, 1976, p. 41; Selwyn Raab, "Pimps Establish Recruiting Link to the Midwest," *New York Times*, Octo-

ber 30, 1977, p. 1; Nathaniel Sheppard, Jr., "Recruiting of Teen-Age Prostitutes Is Increasing in Minneapolis Area," *New York Times*, November 5, 1977, p. 8.

6. Ralph J. Marino, quoted in Selwyn Raab, "State Inquiry to Call the Leaders of Sex Businesses in New York," *New York Times*, August 2, 1977, p. 33.

7. The growing publicity may be measured by the annual indices of the *New York Times*, indicating the annual numbers of articles appearing involving juveniles and pornography. For 1974 there were zero, only one in 1975, and then zero again in 1976. However, in 1977, the year of the clamor and the passage of the Protection of Children Against Sexual Exploitation Act, there were no fewer than twenty-eight articles that appeared in the *New York Times* concerning children's participation in pornography. In 1978, the year the Act was signed, the number of such articles dropped to nine, and by 1979 to only a single such article.

8. William W. Sanger, *The History of Prostitution: Its Extent, Causes and Effects Throughout the World* (New York: Harper & Bros., 1858; reprint, Medical Publishing Co., 1897), p. 70.

9. T. C. Esselstyn, "Prostitution in the United States," *Annals of the American Academy of Political and Social Science* 376 (March 1968): 133.

10. Anatole Broyard, "More Commercial than Lively," review of *The Lively Commerce: Prostitution in the United States*, by Charles Winick and Paul M. Kinsie, in *New York Times*, May 5, 1971, p. 45.

11. Frank J. Prial, Jr., "At Night, Block Belongs to the Male Prostitutes," *New York Times* May 31, 1976, p. 19; "'Chicken-Hawk' Trade Found Attracting More Young Boys to Times Square Area," *New York Times*, February 14, 1977, p. 31; Seth S. King, "Chicago Jury to Probe Pornography and Prostitution Involving Boys," *New York Times*, May 23, 1977, p. 19; Selwyn Raab, "3 Arrested in Raid on Alleged Male Prostitution Ring," *New York Times*, December 1, 1977, sec. B, p. 3.

12. The following discussion of legislative history is drawn from Weisberg, *Children of the Night*, pp. 189–93.

13. Ibid., p. 193.

14. Protection of Children Against Sexual Exploitation Act of 1977, Pub. L. No. 95-225, 92 Stat. 8–9 (signed into law January, 1978).

15. Ronald Kessler, "Customers of Male Prostitutes Face Arrest," *Washington Post*, September 25, 1983, sec. 2, p. 3.

16. Weisberg, *Children of the Night*, p. 207.

17. Ira R. Allen, "Reagan Endorses Anti-discrimination Changes," United Press International, September 8, 1983.

18. 521 F.2d 444 (8th Cir. 1975).

19. 521 F.2d at 446.

20. *United States v. Green*, 554 F.2d 372 (9th Cir. 1977); *United States v. Bankston*, 603 F.2d 528 (5th Cir. 1979).

21. Allen, "Reagan Endorses Anti-discrimination Changes."

22. United Press International, October 1, 1982.

23. The leading articles in the *New York Times* describing the Senate, House, and final congressional approval of the 1978 act, the Protection of Children Against Sexual Exploitation Act of 1977, all described the changes that would be made in the Mann Act. Yet their headlines proclaimed: "Senate, 85-1, Approves Bill to Bar

Use of Minors for Pornography," *New York Times*, October 11, 1977, p. 22; "House Votes Stiff Penalty in Child Pornography Bill," *New York Times*, October 26, 1977, p. 22; and "Child Pornography Measure," *New York Times*, January 25, 1978, p. 10.

24. Vladimir Nabokov, *Lolita*, part two, chapter 1. (Paris: Olympia Press, 1955, and New York: Putnam Publishing, 1958; reprint, New York: Vintage Books, 1989), p. 150. I am grateful to Lisa Harper for this reference.

25. Kitty Kelley, *His Way: The Unauthorized Biography of Frank Sinatra* (Toronto: Bantam Books, 1986), p. 312.

26. Robert H. Williams, "Prisoner of Love," *Washington Post Magazine*, June 8, 1980, p. 8.

27. Daniel Seligman, "A Furtive Flower," *Fortune* (July 28, 1980): 33–34.

28. "The Mann Act at 75," *Boston Globe*, June 25, 1985, p. 14.

29. "Excerpts from Final Report of Attorney General's Panel on Pornography," *New York Times*, July 10, 1986, sec. B, p. 7.

30. October 27, 1944, notation, "white slave" entries, Records of the Department of Justice, New Subject Index, 1930–81, Box 97, Record Group 60, National Archives, Washington National Records Center, Suitland, Maryland; February 12, 1962, notation, "white slave" entries, *loc. cit.*, Box 97 (referring to 1962 bill, identified as H.R. 9853, 87th Cong.).

31. Child Sexual Abuse and Pornography Act of 1986, Pub. L. No. 99-628, 100 Stat. 3511–12.

32. United Press International, releases of September 29, 1986 and November 8, 1986.

33. H.R. Rep. No. 99-910, 99th Cong., 2d Sess. (1986), reprinted in 1986 *U.S. Code Congressional and Administrative News* 5952–59.

34. Ibid., at 5958.

35. 691 F. Supp. 1398 (S.D. Fla. 1988).

36. "U.S. Jury Indicts Man in Youth-Sex Case," *New York Times*, November 19, 1987, sec. B, p. 8.

37. *In re Pine*, 41 So. 2d 546 (Fla. 1949), based upon underlying facts in *Pine v. United States*, 135 F.2d 353 (5th Cir.), *cert. denied*, 320 U.S. 740 (1943).

38. *Spears v. State Bar of California*, 211 Cal. 183, 294 P. 697 (1930).

39. *Scearce v. Field*, 292 F. Supp. 807 (C.D. Cal. 1968); *People v. O'Ward*, 168 Cal. App. 2d 127, 335 P.2d 762 (1959).

40. *People v. Loomis*, 231 Cal. App. 2d 594, 42 Cal. Rptr. 124 (1965).

41. *State v. Phillips*, 102 Ariz. 377, 430 P.2d 139 (1967).

42. *People v. Hurd*, 5 Cal. App. 3d 865, 85 Cal. Rptr. 718 (1970).

43. *Mitchell v. Mitchell*, 133 N.E.2d 79 (Ind. 1956).

44. *Nelson v. Municipal Court*, 28 Cal. App. 3d 889, 105 Cal. Rptr. 46 (1972).

45. *Galloway v. Moreno*, 183 Cal. App. 2d 803, 7 Cal. Rptr. 349 (1960).

46. *Zonver v. Superior Court*, 270 Cal. App. 2d 613, 76 Cal. Rptr. 10 (1969).

47. *Rubenstein v. Kleven*, 150 F. Supp. 47 (D. Mass. 1957).

48. *United States v. Reginelli*, 133 F.2d 595 (3d Cir.), *cert. denied*, 318 U.S. 783 (1943); *Petition of Reginelli*, 86 F. Supp. 599 (D.N.J. 1949); *Petition of Reginelli*, 20 N.J. 266, 119 A.2d 454 (1956).

49. *In the Matter of R——*, 6 I. & N. December 444, 1954 BIA LEXIS 129 (1954).

50. Bates Booth, "The White Slave Traffic Act," *California State Bar Journal* 20 (March–April 1945): 103.

51. "Gravity of the Caminetti Case," *Current Opinion* 55 (August 1913): 77 (also quoting New York *American*).

52. Robert L. Anderson, *The Diggs-Caminetti Case 1913–1917: For Any Other Immoral Purpose* (Lewiston, NY: Edwin Mellen Press, 1990), 1: 197–211, 233, 236, 2: 570, 637–38.

53. "A Verdict Which Is Approved by All Good Men and All Decent Women," *Sacramento Bee*, August 21, 1913, p. 6.

54. *Herald*, August 22, 1913; *Capital*, August 21, 1913; *American*, August 23, 1913; *Tribune*, August 14, 1913, as quoted in "Press Comments on the Diggs-Caminetti Cases," *Vigilance* 27 (October 1913): 8, 11, 14.

55. Senator Tillman, quoted in "Cites Diggs Case Assailing Suffrage," *New York Times*, August 19, 1913, p. 6.

Index